EYEWITNESS TRAVEL
ISTANBUL

EYEWITNESS TRAVEL

ISTANBUL

LONDON, NEW YORK,
MELBOURNE, MUNICH AND DELHI
www.dk.com

PROJECT EDITOR Nick Inman
ART EDITOR Kate Poole
EDITORS Claire Folkard, Jane Oliver, Christine Stroyan
DESIGNERS Jo Doran, Paul Jackson
VISUALIZER Joy FitzSimmons

MAIN CONTRIBUTORS
Rosie Ayliffe, Rose Baring, Barnaby Rogerson, Canan Sılay

MAPS
Paul Bates, Anne Rayski, Glyn Rozier (ESR Cartography Ltd)
Neil Cook, Maria Donnelly, Ewan Watson
(Colourmap Scanning Ltd)

PHOTOGRAPHERS
Anthony Souter, Linda Whitwam, Francesca Yorke

ILLUSTRATORS
Richard Bonson, Stephen Conlin, Gary Cross, Richard Draper,
Paul Guest, Maltings Partnership, Chris Orr & Associates,
Paul Weston, John Woodcock

Reproduced in Singapore by Colourscan
Printed and bound in China by Toppan Printing Co. (Shenzhen Ltd)

First American Edition, 1998
08 09 10 9 8 7 6 5 4 3 2 1

Reprinted with revisions 1999, 2000, 2001, 2002, 2004, 2007

Published in the United States by Dorling Kindersley Publishing,
Inc., 375 Hudson Street, New York 10014

Copyright 1998, 2007 © Dorling Kindersley Limited, London
A Penguin Company

Published in Great Britain by Dorling Kindersley Limited.

A CATALOGING IN PUBLICATION RECORD IS
AVAILABLE FROM THE LIBRARY OF CONGRESS.

ISSN 1542-1554
ISBN 978-0-75662-501-6

THROUGHOUT THIS BOOK, FLOORS ARE REFERRED TO IN ACCORDANCE WITH
EUROPEAN USAGE; I.E., THE "FIRST FLOOR" IS THE FLOOR ABOVE GROUND LEVEL.

Front cover main image: Sülemaniye Mosque

CONTENTS

Madonna mosaic in the Church of
St Saviour in Chora

INTRODUCING ISTANBUL

Tile panel in the Paired Pavilions
of Topkapı Palace's Harem

◁ The Blue Mosque and the church of Haghia Sophia, dominating Sultanahmet Square

The great 6th-century
Byzantine church of
Haghia Sophia

Ferry passing the waterfront of
Karaköy below the Galata Tower

Men smoking bubble pipes in
Çorlulu Ali Paşa Courtyard

Simit seller

Dolmabahçe Mosque with the skyline of Sultanahmet in the distance

HOW TO USE THIS GUIDE

This guide helps you to get the most from your stay in Istanbul. It provides both expert recommendations and detailed practical advice. Introducing Istanbul locates the city geographically, sets Istanbul in its historical and cultural context and gives an overview of the main attractions. Istanbul Area by Area is the main sightseeing section, giving detailed information on all the major sights plus three recommended walks, with photographs, maps and illustrations throughout. Greater Istanbul looks at sights outside the city centre. The Bosphorus guides you through a trip up the straits, and Excursions from Istanbul explores other places within easy reach of the city. Tips for restaurants, hotels, entertainment and shopping are found in Travellers' Needs, while the Survival Guide contains useful advice on everything from personal security to public transport.

FINDING YOUR WAY AROUND ISTANBUL

The centre of Istanbul has been divided into four sightseeing areas, each with its own chapter, colour-coded for easy reference. All sights are numbered and plotted on an area map for each chapter. The major sights are covered in more detail.

1 Area Introduction
This describes the history and character of the area and has a map on which the sights have been plotted. Other key information is also given.

Each area has colour-coded thumb tabs.

Locator Map

The area shaded pink is shown in greater detail on the Street-by-Street map on the following pages.

2 Street-by-Street Map
This gives a bird's-eye view of the heart of each sightseeing area. Interesting features are labelled. There is also a list of "star sights" that no visitor should miss.

A suggested route takes in the most interesting and attractive streets in the area.

3 Detailed information
All the important sights are described individually. They are listed in order, following the numbering on the area map, with practical information about each.

ISTANBUL AREA MAP

The coloured areas shown on this map *(see inside front cover)* are the four main sightseeing areas used in this guide. Each is covered in a full chapter in *Istanbul Area by Area (pp48–107)*. They are highlighted on other maps throughout the book. In *Istanbul at a Glance (see pp34–43)*, they help you to locate the top sights. The introduction to the Street Finder *(see pp246–263)* shows on which detailed street map you will find each area.

Introductory text gives an overview of the main sights in the Greater Istanbul area.

A map of the city shows Greater Istanbul and the areas covered in the chapter's sub-divisions.

4 Introduction to Greater Istanbul
Greater Istanbul has its own introduction, outlining what the city suburbs have to offer the sightseer. It is divided into five districts, shown on a map.

Practical information is provided in an information block. The key to the symbols used is on the back flap.

5 Introduction to Greater Istanbul areas
An introduction places the area in its historical context and provides a map showing the numbered sights.

The Visitors' Checklist provides detailed practical information.

6 The major sights
These are given two or more full pages. Historic buildings are dissected to reveal their interiors. Where necessary, sights are colour-coded to help you locate the most interesting areas.

INTRODUCING
ISTANBUL

FOUR GREAT DAYS IN ISTANBUL

Istanbul is a frenetic city with a wealth of culture, history and nightlife. Split in two by the Bosphorous Strait, it is the only city in the world to straddle two continents, Europe and Asia, and thus has two contrasting atmospheres. These itineraries

Ceramic plate from the Grand Bazaar

are designed to give you a flavour of the city as a whole. All the sights are cross-referenced to the rest of the guide, so you can look up more information and tailor the day to suit your needs. Price guides include meals, transport and admission fees.

A range of exotic spices for sale in the Spice Bazaar

SHOPPING AND SEAFOOD

- **Refresh your senses in the Spice Bazaar**
- **Shop for antiques in Çukurcuma**
- **Haggle in the Grand Bazaar**
- **Enjoy the buzz on Nevizade Sokak**

TWO ADULTS allow US$105

Morning
The **Spice Bazaar** *(see p88)* is a riot of colour, stalls and smells, where you can buy any number of exotic foodstuffs, including hand-made Turkish delight and creamy goats' cheese. From here, head up to the bustling **Grand Bazaar** *(see pp98–9)*, a labyrinthine Ottoman shopping complex housing thousands of leather, rug, ceramics and jewellery shops. Prices are inflated and price tags often absent altogether so remember to bargain. All this shopping is bound to whet your appetite, so head for the waterfront

district of Kumpkapı, where you will find more than 50 fish restaurants vying for your attention. Again, many outlets do not display prices, so ask before you order.

Afternoon
Revived and restored, take a taxi to the Galata Bridge and stroll over to trendy Tünel and Beyoğlu *(see pp101–7)*, soaking up the view as you go. Take time to browse around the cosy cafés and bars in Tünel, before making your way up İstiklâl Cadessi *(see pp102–103)* to shop for clothes, shoes, books and music. Further up, the district of **Çukurcuma** *(see p107)* is a hunting ground for antique furniture and ornaments. Nevizade Sokak, just off İstiklâl Cadessi, is a narrow street lined with dozens of *meyhanes (see p193)*. The area really comes alive at night, when hundreds of locals flock here and passers-by are serenaded by traditional musicians.

A FAMILY DAY OUT

- **See Istanbul in miniature**
- **A boat trip to Büyükada**
- **A horse-drawn carriage ride around Büyükada**

FAMILY OF FOUR allow US$120

Morning
Catch a bus from Taksim Square to Miniatürk *(see pp222–3)* located in Sütlüce on the northern shore of the **Golden Horn** *(see p89)*. The park displays miniatures of the city's most famous sights, such as Haghia Sophia *(see pp72–5)*, as well as other treasures from around the country that reflect Turkey's rich heritage. There is also a children's park and a museum showcasing photographs of Atatürk, the great Turkish leader of the early 20th century, and the wars in Gallipoli. When you get hungry, head to Miniatürk's attractive café-restaurant that overlooks the Golden Horn.

Bustling dock activity at Eminönü

Afternoon

Head back to Istanbul after lunch and hop on a boat bound for the island of Büyükada, one of the nine that make up the **Princes' Islands** *(see p159)*. It is a one-and-a-half hour trip from the docks at Eminönü, so there is plenty of time to admire the view as Istanbul recedes on the horizon. Once you have landed, stroll around the main square of Saat Meydani or take a horse-drawn carriage ride around the island. Climb the hill to St George's Monastery for panoramic views and a meal at the hilltop restaurant.

The Fortress of Europe overlooking the Bosphorus

MOSQUES, MUSEUMS AND HAMAMS

- Byzantine iconography at Haghia Sophia
- Glimpse the past at the Museum of Turkish and Islamic Arts
- An awe-inspiring visit to Topkapi Palace

TWO ADULTS allow US$140

Morning

Start at the **Blue Mosque** *(see pp78–9)*, perhaps Istanbul's most elegant Islamic sight, famous for its slender minarets and blue Iznik tiles. Stroll through the well-tended garden at the front before making your way to imposing **Haghia Sophia** *(see pp72–5)*, another of Istanbul's most renowned mosques. Inside is a marvellous array of Byzantine mosaics, friezes and Iznik blue tile decorations, as well as a huge domed ceiling. Then head to the nearby **Museum of Turkish and Islamic Arts** *(see p77)*, which has a wonderful collection of glass and metalwork, carpets and manuscripts from down the centuries, as well as modern art from Turkey and overseas. Head to Yesil Ev *(see p186)* for lunch, a lovely Ottoman-style restaurant between the museum and Topkapı Palace, serving traditional fare.

Afternoon

You will need at least three hours to appreciate **Topkapi Palace** *(see pp52–9)*, a sprawling complex of courtyards, gardens, fountains, a harem and a collection of priceless antiques. Then, at the end of a long day, indulge in that most Turkish of pleasures, a visit to a Turkish bath *(see p67)*. Çemberlitaş Baths *(see p81)* in Sultanahmet is one of the finest.

Decorative blue tiles in the Haghia Sophia mosque

UP THE BOSPHORUS

- A boat up the Bosphorus
- Enjoy views at Fortress of Europe
- Stroll through the pretty village of Bebek

TWO ADULTS allow US$95

Morning

Catch a bus from Taksim Square or Eminönü bus terminus heading for Sarıyer or Emirgan and get off at Arnavutköy *(see p145)* on the Bosphorous. There are some lovingly restored Ottoman houses and mansions to admire here, most of them painted in pastel shades and trimmed with intricate wooden fretwork. Cafés line the back streets, so sit and linger over a coffee and a pastry. From Arnavutköy, continue walking northwards, past the fishing boats and pleasure cruisers bobbing on the water, until you reach **Bebek** *(see p138 & p146)*, one of Istanbul's most affluent villages. There are more than enough chic clothes and antiques shops here to tempt visitors to part with their cash and work up an appetite for lunch. Dine in style at the **Poseidon** *(see p206)*. Here you can sip an aperitif and enjoy the splendid view before savouring the menu of fresh fish.

Afternoon

Delve into history at the imposing **Fortress of Europe** *(see pp140–1)*, built in the 15th century as part of the Muslim conquest of Constantinople. There is also a fantastic view of the Bosphorus from here. Afterwards, walk around the delightful 19th-century pavilions of nearby **Emirgan Park** *(see p141)* with its hundreds of pine, fir and cypress trees and an ornamental lake.

Putting Istanbul on the Map

Istanbul stands astride the straits of the Bosphorus, straddling the European and Asian parts of Turkey and bordered to the south by the Sea of Marmara. The city is divided not only by the Bosphorus but also by the Golden Horn, an inlet forming a natural harbour. Although no longer the capital of Turkey (*see p31*), Istanbul is still the country's largest and most monumental city.

Satellite view of Greater Istanbul

KEY

☐	Greater Istanbul
✈	Airport
⛴	Ferry port
▆	Motorway
▭	Major road
▆	Other main road
—	Railway
▪▪	International border

0 kilometres 40

0 miles 40

◁ **Miniature depicting the lavish festivities staged for the circumcision of Ahmet III's sons in 1720**

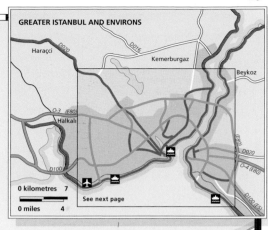

GREATER ISTANBUL AND ENVIRONS

Haraçci
Kemerburgaz
Beykoz
D020
D016
Halkalı
Beykoz

0 kilometres 7

0 miles 4

See next page

Istanbul and its Environs
The sights in central Istanbul are covered in detail on pages 48–107 and a Street Finder is provided on pages 246–63. Sights outside the centre are covered on pages 108–49. Places of interest on the Bosphorus and further afield, still within the city boundaries, are explored on pages 134–71.

Black Sea

Samsun Trabzon

Zonguldak

Ereğli

Devrek

Karabük Yenice Irmağı

Kandıra

Karasu Akçakoca

Kocaeli (İzmit)

Sakarya (Adapazarı)

Düzce

Bolu

Sapanca Gölü

İznik

Bilecik

Sakarya Nehri

Nallıhan

Beypazarı Kirmir Çayı

K   **E**   **Y**

Sarıyar Barajı

ANKARA

Eskişehir

Milhallıçık

EUROPE AND THE MEDITERRANEAN REGION

ESTONIA
SWEDEN
DENMARK
LATVIA
LITHUANIA
RUSSIAN FEDERATION
UNITED KINGDOM
REP. OF IRELAND
BELORUSSIA
NETHERLANDS
GERMANY
POLAND
BELGIUM
LUXEMBOURG CZECH REP.
UKRAINE
FRANCE
AUSTRIA HUNGARY
SLOVAKIA
SWITZERLAND
SLOVENIA
MOLDAVIA
CROATIA
BOSNIA
HERZ.
ROMANIA
ITALY
SERBIA & MONTENEGRO
BULGARIA
MACEDONIA
GEORGIA
ALBANIA
Istanbul
PORTUGAL
SPAIN
GREECE
TURKEY
TUNISIA
SYRIA
LEBANON
MOROCCO
ALGERIA
ISRAEL
IRAQ
JORDAN
LIBYA
EGYPT
SAUDI ARABIA

Tuz Gölü

Greater Istanbul

The expanding metropolis of Istanbul spreads along the Bosphorus to the north, beyond the airport to the west and inland from the Asian shore in the east. Its official population is put at a little over 11 million but the actual population is probably much higher. Transport improvements are being made to make getting around this vast urban area easier. Most visitors, however, stay in the historical central parts where the major sights are located.

Alibeyköy Barajı

TEM YOLU

O-2

Alibey Der

ATATÜRK CADDESI

GAZİOSMANPAŞA

İSTANBUL CADDESİ

D020

Kırklareli

İSTANBUL EDİRNE CADDESİ

ORDU CADDESİ

Edirne

O-2 (E80)

BAYRAMPAŞA

EYÜP

(E80) (E5)

O-3

TRAKYA TEM OTOYOLU

HALKALI CADDESİ

FATİH CADDESİ

ESENLER

Esenler

BAĞLANTI YOLU

MAHMUTBEY CADDESİ

BAĞCILAR

CUMHURİYET CADDESİ

BARIKÖY CADDESİ

ÇİNÇİN CADDESİ

GÜNGÖREN

Balat

FAT

VATAN CADDE

ASFALTI

ATATÜRK CADDESİ

BAHÇELİEVLER

ESKİ LONDRA ASFALTI

LONDRA ASFALTI

K. Mustafa Paşa

Yeı

D100 (E5)

Edirne

LONDRA ASFALTI

O-1 (E5)

SEYİT NİZAM CADDESİ

ZEYTİNBURNU

Yedikule

Kazlıçeşme

BAKIRKÖY

Yeni Mahalle

Zeytinburnu

Bakırköy

ZEYTİNBURNU CADDESİ

HAVAALANI CADDESİ

Ataköy

KENNEDY

RAUF ORBAY CADDESİ

Atatürk

YEŞİLKÖY

Bakırköy

Yeşilköy

FLORYA CADDESİ

Yeşilyurt

Sea of Marmara

0 kilometres   2

0 miles   2

KEY

- Central Istanbul
- Greater Istanbul
- ✈ Airport
- ⛴ Ferry boarding point
- Sea bus boarding point
- 🚉 Railway station
- 🚌 Bus station
- Motorway
- Main road
- Other road
- Railway

Central Istanbul

Shoe shine man outside the New Mosque

This guide divides central Istanbul into four distinct areas, each with its own chapter. Three areas lie on the southern side of the Golden Horn. Seraglio Point is a raised promontory on which stands the sumptuous Topkapı Palace. Two architectural masterpieces, Haghia Sophia and the Blue Mosque, dominate the area of Sultanahmet. The pace of life is quite different in the Bazaar Quarter, a maze of narrow streets filled with frenetic commerce. North of the Golden Horn is Beyoğlu, which for centuries was the preferred place of residence of Istanbul's foreign communities, and is still markedly cosmopolitan in atmosphere.

İstiklâl Caddesi, Beyoğlu
Old-fashioned trams shuttle up and down the pedestrianized street that forms the backbone of this area (see pp100–107).

The Grand Bazaar, in the Bazaar Quarter
This quaint former coffee house stands at a junction in the labyrinthine old shopping complex at the heart of the city's Bazaar Quarter (see pp84–99).

KEY

■	Major sight
⛴	Ferry boarding point
🚊	Railway station
Ⓜ	Metro
🚋	Tram stop
🚋	Nostalgic Tram stop
🚇	Underground funicular stop
ℹ	Tourist information
🛁	Turkish bath
C	Mosque
✝	Church
⊠	Post office

**Topkapı Palace,
Seraglio Point**

*This 18th-century marble
pavilion, the Library of
Ahmet III, stands in one of the
courtyards of Topkapı Palace.
The walls of the palace grounds
now enclose Gülhane Park (see
p61) as well as many other
historic buildings.*

| 0 metres | 500 |
| 0 yards | 500 |

View across Sultanahmet

*The six slender minarets of the Mosque of
Sultan Ahmet I, better known as the Blue
Mosque, soar above the spacious square in
the middle of Sultanahmet (see pp68–83),
Istanbul's most historical district.*

THE HISTORY OF ISTANBUL

*I*stanbul was founded in the 7th century BC on a naturally defensive site from which trade along the Bosphorus could be controlled. For 16 centuries it was a great imperial capital, first of the Byzantine Empire and then of the Ottoman sultans. Some knowledge of the histories of these two civilizations helps the visitor to appreciate the magnificent monuments found throughout the city.

The topography of Istanbul was formed at the end of the last Ice Age, when meltwaters created the Bosphorus. The Stone Age cultures in the area were replaced by Copper Age villages and walled Bronze Age towns (notably Troy, *see p171*). The Bosphorus was an important trade route in the ancient world along which ships carried wine and olive oil north from the Mediterranean, and grain, skins, wool, timber, wax, honey, salted meat and salted fish south from regions around the Black Sea.

Septimius Severus, who devastated the city in the 2nd century AD

The area around the Bosphorus was subjugated by a series of peoples, starting with the Mycenaeans (1400–1200 BC). Between 800 and 680 BC the region was controlled by the kingdom of Phrygia. Later, in 676 BC, Greek expeditionaries founded the city of Chalcedon (on the site where modern Kadıköy now stands).

THE FOUNDATION OF BYZANTION

The foundation of Istanbul is usually dated to 667 BC when, according to legend, a Greek colonist, Byzas, led an expedition from the overcrowded cities of Athens and Megara to establish a colony on the European side of the Bosphorus. This colony, known as Byzantion, grew to be a successful independent city-state, or *polis*, one of the 40 most important such states throughout the Ancient Greek world. During the next few centuries, Byzantion worked in partnership with Chalcedon, using the same coinage and sharing the tolls exacted from passing sea trade.

But Byzantion had to struggle to maintain its independence in the mercurial politics of the ancient world. It endured Lydian (560–546 BC), Persian (546–478 BC), Athenian (478–411 BC) and Macedonian (334–281 BC) rule before briefly regaining its autonomy. In 64 BC it was subsumed into the Roman Empire as Byzantium. The city was almost destroyed in AD 195 by Septimius Severus because of its support for his rival for the imperial throne, Pescennius Niger. It survived the Goths' devastation of Chalcedon in AD 258 but trade in the region dramatically declined in the following years.

TIMELINE

	340 BC Philip II of Macedonia unsuccessfully besieges city				AD 195 Roman emperor Septimius Severus destroys Byzantium but later rebuilds it, laying out the Hippodrome	
c.676 BC Chalcedon, a Greek settlement, founded on Asian shore		*Alexander the Great*				
600 BC	**400 BC**		**200 BC**	**AD 1**		**AD 200**
c.667 BC Byzantion reputedly founded by Greek colonists from Athens and Megara, led by Byzas		**334 BC** Alexander the Great crosses the Hellespont (Dardanelles) and conquers Anatolia		**64 BC** Pompey brings Byzantion into the Roman Empire, renaming it Byzantium	**AD 258** Goths destroy Chalcedon	

◁ The Byzantine emperor Justinian the Great shown with one of his prefects in a mosaic

CONSTANTINE THE GREAT

In AD 324, after defeating his co-emperor Licinius, Constantine the Great (324–37) became sole ruler of the Roman Empire. One of his greatest achievements was to move the capital of the empire from Rome to Byzantium. Initially, Constantine preferred the site of Troy *(see p171)* for his capital, but was persuaded by advisers that Byzantium held a superior position for both defence and trade.

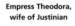

Gold aureus of Constantine

Constantine's city was officially styled the "New Rome" but became widely known as Constantinople. The emperor quickly started on an ambitious programme of construction work, which included the Great Palace *(see pp82–3)* and various public buildings.

Constantine was also instrumental in the spread of Christianity. According to legend, he saw a vision of the cross before a battle in 312. Although not actually baptized until just before his death, he worked hard to create a coherent system of Christian belief out of the variant practices of the day. All the early church councils took place in the city or nearby, the first being held in Nicaea, (modern-day İznik, *see p160*), and the second in Constantinople itself.

A successor of Constantine, Theodosius I (379–95), divided the Empire between his two sons, Honorius and Arcadius. When the Latin-speaking Western Empire fell to barbarian armies during the 5th century, the Greek-speaking Eastern Empire, thereafter known as the Byzantine Empire, survived.

THE AGE OF JUSTINIAN

The 6th century was dominated by the extraordinary genius of Justinian (527–65), who developed Constantinople into a thriving city and almost succeeded in reconquering the lost provinces of the Western Empire from the barbarians. At the time of his death the empire had expanded to its greatest size, and covered Syria, Palestine, Asia Minor, Greece, the Balkans, Italy,

Empress Theodora, wife of Justinian

southern Spain and many territories in northern Africa, including Egypt.

Justinian's formidable wife, the ex-courtesan Theodora, had a great deal of influence over him. In 532 she persuaded the emperor to use mercenaries to put down an angry mob in the most notorious event of his reign, the Nika Revolt. In the carnage that followed 30,000 were killed inside the Hippodrome *(see p80)*.

Justinian was also responsible for much of the city's great architecture, including Haghia Sophia *(see pp72–5)*, Haghia Eirene *(see p60)* and parts of the Great Palace.

Relief from the Egyptian Obelisk *(see p80)*, showing Theodosius I and his courtiers

TIMELINE

300	400	500	600	700
324 Constantine becomes ruler of the Roman Empire	**395** On the death of Theodosius I, the empire is divided into two	**476** The Western Roman Empire falls to barbarians		**674** Five-year long siege of Constantinople initiated by the Saracens
330 Inauguration of Constantinople		**532** Nika Revolt is put down by mercenaries; 30,000 are killed		
325 First church council meets at Nicaea	**412** Construction work begins on the Walls of Theodosius II *(see p22)*	**537** Emperor Justinian dedicates the new Haghia Sophia		
337 Constantine is baptized a Christian on his deathbed			**726** Leo III issues a decree denouncing idolatry, and many icons are destroyed	

Walls of Theodosius II

THE BYZANTINES AT WAR

The Byzantine Empire never again attained the splendour of the reign of Justinian, but throughout the first millennium it remained rich and powerful. During the early Middle Ages, Constantinople was an oasis of learning, law, art and culture at a time when Europe was plunged into a dark age of ignorance and illiteracy. Considering themselves to be the leaders of Christianity, the Byzantine rulers dispatched missionaries to spread their religion and culture among the Slavic nations, especially Russia.

"Greek fire", used by the Byzantines against the Arabs

During this period, Constantinople produced some capable emperors, in particular Heraclius (610–41), Basil the Macedonian (867–86), Leo the Wise (886–912) and Basil the Bulgar-Slayer (976–1025). Between them these rulers contributed a number of buildings to the city and recaptured lost provinces.

Never without enemies greedy for a share of the prodigious riches that had been amassed in the city, Constantinople was besieged by Slavs, Arabs, Avars, Bulgars, Persians and Russians, all without success because of the protection of the land walls. The surrounding seas, meanwhile, were under the control of Constantinople's powerful navy. Its main ship was the dromon, an oared vessel which could ram another ship but above all deliver the dreaded "Greek fire", an early form of napalm.

A 6th-century ivory carving of a Byzantine emperor, possibly Anastasius I (491–518)

In 1059 Constantine X, the first of the Dukas dynasty of emperors, ascended to the throne. The state over which the dynasty presided was a weakened one, divided between the over-privileged bureaucracy in the capital and the feudal landlords of the provinces. At the same time increasing dependency on foreign mercenaries placed the empire's defence in the hands of its most aggressive neighbours. These included the Normans from southern Italy, the Venetians and Turkic nomads from the east. The Byzantine imperial army was totally destroyed at the Battle of Manzikert (1071) and again, a century later, at the Battle of Myriocephalon (1176) by the Seljuk Turks from the east. These losses effectively ended Byzantine rule of Anatolia, which had for so long been the backbone of the empire. The remarkable Comnenus dynasty (1081–1185) ruled for a century after the Dukas emperors, between these two defeats. Their main achievement was to succeed in holding the rest of the empire together.

Haghia Sophia mosaic

843 Icons are permitted again by seventh church council Haghia Sophia

1071 The Byzantine army is destroyed by the Seljuk Turks at the Battle of Manzikert. Emperor Romanus Diogenes is disgraced and deposed

1138 John II Comnenus recovers Serbia

1176 The Seljuk Turks defeat the Byzantine forces at the Battle of Myriocephalon

| 800 | 900 | 1000 | 1100 | 1200 |

1054 The Orthodox and Catholic churches break away from each other because of differences over dogma

1096 The armies of the First Crusade pass through Constantinople and assist Alexius I Comnenus to retake the Anatolian seaboard from the Seljuk Turks

The City of Constantinople

Mosaic of the Virgin, St Saviour in Chora

For almost a thousand years Constantinople was the richest city in Christendom. It radiated out from three great buildings: the church of Haghia Sophia *(see pp72–5)*, the Hippodrome *(see p80)* and the Great Palace *(see pp82–3)*. The city also had a great many other fine churches and palaces, filled with exquisite works of art. Daily life for the populace centred on the four market squares, or *fora*. Meanwhile, their need for fresh water was met by an advanced network of aqueducts and underground water cisterns.

Walls of Theodosius
Theodosius II's great chain of land walls (see p114) *withstood countless sieges until the Ottoman conquest of the city in 1453* (see p26).

THE CITY IN 1200

At its height the magnificent city of Constantinople probably had about 400,000 inhabitants. The population density was relatively low, though, and there was space within the city walls for fields and orchards.

Mocius Cistern

The Golden Gate was a ceremonial gate through the city's ramparts.

Church of St John of Studius *(see p116)*

Walls of Constantine (now totally destroyed)

Forum of Arcadius

Harbour of Theodosius

BYZANTINE CHURCH ARCHITECTURE

Early Byzantine churches were either basilical (like St John of Studius) or built to a centralized plan (as in SS Sergius and Bacchus). From the 9th century, churches, like the typical example shown here, were built around four corner piers, or columns. Exteriors were mostly unadorned brickwork, but interiors were lavishly decorated with golden mosaics. Although the Ottomans converted Constantinople's churches into mosques after their conquest of the city, many original features are clearly discernible today.

TYPICAL LATE BYZANTINE CHURCH

A central apse is flanked by two smaller side apses.

Four columns support the dome.

Brickwork may alternate with layers of stone.

The narthex, a covered porch, forms the entrance to the church.

Golden mosaics cover the ceilings and upper walls.

Church of the Holy Apostles
The domes of what was one of the city's most important churches (see p113) are shown in this 12th-century image of the Ascension.

Aetius Cistern

St Saviour in Chora *(see pp118–19)*

Blachernae Palace *(see p117)*

Monastery of the Pantocrator *(see p113)*

Valens Aqueduct
Water from the Belgrade Forest (see p158) and the mountains west of the city was brought into Constantinople on this great structure (see p89).

Forum of Theodosius *(see p83)*

Forum of Constantine *(see p81)*

Chain across Golden Horn *(see p89)*

Basilica Cistern
This cavernous cistern (see p76) represented a great feat of engineering when it was built in the 6th century.

Church of SS Sergius and Bacchus *(see p82)*

Hippodrome *(see p80)*

Great Palace *(see pp82–3)*

Haghia Eirene *(see p60)*

Haghia Sophia
The great church of Constantinople (see pp72–5) was filled with mosaics, including this one showing the Virgin and Child with the emperors Constantine and Justinian.

Milion, Hippodrome
This stone pillar (see p71) is all that remains of a Byzantine triumphal arch from which road distances to all corners of the empire were once measured.

The capture of Constantinople during the Fourth Crusade of 1202–4

THE FOURTH CRUSADE

In 1202, an army of 34,000 responded to an appeal from Pope Innocent III for a new crusade to the Holy Land. This unruly force of Christians lacked the funds to get beyond Venice, where it needed to hire ships. It consequently fell under the influence of Enrico Dandolo, the manipulative Doge of Venice. With his backing, the crusaders were soon diverted to Constantinople where they helped the young Alexius IV take the throne.

However, six months later, when they realized they were unlikely to receive their promised financial reward from the emperor, the crusaders lost patience and launched a new attack, ousting Alexius in favour

Icon of St Michael, now in Venice, an example of the fine Byzantine art plundered by the Venetians during the Fourth Crusade

of one their own, Baldwin I, Count of Flanders. Through the dark years that followed, known as the Latin Empire, the once great city was reduced by pillage, misrule and emigration to a scattering of disconnected villages grouped behind the city walls. Outside Constantinople, the exiled Byzantine emperors survived the turmoil, biding their time as the rulers of the Empire of Nicaea, just to the south, which included modern-day İznik (see p160).

CONSTANTINOPLE IN DECLINE

In 1261, Constantinople was recaptured for Byzantium by Michael VIII Palaeologus (1258–82), who met almost no resistance in the process. He did this with the aid

TIMELINE

1202 An army assembles in Venice to launch the Fourth Crusade

1204 Alexius IV is deposed and Baldwin I is crowned emperor of a new Latin Empire

1261 Michael VIII Palaeologus recaptures Constantinople from the Venetians

1331 Ottomans capture Nicaea (modern İznik)

1326 Prusa (Bursa) is taken and becomes Ottoman capital

| 1200 | 1225 | 1250 | 1275 | 1300 | 13 |

1203 Dandolo, Doge of Venice, diverts the Fourth Crusade to Constantinople. He cuts the chain across the Golden Horn (see p23) and storms the city

Bronze horses taken by Dandolo from the Hippodrome (see p80) to Venice

1301 Osman I founds the Ottoman Empire

1321 Outbreak of disastrous 33-year-long Byzantine civil war of the Italian city of Genoa, which was naturally disposed to fight against her rival Venice. Yet she still exacted a crippling price for her assistance. The Genoese established the colony of Pera across the Golden Horn from Constantinople, and effectively took control of the city's trade.

Constantinople's recapture and reconstruction caused a flowering of scholarship and artistic activity, known as the Palaeologue Renaissance after the family of emperors. An example of the many beautiful buildings dating from this period is the Church of St Saviour in Chora *(see pp118–19)*.

Two-headed Byzantine eagle

During this period the double-headed eagle was adopted as the imperial crest, with the two heads symbolizing the western and eastern halves of the empire. Yet, within a few decades there was further discord in Constantinople, when a quarrel arose

Mosaic of the Virgin and Child in St Saviour in Chora

between Andronicus II (1282–1328) and his grandson Andronicus III (1328–41) over the succession. This led to the disastrous civil war of 1321–54.

THE RISE OF THE OTTOMANS

The Ottoman state was born in 1301 when Osman I, a leader of warriors who were fighting for the Muslim faith on the eastern frontier of the Byzantine Empire, declared his independence. The new state quickly expanded and in 1326 captured Prusa (modern-day Bursa, *see pp162–8*), which became its capital. The judicious piety of the Ottomans soon won them the support of the general population of their territories, and even of some Christian brotherhoods. Meanwhile, a professional core of Janissaries *(see p127)* was created to add stability to an army which was otherwise too dependent on Turkic and renegade volunteer cavalry.

By 1362, with the Ottoman capture of Adrianople (Edirne, *see pp154–7*), Byzantium had been reduced to the city-state of Constantinople and a few minor outposts, isolated within Ottoman domains. Only a Mongol incursion in 1402 delayed the Ottoman invasion of Constantinople itself. In 1422 the Ottoman army made its first attack on the city's colossal land walls. As the threat increased, the Byzantine emperor made a last ditch effort to win the support of the Latin West in 1439. The Hungarians alone answered his call for help, forming a 25,000-strong crusade. However, in 1444 they were defeated en route by the Ottomans at the Battle of Varna on the Black Sea.

1350	1375		1400	1425	1450

1362 Murat I conquers Adrianople (Edirne), which then becomes the Ottoman capital. Byzantium is reduced to the city of Constantinople

1451 Mehmet II succeeds to the Ottoman throne and orders construction of the Fortress of Europe *(see p140)* to seal the Bosphorus

1348 The Galata Tower is built by the Genoese inhabitants of the city as a watchtower over the Pera quarter

Galata Tower

1422 First Ottoman siege of Constantinople by Murat III

1444 A Hungarian army on its way to help Constantinople is destroyed by the Ottomans at Varna on the Black Sea. Constantinople's last hope of survival is lost

THE CONQUEST OF CONSTANTINOPLE

On 29 May 1453 Sultan Mehmet II (1451–81), known as "the Conqueror", entered Constantinople after a 54-day siege during which his cannon had torn a huge hole in the Walls of Theodosius II *(see p114)*. Mehmet's first task was to rebuild the wrecked city,

Sultan Mehmet II, "the Conqueror"

which would later become known as Istanbul. The Grand Bazaar *(see pp98–9)* and Topkapı Palace *(see pp54–7)* were erected in the years following the Muslim conquest. Religious foundations were endowed to fund the building of mosques such as the Fatih *(see p113)* and their associated schools and baths *(see pp38–9)*. The city had to be repopulated by a mixture of force and encouragement. People from all over the empire moved to Istanbul, and Jews, Christians and Muslims lived together in a cosmopolitan society.

Mehmet and his successors pushed the frontiers of the empire across the Middle East and into Europe. In the early 16th century, Selim I (1512–20) conquered Egypt and assumed the title of caliph *(see p29)*, as well as establishing the Ottomans as a sea power. He is also notorious for killing all his male relatives bar one son, to ensure that there were no rivals for the succession.

SÜLEYMAN THE MAGNIFICENT

Selim's one surviving son was Süleyman I, "the Magnificent" (1520–66), under whose rule the Ottoman Empire reached its maximum extent. At the time of his death the empire stretched from Algiers to the Caspian Sea and from Hungary to the Persian Gulf. Much of western Europe only just escaped conquest when an Ottoman army was driven back from the gates of Vienna in 1529. Süleyman's

OTTOMAN EMPIRE
■ *Maximum extent (1566)*

reign was a time of great artistic and architectural achievements. The architect Sinan *(see p91)* designed many mosques and other great buildings in the city, while the Ottoman arts of ceramics *(see p161)* and calligraphy *(see p95)* also flourished.

Depiction of the unsuccessful siege of Vienna

TIMELINE

1453 Mehmet the Conqueror enters Constantinople on 29 May

1456 The Ottomans occupy Athens

1461 Trebizond on the Black Sea, the last part of the Byzantine Empire, is conquered

1536 Grand Vizier İbrahim Paşa is killed on the orders of Süleyman's wife, Roxelana *(see p76)*

1561 Süleyman executes his son Beyazıt on suspicion of treason

1571 Defeat of the Ottoman navy at the Battle of Lepanto

1450	1475	1500	1525	1550

1455 Yedikule Castle *(see p115)* is built and work begins on the Grand Bazaar

1470 Fatih Mosque is built over the Church of the Holy Apostles

1478 Topkapı Palace completed

1533 Hayrettin Paşa, better known as Barbarossa, is appointed grand admiral

1556 Inauguration of Sinan's Süleymaniye Mosque *(see pp90–91)*

Süleyman I

THE SULTANATE OF WOMEN

Süleyman's son Selim II (1566–74), "the Sot", was not such a capable ruler, although he added Cyprus to the empire. The defeat of his navy by the Venetians at the Battle of Lepanto was a heavy blow to Ottoman ambitions to be a seafaring power. This era was also the start of the so-called "Sultanate of Women", when Selim's mother (the valide sultan, see p28) and Nur Banu, his principal wife (the first *kadın*), effectively took over power and exercised it for their own ends. Corruption and intrigue became endemic, and after Selim's death Nur Banu kept her son, Murat III (1574–95), distracted by the women of the harem so that she could maintain her control over imperial affairs.

The Battle of Lepanto, a defeat for the Ottoman navy

Osman II (1618–22) was the first sultan to try to reverse the decline of the empire. But when the Janissaries *(see p127)* learnt of his plans to abolish their corps, they started a revolt which eventually led to his assassination. Murat IV (1623–40) enjoyed more success in his attempts at reform and significantly reduced corruption during his stable period of rule.

Osman II, who failed to halt Ottoman decline

The late 17th century saw many years of capable government by a succession of grand viziers from the Albanian Köprülü family. Yet their efforts were not sufficient to stem the decline in imperial fortunes, symbolized by a failed attempt to capture Vienna in 1683. The Treaty of Karlowitz in 1699 marked the start of the Ottoman withdrawal from Europe.

THE TULIP PERIOD

Ahmet III (1703–30), on his succession to the throne, left power in the hands of his capable grand vizier, İbrahim Paşa. The sultan preferred pleasure to politics. During his reign, beautiful Baroque palaces, such as Aynalı Kavak Palace *(see p127)*, fountains, mosques and yalis *(see p139)* were built. Formal gardens were laid out and filled with tulips, Ahmet's favourite flower, which lent their name to the period of his rule. The sultan even ordered tulips to be scattered over the floor at the lavish festivals and entertainments that he staged for the Ottoman elite. He also sent an ambassador, Mehmet Çelebi, to France to investigate Western civilization and culture. On his return, Western clothes and costumes became not only acceptable for the first time, but fashionable.

1616 The Blue Mosque *(see pp78–9)* is finished after eight years of construction work by the architect Mehmet Ağa

1699 The loss of Hungary under the Treaty of Karlowitz marks the Ottomans' retreat from Europe

| 00 | 1625 | 1650 | 1700 | 1725 |

Domes of the Blue Mosque

1622 Revolt of the Janissaries. They murder Osman II in Yedikule Castle, the Prison of the Seven Towers

1729 The first Ottoman printing press is set up in Istanbul and begins to print texts in Turkish

Ottoman Society

Beneath the sultan, Ottoman society was divided into a privileged ruling class (the *askeri*, which included the religious hierarchy, or *ulema*) and a tax-paying subject population (*reaya*). Rank and honour, however, were not hereditary but could be gained through education or service in the army or administration. This social structure was modified during the reforms of the 19th century (*see p30*), but Ottoman titles were only finally abolished in 1924 after the Turkish Republic was created (*see p31*).

The grand vizier, the prime minister, was the sultan's right-hand man.

The sultan *was at the apex of the social order and everyone owed allegiance to him. He lived a life of ease and luxury, as seen in this portrait of Mahmut I (1730–54). The Ottoman* (Osmanlı in Turkish) *sultans were always succeeded by one of their sons, but not automatically by the eldest.*

Ağa of the Janissaries

Minister of the Interior

Şeyhülislam (Grand Mufti)

Chief executioner

Men of high rank *could be recognized by their different uniforms, above all their large and distinctive headgear, as seen in this portrait of four Ottoman officials. The turban was abolished by Mahmut II* (see p30) *in 1829 in favour of the more egalitarian fez.*

BAYRAM RECEPTION (c.1800)

In this painting by Konstantin Kapidagi, Selim III (1789–1807, *see p30*) presides over a parade of high-ranking officials during the celebration of a religious festival (*see p47*) at Topkapı Palace.

THE WOMEN OF THE HAREM

Like all other Ottoman institutions the harem was hierarchical. It was presided over by the sultan's mother, the valide sultana. Next in order of importance came the sultan's daughters. Immediately below them were the four *kadıns*, the official wives or favourites. Then came the *gözdes* (girls who had recently caught the sultan's eye), and the *ikbals* (women with whom he had already slept). Apart from the sultan's family members, all these women had entered the harem as slaves. They were kept under a watchful eye by a powerful stewardess, the *kahya kadın*.

One of the sultan's favourites as depicted in a 19th-century engraving

Black eunuchs

Sword bearer to the sultan

The Gate of Felicity *(see p54)*, in the second courtyard of Topkapı Palace, was used for such ceremonial occasions.

The sultan is surrounded by his courtiers. He is the only seated figure.

Şeyhülislam (Grand Mufti)

Chief lackey (footman)

Chief of the sultan's bodyguard

OTTOMAN TITLES

Ağa: leader of an organization. The most influential *ağas* were the commander of the Janissary corps, the sultan's elite troops *(see p127)*, and the Ağa of the Abode of Felicity, or chief black eunuch, who was in charge of the harem *(see pp58–9)*.

Chief black eunuch

Bey: governor of a district or province. The word is now used simply to mean "Mr".

Caliph: spiritual ruler of the Islamic world. The title was assumed by the Ottoman sultans, beginning with Selim the Grim in 1517.

Gazi: honorary title given to a victorious Islamic warrior.

Kadi: judge charged with interpreting Islamic law and Ottoman administrative codes.

Khedive: viceroy of Egypt under Ottoman rule (1867–1914). The autonomous khedives acknowledged the religious leadership of the Ottoman Empire.

Paşa: title bestowed on a senior civil servant or high-ranking army officer. According to his rank, a *paşa* was entitled to display one, two or three horsetails on his standard *(see p56)*.

Sultan: political and religious ruler of the empire.

Şeyhülislam (Grand Mufti): head of the *ulema*, a religious institution which was made up of "learned men" responsible for interpreting and enforcing Islamic law *(sharia)*.

Valide sultana: mother of the ruling sultan.

Vizier: minister of state. The four most senior ministers were called "viziers of the dome" because they attended cabinet meetings in the domed hall of the divan in Topkapı Palace *(see pp54–9)*. From the 16th century, the divan was presided over by the immensely powerful grand vizier (the prime minister).

Grand vizier

Black eunuchs

Dancing women

Valide sultana

Dwarf

The valide sultana, *the most powerful woman in the harem, is the centre of attention in this festive scene. The picture was commissioned 1689 by Madame Giradin, wife of the French ambassador.*

A Janissary leaps to his death in a German painting of the Auspicious Event of 1826

THE REFORMING SULTANS

Abdül Hamit I (1774–89) resumed the work of reform and was succeeded by Selim III, who instituted a wide range of changes to the military and Ottoman society. He was deposed by a Janissary mutiny in 1807. Mahmut II (1808–39) realized that the Janissary corps *(see p127)* could not be reformed, so he replaced them with a modern army, but the Janissaries rebelled and were massacred on 15 June 1826 in the "Auspicious Event". Soon after, in 1829, the sultan introduced further modernizing measures including changes in the dress code.

Later in his reign Mahmut reorganized central government so that a regulated bureaucracy replaced the old system of rule by military and religious powers. By doing this he paved the way for his sons Abdül Mecit (1839–61) and Abdül Aziz (1861–76) to oversee the Tanzimat (Reordering), a series of legislative reforms. Functionaries were given salaries to deter them from taking bribes and the grand vizier's post was replaced by that of prime minister.

A constitution was declared in 1876, creating parliamentary government. However, the Russian-Turkish War of 1877–88 led to Abdül Hamit II suspending it and ruling alone for the next 30 years. In 1908 a bloodless revolution by a collection of educated men – the so-called Young Turks – finally forced the sultan to recall parliament.

ATATÜRK AND WESTERNIZATION

Throughout the 19th- and early 20th-centuries, the Ottoman Empire steadily lost territory through wars with Russia and Austria, and to emerging Balkan nation-states such as Serbia, Greece and Bulgaria. Then, in World War I, despite famously winning the battle for Gallipoli in a valiant defence of the Dardanelles *(see p170)*, the Ottoman Empire found itself on the losing side. Istanbul was occupied by victorious French and British troops and much of Anatolia by Greek forces. The peace

Artillery in action at Gallipoli

TIMELINE

Dolmabahçe clocktower

1807 Much of the city is destroyed during a Janissary revolt against Mahmut II

1845 First (wooden) Galata Bridge is built over the Golden Horn

1870 Schliemann begins excavation of Troy *(see p171)*

1888 Rail link with Paris leads to first run of the Orient Express *(see p66)*

1800	1825	1850	1875	19

1826 Mahmut II finally destroys the Janissaries in their own barracks in the "Auspicious Event"

1856 Abdül Mecit I abandons Topkapı Palace for the new Dolmabahçe Palace *(see pp128–9)*

1875 The Tünel underground railway system, the third built in the world, opens in Galata

Orient Express poster

treaties that followed rewarded the victors with Ottoman territory and as a result stimulated Turkish nationalists to take over power from the sultan.

The history of modern Turkey is dominated by the figure of Mustafa Kemal Paşa (1881–1938), a military hero turned politician, universally known as Atatürk, or "Father of the Turks". It was at his instigation that the Turkish War of Independence was fought to regain territory lost to the Allies and, in particular, Greece. At the conclusion of this war,

A portrait of Atatürk

the present territorial limits of Turkey were established. Atatürk then set in motion an ambitious programme of political and social change. The sultanate was abolished in 1922, and religion and state were formally separated when the country was declared a secular republic in the following year. His reforms included replacing the Arabic alphabet with a Roman one, allowing women greater social and political rights, encouraging Western dress (the fez was banned) and obliging all Turks to choose a surname.

MODERN ISTANBUL

Another part of this process was to move the institutions of state from the old Ottoman city of Istanbul to the more centrally located Ankara, which became the capital of Turkey in 1923. Since then, Istanbul has gone through a dramatic transformation into a modern city. As mi-

grants from Anatolia have poured in, the population has increased, and although small communities of Jews, Arabs, Armenians and Christians remain within the city, they are now vastly outnumbered by Turks.

Modern tram
(see p232)

A booming economy has led to the building of new motorways and bridges, and the public transport network has been revolutionized by the introduction of modern trams, light railways and fast catamaran sea buses *(see p243)*. Meanwhile Istanbul has geared itself up for tourism: its ancient monuments have been restored and many new hotels and restaurants have opened in recent years to accommodate increasing numbers of visitors.

But, like Turkey as a whole, Istanbul is forever wrestling with a divided half-Asian, half-European identity. The influences of these contrasting cultures remain widely evident today and create the city's unique atmosphere.

The 1970s suspension bridge spanning the Bosphorus

1919–22 British and French occupy Istanbul	**1938** Atatürk dies in Dolmabahçe Palace at 9:05am on 10 November *(see p129)*	**1993** The Islamicist Welfare Party takes control of the Greater Istanbul Municipality	**2006** The new Turkish Lira (YTL) becomes the official currency
1922 Sultanate finally ends		*Turkish flag*	

1925	1950	1975	2000

15 Allied ...ces land at ...lipoli but ...e repulsed ...Turkish ...ops

1936 Haghia Sophia becomes a museum. Restoration starts

1973 A suspension bridge is built across the Bosphorus *(see p138)*, linking east and west Turkey

1996 The United Nations Conference on Human Settlement (Habitat II) is held in Istanbul

1928 Istanbul becomes the city's official name

2002 Recep Tayyip Erdoğan is elected Prime Minister

The Ottoman Sultans

The first Ottomans were the leaders of warlike tribes living on the borders of the Byzantine Empire. From the 13th century, however, the dynasty established itself at the head of a large empire. In their heyday, having captured Istanbul in 1453 *(see p26)*, the Ottoman sultans were admired and feared for their military strength and ruthlessness towards opponents and rival pretenders to the throne. Later sultans often led a decadent life-style while power was exercised by their viziers *(see p29)*.

Murat III (1574–95), whose *tuğra (see p95)* is shown above, fathers over 100 children

Selim II, "the Sot" (1566–74), prefers drinking and harem life to the affairs of state

Selim I, "the Grim" (1512–20), seen here at his coronation, assumes the title of caliph after his conquest of Egypt

Osman Gazi (1280–1324), a tribal chieftain, establishes the Ottoman dynasty

1250	1300	1350	1400	1450	1500	1550

Murat I (1360–89)

Mehmet I (1413–21)

Beyazıt II (1481–1512)

1250	1300	1350	1400	1450	1500	1550

Orhan Gazi (1324–59) is the first Ottoman to bear the title of sultan

Beyazıt I (1389–1402) is nicknamed "the Thunderbolt" because of the speed at which he takes strategic decisions and moves his troops from one place to another

Period of Interregnum (1402–13) while Beyazıt's sons fight each other over the succession

Murat II (1421–51), the greatest of the warrior sultans, gains notable victories against the Crusaders

Süleyman I, "the Magnificent" (1520–66), expands the empire and fosters a golden age of artistic achievement

Mehmet II, "the Conqueror" (1451–81), captures Constantinople in 1453. He then rebuilds the city, transforming it into the new capital of the empire

Mehmet III (1595–1603) succeeds the throne after his mother ha but one of his 19 brothers strang

Abdül Mecit I (1839–61) presides over the reforms of the Tanzimat *(see p30)*

ustafa I (1617–18
d 1622–3), a weak and
ompetent ruler, reigns
two short periods and
deposed twice

Mehmet VI (1918–22),
the last Ottoman sultan,
is forced into exile by the
declaration of the Turkish
Republic *(see p31)*

Mahmut II, "the Reformer"
(1808–39), finally defeats
the Janissaries *(see p127)*

Mehmet V
(1909–18)

İbrahim, "the Mad"
(1640–48), much despised,
goes insane at the end of his
short but disastrous reign

Mahmut I
(1730–54)

Murat V
(1876)

Mustafa II
(1695–
1703)

Süleyman II
(1687–91)

Mustafa III
(1757–74)

1650	1700	1750	1800	1850	1900

1650	1700	1750	1800	1850	1900

Osman III
(1754–7)

Abdül Mecit II
(1922–3) is
caliph only,
the sultanate
having been
abolished in
1922 *(see p31)*

Abdül Aziz
(1861–76)

Mehmet IV
(1648–87)

Abdül Hamit I
(1774–89)

Murat IV
(1623–40)

Ahmet III
(1703–30) presides
over a cultural
lowering known
as the Tulip
Period
(see p27)

Mustafa IV
1807–08

)sman II
1618–22)

Abdül Hamit II (1876–1909)
suspends parliament for
30 years and rules an auto-
cratic police state until
toppled from power by
the Young Turk movement

Ahmet I (1603–17)
has the Blue Mosque
(see pp78–9) con-
structed in the
centre of Istanbul

Selim III (1789–1807)
attempts Western-style
reforms but is over-
thrown by a revolt
of the Janissaries

ISTANBUL AT A GLANCE

More than 100 places worth visiting in Istanbul are described in the *Area by Area* section of this book, which covers the sights of central Istanbul as well as those a short way out of the city centre. They range from mosques, churches, palaces and museums to bazaars, Turkish baths and parks. For a breathtaking view across Istanbul, you can climb the Galata Tower *(see p105)*, or take a ride on a ferry *(see pp242–3)* to the city's Asian shore. A selection of the sights you should not miss is given below. If you are short of time you will probably want to concentrate on the most famous monuments, namely Topkapı Palace, Haghia Sophia and the Blue Mosque which are all located conveniently close to each other.

ISTANBUL'S TOP TEN SIGHTS

Topkapı Palace
See pp54–7

Dolmabahçe Palace
See pp128–9

Archaeological Museum
See pp62–5

Blue Mosque
See pp78–9

Haghia Sophia
See pp72–5

Süleymaniye Mosque
See pp90–91

Basilica Cistern
See p76

The Bosphorus Trip
See pp144–9

Grand Bazaar
See pp98–9

Church of St Saviour in Chora
See pp118–19

◁ View of Haghia Sophia in central Sultanahmet, a great Byzantine church later converted into a mosque

Istanbul's Best: Mosques and Churches

Most visitors to Istanbul will immediately be struck by the quantity of mosques, from the imposing domed buildings dominating the skyline to the small neighbourhood mosques which would pass unnoticed were it not for their minarets. Several mosques were built as churches, but converted for Islamic worship after the Ottoman conquest (see p26). Some of the most outstanding of them have since become national monuments, but no longer serve a religious function.

St Saviour in Chora
The Dormition of the Virgin is one of many beautiful mosaics that fill this Byzantine church (see pp118–19).

Eyüp Mosque
The holiest mosque in Istanbul stands beside the tomb of Eyüp Ensari, a companion of the Prophet Mohammed (see p120).

GOLDEN H

Church of the Pammakaristos
An image of Christ Pantocrator gazes down from the main dome of what was one of the most important churches in the city (see p113).

Fatih Mosque
Rebuilt after an earthquake, this mosque was founded by Mehmet the Conqueror after his conquest of the city (see p26). The inner courtyard is especially fine (see p113).

Süleymaniye Mosque
Sinan, the greatest Ottoman imperial architect, built this mosque in honour of his patron Süleyman the Magnificent (see p26). He placed ablution taps in the side arches of the mosque to serve a large number of worshippers (see pp90–91).

Atik Valide Mosque
The last major work of Sinan (see p91), this mosque was built in 1583 for the wife of Selim II. Its mihrab (niche indicating the direction of Mecca) is surrounded by İznik tiles (see p131).

Rüstem Paşa Mosque
The fine tiles decorating this mosque date from the mid-16th century, the greatest period of İznik tile (see p161) production (see p88).

Haghia Sophia
One of the world's greatest feats of architecture, Haghia Sophia dates from AD 537. The calligraphic roundels were added in the 19th century (see pp72–5).

BEYOĞLU

BOSPHORUS

ASIAN SIDE

SERAGLIO
POINT

AZAAR
RTER

SULTANAHMET

Blue Mosque
Istanbul's most famous landmark was built by some of the same stone-masons who later helped construct the Taj Mahal in India (see pp78–9).

Church of SS Sergius and Bacchus
An intricate frieze with a Greek inscription honouring the two dedicatees of this former church has survived for 1,400 years (see p82).

0 metres   500

0 yards   500

Exploring Mosques

Five times a day throughout Istanbul a chant is broadcast over loudspeakers set high in the city's minarets to call the faithful to prayer. Over 99 per cent of the population is Muslim, though the Turkish state is officially secular. Most belong to the Sunni branch of Islam, but there are also a few Shiites. Both follow the teachings of the Koran, the sacred book of Islam, and the Prophet Mohammed (c.570–632), but Shiites accept, in addition, the authority of a line of 12 imams directly descended from Mohammed. Islamic mystics are known as Sufis (see p104).

Overview of the Süleymaniye Mosque complex

The ablutions fountain (*şadırvan*) was used by worshippers for ritual washing.

The caravanserai or han (see p96) provided accommodation for travellers.

The kitchen (*imaret*) catered for mosque officials, students, the sick and the poor.

Hospital (*darüşşifa*)

Colleges (*medreses*) for general and theological education were built adjacent to the mosque. Most now serve other uses.

Turkish baths (*hamam*)

Courtyard (*avlu*)

Prayer hall (*cami*)

A mausoleum (*türbe*) was built for the founder of the mosque.

PLAN OF A TYPICAL MOSQUE COMPLEX (KÜLLİYE)

A large complex such as the Süleymaniye Mosque (see pp90–91), shown here, was built as a charitable foundation as well as a place of worship. It would typically include a hospital, school, Islamic study halls, caravanserai (lodgings for travellers), public kitchen for the poor, and bath house. Today most such buildings no longer fulfil their original functions.

INSIDE A MOSQUE

Visitors will experience a soaring sense of space on entering the prayer hall of one of Istanbul's great mosques. Islam forbids images of living things (human or animal) inside a mosque, so there are never any statues or figurative paintings; but the geometric and abstract architectural details of the interior can be exquisite. Men and women pray separately. Women often use a screened off area or a balcony.

The müezzin mahfili *is a raised platform found in large mosques. The muezzin (mosque official) stands on this when chanting responses to the prayers of the imam (head of the mosque).*

The mihrab, *an ornate niche in the wall, marks the direction of Mecca. The prayer hall is laid out so that most people can see it.*

The minbar *is a lofty pulpit to the right of the mihrab. This is used by the imam when he delivers the Friday sermon (khutba).*

MUSLIM BELIEFS AND PRACTICES

Muslims believe in God (Allah), and the Koran shares many prophets and stories with the Bible. However, whereas for Christians Jesus is the son of God, Muslims hold that he was just one in a line of prophets – the last being Mohammed, who brought the final revelation of God's truth to mankind. Muslims believe that Allah communicated the sacred texts of the Koran to Mohammed, via the archangel Gabriel.

There are five basic duties for Muslims. The first of these is the profession of faith: "There is no God but God, and Mohammed is his Prophet". Muslims are also enjoined to pray five times a day, give alms to the poor, and fast during the month of Ramazan (see p47). Once in their lifetime, if they can afford it, they should make the pilgrimage (hajj) to Mecca (in Saudi Arabia), the site of the Kaaba, a sacred shrine built by Abraham, and also the birthplace of the Prophet.

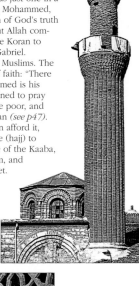

PRAYER TIMES

The five daily prayer times are calculated according to the times of sunrise and sunset, and so change throughout the year. Exact times will be posted up on boards outside large mosques. Those given here are a guide.

Prayer	Summer	Winter
Sabah	5am	7am
öğle	1pm	1pm
İkindi	6pm	4pm
Akşam	8pm	6pm
Yatsı	9:30pm	8pm

The call to prayer *used to be given by the muezzin from the balcony of the minaret. Now-adays loudspeakers broadcast the call across the city. Only imperial mosques have more than one minaret.*

Ritual ablutions *must be undertaken before prayer. Worshippers wash their head, hands and feet either at the fountain in the courtyard or, more usually, at taps set in a discreet wall of the mosque.*

When praying, *Muslims always face the Kaaba in the holy city of Mecca, even if they are not in a mosque, where the mihrab indicates the right direction. Kneeling and lowering the head to the ground are gestures of humility and respect for Allah.*

The loge (hünkar mahfili) *provided the sultan with a screened-off balcony where he could pray, safe from would-be assassins.*

The kürsü, *seen in some mosques, is a chair or throne used by the imam while he reads extracts from the Koran.*

VISITING A MOSQUE

Visitors are welcome at any mosque in Istanbul, but non-Muslims should try to avoid prayer times, especially the main weekly congregation and sermon on Fridays at 1pm. Take off your shoes before entering the prayer hall. Shoulders and knees should be covered. Some mosques require women to cover their hair, and scarves can usually be borrowed. Do not eat, take photographs with a flash or stand close to worshippers. A contribution to a donation box or mosque official is courteous.

Board outside a mosque giving times of prayer

Istanbul's Best: Palaces and Museums

As the former capital of an empire that spanned
from Algeria to Iraq and from Arabia to Hungary,
Istanbul is home to a huge and diverse collection of
treasures. Some, from musical instruments to priceless
jewels, are housed in the beautiful former imperial
palaces of the Ottoman sultans, which are worth visiting
in any case for their architecture and opulent
interiors. Topkapı and Dolmabahçe are the most
famous palaces in Istanbul. The Archaeological
Museum should also be on any itinerary of the
city. This map points out these and other
palaces and museums which are worth
visiting for their splendid buildings or the
exceptional collections they contain.

Aynalı Kavak Palace
*This reclusive palace,
with its airy feel and
intimate proportions,
shows subtler aspects of
Ottoman taste. It houses
a collection of Turkish
musical instruments.*

Archaeological Museum
*Purpose-built in 1896, this
superb museum has exhibits
ranging from prehistory to
the Byzantine era. They
include this classical sculpture of the 2nd-century
Roman Emperor Hadrian.*

Museum of Calligraphy
*Some of the texts in Istanbul's
collection of Ottoman calligraphy
(see p95) are by sultans, such as this
panel by Ahmet III (1703–30).*

THE BAZAAR
QUARTER

GOLDEN HORN

BEYOĞLU

SERAGL
POIN

SULTANAHMET

**Museum of Turkish
and Islamic Arts**
*This Seljuk example is
one of the many carpets
(see pp218–19) included
in this museum's display
of Turkish heritage. Other
collections include glassware and ceramics.*

Mosaic Museum
*Gladiators fighting
a lion are shown in
one of the floors from
the Great Palace (see
pp82–3) displayed in
this small museum.*

Military Museum
A highlight of this museum is the famous Mehter Band, which gives regular outdoor concerts of Ottoman military music.

Şale Pavilion
One of a group of pavilions built in leafy Yildiz Park by 19th-century sultans, the Şale Pavilion has around 50 splendid rooms, including the Mother-of-Pearl Hall.

BOSPHORUS

THE ASIAN SIDE

Dolmabahçe Palace
This opulent 19th-century palace is home to such marvels as 2-m (7-ft) high vases, a crystal staircase and an alabaster bathroom.

Topkapı Palace
This huge palace was used as the official royal residence for 400 years. The treasury contains a myriad of precious objects such as jewel-encrusted thrones and this ornate ceremonial canteen.

Beylerbeyi Palace
Adorning one of the principal atriums of this 19th-century imperial summer palace is this elegant marble fountain. The palace was built to entertain visiting foreign dignitaries.

0 metres	750
0 yards	750

Exploring Istanbul's Collections

Each museum in Istanbul contributes a piece to the vast cultural jigsaw of this cosmopolitan city. From Ancient Greek remains and early Chinese ceramics, which arrived in the city along the Silk Route, to 16th-century tiles commissioned for the great mosques and modern industrial machinery, each has its place in the history of Istanbul. Many of the larger museums have a wide range of exhibits and therefore feature under several of the headings below.

The *saz*, a type of lute

The Sarcophagus of the Mourning Women, Archaeological Museum

ARCHAEOLOGY

The archaeological fruits of the expansive Ottoman Empire are displayed in the **Archaeological Museum**, where the exhibits range from monumental 6th-century BC Babylonian friezes to exquisite classical sarcophagi and statues. Classical sculpture fills the ground floor. Upstairs there is a gallery for the archaeology of Syria and Cyprus. Ancient oriental finds are housed in an annexe. The **Museum of Turkish and Islamic Arts** features specifically Muslim artifacts, including early Iraqi and Iranian ceramics as well as beautiful displays of glassware, metalwork and woodwork.

Byzantine mosaic floor in the Mosaic Museum

BYZANTINE ANTIQUITIES

Although Constantinople was the capital of the Byzantine Empire *(see pp20–25)* for over 1,000 years, it can be hard to get a full picture of the city in that period. The best place to start is the **Archaeological Museum**, which has displays illustrating the city's Byzantine history. Its courtyard contains the purple sarcophagi of the Byzantine emperors.

For Byzantine church mosaics, visit the **Church of St Saviour in Chora** near the city walls which has some particularly fine examples vividly depicting the lives of Christ and the Virgin Mary. The impressive **Haghia Sophia** has a few brilliant gold mosaics remaining, some dating back to the reign of Justinian *(see p20)*.

Mosque lamp from the Archaeological Museum

The galleries and upper walls of the **Church of the Pammakaristos** are covered with mosaics, although public access is restricted.

The **Mosaic Museum** houses mosaic floors and murals from the now-vanished Byzantine Great Palace *(see pp82–3)*, which were discovered by archaeologists in 1938. The **Sadberk Hanım Museum** also houses several Byzantine antiquities, including icons, ceramics and jewellery.

CALLIGRAPHY

In the days before the printed word, Ottoman calligraphy *(see p95)* developed into a highly skilled artform, widely used both to ornament religious texts and legal documents and decrees. The **Museum of Calligraphy** mounts a continuous series of temporary exhibitions. Early Koranic calligraphy can be viewed in **Topkapı Palace**, the **Museum of Turkish and Islamic Arts** and the **Sakıp Sabancı Museum** *(see p141)*.

CERAMICS

Experts and amateurs come from all over the world to view the collection of Chinese ceramics and porcelain on display in the kitchens of **Topkapı Palace**. The earliest examples provided the inspiration for Turkey's indigenous ceramic production at İznik *(see p161)*. Examples of İznik tiles can be seen on the walls of Topkapı Palace and in the city's mosques. İznik tiles and also pottery are on display in the çinili Pavilion, an annexe of the **Archaeological Museum**, and at the **Sadberk Hanım Museum**.

A wider selection of ceramics from all over the Islamic world can be found in the **Museum of Turkish and Islamic Arts**.

OTTOMAN INTERIORS

The interiors that can be visited in Istanbul run the gamut from the classical Ottoman styling of the older parts of **Topkapı Palace** to extravagant European-inspired 19th-century decor. In the latter category, the huge **Dolmabahçe Palace** set the style. It was decorated with Bohemian glass and Hereke carpets and has an

The opulent Süfera Salon in Dolmabahce Palace

ornate central stairway fashioned of crystal and brass. The **Pavilion of the Linden Tree** and the Rococo **Küçüksu Palace**, although more intimate in scale, are equally lavish in their interior style.

TEXTILES

The Ottomans were justifiably proud of their textile tradition, which can be admired in the huge imperial costume collection at **Topkapı Palace**, begun in 1850. The palace collection houses older materials, including kaftans dating back to the 15th century. The **Sadberk Hanım Museum** houses magnificent, mostly 19th-century pieces on the top floor and some fine examples of embroidery.

On a larger scale, there are huge imperial campaign tents in the **Military Museum**, which also has a collection of miniature Janissary (see p127) costumes. Uniforms, nomadic tents and fine carpets are on display in the **Museum of Turkish and Islamic Arts**. Antique carpets can also be seen in the **Vakıflar Carpet Museum**, housed in an annexe of the Blue Mosque. It contains some valuable old carpets that come originally from mosques all over Turkey.

Costume from
Topkapı Palace

MUSICAL INSTRUMENTS

Examples of typical Turkish instruments, such as the *saz* (lute), can be found in a museum devoted to them at **Aynalı Kavak Palace**. Those played by the Whirling Dervishes are on display at the **Mevlevi Monastery**. Instruments can also be seen, and bought, in two shops situated near the entrance to Gülhane Park (see p61). Traditional Turkish military instruments can be heard being played at the **Military Museum**.

MILITARIA

The beautiful barges in which the Ottoman sultans were rowed around the Golden Horn and the Bosphorus are part of the **Naval Museum** collection. Currently closed for renovations, the museum is due to re-open in 2008. Weapons and armour from the 12th–20th centuries can be found in the **Military Museum**, along with a cannon, captured by the Turks during their European campaigns. There is a smaller selection of weaponry in the armoury of **Topkapı Palace**. The **Florence Nightingale Museum** (in the Selimiye Barracks on the Asian Side) commemorates the work of the nurse during the Crimean War. It also has some interesting military exhibits.

PAINTING

Close to Dolmabahçe Palace is Istanbul's **Museum of Fine Arts**, which offers a collection of largely late 19th- and early 20th-century Turkish paintings. Those interested in more contemporary works of art may also like to visit the changing exhibitions at the **Taksim Art Gallery**.

SCIENCE AND TECHNOLOGY

Located in a converted warehouse in the heart of Istanbul's docks is the **Rahmi Koç Museum**. It is home to a selection of mechanical and scientific instruments dating from the early years of the Industrial Revolution, as well as an entire reconstructed bridge taken from an early 20th-century ship.

ISTANBUL THROUGH THE YEAR

Istanbul is at its best in late May and early September, when temperatures are mild and sunshine is plentiful. High season, from June to August, is the most expensive, crowded and hottest time to visit, but the summer arts and music festivals are highlights in the city's cultural calendar. Late November until March or April can be damp and dreary. However, Istanbul is still mild in autumn

National Sovereignty Day in Istanbul

and winter and, with fewer tour parties around, you can enjoy the sights in peace. As well as arts and sporting events, several public holidays and religious festivals punctuate the year. It is wise to be aware of these when planning an itinerary as some sights may be closed or else crammed with locals enjoying a day out. Some of these celebrations are also fascinating spectacles in their own right.

Tulips growing in Emirgan Park, scene of the spring Tulip Festival

SPRING

As the winter smog fades and sunshine increases, cafés and restaurants prepare for the first wave of alfresco dining. After a winter's diet of apples and oranges, a welcome crop of spring fruits, including fresh figs, strawberries and tart green plums, arrives in the shops. Toasted sweetcorn is sold from carts *(see p208)*, and a spring catch of sea bream, sea bass and turbot is on the menu. Tulips, hyacinths, daffodils and pansies fill parks and gardens, and the distinctive pink buds of the Judas tree are seen along the Bosphorus. Monuments and museums are generally uncrowded in spring, and discounts are available at many hotels. In May the popular son et lumière shows outside the Blue Mosque *(see pp78–9)* begin and continue until September.

EVENTS

Easter *(March or April)*. Pilgrimage to the Monastery of St George on Büyükada in the Princes' Islands *(see p159)*.
International Istanbul Film Festival *(late March–mid-April)*, selected cinemas. Screening of Turkish and foreign films and related events.
Tulip Festival *(April)*, Emirgan Park *(see p141)*. Displays of springtime blooms.
National Sovereignty Day *(23 April)*. Public holiday marking the inauguration of the Turkish Republic in 1923 *(see pp30–31)*. Children take to the streets in folk costume.
Commemoration of the Anzac Landings *(25 April)*, Gallipoli. Britons, Australians and New Zealanders gather at the location of the Anzac landings at Gallipoli during World War I *(see pp170–71)*.

Spring Day and Workers' Day *(1 May)*. Unofficial public holiday when workers usually attend union-organized rallies.
Kakava Festival *(early May)*, Edirne. A celebration of gypsy music and dance.
Youth and Sports Day *(19 May)*. Public holiday in commemoration of the start of the War of Independence *(see p31)* in 1919, with sporting events and other activities held throughout the city in stadiums and on the streets.
International Istanbul Theatre Festival *(May–June)*, various venues. European and Turkish productions.
Conquest of Istanbul *(29 May)*, between Tophane and Karaköy and on the shores of the upper Bosphorus. Mehmet the Conqueror's taking of the city in 1453 *(see p26)* is re-enacted in street parades and mock battles.

Colourful evening son et lumière show at the Blue Mosque

AVERAGE DAILY HOURS OF SUNSHINE

Hours

Sunshine Chart
One of Istanbul's attractions is its summer sunshine – there are about 2,500 hours each year. From May to October the city is bathed in light well into the evening, however, bursts of heavy rain are common in high summer. Winter, by contrast, is notoriously deprived of sun.

SUMMER

In contrast to an all-too-brief spring, the warm weather and clear skies of summer can linger on in Istanbul until November. In July and August temperatures soar and although luxury hotels have air conditioning, cheaper ones do not. Popular sights are packed with tourists throughout the high season. Picturesque locations outside Istanbul may, on the other hand, be overrun by locals. At weekends city dwellers trek out to the Belgrade Forest and Black Sea beaches *(see p158)* or to health clubs along the Bosphorus. Those who can afford it flee to their coastal summer homes until autumn.

For those who stay behind there is a strong summer culture. This includes a wild nightlife in hundreds of bars and night spots *(see p213)*, and enthusiastic support for many arts festivals, which attract world-famous performers. Look out, too, for events taking place in historical buildings. You may be able to listen to classical music in Haghia Eirene *(see p60)* or enjoy a pop concert in the Fortress of Europe on the Bosphorus *(see pp140–41)*. This is also the best time of year for outdoor sports such as hiking, horse-riding, water sports, golf and parachuting.

In summer, the menu focuses more on meat than fish, but vegetables and fresh fruit – such

Silk Market in Bursa, which operates all year round

as honeydew melons, cherries, mulberries, peaches and apricots – are widely available. In July and August many shops have summer sales *(see p203)*.

EVENTS

Silk Market *(June–July)*, Bursa. Special market for the sale of silk cocoons *(see p164)*.
International Istanbul Music and Dance Festival *(mid-June–July)*. Classical music, opera and dance performed in historic locations. Mozart's *Abduction from the*

Performance of Mozart's *Abduction from the Seraglio* in the Harem of Topkapı Palace

Seraglio is staged annually in Topkapı Palace *(see pp54–9)*.
Bursa Festival *(June–July)*, Bursa Park. Music, folk dancing, plays, opera and shadow puppetry.
Navy Day *(1 July)*. Parades of old and new boats along the Bosphorus.
International Istanbul Jazz Festival *(July)*, various venues. International event with a devoted following.
International Sailing Races *(July)*. Regatta held at the Marmara Islands *(see p169)*.
Grease Wrestling *(July)*, Kırkpınar, Edirne. Wrestlers smeared in olive oil grapple with each other *(see p154)*.
Hunting Festival *(3 days, late July)*, Edirne. Music, art and fishing displays.
Folklore and Music Festival *(late July)*, Bursa. Ethnic dances and crafts displays.
Festival of Troy *(August)*, Çanakkale. Re-enactment of the tale of Troy *(see p171)*.
Victory Day *(30 August)*. Public holiday commemorating victory over Greece in 1922.

AVERAGE MONTHLY RAINFALL

Rainfall Chart
Winter is the wettest season in Istanbul. Heavy showers of rain can sometimes continue into April and May, making spring seem shorter. Sudden snowstorms are not uncommon in winter, but these are short-lived and snowfalls will usually melt away as quickly as they come.

AUTUMN

Residents of Istanbul often consider their city to be at its best in autumn. As the summer heat loses its grip, chestnut sellers appear on the streets *(see p208)*, pumpkins are sold in the markets, and fresh figs are eaten in abundance. In the surrounding countryside, cotton, wheat and sunflowers are harvested. Migratory grouper and bonito are among the tastiest types of fish which are caught at this time of year.

A popular beauty spot for its array of autumn colours is Lake Abant, 200 km (125 miles) east of Istanbul. Meanwhile, bird-watchers converge on the hills overlooking the Bosphorus to view great flocks of migratory birds heading for their warm wintering grounds in Africa *(see p141)*.

On the cultural agenda is a world-class arts biennial and an antiques fair which blends

Turkish and Western aesthetics. Several public holidays reaffirm Turkey's commitment to secularism, including Republic Day in late October, during which flags are hung from balconies. The bridges over the Bosphorus *(see p138)* are hung with particularly huge flags.

Street-side roasting of seasonal chestnuts

EVENTS

Tüyap Arts Fair *(September)*, opposite the Pera Palas Hotel *(see p104)*. A showcase of Istanbul's artistic talent.
Yapı Kredi Festival *(September)*, various venues. A celebration of music and dance promoting young performers.

Republic Day *(29 October)*. Public holiday commemorating Atatürk's proclamation of the Republic in 1923 *(see p31)*. The Turkish flag adorns buildings in the city.
Akbank Jazz Festival *(October)*, various venues. Jazz music *(see p221)*.
International Istanbul Fine Arts Biennial 2007 *(October–November every two years)*. International and local avant-garde artists exhibit work in historic locations such as Haghia Eirene and the Imperial Mint *(see p60)*, and the Basilica Cistern *(see p76)*.
Anniversary of Death *(10 November)*. A minute's silence is observed at 9:05am, the precise time of Atatürk's death in Dolmabahçe Palace *(see pp128–9)* in 1938.
Tüyap Book Fair *(October)*, Belikduzu Fair and Congress Centre. Istanbul's premier publishing event showcases prominent writers.
Efes Pilsen Blues Festival *(early November)*, selected venues. Foreign and local blues bands play in popular music venues throughout the city.
Interior Design Fair *(first week of November)*, çirağan Palace Hotel Kempinski *(see p123)*. Interior designers and antique dealers display up-market wares in this popular annual show.
Elit's Küsav Antiques Fair *(mid-November)*, Military Museum *(see p126)*. Sale of local and foreign paintings, furniture, carpets, maps, books, porcelain, textiles, silver, clocks and bronze statuary.

Crowds gathering to celebrate Republic Day on 29 October

AVERAGE MONTHLY TEMPERATURE

Temperature Chart
The temperature of the city rarely drops below freezing in winter, and even very cold snaps seldom last longer than three days. The heat of the long, humid summer is intensified by the lodos wind, which blows in from the Sea of Marmara. However, the northerly poyraz occasionally provides a cooling breeze.

WINTER

There are distinct bonuses to visiting Istanbul in the winter, when even major sights are uncrowded, although the rain, fog and pollution may be off-putting. Shops in the Akmerkez, Galleria, Capitol and Carousel malls *(see p211)* hold sales, making the city a shopper's paradise for leather, woollens and fashion.

Outside Istanbul, when enough snow has fallen on the mountains, the ski season begins in Uludağ *(see p169)*, one of Turkey's most important winter sports resorts. Meanwhile, tea with baklava and cream cakes is consumed in the cosy cafés along the Bosphorus and in the old quarter of Beyoğlu *(see pp100–7)*.

View of Bebek on the Bosphorus *(see pp136–49)* in winter

Multitude of lights to welcome in the New Year in Beyoğlu

EVENTS

Mevlâna Festival *(17–24 December)*, Mevlevi Monastery *(see p104)*. Enthusiastic Istanbul devotees perform special dances in honour of the founder of the famous Whirling Dervishes.
Christmas *(late December)*. Though Christmas Day is not a public holiday, major hotels organize seasonal festivities.
New Year's Day *(1 January)*. Public holiday incorporating European Christmas traditions including eating turkey, decorating trees and partying. Strings of lights adorn the main roads.
Karadam Ski Festival *(second half of February)*, Uludağ Mountain. Competitions organized by local radio stations and the Uludağ Ski Instructors' Association.

MUSLIM HOLIDAYS

The dates of Muslim holidays vary according to the phases of the moon and therefore change from year to year. In the holy month of **Ramazan**, Muslims refrain from eating and drinking between dawn and dusk. Some restaurants are closed during the day, and tourists should be discreet when eating in public. Straight after this is the three-day **Şeker Bayramı** (Sugar Festival), when sweetmeats are prepared. Two months later the four-day **Kurban Bayramı** (Feast of the Sacrifice) commemorates the Koranic version of Abraham's sacrifice. This is the main annual public holiday in Turkey, and hotels, trains and roads are packed. Strict Muslims also observe the festivals of **Regaip Kandili, Miraç Kandili, Berat Kandili** and **Mevlid-i-Nebi**.

Festivities during Şeker Bayramı

ISTANBUL AREA BY AREA

SERAGLIO POINT

The hilly, wooded promontory that marks the meeting point of the Golden Horn, the Sea of Marmara and the Bosphorus occupies a natural strategic position. In Byzantine times, monasteries and public buildings stood on this site. Today it is dominated by the grandiose complex of buildings forming Topkapı Palace, the residence of the Ottoman sultans and the women of the harem for 400 years.

Lion relief from the Ishtar Gate

The palace is now open to the public as a rambling museum, with lavish apartments and glittering collections of jewels and other treasures. Originally, the palace covered almost the whole of the area with its gardens and pavilions. Part of the grounds have now been turned into a public park. Adjacent to it is the Archaeological Museum, a renowned collection of finds from Turkey and the Near East.

SIGHTS AT A GLANCE

Museums and Palaces
*Archaeological Museum
pp62–5* ❷
Topkapı Palace pp54–9 ❶

Churches
Haghia Eirene ❹

Historic Buildings and Monuments
Fountain of Ahmet III ❺
Imperial Mint ❸
Sirkeci Station ⓫
Sublime Porte ❾

Streets and Courtyards
Cafer Ağa Courtyard ❼
Soğukçeşme Sokağı ❻

Parks
Gülhane Park ❽

Turkish Baths
Cağaloğlu Baths ❿

GETTING AROUND
With little traffic, this area is easily explored on foot. Trams between the Grand Bazaar and the ferry piers at Eminönü stop outside Gülhane Park.

0 metres 400
0 yards 400

KEY

▨	Street-by-Street map *See pp52–3*
⛴	Ferry boarding point
🚉	Railway station
🚊	Tram stop
ℹ	Tourist information
C	Mosque
—	Walls

◁ **The Circumcision Pavilion in the third courtyard of Topkapı Palace**

Street-by-Street: The First Courtyard of Topkapı

The juxtaposition of Ottoman palace walls, intimately proportioned wooden houses and a soaring Byzantine church lends plenty of drama to the First Courtyard, the outer part of Topkapı Palace. This was once a service area, housing the mint, a hospital, college and a bakery. It was also the mustering point of the Janissaries *(see p127)*. Nowadays, the Cafer Ağa Courtyard and the Fatih Büfe, just outside the courtyard wall, offer unusual settings for refreshments. Gülhane Park, meanwhile, is one of the few shady open spaces in a city of monuments.

Gülhane Park
Once a rose garden in the outer grounds of Topkapı Palace, the wooded Gülhane Park provides welcome shade in which to escape from the heat of the city **8**

Soğukçeşme Sokağı
Traditional, painted wooden houses line this narrow street **6**

Museum of the Ancient Orient

Sublime Porte
A Rococo gate stands in place of the old Sublime Porte, once the entrance to (and symbol of) the Ottoman government **9**

Entrance to Gülhane Park

Gülhane tram stop

Alay Pavilion

ALEMDAR CAD

0 metres	75
0 yards	75

KEY

– – – Suggested route

SOĞUKÇEŞME

Zeynep Sultan Mosque
Resembling a Byzantine church, this mosque was built in 1769 by the daughter of Ahmet III, Princess Zeynep.

Fatih Büfe, a tiny ornate kiosk, sells drinks and snacks.

Otağ Music Shop sells traditional Turkish instruments.

Cafer Ağa Courtyard
The cells of this former college, ranged round a tranquil courtyard café, are now occupied by jewellers, calligraphers and other artisans selling their wares **7**

STAR SIGHTS

★ Archaeological Museum

★ Topkapı Palace

★ Archaeological Museum

Classical statues, dazzling carved sarcophagi, Turkish ceramics and other treasures from all over the former Ottoman Empire make this one of the world's great collections of antiquities ❷

LOCATOR MAP
See Street Finder maps 3 and 5

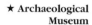

Çinili Pavilion
(see p65)

The Executioner's Fountain is so named because the executioner washed his hands and sword here after a public beheading.

★ Topkapı Palace

For 400 years the Ottoman sultans ruled their empire from this vast palace. Its fine art collections, opulent rooms and leafy courtyards are among the highlights of a visit to Istanbul ❶

Entrance to Topkapı Palace

Topkapı Palace ticket office

Imperial Mint

This museum houses exhibitions on the historical background to Istanbul ❸

Haghia Eirene
The Byzantine church of Haghia Eirene dates from the 6th century. Unusually, it has never been converted into a mosque ❹

Imperial Gate

Fountain of Ahmet III
Built in the early 18th century, the finest of Istanbul's Rococo fountains is inscribed with poetry likening it to the fountains of paradise ❺

Topkapı Palace ❶

Topkapı Sarayı

Süleyman I's
tuğra over
the main gate

Between 1459 and 1465, shortly after his conquest of Constantinople *(see p26)*, Mehmet II built Topkapı Palace as his principal residence. Rather than a single building, it was conceived as a series of pavilions contained by four enormous courtyards, a stone version of the tented encampments from which the nomadic Ottomans had emerged. Initially, the palace served as the seat of government and contained a school in which civil servants and soldiers were trained. In the 16th century, however, the government was moved to the Sublime Porte *(see p61)*. Sultan Abdül Mecit I abandoned Topkapı in 1853 in favour of Dolmabahçe Palace *(see pp128–9)*. In 1924 it was opened to the public as a museum.

★ Harem
The labyrinth of exquisite rooms where the sultan's wives and concubines lived can be visited on a guided tour (see pp58–9).

Exhibition of arms
and armour *(see p56)*

Entrance to
Harem

Harem ticket
office

Gate of
Salutations:
entrance to
the palace

Divan
The viziers of the imperial council met in this chamber, sometimes watched covertly by the sultan.

Second
courtyard

**The Gate
of Felicity** is also
called the Gate of the
White Eunuchs.

The kitche
contain an
exhibition
ceramics, g
and silverv
(see p56).

İftariye Pavilion
Standing between the Baghdad and Circumcision pavilions, this canopied balcony provides views down to the Golden Horn.

VISITORS' CHECKLIST

Babıhümayun Cad. **Map** 3 F3.
Tel (0212) 512 04 80.
Sultanahmet. ◯ 9:30am–4pm Wed–Mon. **Harem**
◯ 9:30am–4pm Wed–Mon.
(book early)

Baghdad Pavilion
In 1639 Murat IV built this pavilion to celebrate his capture of Baghdad. It has exquisite blue-and-white tilework.

Circumcision Pavilion

Exhibition of clocks *(see p57)*

lion of the / Mantle p57)

Exhibition of miniatures and manuscripts *(see p57)*

Konyalı Restaurant *(see p198)*

The fourth courtyard is a series of gardens dotted with pavilions.

Third courtyard

Library of Ahmet III
Erected in 1719, the library is an elegant marble building. This ornamental fountain is set into the wall below its main entrance.

Exhibition of imperial costumes *(see p56)*

Throne Room

★ Treasury
This 17th-century jewel-encrusted jug is one of the precious objects exhibited in the former treasury (see p57).

STAR FEATURES

★ Harem

★ Treasury

Exploring the Palace's Collections

During their 470-year reign, the Ottoman sultans amassed a glittering collection of treasures. After the foundation of the Turkish Republic in 1923 (see p31), this was nationalized and the bulk of it put on display in Topkapı Palace. As well as diplomatic gifts and articles commissioned from the craftsmen of the palace workshops, a large number of items in the collection were brought back as booty from successful military campaigns.

Many such trophies date from the massive expansion of the Ottoman Empire during the reign of Selim the Grim (1512–20), when Syria, Arabia and Egypt were conquered.

Royal crib displayed in the Treasury

CERAMICS, GLASS AND SILVERWARE

The kitchens contain the palace's collection of ceramics, glass and silverware. Turkish and European pieces are massively overshadowed here by the vast display of Chinese and, to a lesser extent, Japanese porcelain. This was brought to Turkey along the Silk Route, the overland trading link between the Far East and Europe. Topkapı's collection of Chinese porcelain is the world's second best after China itself.

Japanese porcelain plate

The Chinese porcelain on display spans four dynasties: the Sung (10–13th centuries), followed by the Yüan (13–14th centuries), the Ming (14–17th centuries) and the Ching (17–20th centuries). Celadon, the earliest form of Chinese porcelain collected by the sultans, was made to look like jade, a stone believed by the Chinese to be lucky. The Ottomans prized it because it was said to neutralize poison in food. More delicate than these are a number of exquisite blue-and-white pieces, mostly of the Ming era.

Chinese aesthetics were an important influence on Ottoman craftsmen, particularly in

the creation of designs for their fledgling ceramics industry at İznik (see p161). Although there are no İznik pieces in the Topkapı collection, many of the tiles on the palace walls originated there. These clearly show the influence of designs used for Chinese blue-and-white porcelain, such as stylized flowers and cloud scrolls. Much of the later porcelain, particularly the Japanese Imari ware, was made specifically for the export market. The most obvious examples of this are some plates decorated with quotations from the Koran.

A part of the kitchens, the old confectioners' pantry, has been preserved as it would have been when in use. On display are huge cauldrons and other utensils wielded by the palace's chefs as they prepared to feed its 12,000 residents and guests.

ARMS AND ARMOUR

Taxes and tributes from all over the empire were once stored in this chamber, which was known as the Inner Treasury. Straight ahead as you enter are a series of horse-tail standards. Carried in processions or displayed outside tents, these proclaimed the rank of their owners. Viziers

(see p29), for example, merited three, and the grand vizier five, while the sultan's banner would flaunt nine.

The weaponry includes ornately embellished swords and several bows made by sultans themselves (Beyazıt II was a particularly fine craftsman). Seen next to these exquisite items, the huge iron swords used by European crusaders look crude by comparison. Also on view are pieces of 15th-century Ottoman chainmail and colourful shields. The shields have metal centres surrounded by closely woven straw painted with flowers.

IMPERIAL COSTUMES

A collection of imperial costumes is displayed in the Hall of the Campaign Pages, whose task was to look after the royal wardrobe. It was a palace tradition that on the death of a sultan his clothes were carefully folded and placed in sealed bags. As a result, it is possible to see a perfectly preserved kaftan once worn by Mehmet the Conqueror (see p26). The reforms of Sultan Mahmut II included a revolution in the dress code (see p30). The end of an era came as plain grey serge replaced the earlier luxurious silken textiles.

Sumptuous silk kaftan once worn by Mehmet the Conqueror

TREASURY

Of all the exhibitions in the palace, the Treasury's collection is the easiest to appreciate, glittering as it does with thousands of precious and semi-precious stones. The only surprise is that there are so few women's jewels here. Whereas the treasures of the sultans and viziers were owned by the state and reverted to the palace on their deaths, those belonging to the women of the court did not.

In the first hall stands a full, diamond-encrusted suit of chainmail, designed for Mustafa III (1757–74) for ceremonial use. Diplomatic gifts include a fine pearl statuette of a prince seated beneath a canopy, which was sent to Sultan Abdül Aziz (1861–76) from India.

The Topkapı dagger

The greatest pieces are in the second hall. Foremost among these is the Topkapı dagger (1741). This splendid object was commissioned by the sultan from his own jewellers. It was intended as a present for the Shah of Persia, but he died before it reached him. Among other exhibits here are a selection of the bejewelled aigrettes (plumes) which added splendour to imperial turbans.

In the third hall, the 86-carat Spoonmaker's diamond is said to have been discovered in a rubbish heap in Istanbul in the 17th century, and bought from a scrap merchant for three spoons. The gold-plated Bayram throne was given to Murat III *(see p32)* by the Governor of Egypt in 1574 and used for state ceremonies until early this century.

It was the throne in the fourth hall, given by the Shah of Persia, which was to have been acknowledged by the equally magnificent gift of the Topkapı dagger. In a cabinet near the throne is an unusual relic: a case containing bones said to be from the hand of St John the Baptist.

MINIATURES AND MANUSCRIPTS

It is possible to display only a tiny fraction of Topkapı's total collection of over 13,000 miniatures and manuscripts at any one time. Highlights of it include a series of depictions of warriors and fearsome creatures known as *Demons and Monsters in the Life of Nomads*, which was painted by Mohammed Siyah Qalem, possibly as early as the 12th century. It is from this Eastern tradition of miniature painting, which was also prevalent in Mogul India and Persia, that the ebullient Ottoman style of miniatures developed.

Also on show are some fine examples of calligraphy *(see p95)*, including texts of the Koran, manuscripts of poetry and several firmans, the imperial decrees by which the sultan ruled his empire.

Cover of a Koran, decorated in gold filigree work

CLOCKS

European clocks given to, or bought by, various sultans form the majority of this collection, despite the fact that there were makers of clocks and watches in Istanbul from the 17th century. The clocks

A 17th-century watch made of gold, enamel and precious stones

range from simple, weight-driven 16th-century examples to an exquisite 18th-century English mechanism encased in mother-of-pearl and featuring a German organ which played tunes on the hour to the delight of the harem.

Interestingly, the only male European eyewitness accounts of life in the harem were written by the mechanics sent to service these instruments.

PAVILION OF THE HOLY MANTLE

Some of the holiest relics of Islam are displayed in these five domed rooms, which are a place of pilgrimage for Muslims. Most of the relics found their way to Istanbul as a result of the conquest by Selim the Grim *(see p26)* of Egypt and Arabia, and his assumption of the caliphate (the leadership of Islam) in 1517.

The most sacred treasure is the mantle once worn by the Prophet Mohammed. Visitors cannot actually enter the room in which it is stored; instead they look into it from an antechamber through an open doorway. Night and day, holy men continuously chant passages from the Koran over the gold chest in which the mantle is stored. A stand in front of the chest holds two of Mohammed's swords.

A glass cabinet in the anteroom contains hairs from the beard of the Prophet, a letter written by him and an impression of his footprint.

In the other rooms you can see some of the ornate locks and keys for the Kaaba *(see p39)* which were sent to Mecca by successive sultans.

Topkapı Palace: The Harem

Stained-glass window in the Paired Pavilions

The word Harem comes from the Arabic for "forbidden". It was the residence of the sultan's wives, concubines and children, who were guarded by black slave eunuchs. The sultan and his sons were the only other men allowed access to the Harem, which also included the Cage, a set of rooms where the sultan's brothers were confined to avoid succession contests. Topkapı's Harem was laid out by Murat III in the late 16th century and is a labyrinth of brilliantly tiled corridors and chambers. Visitors must take a guided tour. These last a little over half an hour and often get booked up early in the day.

LOCATOR MAP
See main illustration of the palace on pp54–5

Apartments and courtyard of the favourites

Sultan's bathroom

★ Paired Pavilions
These twin apartments, built in the 17th century for the crown prince, boast superb İznik tiles (see p161) and a dome lined with gilded canvas.

The Library of Ahmet I is pleasantly light and airy, with ivory-faced shutters.

The Salon of Murat III, built by Sinan *(see p91)*, has fine tiled walls, a handsome fountain and a large hearth.

★ Dining Room of Ahmet III
A sumptuous array of fruit and flowers is painted on to the walls of this 18th-century chamber, which is also known as the Fruit Room.

Imperial Hall
The largest room in the Harem, this hall was used for entertainments. Against one wall stands a large throne, from which the sultan would view the proceedings.

LIFE IN THE HAREM

The women of the Harem were slaves, gathered from the furthest corners of the Ottoman Empire and beyond. Their dream was to become a favourite of the sultan *(see p28)* and bear him a son, which on some occasions led to marriage. Competition was stiff, however, for at its height the Harem contained over 1,000 concubines, many of whom never rose beyond the service of their fellow captives. The last women eventually left in 1909.

A western view of Harem life in a 19th-century engraving

Salon of the Valide Sultana
The sultan's mother, the valide sultana (see p29), was the most powerful woman in the Harem and had some of the best rooms.

The Tower of Justice offers a superb view of Topkapı's rooftops and beyond.

Courtyard of the valide sultan

The Golden Way is so called because new sultans reputedly threw gold coins to their concubines here.

Exit

Entrance

Courtyard of the concubines

Valide sultan's bedchamber

de sultan's
er room

The Harem baths were where the concubines bathed and relaxed.

Barracks of the black eunuchs

— — Route of guided tour

Rooms on guided tour

Areas closed to the public

STAR FEATURES

★ Paired Pavilions

★ Dining Room of Ahmet III

Courtyard of the Black Eunuchs
Marble columns line this courtyard, which still has some old-fashioned, wrought-iron lamps.

Archaeological Museum ❷

See pp62–5.

Imperial Mint ❸
Darphane-i Amire

First courtyard of Topkapı Palace.
Map 3 E4 (5 F3). 🚋 *Gülhane or Sultanahmet.*

The Ottoman Mint opened here in 1727, but most of what can be seen today dates from the reign of Mahmut II (1808–39), when the complex was extended. In 1967, the mint moved to a new location. The buildings now house laboratories for the state restoration and conservation department, but visitors can look around the exterior of the building during office hours.

Haghia Eirene ❹
Aya İrini Kilisesi

First courtyard of Topkapı Palace.
Map 3 E4 (5 F3). *Tel (0212) 522 17 50.* 🚋 *Gülhane or Sultanahmet.* 🔲 *for concerts.*

Though the present church dates only from the 6th century, it is at least the third building to be erected on what is thought to be the oldest site of Christian worship in Istanbul. Within a decade of the Muslim conquest of the city in 1453 *(see p26)* it had

One of the four elaborately decorated sides of the Fountain of Ahmet III

been included within the Topkapı Palace complex and pressed into use as an arsenal. Today the building, which has good acoustics, is the setting for concerts during the Istanbul Music Festival *(see p45)*.

Inside are three fascinating features that have not survived in any other Byzantine church in the city. The *synthronon*, the five rows of built-in seats hugging the apse, were occupied by clergymen officiating during services. Above this looms a simple black mosaic cross on a gold background, which dates from the iconoclastic period *(see p20)*, when figurative images were forbidden. At the back of the church is a cloister-like courtyard where deceased Byzantine emperors once lay in their porphyry sarcophagi. Most have been moved to the Archaeological Museum.

Fountain of Ahmet III ❺
Ahmet III Çeşmesi

Junction of İshak Paşa Cad & Babıhümayun Cad. **Map** 3 E4 (5 F4). 🚋 *Gülhane or Sultanahmet.*

Built in 1728, the most beautiful of Istanbul's countless fountains survived the violent deposition of Sultan Ahmet III two years later. Many of the other monuments constructed by the sultan during his reign, which has become known as the Tulip Period *(see p27)*, were destroyed. The fountain is in the delicate Turkish Rococo style, with five small domes, mihrab-shaped niches and dizzying floral reliefs.

Ottoman "fountains" do not spout jets of water, but are more like ornate public taps. They sometimes incorporated a counter, or *sebil*, from which refreshments would be served.

In this case, each of the fountain's four walls is equipped with a tap, or *çeşme*, above a carved marble basin. Over each tap is an elaborate calligraphic inscription by the 18th-century poet Seyit Vehbi Efendi. The inscription, in gold on a blue-green background, is in honour of the fountain and its founder. At each of the four corners there is a *sebil* backed by three windows covered by ornate marble grilles. Instead of the customary iced water, passersby at this fountain would have been offered sherbets and flavoured waters in silver goblets.

The apse of Haghia Eirene, with its imposing black-on-gold cross

Soğukçeşme Sokağı ❻

Map 3 E4 (5 F3). 🚊 *Gülhane.*

Charming old wooden houses line this narrow, sloping cobbled lane ("the street of the cold fountain"), which squeezes between the outer walls of Topkapı Palace and the towering minarets of Haghia Sophia. Traditional houses like these were built in the city from the late 18th century onwards.

The buildings in the lane were renovated by the Turkish Touring and Automobile Club (TTOK, *see p181*) in the 1980s. Some of them now form the Ayasofya Pansiyonları *(see p184)*, a series of attractive pastel-painted guesthouses popular with tourists. Another building has been converted by the TTOK into a library of historical writings on Istanbul, and archive of engravings and photographs of the city. A Roman cistern towards the bottom of the lane has been converted into the Sarnıç restaurant *(see p198)*.

Traditional calligraphy on sale in Cafer Ağa Courtyard

Cafer Ağa Courtyard ❼

Cafer Ağa Medresesi

Caferiye Sok. **Map** 5 E3. *Tel (0212) 513 18 43.* 🚊 *Gülhane.*
🕐 *8:30am–8pm daily.*

This peaceful courtyard at the end of an alley was built in 1559 by Sinan *(see p91)* for the chief black eunuch *(see p29)* as a *medrese* (theological college, *see p38*). Sinan's bust presides over the café tables in the courtyard. The former students' lodgings

Restored Ottoman house on Soğukçeşme Sokağı

OTTOMAN HOUSES

The typical, smart town house of 19th-century Istanbul had a stone ground floor above which were one or two wooden storeys. The building invariably sported a *çıkma,* a section projecting out over the street. This developed from the traditional Turkish balcony, which was enclosed in the northern part of the country because of the colder climate. Wooden lattice covers, or *kafesler,* over the windows on the upper storeys ensured that the women of the house were able to watch life on the street below without being seen themselves. Few wooden houses have survived. Those that remain usually owe their existence to tourism and many have been restored as hotels. While the law forbids their demolition, it is extremely hard to obtain insurance for them in a city that has experienced many devastating fires.

---

are now used to display a variety of craft goods typically including jewellery, silk prints, ceramics and calligraphy.

Gülhane Park ❽

Gülhane Parkı

Alemdar Cad. **Map** 3 E3 (5 F2).
🚊 *Gülhane.* 🕐 *daily.*

Gülhane Park occupies what was the lower grounds of Topkapı Palace. Today it has a neglected air but it is still a shady place to stroll and it includes a couple of interesting landmarks.

Ignore the ill-kept zoo on the left of the road through the park, but seek out the aquarium by the disused cascade on the right. It is in the cavernous vaults of a Roman water cistern. At the far end of the park is the Goths' Column, a well-preserved 3rd-century victory monument, surrounded by a cluster of clapboard teahouses. Its name comes from the Latin inscription on it which reads: "Fortune is restored to us because of victory over the Goths".

Across Kennedy Caddesi, the main road running along the northeast side of the park, there is a viewpoint over the busy waters where the Golden Horn meets the Bosphorus.

Sublime Porte ❾

Bab-ı Ali

Alemdar Cad. **Map** 3 E3 (5 E2).
🚊 *Gülhane.*

Foreign ambassadors to Ottoman Turkey were known as Ambassadors to the Sublime Porte, after this monumental gateway which once led into the offices and palace of the grand vizier. The institution of the Sublime Porte filled an important role in Ottoman society because it could often provide an effective counterbalance to the whims of sultans.

The Rococo gateway you see today was built in the 1840s. Its guarded entrance now shields the offices of Istanbul's provincial government.

Rococo decoration on the roof of the Sublime Porte

Archaeological Museum ❷

Arkeoloji Müzesi

Roman statue of Apollo

Although this collection of antiquities was begun only in the mid-19th century, provincial governors were soon sending in objects from the length and breadth of the Ottoman Empire. Today the museum has one of the world's richest collections of classical artifacts, and also includes treasures from the pre-classical world. The main building was erected under the directorship of Osman Hamdi Bey (1881–1910), to house his finds. This archaeologist, painter and polymath discovered the exquisite sarcophagi in the royal necropolis at Sidon in present-day Lebanon. A new four-storey wing of the museum was opened in 1991.

★ Alexander Sarcophagus
This fabulously carved marble tomb from the late 4th century BC is thought to have been built for King Abdalonymos of Sidon. It is called the Alexander Sarcophagus because Alexander the Great is depicted on it winning a victory over the Persians.

KEY

- ☐ Classical Archaeology
- ☐ Children's Museum
- ☐ Thracian, Bithynian and Byzantine Collections
- ☐ Istanbul Through the Ages
- ☐ Anatolia and Troy
- ☐ Anatolia's Neighbouring Cultures
- ☐ Turkish Tiles and Ceramics
- ☐ Museum of the Ancient Orient
- ☐ Non-exhibition space

GALLERY GUIDE

The 20 galleries of the main building house the museum's important collection of classical antiquities. The new wing has displays on the archaeology of Istanbul and nearby regions, and includes the Children's Museum. There are two other buildings within the grounds: the çinili Pavilion, which contains Turkish tiles and ceramics, and the Museum of the Ancient Orient.

The porticoes of the museum take their design from the 4th-century BC Sarcophagus of the Mourning Women.

Sarcophagus of the Mourning Women

Çinili Pavilion

Outdoor café

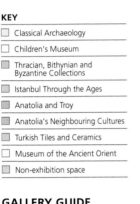

★ Karaman Mihrab
This blue, richly tiled mihrab (see p38) comes from the city of Karaman in southeast Turkey, which was the capital of the Karamanid state from 1256–1483. It is the most important artistic relic of that culture.

STAR EXHIBITS

- ★ Alexander Sarcophagus
- ★ Karaman Mihrab
- ★ Treaty of Kadesh

Geometric Period Cypriot Jug
Stylized fish decorate this jug, in a design typical of the Geometric Period (1050–750 BC), when a vibrant ceramics culture flourished on Cyprus.

Stairs to main building

Third floor

Second floor

First floor

Ground floor of the new wing

Statue of Marsyas

Statue and bust of Alexander the Great

Entrance

Mosaic Icon of the Presentation
Dating from the 6th–7th centuries AD, this battered panel from Kalenderhane Mosque (see p92) is the only religious figurative mosaic to have survived Byzantium's iconoclastic period (see p20).

Porphyry Sarcophagi
These monumental purple sarcophagi (4th–5th centuries AD) are thought to have held the bodies of some of the early Byzantine emperors.

★ Treaty of Kadesh
This tablet constitutes the world's earliest surviving peace treaty, agreed between the Egyptians and Hittites in 1269 BC. Among its many clauses are provisions for the return of political refugees.

Exploring the Archaeological Museum

This enormous collection spans over 5,000 years, from figurines of the Mother Goddess modelled in the 3rd millennium BC to Turkish pottery thrown in the 19th century. To cover everything in one visit is impossible. Visitors with little time should not miss the breathtaking sarcophagi from the royal necropolis at Sidon. To learn more about the history of Istanbul itself you should head for the gallery exploring this theme, on the first floor of the new wing. Youngsters may enjoy the displays in the Children's Museum.

CLASSICAL ARCHAEOLOGY

Monumental Bes, the ancient Egyptian god, greets visitors at the door to the main building. Hugely popular in the 1st–3rd centuries, Bes' comically grotesque appearance was an effective deterrent for evil spirits. Rooms 9 and 8 contain the highlights of the museum's entire collection: a group of sarcophagi unearthed in 1887 at Sidon (in present-day Lebanon). These are thought to have been made for a line of Phoenician

Marble bust of Emperor Augustus

kings who ruled in the 6th–4th centuries BC. Their decoration vividly shows the transition from Egyptian to Greek influence in the art of the Near East at that time.

The latest and finest of them is the so-called Alexander Sarcophagus (late 4th century BC). Alexander the Great features in two decorative, high-relief friezes on the longest sides. These show a battle scene and a hunting scene. The friezes survive in almost perfect condition, showing traces of their original colouring, though the metal weapons of the soldiers and hunters have been lost.

The Sarcophagus of the Mourning Women is thought to have been made for King Straton (374–358 BC), who was known for his fondness for women. The grief-stricken females may have been members of his harem.

Rooms 14–20 contain some remarkable statues. Among them is a Roman copy of a 3rd century BC statue of Marsyas, depicting the satyr about to be flayed after daring to challenge Apollo's musical ability. A statue and bust of Alexander the Great (3rd–2nd centuries BC) show the conqueror as the perfect hero, with a meditative expression on his face. Room 18 contains realistic busts of Roman emperors.

CHILDREN'S MUSEUM

Special low cabinets are used in this part of the museum, which is designed for visiting schoolchildren. Paper and coloured crayons are to hand in a bid to stimulate future archaeologists.

THRACIAN, BITHYNIAN AND BYZANTINE COLLECTIONS

This gallery on the ground floor of the new wing displays religious and other artifacts from the ancient civilizations of Thrace and Bithynia, and from Byzantium *(see pp20–25)* – including a statue of Byzantine Emperor Valens. This section of the musuem also covers the architecture of the ancient world.

Bronze head of a snake from the Serpentine Column

ISTANBUL THROUGH THE AGES

With a few well-chosen pieces and explanatory texts in Turkish and English, this gallery brilliantly chronicles Istanbul's archaeological past.

The rare Mosaic Icon of the Presentation (c.AD 600) originally adorned the Kalenderhane Mosque *(see p92)*. One of the three snakes' heads from the Serpentine Column, which has stood headless in the Hippodrome *(see p80)* since the 18th century, is also displayed here. Look out too for a section of the iron chains that the Byzantines hung across both the Bosphorus and the Golden Horn to stop hostile ships *(see p23)*.

Frieze showing the battle of Issus (333 BC), on the side panel of the Alexander Sarcophagus

Reconstruction of a mausoleum discovered at Palmyra in Syria

ANATOLIA AND TROY

One side of this narrow, long hall chronicles the history of Anatolia (the Asiatic part of modern Turkey) from the Palaeolithic era to the Iron Age. It culminates with a room devoted to the Phrygian culture, which centred on the city of Gordion. The highlight is a recreation of an 8th-century BC royal tomb, which was housed beneath a tumulus in a juniper-wood chamber. As well as cooking utensils, the king was buried with furniture made of oak, box, yew and juniper.

The other side of the gallery traces the excavations of nine different civilizations at Troy (see p171), from 3000 BC to the time of Christ. On display are a few pieces of the gold hoard known as the Schliemann treasure, after the archaeologist who first discovered it in the late 19th century. Most of the pieces were smuggled out of Turkey, however, and are now in museums around the world.

ANATOLIA'S NEIGHBOURING CULTURES

This long gallery is also divided in two, with one side devoted to Cyprus and the other to Syria-Palestine. The Cypriot collection was assembled by the joint American and Russian consul to Cyprus, Luigi Palma di Cesnola, who systematically looted its tombs from 1865–73. Apart from some beautiful pots, the most interesting objects are the figures of plump, naked temple boys (3rd century BC). They are thought to represent boy prostitutes at temples to Aphrodite, the Greek goddess of love.

Among the Syrian exhibits are funerary reliefs, the Gezer Calendar (925 BC) – a limestone tablet bearing the oldest known Hebrew inscription – and a reconstruction of a 1st–3rd-century mausoleum from the trading oasis of Palmyra.

16th-century İznik tiled lunette in the Çinili Pavilion

TURKISH TILES AND CERAMICS

Apart from carpets, the most distinctive Turkish art form is ceramics. This is particularly seen in the sheets of tiles used to decorate the walls of mosques and pavilions such as the Çinili Pavilion, where the entrance archway is plastered with geometric and calligraphic tiles.

In the main room there is an exquisite early 15th-century tiled mihrab from central Anatolia. Rooms 3 and 4 contain tiles and mosque lamps from the famed İznik potteries, the hub of Turkish ceramics production (see p161). With the decline in quality of İznik ceramics in the late 16th century, other centres took over. One of these, Kütahya, also produced pieces of beauty and high quality (rooms 5 and 6).

MUSEUM OF THE ANCIENT ORIENT

Although this collection contains antiquities of great rarity and beauty from the Egyptian and Hittite cultures, pride of place goes to the artifacts from the early civilizations of Mesopotamia (present-day Iraq).

The monumental glazed brick friezes from Babylon's main entrance, the Ishtar Gate, (rooms 3 and 9) date from the reign of Nebuchadnezzar II (605–562 BC), when the capital of Babylon experienced its final flowering. The elegant, 30-kg (65-lb) duck-shaped weight in Room 4 comes from a much earlier Babylonian temple (c.2000 BC).

Room 5 contains some of the earliest known examples of writing, in the form of cuneiform inscriptions on clay tablets, dating from 2700 BC. The famous Treaty of Kadesh (room 7), concluded around 1269 BC between the Egyptian and Hittite empires, was originally written on a sheet of silver. The one in this collection is a Hittite copy. The treaty includes many sophisticated clauses, including one providing for the return of a political refugee, who was "not to be charged with his crime, nor his house and wives and his children be harmed".

Glazed frieze of a bull from Ishtar Gate, Babylon

Cağaloğlu Baths ❿
Cağaloğlu Hamamı

Prof Kazım İsmail Gürkan Cad 34, Cağaloğlu. **Map** 3 E4 (5 D3). *Tel* (0212) 522 24 24.
🚇 *Sultanahmet.* ⬡ *daily 8am–8pm.* www.cagalogluhamami.com.tr

Among the city's more sumptuous Turkish baths, the ones in Cağaloğlu were built by Sultan Mahmut I in 1741. The income from them was designated for the maintenance of Mahmut's library in Haghia Sophia *(see pp72–5).*

The city's smaller baths have different times at which men and women can use the same facilities. But in larger baths,

Corridor leading into the Cağaloğlu Baths, built by Mahmut I

such as this one, there are entirely separate sections. In the Cağaloğlu Baths the men's and women's sections are at right angles to one another and entered from different streets. Each consists of three parts: a *camekan,* a *soğukluk* and the main bath chamber or *hararet,* which centres on a massive octagonal massage slab.

The Cağaloğlu Baths are popular with foreign visitors because the staff are happy to explain the procedure. Even if you do not want to sweat it out, you can still take a look inside the entrance corridor and *camekan* of the men's section. Here you will find a small display of Ottoman bathing regalia, including precarious wooden clogs once worn by women on what would frequently be their only outing from the confines of the home. You can also sit and have a drink by the fountain in the peaceful *camekan.*

Sirkeci Station ⓫
Sirkeci Garı

Sirkeci İstasyon Cad, Sirkeci. **Map** 3E3 (5 E1). *Tel* (0212) 527 00 50 or 520 65 75. 🚆 *Sirkeci.* ⬡ *daily.*

This magnificent railway station was built to receive the long-anticipated Orient Express from Europe. It was officially opened in 1890, even

Sirkeci Station, final destination of the historic Orient Express

though the luxurious train had been running into Istanbul for a year by then. The design, by the German architect Jasmund, successfully incorporates features from the many different architectural traditions of Istanbul. Byzantine alternating stone and brick courses are combined with a Seljuk-style monumental recessed portal and Muslim horseshoe arches around the windows.

The station café is a good place in which to escape the bustle of the city for a while. Sirkeci serves Greece and other destinations in Europe as well as the European part of Turkey. Istanbul's other mainline railway station is Haydarpaşa *(see p133),* on the Asian side of the city.

THE WORLD-FAMOUS ORIENT EXPRESS

The Orient Express made its first run from Paris to Istanbul in 1889, covering the 2,900-km (1,800-mile) journey in three days. Both Sirkeci Station and the Pera Palas Hotel *(see p104)* in Istanbul were built especially to receive its passengers. The wealthy and often distinguished passengers of "The Train of Kings, the King of Trains" did indeed include kings among the many presidents, politicians, aristocrats and actresses. King Boris III of Bulgaria even made a habit of taking over from the driver of the train when he travelled on it through his own country.

A byword for exoticism and romance, the train was associated with the orientalist view of Istanbul as a treacherous melting pot of diplomats and arms dealers. It inspired no fewer than 19 books – *Murder on the Orient Express* by Agatha Christie and *Stamboul Train* by Graham Greene foremost among them – six films and one piece of music. During the Cold War standards of luxury crashed, though a service of sorts, without even a restaurant car, continued twice weekly to Istanbul until 1977.

A 1920s poster for the Orient Express, showing a romantic view of Istanbul

Turkish Baths

No trip to Istanbul is complete without an hour or two spent in a Turkish bath *(hamam)*, which will leave your whole body feeling rejuvenated. Turkish baths differ little from the baths of ancient Rome, from which they derive, except there is no pool of cold water to plunge into at the end.

A full service will entail a period of relaxation in the steam-filled hot room, punctuated by bouts of vigorous soaping and massaging. There is no time limit, but allow at least an hour and a half for a leisurely bath. Towels and soap will be provided, but you can take special toiletries with you.

Two historic baths located in the old city, Çemberlitaş *(see p81)* and Cağaloğlu (illustrated below), are used to catering for foreign tourists. Most luxury hotels have their own baths *(see pp180–91)*.

Ornate wash basin

Choosing a Service
Services, detailed in a price list at the entrance, range from a self-service option to a luxury body scrub, shampoo and massage.

The *camekan* (entrance hall) is a peaceful internal courtyard near the entrance of the building. Bathers change clothes in cubicles surrounding it. The *camekan* is also the place to relax with a cup of tea after bathing.

Changing Clothes
Before changing you will be given a cloth (peştemal), *to wrap around you, and a pair of slippers for walking on the hot, wet floor.*

Corridor from street

Basin and tap for washing

Small, star-like windows piercing the domes

CAĞALOĞLU BATHS
The opulent, 18th-century Turkish baths at Cağaloğlu have separate, identical sections for men and women. The men's section is shown here.

The *soğukluk* (intermediate room) is a temperate passage between the changing room and the *hararet*. You will be given dry towels here on your way back to the *camekan*.

In the *hararet* (hot room), the main room of the Turkish bath, you are permitted to sit and sweat in the steam for as long as you like.

The Exfoliating Body Scrub
In between steaming, you (or the staff at the baths) scrub your body briskly with a coarse, soapy mitt (kese).

The Body Massage
A marble plinth (göbek taşı) *occupies the centre of the hot room. This is where you will have your pummelling full-body massage.*

SULTANAHMET

I stanbul's two principal monuments face each other across an area of gardens known informally as Sultanahmet Square. This part of the city gets its name from Sultan Ahmet I, who built the Blue Mosque. Opposite is Haghia Sophia, an outstanding example of early Byzantine architecture, and still one of the world's most remarkable churches. A neat oblong square

Mosaic of Empress Irene in Haghia Sophia

next to the Blue Mosque marks the site of the Hippodrome, a chariot-racing stadium built by the Romans in around AD 200. On the other side of the Blue Mosque, Sultanahmet slopes down to the Sea of Marmara in a jumble of alleyways. Here, traditional-style Ottoman wooden houses have been built over the remains of the Great Palace of the Byzantine emperors.

SIGHTS AT A GLANCE

Mosques and Churches
Blue Mosque pp78–9 ❼
Church of SS Sergius and Bacchus ⓴
Haghia Sophia pp72–5 ❶
Sokollu Mehmet Paşa Mosque ⓭

Museums
Mosaic Museum ❻
Museum of Turkish and Islamic Arts ❽
Vakıflar Carpet Museum ❺

Squares and Courtyards
Hippodrome ❾
Istanbul Crafts Centre ❸

Historic Buildings and Monuments
Basilica Cistern ❷
Baths of Roxelana ❹
Bucoleon Palace ⓯
Cistern of 1,001 Columns ❿
Constantine's Column ⓬
Tomb of Sultan Mahmut II ⓫

KEY

▨	Street-by-Street map *See pp70–71*
🚋	Tram stop
ℹ	Tourist information
🄲	Mosque
—	Walls

GETTING AROUND
Trams between Eminönü and Beyazıt stop in Sultanahmet by the Firuz Ağa Mosque on Divanyolu Caddesi. From there, most of the sights are easily reached on foot. A city bus runs between Taksim and Sultanahmet.

◁ **The elegant domes of the Blue Mosque, catching the evening sun**

Street-by-Street: Sultanahmet Square

Two of Istanbul's most venerable monuments, the Blue Mosque and Haghia Sophia, face each other across a leafy square, informally known as Sultanahmet Square (Sultanahmet Meydanı), next to the Hippodrome of Byzantium. Also in this fascinating historic quarter are a handful of museums, including the Mosaic Museum, built over part of the old Byzantine Great Palace *(see pp82–3)*, and the Museum of Turkish and Islamic Arts. No less diverting than the cultural sights are the cries of the *simit* (bagel) hawkers and carpet sellers, and the chatter of children selling postcards.

Tomb of Sultan Ahmet I
Stunning 17th-century İznik tiles (see p161) *adorn the inside of this tomb, which is part of the outer complex of the Blue Mosque.*

★ Blue Mosque
Towering above Sultanahmet Square are the six beautiful minarets of this world-famous mosque. It was built in the early 17th century for Ahmet I ❼

Museum of Turkish and Islamic Arts
Yurts, used by Turkey's nomadic peoples, and rugs are included in this impressive collection ❽

KEY

– – – Suggested route

Hippodrome
This stadium was the city's focus for more than 1,000 years before it fell into ruin. Only a few sections, such as the central line of monuments, remain ❾

Vakıflar Carpet Museum
Part of the Blue Mosque complex, this museum displays fine antique carpets ❺

Mosaic Museum
Hunting scenes are one of the common subjects that can be seen in some of the mosaics from the Great Palace ❻

★ Basilica Cistern
This marble Medusa head is one of two classical column bases found in the Basilica Cistern. The cavernous cistern dates from the reign of Justinian (see p20) in the 6th century ❷

A stone pilaster next to the remains of an Ottoman water tower is all that survives of the Milion *(see p83)*, a triumphal gateway.

LOCATOR MAP
See Street Finder, maps 3 and 5

★ Haghia Sophia
The supreme church of Byzantium is over 1,400 years old but has survived in a remarkably good state. Inside it are several glorious figurative mosaics ❶

Baths of Roxelana
Sinan (see p91) designed these beautiful baths in the mid-16th century. They no longer serve their original function, however, having been converted into a state-run carpet shop ❹

Yeşil Ev Hotel
(see p186)

Istanbul Crafts Centre
Visitors have a rare opportunity here to observe Turkish craftsmen practising a range of skills ❸

Cavalry Bazaar
Eager salesmen will call you over to peruse their wares – mainly carpets and handicrafts – in this bazaar. With two long rows of shops on either side of a lane, the bazaar was once a stable yard.

STAR SIGHTS

★ Blue Mosque

★ Basilica Cistern

★ Haghia Sophia

Haghia Sophia ❶

Aya Sofya

The "church of holy wisdom," Haghia Sophia is among the world's greatest architectural achievements. More than 1,400 years old, it stands as a testament to the sophistication of the 6th-century Byzantine capital and was of paramount influence on architecture in the following centuries. The vast edifice was built over two earlier churches and inaugurated by Emperor Justinian in 537. In the 15th century the Ottomans converted it into a mosque: the minarets, tombs, and fountains date from this period. To help support the structure's great weight, the exterior has been buttressed on numerous occasions, which has partly obscured its original shape.

Print of Haghia Sophia from the mid-19th century

Seraphims adorn the pendentives at the base of the dome.

Calligraphic roundel

Kürsü *(see p39)*

Byzantine Frieze
Among the ruins of the monumental entrance to the earlier Haghia Sophia (dedicated in AD 415) is this frieze of sheep.

Buttresses

Imperial Gate

Outer Narthex

Inner Narthex

The galleries were originally used by women during services.

Entrance

HISTORICAL PLAN OF HAGHIA SOPHIA

Nothing remains of the first 4th-century church on this spot, but there are traces of the second one from the 5th century, which burnt down in AD 532. Earthquakes have taken their toll on the third structure, strengthened and added to many times.

KEY

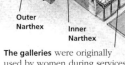

☐	5th-century church
▨	6th-century church
☐	Ottoman additions

STAR FEATURES

★ Nave

★ The Mosaics

★ Ablutions Fountain

★ Nave
Visitors cannot fail to be staggered by this vast space which is covered by a huge dome reaching to a height of 56 m (184 ft).

Brick minaret

★ The Mosaics
The church's splendid Byzantine mosaics include this one at the end of the south gallery. It depicts Christ flanked by Emperor Constantine IX and his wife, the Empress Zoe.

VISITORS' CHECKLIST

Ayasofya Meydanı, Sultanahmet.
Map 3 E4 (5 F3). **Tel** (0212) 522
17 50. 🚇 *Sultanahmet.*
⬜ 9:15am–4:30pm Tue–Sun.
📷 🚫 ♿ *ground floor only.*

Sultan's loge

**Müezzin mahfili
(see p38)**

The Coronation Square served for the crowning of emperors.

Mausoleum of Mehmet III

Library of Sultan Mahmut I

Exit

The mausoleum of Murat III was used for his burial in 1599. Murat had by that time sired 102 children.

The Baptistry, part of the 6th-century church, now serves as the tomb of two sultans.

Mausoleum of Selim II
The oldest of the three mausoleums was completed in 1577 to the plans of Sinan (see p91). Its interior is entirely decorated with İznik tiles (see p161).

★ Ablutions Fountain
Built around 1740, this fountain is an exquisite example of Turkish Rococo style. Its projecting roof is painted with floral reliefs.

Exploring Haghia Sophia

Calligraphic roundel

Designed as an earthly mirror of the heavens, the interior of Haghia Sophia succeeds in imparting a truly celestial feel. The artistic highlights are a number of glistening figurative mosaics – remains of the decoration that once covered the upper walls but which has otherwise mostly disappeared. These remarkable works of Byzantine art date from the 9th century or later, after the iconoclastic era *(see p20)*. Some of the patterned mosaic ceilings, however, particularly those adorning the narthex and the neighbouring Vestibule of the Warriors, are part of the cathedral's original 6th-century decoration.

Interior as it looked after restoration in the 19th century

GROUND FLOOR

The first of the surviving Byzantine mosaics can be seen over the Imperial Gate. This is now the public entrance into the church, although previously only the emperor and his entourage were allowed to pass through it. The mosaic shows **Christ on a throne with an emperor kneeling beside him** ① and has been dated to between 886 and 912. The emperor is thought to be Leo VI, the Wise *(see p21)*.

The most conspicuous features at ground level in the nave are those added by the Ottoman sultans after the conquest of Istanbul in 1453, when the church was converted into a mosque.

The **mihrab** ②, the niche indicating the direction of Mecca, was installed in the apse of the church directly opposite the entrance. The **sultan's loge** ③, on the left of the mihrab as you face it, was built by the Fossati brothers. These Italian-Swiss architects undertook a major restoration of Haghia Sophia for Sultan Abdül Mecit in 1847–9.

To the right of the mihrab is the **minbar** ④, or pulpit, which was installed by Murat III (1574–95). He also erected the four **müezzin mahfilis** ⑤, marble platforms for readers of the Koran *(see p39)*. The largest of these is adjacent to the *minbar*. The patterned marble **coronation square** ⑥ next to it marks the supposed site of the Byzantine emperor's throne, or omphalos (centre of the world). Nearby, in the south aisle, is the **library of Mahmut I** ⑦, which was built in 1739 and is entered by a decorative bronze door.

Across the nave, between two columns, is the 17th-century marble **preacher's throne** ⑧, the contribution of Murat IV (1623–40). Behind it is one of several **maqsuras** ⑨. These low, fenced platforms were placed beside walls and pillars to provide places for elders to sit, listen and read the Koran.

In the northwestern and western corners of the church are two **marble urns** ⑩, thought to date from the Hellenistic or early Byzantine period. A rectangular pillar behind one of the urns, the **pillar of St Gregory the Miracle-Worker** ⑪, is believed to have healing powers. As you leave the church you pass through the Vestibule of the Warriors, so called because the emperor's bodyguards would wait here for him when he came to worship. Look behind you as you enter it at the wonderful mosaic of the **Virgin with Constantine and Justinian** ⑫ above the door. It shows Mary seated

FLOORPLAN OF HAGHIA SOPHIA

- ☐ Upper walls and domes
- ☐ Galleries
- ☐ Ground floor

Apse

Upper walls and domes

North gallery

West gallery

Ramp to gallery

South gallery

Apse

Nave

Entrance

Outer narthex

Narthex

Vestibule of the Warriors

on a throne holding the infant Jesus and flanked by two of the greatest emperors of the city. Constantine, on her right, presents her with the city of Constantinople, while Justinian offers her Haghia Sophia. This was made long after either of these two emperors lived, probably in the 10th century, during the reign of Basil II *(see p21)*. Visitors exit the church by the door that was once reserved for the emperor due to its proximity to the Great Palace *(see pp82–3)*.

Figure of Christ, detail from the Deesis Mosaic in the south gallery

GALLERIES

A ramp leads from the ground floor to the north gallery. Here, on the eastern side of the great northwest pier, you will find the 10th-century mosaic of **Emperor Alexander holding a skull** ⑬. On the west face of the same pier is a medieval drawing of a galleon in full sail. The only point of interest in the western

gallery is a green marble disk marking the location of the Byzantine **Empress's throne** ⑭.

There is much more to see in the south gallery. You begin by passing through the so-called **Gates of Heaven and Hell** ⑮, a marble doorway of which little is known except that it predates the Ottoman conquest *(see p26)*.

Around the corner to the right after passing through this dooorway is the **Deesis Mosaic** ⑯ showing the Virgin Mary and John the Baptist with Christ Pantocrator (the All-Powerful). Set into the floor opposite it is the tomb of Enrico Dandalo, the Doge of Venice responsible for the sacking of Constantinople in 1204 *(see p24)*.

In the last bay of the southern gallery there are two more mosaics. The right-hand one of these is of the **Virgin holding Christ, flanked by Emperor John II Comnenus and Empress Irene** ⑰. The other shows **Christ with Emperor Constantine IX Monomachus and Empress Zoe** ⑱. The faces of the emperor and empress have been altered.

Eight great **wooden plaques** ⑲ bearing calligraphic inscriptions hang over the nave at the level of the gallery. An addition of the Fossati brothers, they bear the names of Allah, the Prophet Mohammed, the first four caliphs and Hasan and Hussein, two of the Prophet's grandsons who are revered as martyrs.

Mosaic depicting the archangel Gabriel, adorning the lower wall of the apse

UPPER WALLS AND DOMES

The apse is dominated by a large and striking mosaic showing the **Virgin with the infant Jesus on her lap** ⑳. Two other mosaics in the apse show the archangels **Gabriel** ㉑ and, opposite him, Michael, but only fragments of the latter now remain. The unveiling of these mosaics on Easter Sunday 867 was a triumphal event celebrating victory over the iconoclasts *(see p21)*.

Three mosaic portraits of **saints** ㉒ adorn niches in the north tympanum and are visible from the south gallery and the nave. From left to right they depict: St Ignatius the Younger, St John Chrysostom and St Ignatius Theophorus.

In the four pendentives (the triangular, concave areas at the base of the dome) are mosaics of six-winged **seraphim** ㉓. The ones in the eastern pendentives date from 1346–55, but may be copies of much older ones. Those on the western side are 19th-century imitations that were added by the Fossati brothers.

The great **dome** ㉔ itself is decorated with Koranic inscriptions. It was once covered in golden mosaic and the tinkling sound of pieces dropping to the ground was familiar to visitors until the building's 19th-century restoration.

Mosaic of the Virgin with Emperor John II Comnenus and Empress Irene

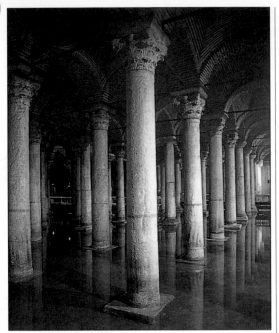

The cavernous interior of the Byzantine Basilica Cistern

Basilica Cistern ❷
Yerebatan Sarayı

13 Yerebatan Cad, Sultanahmet.
Map 3 E4 (5 E4). *Tel* (0212) 522
12 59. 🚊 Sultanahmet. ⬤ 9am–
5pm daily (Oct–Apr 8:30am–4pm).

This vast underground water
cistern, a beautiful piece of
Byzantine engineering, is the
most unusual tourist attraction
in the city. Although there may
have been an earlier, smaller
cistern here, this cavernous
vault was laid out under Justinian in 532, mainly to satisfy
the growing demands of the
Great Palace *(see pp82–3)* on
the other side of the Hippodrome *(see p80)*. For a century
after the conquest *(see p24)*,
the Ottomans did not know
of the cistern's existence. It
was rediscovered after people
were found to be collecting
water, and even fish, by
lowering buckets through
holes in their basements.
    Visitors tread walkways, to
the mixed sounds of classical
music and dripping water. The
cistern's roof is held up by 336
columns, each over 8 m (26ft)
high. Only about two thirds of

the original structure is visible
today, the rest having been
bricked up in the 19th century.
    In the far left-hand corner
two columns rest on Medusa
head bases. These bases are
evidence of plundering by the
Byzantines from earlier monuments. They are thought to
mark a *nymphaeum*, a shrine
to the water nymphs.

Istanbul Crafts Centre ❸
Mehmet Efendi Medresesi

Kabasakal Cad 5, Sultanahmet.
Map 3 E4 (5 E4).
Tel (0212) 517 67 82. 🚊 Adliye.
⬤ 9:30am–5:30pm daily.

If you are interested in
Turkish craftwork, this former Koranic college is worth
a visit. You can watch skilled
artisans at work: they may be
binding a book, executing an
elegant piece of calligraphy
or painting glaze onto ceramics. Items produced here are
all for sale. Others include
exquisite dolls, meerschaum
pipes and jewellery based
on Ottoman designs.
    Next door is the Yeşil Ev
Hotel *(see p182)*, a restored
Ottoman building with a
pleasant café in its courtyard.

Baths of Roxelana ❹
Haseki Hürrem Hamamı

Ayasofya Meydanı, Sultanahmet.
Map 3 E4 (5 E4). *Tel* (0212) 638 00
35. 🚊 Sultanahmet. ⬤ 8:30am–
5pm Wed–Mon.

These baths were built for
Süleyman the Magnificent
(see p26) by Sinan *(see p91)*,
and are named after Roxelana,
the sultan's scheming wife.
They were designated for the

ROXELANA

Süleyman the Magnificent's
power-hungry wife Roxelana
(1500–58, Haseki Hürrem
in Turkish), rose from being
a concubine in the imperial
harem to become his chief
wife, or first *kadın (see p28)*.
Thought to be of Russian
origin, she was also the first
consort permitted to reside
within the walls of Topkapı
Palace *(see pp54–9)*.
    Roxelana would stop at
nothing to get her own way.
When Süleyman's grand vizier and friend from youth,
İbrahim Paşa, became a threat to her position, she
persuaded the sultan to have him strangled. Much later,
Roxelana performed her *coup de grâce*. In 1553 she
persuaded Süleyman to have his handsome and popular
heir, Mustafa, murdered by deaf mutes to clear the way
for her own son Selim *(see p26)* to inherit the throne.

The 16th-century Baths of Roxelana, now housing an exclusive carpet shop

use of the congregation of Haghia Sophia (*see pp72–5*) when it was used as a mosque. With the women's entrance at one end of the building and the men's at the other, their absolute symmetry makes them perhaps the most hand-some baths in the city.

The building is now a government-run carpet shop, but the baths' original features are still clearly visible. A look around it is a must for those who have no intention of baring themselves in a public bath, but are curious about what the interior of a Turkish baths (*see p67*) is like.

Each end starts with a *camekan*, a massive domed hall which would originally have been centred on a foun-tain. Next is a small *soğukluk*, or intermediate room, which opens into a *hararet*, or steam room. The hexagonal massage slab in each *hararet*, the *göbek taşi*, is inlaid with coloured marbles, indicating that the baths are of imperial origin.

Vakıflar Carpet Museum ❺
Vakıflar Halı Müzesi

Imperial Pavilion, Blue Mosque, Sultanahmet. **Map** 3 E5 (5 E4). **Tel** *(0212) 518 13 30.* ☐ *9am–noon, 1–4pm Tue–Sat.* ● *public & religious hols.*

A ramp to the left of the main doorway into the Blue Mosque (*see pp78–9*) leads up to the Vakıflar Carpet

Museum. It has been installed in what was formerly the mosque's imperial pavilion. This pavilion was built by Ahmet I and used on Fridays by him and his successors when they attended prayers.

The carpets (*see pp218–19*) are hidden from potentially de-structive sunlight by stained-glass windows. They date from the 16th to the 19th centuries and are mostly from the western Anatolian regions of Uşak, Bergama and Konya. For many years mosques have played a vital role in the preservation of early rugs: all the carpets in this museum lay inside mosques until recently.

Detail of a 5th-century mosaic in the Mosaic Museum

Mosaic Museum ❻
Mozaik Müzesi

Arasta çarşısı, Sultanahmet. **Map** 3 E5 (5 E5). **Tel** *(0212) 518 12 05.* ☐ *Sultanahmet.* ☐ *9am–5pm Tue–Sun.*

This museum was created simply by roofing over a part of the Great Palace of the Byzantine Emperors (*see pp82–3*) which was discovered in the 1930s. In its heyday the palace boasted hundreds of rooms, many of them glit-tering with gold mosaics.

The surviving mosaic floor shows a lively variety of wild and domestic beasts and includes some hunting and fighting scenes. It is thought to have adorned the colon-nade leading from the royal apartments to the imperial enclosure beside the Hippo-drome, and dates from the late 5th century AD.

Blue Mosque ❼
See pp78–9.

Museum of Turkish and Islamic Arts ❽
Türk ve İslam Eserleri Müzesi

Atmeydanı Sok, Sultanahmet. **Map** 3 D4 (5 D4). **Tel** *(0212) 518 18 05.* ☐ *Sultanahmet.* ☐ *9am–4:30pm Tue–Sun.* **www**.tiem.org

Over 40,000 items are on display in the former pal-ace of İbrahim Paşa (c.1493–1536), the most gifted of Süleyman's many grand viziers. The collection was begun in the 19th century and ranges from the earliest period of Islam, under the Omayyad caliphate (661–750), through to modern times.

Each room concentrates on a different chronological period or geographical area of the Islamic world, with detailed explanations in both Turkish and English. The museum is particularly re-nowned for its collection of rugs. These range from 13th-century Seljuk fragments to the palatial Persian silks that cover the walls from floor to ceiling in the palace's great hall.

On the ground floor, an ethnographic section focuses on the lifestyles of different Turkish peoples, particularly the nomads of central and eastern Anatolia. The exhibits include recreations of a round felt *yurt* (Turkic nomadic tent) and a traditional brown tent.

Recreated yurt interior, Museum of Turkish and Islamic Arts

Blue Mosque ❼

Sultan Ahmet Camii

The blue mosque, which takes its name from the mainly blue İznik tilework *(see p161)* decorating its interior, is one of the most famous religious buildings in the world. Serene at any time, it is at its most magical when floodlit at night, its minarets circled by keening seagulls. Sultan Ahmet I *(see p33)* commissioned the mosque during a period of declining Ottoman fortunes, and it was built between 1609–16 by Mehmet Ağa, the imperial architect. The splendour of the plans provoked great hostility at the time, especially because a mosque with six minarets was considered a sacrilegious attempt to rival the architecture of Mecca itself.

A 19th-century engraving showing the Blue Mosque viewed from the Hippodrome *(see p80)*

Thick piers support the weight of the dome.

Mihrab

The loge *(see p39)* accommodated the sultan and his entourage during mosque services.

The Imperial Pavilion now houses the Vakıflar Carpet Museum *(see p77)*.

Minbar
The 17th-century minbar is intricately carved in white marble. It is used by the imam during prayers on Friday (see pp38–9).

Prayer hall

Exit for tourists

Müezzin mahfili *(see p38)*

Entrance to courtyard

★ İznik Tiles
No cost was spared in the decoration of the mosque. The tiles were made at the peak of tile production in İznik (see p161).

STAR FEATURES

★ İznik Tiles

★ Inside of the Dome

★ View of the Domes

★ Inside of the Dome

Mesmeric designs, employing flowing arabesques, are painted onto the interior of the mosque's domes and semidomes. The windows which pierce the domes no longer have their original 17th-century stained glass.

VISITORS' CHECKLIST

Meydanı 21, Sultanahmet. **Map** 3 E5 (5 E5). **Tel** *(0212) 458 07 76.* ⊞ *Sultanahmet.* ☐ *8:30am–noon, 1.45–4:30pm daily.* ● *prayer times.* **Son et Lumière** *May–Sep: daily after dusk (see the board on Mimar Mehmet Ağa Caddesi).*

★ View of the Domes

The graceful cascade of domes and semidomes makes a striking sight when viewed from the courtyard below.

Over 250 windows allow light to flood into the mosque.

Entrance

Ablutions Fountain
The hexagonal şadırvan is now purely ornamental since ritual ablutions are no longer carried out at this fountain.

Each minaret has two or three balconies.

Exit to Hippodrome

Washing the Feet
The Muslim's ritual ablutions conclude with the washing of the feet (see p39). Taps outside the mosque are used by the faithful for this purpose.

The courtyard covers the same area as the prayer hall, balancing the whole building.

Egyptian Obelisk and the Serpentine Column in the Hippodrome

Hippodrome ❾
At Meydanı

Sultanahmet. **Map** 3 E4 (5 D4).
🚇 *Sultanahmet.*

Little is left of the gigantic
stadium which once stood
at the heart of the Byzantine
city of Constantinople *(see
pp22–3)*. It was originally laid
out by Emperor Septimus
Severus during his rebuilding
of the city in the 3rd century
AD *(see p19)*.
Emperor Con-
stantine *(see p20)*
enlarged the
Hippodrome and
connected its
kathisma, or royal
box, to the near-
by Great Palace
(see pp82–3). It
is thought that
the stadium held
up to 100,000 people. The site
is now an elongated public
garden, At Meydanı, Cavalry
Square. There are, however,
enough remains of the
Hippodrome to get a sense of
its scale and importance.

The road running around the
square almost directly follows
the line of the chariot racing
track. You can also make out

**Relief carved on the base
of the Egyptian Obelisk**

some of the arches of the
sphendone (the curved end of
the Hippodrome) by walking
a few steps down İbret Sokağı.
Constantine adorned the
spina, the central line of the
stadium, with obelisks and
columns from Ancient Egypt
and Greece, importing a sense
of history to his new capital.
Conspicuous by its absence
is the column which once
stood on the spot where the
tourist information office is
now located. This
was topped by
four bronze horses
which were pill-
aged during the
Fourth Crusade
(see p24) and
taken to St Mark's
in Venice. Three
ancient monu-
ments remain,
however. The
Egyptian Obelisk, which
was built in 1500 BC, stood
outside Luxor until Constantine
had it brought to his city. This
beautifully carved monument
is broken and is probably only
one third of its original height.
It stands on a base, made in
the 4th century AD, showing
Theodosius I *(see p20)* and
his family in the *kathisma*

watching various events. The
four sides depict a chariot race;
Theodosius preparing to crown
the winner with a wreath of
laurel; prisoners paying hom-
age to the emperor; and the
erection of the obelisk itself.

Next to it is the **Serpentine
Column**, believed to date
from 479 BC, which was
shipped here from Delphi.
The heads of the serpents
were knocked off in the 18th
century by a drunken Polish
nobleman. One of them can
be seen in the Archaeological
Museum *(see pp62–5)*.

Another obelisk still standing, but of unknown date, is
usually referred to as the
**Column of Constantine
Porphyrogenitus**, after the
emperor who restored it in
the 10th century AD. It is also
sometimes called the Brazen
Column, because it is thought
to have once been sheathed
in a case of bronze. Its dilapi-
dated state owes much to the
fact that young Janissaries *(see
p127)* would routinely scale
it as a test of their bravery.

The only other structure in
the Hippodrome is a domed
fountain which commemorates
the visit of Kaiser Wilhelm II
to Istanbul in 1898.

The Hippodrome was the
scene of one of the bloodiest
events in Istanbul's history.
In 532 a brawl between rival
chariot-racing teams developed into the Nika Revolt,
during which much of the
city was destroyed. The end
of the revolt came when an
army of mercenaries, under
the command of Justinian's
general Belisarius, massacred
an estimated 30,000 people
trapped in the Hippodrome.

Cistern of 1001
Columns ❿
Binbirdirek Sarnıcı

Klodfarer Cad, Sultanahmet. **Map** 3
D4 (5 D4). **Tel** *(0212)* 638 22 38. 🚇
çemberlitaş. ⬜ *due to open summer
1999 after restoration phone for details*

This cistern, dating back to
the 4th century AD, is the
second largest underground
Byzantine cistern in Istanbul
after the Basilica Cistern *(see
p76)*. Spanning an area of

CEREMONIES IN THE HIPPODROME

Beginning with the inauguration of Constantinople on 11th May 330 *(see p20)*, the Hippodrome formed the stage for the city's greatest public events for the next 1,300 years. The Byzantines' most popular pastime was watching chariot racing in the stadium. Even after the Hippodrome fell into ruins following the Ottoman conquest of Istanbul *(see p26)*, it continued to be used for great public occasions. This 16th-century illustration depicts Murat III watching the 52-day-long festivities staged for the circumcision of his son Mehmet. All the guilds of Istanbul paraded before the Sultan displaying their crafts.

Sultan Murat III

Palace of İbrahim Paşa (Museum of Turkish and Islamic Arts, *see p77*)

Column of Constantine Porphyrogenitus

Serpentine Column

Egyptian Obelisk

---

64 m (210 ft) by 56 m (185 ft), the herring-bone brick roof vaults are held up by 264 marble columns – the 1,001 columns of its name is poetic exaggeration. Until not long ago, the cistern was filled with rubble and only explored by adventurous visitors. It has recently been transformed into an atmospheric shopping complex specializing in jewellery, carpets and tiles and other merchandise inspired by Ottoman culture.

Tomb of Sultan Mahmut II ⓫
Mahmut II Türbesi

Divanyolu Cad, Çemberlitaş.
Map 3 D4 (4 C3). 🚊 Çemberlitaş.
◯ 9:30am–4:30pm daily.

This large octagonal mausoleum is in the Empire style (modelled on Roman architecture), made popular by Napoleon. It was built in 1838, the year before Sultan Mahmut II's death and is shared by sultans Mahmut II, Abdül Aziz and Abdül Hamit II *(see pp32–3)*. Within, Corinthian pilasters divide up walls which groan with symbols of prosperity and victory. The huge tomb dominates a cemetery that has beautiful headstones, a fountain and, at the far end, a good café.

Constantine's Column ⓬
Çemberlitaş

Yeniçeriler Cad, Çemberlitaş.
Map 3 D4 (4 C3). 🚊 Çemberlitaş.
Çemberlitaş Baths Vezirhani Cad 8. **Tel** *(0212) 511 25 35.* ◯ *6am–midnight daily.*

A survivor of both storm and fire, this 35-m (115-ft) high column was constructed in AD 330 as part of the celebrations to inaugurate the new Byzantine capital *(see p20)*. It once dominated the magnificent Forum of Constantine *(see p23)*.

Made of porphyry brought from Heliopolis in Egypt, it was originally surmounted by a Corinthian capital bearing a statue of Emperor Constantine dressed as Apollo. This was brought down in a storm in 1106. Although what is left is relatively unimpressive, it has been carefully preserved. In the year 416 the 10 stone drums making up the column were reinforced with metal rings. These were renewed in 1701 by Sultan Mustafa III, and consequently the column is

Constantine's Column

known as çemberlitaş (the Hooped Column) in Turkish. In English it is sometimes referred to as the Burnt Column because it was damaged by several fires, especially one in 1779 which decimated the Grand Bazaar *(see pp98–9)*.

A variety of fantastical holy relics were supposedly entombed in the base of the column, which has since been encased in stone to strengthen it. These included the axe which Noah used to build the ark, Mary Magdalen's flask of anointing oil, and remains of the loaves of bread with which Christ fed the multitude.

Next to Constantine's Column, on the corner of Divanyolu Caddesi, stand the Çemberlitaş Baths. This splendid *hamam* complex *(see p67)* was commissioned by Nur Banu, wife of Sultan Selim II, and built in 1584 to a plan by the great Sinan *(see p91)*. Although the original women's section no longer survives, the baths still have separate facilities for men and women. The staff are used to foreign visitors, so this is a good place for your first experience of a Turkish bath.

Sokollu Mehmet Paşa Mosque ⓭
Sokollu Mehmet Paşa Camii

Şehit Çeşmesi Sok, Sultanahmet.
Map 3 D5 (4 C5). 🚊 Çemberlitaş or Sultanahmet. ⬭ daily.

Built by the architect Sinan (see p91) in 1571–2, this mosque was commissioned by Sokollu Mehmet Paşa, grand vizier to Selim II (see p32). The simplicity of Sinan's design solution for the mosque's sloping site has been widely admired. A steep entrance stairway leads up to the mosque courtyard from the street, passing beneath the teaching hall of its medrese (see p38), which still functions as a college. Only the tiled lunettes above the windows in the portico give a hint of the jewelled mosque interior to come.

Inside, the far wall around the carved mihrab is entirely covered in İznik tiles (see p161) of a sumptuous green-blue hue. This tile panel, designed specifically for the space, is complemented by six stained-glass windows. The "hat" of the minbar is covered with the same tiles. Most of the mosque's other walls are of plain stone, but they are enlivened by a few more tile panels. Set into the wall over the entrance there is a small piece of greenish stone which is supposedly from the Kaaba, the holy stone at the centre of Mecca.

Interior of the 16th-century Sokollu Mehmet Paşa Mosque

The Byzantine Church of SS Sergius and Bacchus, now a mosque

SS Sergius and Bacchus' Church ⓮
Küçük Ayasofya Camii

Küçük Ayasofya Cad. **Map** 3 D5 (4 C5). 🚊 Çemberlitaş or Sultanahmet. ⬭ daily. ♿

Commonly referred to as "Little Haghia Sophia", this church was built in 527, a few years before its namesake (see pp72–5). It too was founded by Emperor Justinian (see p20), together with his empress, Theodora, at the beginning of his long reign. Ingenious and highly decorative, the church gives a somewhat higgledy-piggledy impression both inside and out and is one of the most charming of all the city's architectural treasures.

Inside, an irregular octagon of columns on two floors supports a broad central dome composed of 16 vaults. The

RECONSTRUCTION OF THE GREAT PALACE

In Byzantine times, present-day Sultanahmet was the site of the Great Palace, which, in its heyday, had no equal in Europe and dazzled medieval visitors with its opulence. This great complex of buildings – including royal apartments, state rooms, churches, courtyards and gardens – extended over a sloping, terraced site from the Hippodrome to the imperial harbour on the shore of the Sea of Marmara. The palace was built in stages, beginning under Constantine in the 4th century. It was enlarged by Justinian following the fire caused by the Nika Revolt in 532 (see p80). Later emperors, especially the 9th-century Basil I (see p21), extended it further. After several hundred years of occupation, it was finally abandoned in the second half of the 13th century in favour of Blachernae Palace (see p117).

The Mese was a colonnaded street lined with shops and statuary.

Hippodrome (see p80)

Hormisdas Palace

Church of SS Peter and Paul

Church of SS Sergius and Bacchus

mosaic decoration which once adorned some of the walls has long since crumbled away. However, the green and red marble columns, the delicate tracery of the capitals and the carved frieze running above the columns are original features of the church.

The inscription on this frieze, in boldly carved Greek script, mentions the founders of the church and St Sergius, but not St Bacchus. The two saints were Roman centurions who converted to Christianity and were martyred. Justinian credited them with saving his life when, as a young man, he was implicated in a plot to kill his uncle, Justin I. The saints supposedly appeared to Justin in a dream and told him to release his nephew.

The Church of SS Sergius and Bacchus was built between two important edifices to which it was connected, the Palace of Hormisdas and the Church of SS Peter and Paul, but has outlived them both. After the conquest of Istanbul in 1453 (see p26) it was converted into a mosque.

Bucoleon Palace ⑮
Bukoleon Sarayı

Kennedy Cad, Sultanahmet.
Map 3 E5. 🚊 *Sultanahmet.*

Finding the site of what remains of the Great Palace of the Byzantine emperors requires precision. It is not advisable to visit the ruins alone as they are usually inhabited by tramps.

Take the path under the railway from the Church of SS Sergius and Bacchus, turn left and walk beside Kennedy Caddesi, the main road along the shore of the Sea of Marmara for about 400 m (450 yards). This will bring you to a stretch of the ancient sea walls, constructed to protect the city from a naval assault. Within these walls you will find a creeper-clad section of stonework pierced by three vast windows framed in

marble. This is all that now survives of the Bucoleon Palace, a maritime residence that formed part of the sprawling Great Palace. The waters of a small private harbour lapped right up to the palace and a private flight of steps led down in to the water, allowing the emperor to board imperial caïques. The ruined tower just east of the palace was a lighthouse, called the Pharos, in Byzantine times.

Wall of Bucoleon Palace, the only part of the Byzantine Great Palace still standing

The Kathisma was the imperial box of the Hippodrome.

The Milion was the point from which road distances were measured (see p71).

Haghia Sophia *(see pp72–5)*

The Augusteum was a porticoed public square.

Chalke Gate was the main entrance to the palace.

Hall of Gold (site of Mosaic Museum, see p77)

Lighthouse

Magnaura Palace

The Bucoleon Palace had a magnificent façade looking out over the sea.

The Nea Ekklesia, erected by Basil I, set the style for all subsequent Byzantine churches.

Daphne Palace

THE BAZAAR QUARTER

Trade has always been important in a city straddling the continents of Asia and Europe. Nowhere is this more evident than in the warren of streets lying between the Grand Bazaar and Galata Bridge. Everywhere, goods tumble out of shops onto the pavement. Look through any of the archways in between shops and you will discover hidden courtyards or hans (*see p96*) containing feverishly

Window from Nuruosmaniye Mosque

industrious workshops. With its seemingly limitless range of goods, the labyrinthine Grand Bazaar is at the centre of all this commercial activity. The Spice Bazaar is equally colourful but smaller and more manageable.

Up on the hill, next to the university, is Süleymaniye Mosque, a glorious expression of 16th-century Ottoman culture. It is just one of numerous beautiful mosques in this area.

SIGHTS AT A GLANCE

Mosques and Churches
Atik Ali Paşa Mosque ⓴
Bodrum Mosque ⓬
Church of St Theodore ❻
Kalenderhane Mosque ❿
Mahmut Paşa Mosque ㉒
New Mosque ❶
Nuruosmaniye Mosque ㉑
Prince's Mosque ❾
Rüstem Paşa Mosque ❸
Sülemaniye Mosque pp90–91 ❺
Tulip Mosque ⓫

Bazaars, Hans and Shops
Book Bazaar ⓰
Grand Bazaar pp98–9 ⓲
Spice Bazaar ❷
Valide Hanı ⓱
Vefa Bozacısı ❽

Museums and Monuments
Forum of Theodosius ⓭
Museum of Calligraphy ⓮
Valens Aqueduct ❼

Squares and Courtyards
Beyazıt Square ⓯
Çorlulu Ali Paşa Courtyard ⓳

Waterways
Golden Horn ❹

KEY

- ▨ Street-by-Street map *See pp86–7*
- ⛴ Ferry boarding point
- 🚋 Tram stop
- 🚌 Main bus stop
- C Mosque

GETTING AROUND

Trams from Sultanahmet run down Yeniçeriler Caddesi, and stop outside the Grand Bazaar. Ferries from various destinations dock at Eminönü, opposite the Spice Bazaar.

0 metres   500
0 yards   500

◁ **The inside of the Grand Bazaar, always thronging with bargain-hunters**

Street-by-Street:Around the Spice Bazaar

The narrow streets around the Spice Bazaar encapsulate the spirit of old Istanbul. From here buses, taxis and trams head off across the Galata Bridge and into the interior of the city. The blast of ships' horns signals the departure of ferries from Eminönü to Asian Istanbul. It is the quarter's shops and markets, though, that are the focus of attention for the eager shoppers who crowd the Spice Bazaar and the streets around it, sometimes breaking for a leisurely tea beneath the trees in its courtyard. Across the way, and entirely aloof from the bustle, rise the domes of the New Mosque. On one of the commercial alleyways which radiate out from the mosque, an inconspicuous doorway leads up stairs to the terrace of the serene, tile-covered Rüstem Paşa Mosque.

Nargile on sale near the Spice Bazaar

★ **Rüstem Pasa Mosque**
The interior of this secluded mosque is a brilliant pattern-book made of İznik tiles (see p161) of the finest quality ❸

The *pastırma* shop at 11 Hasırcılar Caddesi sells thin slices of dried beef, spiced with fenugreek – a Turkish delicacy.

Tahtakale Hamamı Çarşısı, now a bazaar, was formerly a Turkish bath.

Kurukahveci Mehmet Efendi is one of Istanbul's oldest and most popular coffee shops. You can drink coffee on the premises or buy a packet to take away with you *(see p213)*.

KUTUCULAR CAD

UZUNÇARŞILI CAD

BALKAPANI SOK

HASIRCILAR CAD

TAHTAKALE CAD

SABUNCUHANI SOK

MARPUÇC

0 metres   75
0 yards   75

STAR SIGHTS

★ Rüstem Pasa Mosque

★ New Mosque

★ Spice Bazaar

Stall holders and street traders, such as this man selling garlic cloves, ply their wares in Sabuncuhanı Sokağı and the other narrow streets around the Spice Bazaar.

Eminönü is the port from which ferries depart to many destinations *(see p244)* and for trips along the Bosphorus *(see pp144–9)*. It bustles with activity as traders compete to sell drinks and snacks.

LOCATOR MAP
See Street Finder map 2

Galata Bridge

Pandeli's Restaurant *(see p200)*

The royal pavilion, a suite of beautifully tiled private rooms, is linked by a passage to the sultan's loge inside the New Mosque.

Eminönü sea bus boarding point

Eminönü bus terminus

Eminönü tram stop

RESADIYE CAD

CAMI MEYDANI SOK

CAD

PAZARI SOK

YENI CAMI CAD

Tea Gardens

★ **New Mosque**
This mosque, which dominates the Eminönü waterfront, was completed in the 17th century by the mother of Sultan Mehmet IV (see p33) ❶

Mausoleum of Turhan Hatice Valide Sultan, mother of Mehmet IV

★ **Spice Bazaar**
This market was built in 1660 as part of the New Mosque complex, and it has always been associated with the sale of spices, though today there is much more on offer ❷

Pet market and garden centre

KEY

— — — Suggested route

New Mosque ❶
Yeni Cami

Yeni Cami Meydanı, Eminönü.
Map 3 D2. 🚇 *Eminönü.* ⬭ *daily.*

Situated at the southern end of Galata Bridge, the New Mosque is one of the most prominent mosques in the city. It dates from the time when a few women from the harem became powerful enough to dictate the policies of the Ottoman sultans *(see p27)*. The mosque was started in 1597 by Safiye, mother of Mehmet III, but building was suspended on the sultan's death as his mother then lost her position. It was not completed until 1663, after Turhan Hadice, mother of Mehmet IV, had taken up the project.

Though the mosque was built after the classical period of Ottoman architecture, it shares many traits with earlier imperial foundations, including a monumental courtyard. The mosque once had a hospital, school and public baths.

The turquoise, blue and white floral tiles decorating the interior are from İznik *(see p161)* and date from the mid-17th century, though by this time the quality of the tiles produced there was already in decline. More striking are the tiled lunettes and bold Koranic frieze decorating the porch between the courtyard and the prayer hall.

At the far left-hand corner of the upper gallery is the sultan's loge *(see p39)*, which is linked to his personal suite of rooms *(see p87)*.

A selection of nuts and seeds for sale in the Spice Bazaar

Spice Bazaar ❷
Mısır Çarşısı

Cami Meydanı Sok. **Map** 3 D2 (4 C1). 🚇 *Eminönü.* ⬭ *8am–7pm Mon–Sat.*

This cavernous, L-shaped market was built in the early 17th century as an extension of the New Mosque complex. Its revenues once helped maintain the mosque's philanthropic institutions.

In Turkish the market is named the Mısır Çarşısı – the Egyptian Bazaar – because it was built with money paid as duty on Egyptian imports. In English it is usually known as the Spice Bazaar. From medieval times spices were a vital and expensive part of cooking and they became the market's main produce. The bazaar came to specialize in spices from the orient, taking advantage of Istanbul's site on the trade route between the East (where most spices were grown) and Europe.

Stalls in the bazaar stock spices, herbs and other foods such as honey, nuts, sweetmeats and *pastirma* (cured beef). Today's expensive Eastern commodity, caviar, is also available, the best variety being Iranian.

Nowadays an eclectic range of other items can be found in the Spice Bazaar, including everything from household goods, toys and clothes to exotic aphrodisiacs. The square between the two arms of the bazaar is full of commercial activity, with cafés, and stalls selling plants and pets.

Floral İznik tiles adorning the interior of Rüstem Paşa Mosque

Rüstem Paşa Mosque ❸
Rüstem Paşa Camii

Hasıcılar Cad, Eminönü.
Map 3 D2. 🚇 *Eminönü.* ⬭ *daily.*

Raised above the busy shops and warehouses around the Spice Bazaar, this mosque was built in 1561 by the great architect Sinan *(see p91)* for Rüstem Paşa, son-in-law of and grand vizier to Süleyman I *(see p26)*. Rents from the businesses in the bazaar were intended to pay for the upkeep of the mosque.

The staggering wealth of its decoration says something about the amount of money that the corrupt Rüstem managed to salt away during his career. Most of the interior is covered in İznik tiles of the very highest quality.

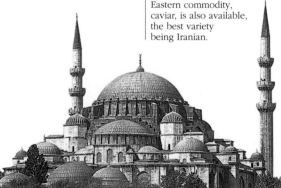

The New Mosque, a prominent feature on the Eminönü waterfront

The four piers are adorned with tiles of one design but the rest of the prayer hall is a riot of different patterns, from abstract to floral. Some of the finest tiles can be found on the galleries. All in all, there is no other mosque in the city adorned with such a magnificent blanket of tiles.

The mosque is also notable for its numerous windows: it was built with as many as the structure would allow.

Golden Horn ❹
Haliç

Map 3 D2. 🚇 *Eminönü.* 🚌 *55T, 99A.*

Often described as the world's greatest natural harbour, the Golden Horn is a flooded river valley which flows southwest into the Bosphorus. The estuary attracted settlers to its shores in the 7th century BC and later enabled Constantinople to become a rich and powerful port. According to legend, the Byzantines threw so many valuables into it during the Ottoman conquest *(see p26)*, that the waters glistened with gold. Today, however, belying its name, the Golden Horn has become polluted by the numerous nearby factories.

For hundreds of years the city's trade was conducted by ships that off-loaded their goods into warehouses lining the Golden Horn. Nowadays, though, the great container ships coming to Istanbul use ports on the Sea of Marmara. Spanning the mouth of the Horn is the Galata Bridge, which joins Eminönü to Galata. The bridge, built in 1992, opens in the middle to allow access for tall ships. It is a good place from which to appreciate the complex geography of the city and admire the minaret-filled skyline.

The functional Galata Bridge replaced the raffish charm of a pontoon bridge with a busy lower level of restaurants. The old bridge has been reconstructed just south of the Rahmi Koç Museum *(see p127)*. There is another bridge, Atatürk, between these, and a fourth, Fatih, further up the Horn near the end of the city walls. Between Sütlüce and Eyüp, the da Vinci pedestrian bridge will soon be finished.

Süleymaniye Mosque ❺

See pp90–91.

Church of St Theodore ❻
Kilise Camii

Vefa Cad, Cami Sok, Vefa.
Map 2 B2. 🚌 *28, 61B, 87.*

Apart from its delightfully dishevelled ancient exterior, very little else remains of the former Byzantine Church of St Theodore. The elaborate church was built in the 12th–14th centuries, the last great era of Byzantine construction. It was converted into a mosque following the Ottoman conquest of the city in 1453 *(see p26)*.

One feature that is still evident in the south dome in its outer porch is a 14th-century mosaic of the Virgin Mary surrounded by the Prophets. The fluted minaret makes a sympathetic addition.

The 4th-century Valens Aqueduct crossing Atatürk Bulvarı

Valens Aqueduct ❼
Bozdoğan Kemeri

Atatürk Bulvarı, Saraçhane.
Map 2 A3. 🚇 *Laleli.* 🚌 *28, 61B, 87.*

Emperor Valens built this mighty aqueduct, supported by two imposing rows of arches, in the late 4th century AD. Part of the elaborate water system feeding the palaces and fountains of the Byzantine capital, it brought water from the Belgrade Forest *(see p158)* and mountains over 200 km (125 miles) away to a vast cistern which stood in the vicinity of what is now Beyazıt Square *(see p94)*.

The aqueduct supplied the city's water until the late 19th century, when it was made obsolete by a modern water distribution network. The original open channels, however, had by this stage already been replaced first by clay pipes and then by iron ones.

The structure was repaired many times during its history, latterly by sultans Mustafa II (1695–1703) and Ahmet III *(see p25)*. It was originally 1,000 m (3,300 ft) long, of which 625 m (2,050 ft) remain.

Fisherman on the modern Galata Bridge spanning the Golden Horn

Süleymaniye Mosque ❺

Süleymaniye Camii

Istanbul's most important mosque is both a tribute to its architect, the great Sinan, and a fitting memorial to its founder, Süleyman the Magnificent *(see p26)*. It was built above the Golden Horn in the grounds of the old palace, Eski Saray *(see p94)*, between 1550–57. Like the city's other imperial mosques, the Süleymaniye Mosque was not only a place of worship, but also a charitable foundation, or *külliye (see p38)*. The mosque is surrounded by its former hospital, soup kitchen, schools, caravanserai and bath house. This complex provided a welfare system which fed over 1,000 of the city's poor – Muslims, Christians and Jews alike – every day.

Courtyard
The ancient columns that surround the courtyard are said to have come originally from the kathisma, the Byzantine royal box in the Hippodrome (see p80).

Muvakkithane Gateway
The main courtyard entrance (now closed) contained the rooms of the mosque astronomer, who determined prayer times.

Minaret

Tomb of Sinan

The caravanserai provided lodging and food for travellers and their animals.

İmaret Gate

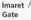

Café in a sunken garden

İmaret
The kitchen – now a restaurant (see p200) – fed the city's poor as well as the mosque staff and their families. The size of the millstone in its courtyard gives some idea of the amount of grain needed to feed everyone.

★ **Mosque Interior**
A sense of soaring space and calm strikes you as you enter the mosque. The effect is enhanced by the fact that the height of the dome from the floor is exactly double its diameter.

VISITORS' CHECKLIST

Prof Siddik Sami Onar Caddesi, Vefa. **Map** 2 C3 (4 A1). **Tel** (0212) 522 02 98. 🚇 Beyazıt or Eminönü, then 10 mins' walk. ⬜ daily. ⬤ at prayer times.

The Tomb of Roxelana contains Süleyman's beloved wife *(see p76)*.

Entrance

Graveyard

★ **Tomb of Süleyman**
Ceramic stars said to be set with emeralds sparkle above the coffins of Süleyman, his daughter Mihrimah and two of his successors, Süleyman II and Ahmet II.

These marble benches were used to support coffins before burial.

"Addicts Alley" is so called because the cafés here once sold opium and hashish as well as coffee and tea.

The medreses *(see p38)* to the south of the mosque house a library containing 110,000 manuscripts.

Former hospital and asylum

SINAN, THE IMPERIAL ARCHITECT

Like many of his eminent contemporaries, Koca Mimar Sinan (c.1491–1588) was brought from Anatolia to Istanbul in the *devşirme*, the annual roundup of talented Christian youths, and educated at one of the elite palace schools. He became a military engineer but won the eye of Süleyman I, who made him chief imperial architect in 1538. With the far-sighted patronage of the sultan, Sinan – the closest Turkey gets to a Renaissance architect – created masterpieces which demonstrated his master's status as the most magnificent of monarchs. Sinan died aged 97, having built 131 mosques and 200 other buildings.

Bust of the great architect Sinan

STAR FEATURES

★ Mosque Interior

★ Tomb of Süleyman

Vefa Bozacısı ❽

Katip Çelebi Cad 102, Vefa. **Map** 2
B2. **Tel** (0212) 519 49 22. 🚌 61B,
90. ⬭ 8am–5:30pm daily.

With its wood-and-tile
interior and glittering
glass-mosaic columns, this
unusual shop and bar has
changed little since the 1930s.
It was founded in 1876 to sell
boza, a popular winter drink
made from bulgur (cracked
wheat, *see p197*). In summer
a slightly fermented grape
juice known as *şıra* is sold.
The shop's main trade throughout the whole year, however,
is in wine vinegar.

Inside the shop you will
see a glass from which Kemal
Atatürk *(see p31)* drank *boza*
in 1937, enshrined in a display
beneath a glass dome.

**Bottles of *boza*, a wheat-based drink, lining
the interior of Vefa Bozacısı**

Prince's Mosque ❾
Şehzade Camii

Şehzade Başı Cad 70, Saraçhane.
Map 2 B3. 🚇 Laleli. ⬭ daily.
Tombs ⬭ 9am–5pm Tue–Sun.

This mosque complex was
erected by Süleyman the
Magnificent *(see p26)* in
memory of his eldest son by
Roxelana *(see p76)*, Şehzade
(Prince) Mehmet, who died of
smallpox at the age of 21. The
building was Sinan's *(see p91)*
first major imperial commission
and was completed in 1548.
The architect used a delightful
decorative style in designing
this mosque before abandon-
ing it in favour of the classical
austerity of his later work.
The mosque is approached

**Dome of the Prince's Mosque,
Sinan's first imperial mosque**

through an elegant porticoed
inner courtyard, while the
other institutions making up
the mosque complex, including a *medrese (see p38)*, are
enclosed within an
outer courtyard.

The interior of the
mosque is unusual and
was something of an
experiment in that it
is symmetrical, having
a semidome on each
of its four sides.

The three tombs
located to the rear of
the mosque, belonging
to Şehzade Mehmet
himself and grand vi-
ziers İbrahim Paşa and
Rüstem Paşa *(see p88)*,
are the finest in the
city. Each has beauti-
ful İznik tiles *(see
p161)* and lustrous original
stained glass. That of Şehzade
Mehmet also boasts the finest
painted dome in Istanbul.

On Fridays you will notice
a crowd of women flocking
to another tomb within the

complex, that of Helvacı
Baba, as they have done for
over 400 years. Helvacı Baba
is said to miraculously cure
crippled children, solve fertil-
ity problems and find husbands
or accommodation for those
who beseech him.

Kalenderhane
Mosque ❿
Kalenderhane Camii

16 Mart Şehitleri Cad, Saraçhane.
Map 2 B3. 🚇 Üniversite.
⬭ prayer times only.

Sitting in the lee of the
Valens Aqueduct *(see p89)*,
on the site where a Roman
bath once stood, is this Byzantine church with a chequered
history. It was built and rebuilt several times between
the 6th and 12th centuries,
before finally being converted
into a mosque shortly after
the conquest in 1453 *(see
p26)*. The mosque is named
after the Kalender brotherhood
of dervishes which used the
church as its headquarters for
some years after the conquest.

The building has the cruci-
form layout characteristic of
Byzantine churches of the
period. Some of the decoration remaining from its last
incarnation, as the Church
of Theotokos Kyriotissa (her
Ladyship Mary, Mother of
God), also survives in the
prayer hall with its marble
panelling and in the fragments of fresco in the narthex
(entrance hall). A series of
frescoes depicting the life of
St Francis of Assisi were removed in the 1970s and are
no longer on public view.

A shaft of light illuminating the interior of Kalenderhane Mosque

The Baroque Tulip Mosque, housing a marketplace in its basement

Tulip Mosque ⓫
Lâleli Camii

Ordu Cad, Lâleli. **Map** 2 B4.
🚇 *Lâleli.* ⃝ *prayer times only.*

Built in 1759–63, this
mosque complex is the
best example in the city of
the Baroque style, of which
its architect, Mehmet Tahir Ağa,
was the greatest exponent.
Inside the mosque, a variety
of gaudy, coloured marble
covers all of its surfaces.

More fascinating is the area
underneath the main body of
the mosque. This is a great
hall supported on eight piers,
with a fountain in the middle.
The hall is now used as a
subterranean marketplace,
packed with Eastern Europeans
and Central Asians haggling
over items of clothing.

The nearby Büyük Taş Hanı
(see p96), or Big Stone Han,
is likely to have been part
of the mosque's original
complex but now houses a
number of leather shops and
a restaurant. To get to it turn
left outside the mosque into
Fethi Bey Caddesi and then
take the second left into
Çukur Çeşme Sokağı. The
main courtyard of the han is
at the end of a long passage
situated off this lane.

Bodrum Mosque ⓬
Bodrum Camii

Sait Efendi Sok, Laleli. **Map** 2 A4.
🚇 *Laleli.* ⃝ *prayer times only.*

Narrow courses of brick
forming the outside walls,
and a window-pierced dome,
betray the early origins of this
mosque as a Byzantine church.
It was built in the early 10th
century by co-Emperor Romanus I Lacapenus (919–44)
as part of the Monastery of
Myrelaion and adjoined a
small palace. The palace was
later converted into a nunnery
where the emperor's widow,
Theophano, lived out her
final years. She was eventually buried in a sanctuary
chapel beneath the church,
which is closed to the public.

In the late 15th century the
church was converted into a
mosque by Mesih Paşa, a
descendant of the Palaeologus
family, the last dynasty to rule
Byzantium. The building was
gutted by fire several times
and nothing remains of its
internal decoration. Today
it is still a working mosque
and is accessed via a stairway
which leads up to a raised
piazza filled with coat stalls.

Forum of
Theodosius ⓭

Ordu Cad, Beyazıt. **Map** 2 C4 (4 A3).
🚇 *Üniversite or Beyazıt.*

Constantinople *(see p20)*
was built around several
large public squares or forums.
The largest of them stood on
the site of present-day Beyazıt
Square. It was originally known
as the Forum Tauri (the Forum
of the Bull) because of the
huge bronze bull in the middle of it in which sacrificial
animals, and sometimes even
criminals, were roasted.

After Theodosius the Great
enlarged it in the late 4th
century, the forum took his
name. Relics of the triumphal
arch and other structures can
be found lying and stacked
on either side of the tram
tracks along Ordu Caddesi.
The huge columns, decorated
with a motif reminiscent of a
peacock's tail, are particularly
striking. Once the forum had
become derelict, these columns were reused all over
the city. Some can be seen in
the Basilica Cistern *(see p76)*.
Other fragments from the
forum were built into Beyazıt
Hamamı, a Turkish bath *(see
p67)* further west down Ordu
Caddesi, now a bazaar.

Peacock feather design on a column
from the Forum of Theodosius

Museum of Calligraphy ⑭

Türk Vakıf Hat Sanatları Müzesi

Beyazıt Meydanı, Beyazıt. **Map** 2 C4
(4 A3). **Tel** *(0212) 527 58 51.*
🚇 *Üniversite.* ◯ *9am–4pm
Tue–Sat.* 🈵 ♿ *with assistance.*

The delightful courtyard in which this museum has been installed was once a *medrese (see p38)* of Beyazıt Mosque, situated on the other side of the square.

Its changing displays are taken from the massive archive belonging to the Turkish Calligraphy Foundation. As well as some beautiful manuscripts there are also examples of calligraphy on stone and glass. There is also an exhibition of tools used in calligraphy. One of the cells in the *medrese* now contains a waxwork tableau of a master calligrapher with his pupils.

Beyazıt Tower, within the wooded grounds of Istanbul University

Beyazıt Square ⑮

Beyazıt Meydanı

Ordu Cad, Beyazıt. **Map** 2 C4 (4
A3). 🚇 *Beyazıt.*

Always filled with crowds of people and huge flocks of pigeons, Beyazıt Square is the most vibrant space in the old part of the city. Throughout the week the square is the venue for a flea market, where everything from carpets *(see pp218–19)* and Central Asian silks to general bric-a-brac can be purchased. When

The fortress-like entrance to Istanbul University, Beyazıt Square

you have tired of rummaging, there are several cafés.

On the northern side of the square is the Moorish-style gateway leading into Istanbul University. The university's main building dates from the 19th century and once served as the Ministry of War. Within the wooded grounds rises Beyazıt Tower. This marble fire-watching station was built in 1828 on the site of Eski Saray, the palace first inhabited by Mehmet the Conqueror *(see p26)* after Byzantium fell to the Ottomans. Two original timber towers were destroyed by fire. At one time, you could climb to the top of the tower but it is now closed to the public.

On the square's eastern side is Beyazıt Mosque, which was commissioned by Beyazıt II and completed in 1506. It is the oldest surviving imperial mosque in the city. Behind the impressive outer portal is a harmonious courtyard with an elegant domed fountain at its centre. Around the courtyard are columns made of granite and green and red Egyptian porphyry, and a pavement of multi-coloured marble. The layout of the mosque's interior, with its central dome and surrounding semi-domes, is heavily inspired by the design of Haghia Sophia *(see pp72–5)*.

Book Bazaar ⑯

Sahaflar Çarşısı

Sahaflar Çarşısı Sok, Beyazıt.
Map 2 C4 (4 A3). 🚇 *Üniversite.*
◯ *8am–8pm daily.* ♿

This charming booksellers' courtyard, on the site of the Byzantine book and paper market, can be entered either from Beyazıt Square or from inside the Grand Bazaar *(see pp98–9)*. Racks are laden with all sorts of books, from tourist guides to academic tomes.

During the early Ottoman period *(see pp25–7)*, printed books were seen as a corrupting European influence and were banned in Turkey. As a result the bazaar only sold manuscripts. Then on 31 January 1729 İbrahim Müteferrika (1674–1745) produced the first printed book in the Turkish language, an Arabic dictionary. His bust stands in the centre of the market today. Note that book prices are fixed and cannot be haggled over.

Customers browsing in the Book Bazaar

The Art of Ottoman Calligraphy

Calligraphy is one of the noblest of Islamic arts. Its skills were handed down from master to apprentice, with the aim of the pupil being to replicate perfectly the hand of his master. In Ottoman Turkey, calligraphy was used to ornament firmans (imperial decrees) as well as poetry and copies of the Koran. However, many examples are also to be found on buildings, carved in wood and applied to architectural ceramics. The art of the calligrapher in all cases was to go as far as possible in beautifying the writing without altering the sense of the text. It was particularly important that the text of the Koran should be accurately transcribed. With the text of a firman, made to impress as much as to be read, the calligrapher could afford to add more flourishes.

The great calligraphers *of the Ottoman period were Şeyh Hamdullah (1436–1520), whose work is seen in this Koran, Hafiz Osman (1642–98) and Ahmet Karahisari (d.1556). Their pupils also achieved great renown.*

Floral decorations

Ornamental loops

The sultan's tuğra *was his personal monogram, used in place of his signature. It would either be drawn by a calligrapher or engraved on a wooden block and then stamped on documents. The tuğra incorporated the sultan's name and title, his patronymic and wishes for his success or victory – all highly stylized. This is the tuğra of Selim II (1566–74).*

Calligraphy *developed further in the 19th and early 20th centuries when artists explored more creative forms and worked with new media. There was greater freedom to depict human faces and animal forms. Calligraphers also began to practise the technique of découpage (cutting out the letters) and, as seen here, wrote inscriptions on delicate leaf skeletons.*

The later sultans *were taught calligraphy as part of their education and became skilled artists. This panel, from the 19th century, is by Mahmut II (1808–39).*

Breathing techniques *were probably practised by some calligraphers in order to achieve the steadiness of hand required for their craft.*

Burnisher

Knife for cutting pen nib

The calligrapher's tools *and materials included a burnisher, usually made of agate, which was used to prepare the paper. A knife was used to slit the reed nib of the pen before writing.*

Valide Han ⓱
Valide Hanı

Junction of çakmakçılar Yokuşu & Tarakçılar Cad, Beyazıt. **Map** 2 C3 (4 B2). 🚊 *Beyazıt, then 10 mins walk.* 🕐 *9:30am–5pm Mon–Sat.*

If the Grand Bazaar *(see pp98–9)* seems large, it is sobering to realize that it is only the covered part of an huge area of seething commercial activity which reaches all the way to the Golden Horn *(see p89)*. As in the Grand Bazaar, most manufacturing and trade takes place in hans, courtyards hidden away from the street behind shaded gateways.

The largest han in Istanbul is Valide Han. It was built in 1651 by Kösem, the mother of Sultan Mehmet IV. You enter it from Çakmakçılar Yokuşu through a massive portal. After passing through an irregularly shaped forecourt, you come out into a large courtyard centring on a Shiite mosque. This was built when the han became the centre of Persian trade in the city. Today, the han throbs to the rhythm of hundreds of weaving looms.

A short walk further down Çakmakçılar Yokuşu is Büyük Yeni Han, hidden behind another impressive doorway. This Baroque han, built in

Carpet shops in Çorlulu Ali Paşa Courtyard

1764, has three arcaded levels. The entrance is on the top level, where distinctive bird cages are among the wares.

In the labyrinth of narrow streets around these hans, artisans are grouped according to their wares: on Bakırcılar Caddesi, for instance, you will find metal workers, while the craftsmen of Uzunçarşı Caddesi make wooden items.

Grand Bazaar ⓲

See pp98–9.

HANS OF ISTANBUL
The innumerable hans that dot the centre of Istanbul originally provided temporary accommodation for travellers, their pack animals and their wares. The typical han was built as part of a mosque complex *(see pp38–9)*. It consists of two- or three-storey buildings around a courtyard. This is entered via a large gateway which can be secured by a heavy wooden door at night. When vans and lorries replaced horses and mules, the city's hans lost their original function and most of them were converted into warrens of small factories and workshops. These working hans are frequently in bad repair, but in them you can still sense the entrepreneurial, oriental atmosphere of bygone Istanbul.

Café in Büyük Taş Han, near the Tulip Mosque *(see p93)*

Çorlulu Ali Paşa Courtyard ⓳
Çorlulu Ali Paşa Külliyesi

Yeniçeriler Cad, Beyazıt. **Map** 4 B3. 🚊 *Beyazıt.* 🕐 *daily.*

Like many others in the city, the *medrese (see p38)* of this mosque complex outside the Grand Bazaar has become the setting for a tranquil outdoor café. It was built for Çorlulu Ali Paşa, son-in-law of Mustafa II, who served as grand vizier under Ahmet III *(see p27)*. Ahmet later exiled him to the island of Lésvos and had him executed there in 1711. Some years later his family smuggled his head back to Istanbul and interred it in the tomb built for him.

The complex is entered from Yeniçeriler Caddesi by two alleyways. Several carpet shops now inhabit the *medrese* and rugs are hung and spread all around, waiting for prospective buyers. The carpet shops share the *medrese* with a *kahve*, a traditional café *(see p208)*, which is popular with locals and students from the nearby university. It advertises itself irresistibly as the "Traditional Mystic Water Pipe and Erenler Tea Garden". Here you can sit and drink tea, and perhaps smoke a nargile (bubble pipe), while deciding which carpet to buy *(see pp218–19)*.

Situated across Bıleycıler Sokak, an alleyway off Çorlulu Ali Paşa Courtyard, is the Koca Sinan Paşa tomb complex, the courtyard of which is another tea garden. The charming *medrese*, mausoleum and *sebil* (a fountain where water was handed out to passers-by) were built in 1593 by Davut Ağa, who succeeded Sinan *(see p91)* as chief architect of the empire. The tomb of Koca Sinan Paşa, grand vizier under Murat III and Mehmet III, is a striking 16-sided structure.

Just off the other side of Yeniçeriler Caddesi is Gedik Paşa Hamamı, thought to be the oldest working Turkish baths *(see p67)* in the city. It was built around 1475 for Gedik Ahmet Paşa, grand vizier under Mehmet the Conqueror *(see p26)*.

The dome and minaret of the mosque of Atik Ali Paşa, dating from 1496

Atik Ali Paşa Mosque ⑳

Atik Ali Paşa Camii

Yeniçeriler Cad, Beyazıt. **Map** 3 D4 (4 C3). 🚋 Çemberlitaş. 🚌 *61B.* ⬜ *daily.* 📷

Secreted behind walls in the area south of the Grand Bazaar, this is one of the oldest mosques in the city. It was built in 1496 during the reign of Beyazıt II, the successor of Mehmet the Conqueror, by his eunuch grand vizier, Atik Ali Paşa. The mosque stands in a small garden. It is a simple rectangular structure entered through a deep stone porch. In an unusual touch, its mihrab

is contained in a kind of apse. The other buildings which formed part of the mosque complex – its kitchen (*imaret*), *medrese* and Sufi monastery (*tekke*) – have all but disappeared during the widening of the busy Yeniçeriler Caddesi.

Nuruosmaniye Mosque ㉑

Nuruosmaniye Camii

Vezirhanı Cad, Beyazıt. **Map** 3 D4 (4 C3). 🚋 Çemberlitaş. 🚌 *61B.* ⬜ *daily.* 📷

Nuruosmaniye Caddesi, a street lined with carpet and antique shops, leads to the gateway of the mosque from which it gets its name. Mahmut I began the mosque in 1748, and it was finished by his brother, Osman III. It was the first in the city to exhibit the exaggerated traits of the Baroque, as seen in its massive cornices. Its most striking features, however, are the enormous unconcealed arches supporting the dome, each pierced by a mass of windows.

Light floods into the plain square prayer hall, allowing you to see the finely carved wooden calligraphic frieze which runs around the walls above the gallery.

On the other side of the mosque complex is the Nuruosmaniye Gate. This leads into Kalpakçılar Caddesi, the Grand Bazaar's street of jewellery shops (*see p212*).

The tomb of Mahmut Paşa, behind the mosque named after him

Mahmut Paşa Mosque ㉒

Mahmut Paşa Camii

Vezirhanı Cad, Beyazıt. **Map** 3 D3 (4 C3). 🚋 Çemberlitaş. 🚌 *61B.* ⬜ *daily.* 📷

Built in 1462, just nine years after Istanbul's conquest by the Ottomans, this was the first large mosque to be erected within the city walls. Unfortunately, it has been over-restored and much of its original charm lost.

The mosque was funded by Mahmut Paşa, a Byzantine aristocrat who converted to Islam and became grand vizier under Mehmet the Conqueror. In 1474 his disastrous military leadership incurred the sultan's fury, and he was executed. His tomb, behind the mosque, is unique in Istanbul for its Moorish style of decoration, with small tiles in blue, black, turquoise and green set in swirling geometric patterns.

Rows of windows illuminating the prayer hall of Nuruosmaniye Mosque

Grand Bazaar ⑱

Kapalı Çarşı

Nothing can prepare you for the Grand Bazaar. This labyrinth of streets covered by painted vaults is lined with thousands of booth-like shops, whose wares spill out to tempt you and whose shopkeepers are relentless in their quest for a sale. The bazaar was established by Mehmet II shortly after his conquest of the city in 1453 *(see p26)*. It can be entered by several gateways, two of the most useful being Çarşıkapı Gate (from Beyazıt tram stop) and Nuruosmaniye Gate (from Nuruosmaniye Mosque). It is easy to get lost in the bazaar in spite of the signposting. Most of the bazaar's goods were once behind the scenes in secluded hans *(see p96)*.

Muhlis Günbattı is a well known textile and carpet shop *(see p212)*.

The Rooftops of the Grand Bazaar
Cafés, restaurants, toilets, banks, a post office, a police station and a mosque serve those who work and shop inside the bazaar.

Beyazıt Gate

Çadırcılar Caddesi, Book Bazaar *(see p94)*

Havuzlu Lokanta is the best restaurant in the bazaar *(see p200).*

Şark Kahvesi
This traditional Turkish café is a popular choice with local bazaar traders.

Çarşıkapı Gate

Beyazıt tram stop

Marble Fountain
Two copper and marble fountains once provided the bazaar with fresh water.

Örücüler Gate

Spice Bazaa Valide *(p96)*

ASTARCI HANI

İÇ CEBECİ HAN

PERDAHÇILA

YORGANCILAR CAD

YAĞLIKÇILAR SOK

KAVAFLAR

HACI HASAN SOK

ZENNECİLER SOK

BODRUM HANI

FERACECİLER SOK

FESÇİLER CAD

KALPAKÇILAR

Zincirli Han

This is one of the prettiest hans in the bazaar. Here a piece of jewellery can be made to your own choice of design.

VISITORS' CHECKLIST

Çarşıkapı Cad, Beyazıt. **Map** 2 C4 (4 B3). ⓜ Beyazıt (for Çarşıkapı Gate), Çemberlitaş (for Nuruosmaniye Gate). ⏹ 61B. ⏲ 9am–8pm Mon–Sat.

The İç Bedesten is the oldest part of the bazaar. Once a locked warehouse, it also served as a place where jewellers could make and sell their wares.

The Oriental Kiosk was built as a coffee house in the 17th century and is now a jewellery shop.

Rugs on Display

Carpets and kilims (see pp218–19) from all over Turkey and Central Asia are on sale in the bazaar.

ZİNCİRLİ HAN

AYNACILAR SOK

ICILAR ÇARŞISI CAD

EDESTEN

AĞA SOK

MUHAFAZACILAR SOK

SECİLER CAD

TERZİ BAŞI SOK

SANDAL BEDESTENİ SOK

SANDAL BEDESTENİ

Mahmut Paşa Gate

Money trading is conducted on mobile phones.

Gateway to the İç Bedesten

Though the eagle was a symbol of the Byzantine emperors (see p25), this eagle, like the bazaar itself, postdates the Byzantine era.

The Sandal Bedesteni dates from the 16th century and is covered by 20 brick domes supported on piers.

↖ **Nuruosmaniye Mosque** *(see p97),* Çemberlitaş tram stop

Nuruosmaniye Gate

Kalpakçılar Başı Caddesi, the widest of the streets in the bazaar, is lined with the glittering windows of countless jewellery shops.

Souvenirs

Traditionally crafted items, such as this brass coffee pot, are for sale in the bazaar.

0 metres 40

0 yards 40

KEY

— Suggested route

▢ Antiques and carpets

▢ Leather and denim

▢ Gold and silver

▢ Fabrics

▢ Souvenirs

▢ Household goods and workshops

▢ Boundary of the bazaar

BEYOĞLU

For centuries Beyoğlu, a steep hill north of the Golden Horn, was home to the city's foreign residents. First to arrive here were the Genoese. As a reward for their help in the reconquest of the city from the Latins in 1261 *(see p24)*, they were given the Galata area, which is now dominated by the Galata Tower. During the Ottoman period, Jews from Spain, Arabs, Greeks and Armenians settled in communities here. From the 16th century the great European powers established embassies in the area to further their own interests within the lucrative territories of the Ottoman Empire. The district has not changed much in character over the centuries and is still a thriving commercial quarter today.

Monument of Independence, Taksim Square

SIGHTS AT A GLANCE

Historic Buildings and Monuments
Galata Tower ❹
Mevlevi Lodge ❸
Pera Palas Hotel ❶
Tophane Fountain ⓫

Mosques and Churches
Arab Mosque ❻
Azap Kapı Mosque ❼
Church of SS Peter and Paul ❺
Kılıç Ali Paşa Mosque ❿
Nusretiye Mosque ⓬
Yeraltı Mosque ❾

Museums
Istanbul Museum of Modern Art ⓭
Ottoman Bank Museum ❽
Pera Museum ❷

Quarters
Çukurcuma ⓮
Taksim ⓯

KEY

▢ Street-by-Street map See pp102–3	ℹ Tourist information
⛴ Ferry boarding point	Ⓒ Mosque
Ⓜ Metro station	✝ Church
🚊 Tram stop	Underground funicular station
🚌 Bus stop	Nostalgic Tram stop

GETTING AROUND

The Tünel underground funicular climbs the hill between the bottom station (Karaköy) on Tersane Caddesi and the top station on Tünel Square at the beginning of İstiklâl Caddesi. An old-fashioned tram travels the length of İstiklâl Caddesi but it is equally pleasant to walk. Taksim Square is a centre for buses, taxis and dolmuşes.

◁ The Galata Tower and backstreets of Beyoğlu, seen from the mouth of the Golden Horn

Street-by-Street: İstiklâl Caddesi

Crest on top of the Russian Consulate gate

The pedestrianized İstiklal Caddesi is Beyoğlu's main street. Once known as the Grande Rue de Pera, it is lined by late 19th-century apartment blocks and European embassy buildings whose grandiose gates and façades belie their use as mere consulates since Ankara became the Turkish capital in 1923 (see p31). Hidden from view stand the churches which used to serve the foreign communities of Pera (as this area was formerly called), some still buzzing with worshippers, others just quiet echoes of a bygone era. Today, the once seedy backstreets of Beyoğlu, off İstiklâl Caddesi, are taking on a new lease of life, with trendy jazz bars opening and shops selling handcrafted jewellery, furniture and the like. Crowds are also drawn by the area's cinemas and numerous stylish restaurants.

St Mary Draperis is a Franciscan church dating from 1789. This small statue of the Virgin stands above the entrance from the street. The vaulted interior of the church is colourfully decorated. An icon of the Virgin, said to perform miracles, hangs over the altar.

★ **Pera Palas Hotel**
This hotel is an atmospheric period piece. Many famous guests, including Agatha Christie, have stayed here since it opened in 1892. Non-residents can enjoy a drink in the bar ❶

Tünel underground funicular to Karaköy

Tünel Square

★ **Mevlevi Lodge**
A peaceful garden surrounds this small museum of the Mevlevi Sufi sect (see p104). On the last Sunday of every month visitors can see dervishes perform their famous swirling dance ❸

Russian Consulate

Swedish Consulate

KEY

– – – Suggested route

0 metres	75
0 yards	75

Galatasaray Fish Market
(Balık Pazarı) mainly sells fresh fish, but inside you will also discover numerous delicatessens offering everything from meats and cheeses through to delicious sweetmeats and pickles.

LOCATOR MAP
See Street Finder map 7

British Consulate

HAMALBAŞI CAD

Armenian church

T CAD

İSTİKLAL CAD

YENİ ÇARŞI CAD

Galatasaray High School

Çiçek Pasajı was originally a flower market. Its stalls have now been replaced by bars and restaurants, which are particularly lively in the evenings.

Dutch Consulate

Pera Museum
Oriental paintings, Anatolian weights and measures and Kütahya tiles and ceramics are part of the collection ❷

STAR SIGHTS

★ Pera Palas Hotel

★ Mevlevi Lodge

The Church of the Panaghia serves the now much reduced Greek Orthodox population of Beyoğlu. Dedicated to the Virgin Mary, it contains this beautiful classical iconostasis.

The elegant Grand Orient bar in the Pera Palas Hotel

Pera Palas Hotel **❶**
Pera Palas Oteli

Meşrutiyet Cad 98–100, Tepebaşı.
Map 7 D5. *Tel (0212) 251 45 60.*
Tünel. by arrangement.
by appointment only.
www.perapalas.com

There are hotels that have attained a legendary status; one such is the Pera Palas *(see p189)*. Relying on the hazy mystique of yesteryear, it has changed little since it opened in 1892, principally to cater for travellers on the Orient Express *(see p66)*. It still evokes images of uniformed porters and exotic onward destinations such as Baghdad. The Grand Orient bar serves cocktails beneath its original chandeliers, while the patisserie attracts customers with its irresistible cakes and genteel ambience.

Former guests who have contributed to the hotel's reputation include Mata Hari, Greta Garbo, Jackie Onassis, Sarah Bernhardt, Josephine Baker and Atatürk *(see p31)*. A room used by the thriller writer Agatha Christie can be visited on request.

The peaceful courtyard of the Mevlevi Lodge

SUFISM AND THE WHIRLING DERVISHES
Sufism is the mystical branch of Islam *(see pp38–9)*. The name comes from *suf*, the Arabic for wool, for Sufis were originally associated with poverty and self-denial, and often wore rough woollen clothes next to the skin. Sufis aspire to a personal experience of the divine. This takes the form of meditative rituals, involving recitation, dance and music, to bring the practitioner into direct, ecstatic communion with Allah. There are several sects of Sufis, the most famous of which are the Mevlevi, better known as the Whirling Dervishes on account of their ritual spinning dance.

Painting of the Whirling Dervishes (1837) at the Mevlevi Lodge

Pera Museum **❷**
Pera Müzesi

Meşrutiyet Cad 141, Tepebaşı.
Map 7 D4. *Tel (0212) 334 99 00.*
Tünel. From Taksim Square down Tarlabaşı. 10am–7pm Tue–Sat, noon–6pm Sun. 1 Jan, first day of Religious Holidays. (disabled visitors enter free).
www.peramuzesi.org.tr

The Pera Museum was opened in June 2005 by the Suna and İnan Kıraç Foundation, with the aim of providing a cultural centre. The historic building, formerly the Hotel Bristol, has been transformed into a fully equipped modern museum. Notable collections include Ottoman weights and measures, over 400 examples of 18th-century Kütahya tiles and ceramics and the Suna and İnan Kıraç Foundation's exhibition of Orientalist art. This collection brings together works by European artists inspired by the Ottoman world from the 17th century to the early 19th century. It also covers the last two centuries of the Ottoman Empire and provides an insight into upper class lives, customs and dress.

Mevlevi Lodge **❸**
Mevlevi Tekkesi

Galip Dede Cad 15, Beyoğlu. **Map** 7 D5. *Tel (0212) 245 41 41.* Tünel. 9am–4pm Wed–Mon.

Although Sufism was banned by Atatürk in 1924, this monastery has survived as the Divan Edebiyatı Müzesi, a museum of *divan* literature (classical Ottoman poetry). The monastery belonged to the most famous sect of Sufis, who were known as the Whirling Dervishes. The original dervishes were disciples of the mystical poet and great Sufi master "Mevlana" (Our Leader) Jelaleddin Rumi, who died in Konya, in central Anatolia in 1273.

Tucked away off a street named after one of the great poets of the sect, Galip Dede, the museum centres on an 18th-century lodge, within which is a beautiful octagonal wooden dance floor. Here, for the benefit of visitors, the *sema* (ritual dance) is performed by a group of latter-day Sufi devotees on the last Sunday of every month. At 3pm a dozen or so dancers unfurl their great circular skirts to whirl round the room in an extraordinary state of ecstatic meditation, accompanied by haunting music.

Around the dance floor are glass cases containing a small exhibition of artifacts belonging to the sect, including hats, clothing, manuscripts, photographs and musical instruments. Outside, in the calm, terraced garden, stand the ornate tombstones of ordinary sect members and prominent sheikhs (leaders).

Galata Tower ❹
Galata Kulesi

Büyük Hendek Sok, Beyoğlu. **Map** 3 D1. **Tel** (0212) 293 81 80. 🚇 *Tünel*. ⬜ *9am–7pm daily.* 🍴 **Restaurant & Nightclub** ⬜ *8pm–midnight daily.* **www**.galatatower.net

The most recognizable feature on the Golden Horn, the Galata Tower is 60-m

Doorway into the main courtyard of the Church of SS Peter and Paul

(196-ft) high and topped by a conical tower. Its origins date from the 6th century when it was used to monitor shipping. After the conquest of Istanbul in 1453, the Ottomans turned it into a prison and naval depot. In the 18th century, aviation pioneer, Hezarifen Ahmet Çelebi, attached wings to his arms and "flew" from the tower to Üsküdar. The building was subsequently used as a fire watchtower.

The tower has been renovated and on the ninth floor there is now a restaurant and nightclub. The unmissable view from the top encompasses the Istanbul skyline and beyond as far as Princes' Islands *(see p159)*.

The distinctive Galata Tower, as seen from across the Golden Horn

Church of SS Peter and Paul ❺
Sen Piyer Kilisesi

Galata Kulesi Sok 44, Karaköy. **Map** 3 D1. **Tel** (0212) 249 23 85. 🚇 *Tünel*. ⬜ *7am–5pm Mon–Sat & 10.30am–noon Sun.*

When their original church was requisitioned as a mosque (to become the nearby Arab Mosque) in the early 16th century, the Dominican brothers of Galata moved to this site, just below the Galata Tower. The present building, dating from 1841, was built by the Fossati brothers, architects of Italian-Swiss origin who also worked on the restoration of Haghia Sophia *(see pp72–5)*. The church's rear wall is built into a section of Galata's old Genoese ramparts.

According to Ottoman regulations, the main façade of the building could not be directly on a road, so the church is reached through a courtyard, the entrance to which is via a tiny door on the street. Ring the bell to gain admittance.

The church is built in the style of a basilica, with four side altars. The cupola over the choir is sky blue, studded with gold stars. Mass is said here in Italian every morning.

Arab Mosque ❻
Arap Camii

Kalyon Sok 1, Galata. **Map** 3 D1. 🚇 *Tünel*. ⬜ *prayer times only.*

The Arabs after whom this mosque was named were Moorish refugees from Spain. Many settled in Galata after their expulsion from Andalusia following the fall of Granada in 1492. The church of SS Paul and Dominic, built in the first half of the 14th century by Dominican monks, was given to the settlers for use as a mosque. It is an unusual building for Istanbul: a vast, strikingly rectangular Gothic church with a tall square belfry which now acts as a minaret. The building has been restored several times, but of all the converted churches in the city it makes the least convincing mosque.

Azap Kapı Mosque, built by the great architect Sinan

Azap Kapı Mosque 7
Azap Kapı Camii

Tersane Cad, Azapkapı. **Map** 2 C1. Tünel. 46H, 61B. prayer times only.

Delightful though they are, this little mosque complex and fountain are somewhat overshadowed by the stream of traffic thundering over the adjacent Atatürk Bridge. The trees surrounding the mosque, however, help to screen it from the noise. It was built in 1577–8 by Sinan (see p91) for Grand Vizier Sokollu Mehmet Paşa and is considered to be one of Sinan's more attractive mosques. Unusually, the entrance is up a flight of internal steps.

Ottoman Bank Museum 8
Osmanlı Bankası Müzesi

Voyvoda Cad 35–37, Karaköy. **Map** 3 D1. **Tel** (0212) 334 22 70. Tünel. 25E, 56. 10am–6pm daily. **www**.obmuseum.com

The Ottoman Bank Museum has the most interesting collection of state archives in Turkey. Exhibits include Ottoman banknotes, promissory notes from officials at the imperial palace and photos of the Empire's ornately crafted branches.

Outstanding are the 6,000 photographs of the bank's employees – a unique social registry.

Yeraltı Mosque 9
Yeraltı Camii

Karantina Sok, Karaköy. **Map** 3 E1. Tünel. daily.

This mosque, literally "the underground mosque", contains the shrines of two Muslim saints, Abu Sufyan and Amiri Wahibi, who died during the first Arab siege of the city in the 7th century (see p21). It was the discovery of their bodies in the cellar of an ancient Byzantine fortification in 1640 that led to the creation of first a shrine on the site and later, in 1757, a mosque.

The tombs of the saints are behind grilles at the end of a low, dark prayer hall, the roof of which is supported by a forest of pillars.

Kılıç Ali Paşa Mosque 10
Kılıç Ali Paşa Camii

Necatibey Cad, Tophane. **Map** 7 E5. 25E, 56. Tophane. daily.

This mosque was built in 1580 by Sinan, who was by then in his 90s. The church of Haghia Sophia (see pp72–5) provided the architect with his inspiration. İznik tiles adorn the mihrab and there is a delightful deep porch before the main door. Above the entrance portal is an inscription giving the date when the mosque was completed.

Kılıç Ali Paşa, who commissioned the mosque, had a colorful life. Born in Italy, he was captured by Muslim pirates

Koranic inscription in İznik tiles at the Kılıç Ali Paşa Mosque

and later converted to Islam in the service of Süleyman the Magnificent (1520–66). He served as a naval commander under three sultans and after retiring asked Murat III (see p27) where to build his mosque. The sultan is said to have replied "in the admiral's domain, the sea". Taking him at his word, Kılıç Ali Paşa reclaimed part of the Bosphorus for his complex.

Tophane Fountain 11
Tophane Çeşmesi

Tophane İskele Cad, Tophane. **Map** 7 E5. 25E, 56. Tophane.

Beside Kılıç Ali Paşa Mosque stands a beautiful but abandoned Baroque fountain, built in 1732 by Mahmut I. With its elegant roof and dome, it resembles the fountain of Ahmet III (see p60). Each of the four walls is entirely covered in low-relief floral carving, which would once have been gaily painted.

Detail of a carved panel on Tophane Fountain

The name, meaning "cannon foundry fountain", comes from the brick and stone foundry building on the hill nearby. Established in 1453 by Mehmet the Conqueror (see p26) and rebuilt several times, the foundry no longer produces weapons but is still owned by the military.

Nusretiye Mosque 12
Nusretiye Camii

Necatibey Cad, Tophane. **Map** 7 E5. 25E, 56. daily.

The baroque "Mosque of Victory" was built in the 1820s by Kirkor Balyan (see p128), who went on to found a dynasty of architects. This ornate building seems more like a large palace pavilion

The window-filled dome and arches of Nusretiye Mosque

than a mosque, with its decorative out-buildings and marble terrace.

Commissioned by Mahmut II to commemorate his abolition of the Janissary corps in 1826 *(see p30)*, it faces the Selimiye Barracks *(see p132)*, across the Bosphorus, which housed the New Army that replaced the Janissaries. The Empire-style swags and embellishments celebrate the sultan's victory. The marble panel of calligraphy around the interior of the mosque is particularly fine, as is the pair of *sebils* (kiosks for serving drinks) outside.

Istanbul Museum of Modern Art **⑬**
İstanbul Modern Sanat Müzesi

Meclis-i Mebusan Cad, Liman İşletmeleri Sahası, Antrepo 4, Karaköy. **Map** 7 F5. *Tel (0212) 234 73 00.* 🚇 *Tophane.* 🚌 *56.* ⭕ *10am–6pm Tue–Sun.* 📷 ♿ 🏬 🎁 www.istanbulmodern.org

The Istanbul Modern, a new building perched on the Golden Horn, opened in 2005 as the most upbeat and thoroughly contemporary museum in Turkey. It houses both permanent collections and temporary exhibitions, providing a showcase for many of the eccentric and talented personalities who have shaped modern art in Turkey from the early 20th

century to the present day. Many of the works are from the private collection of the Ecacıbaşı family, who founded the museum. Exhibits include abstract art, landscapes and watercolours as well as a sculpture garden and a stunning display of black and white photography.

Çukurcuma **⑭**

Map 7 E4.
🚇 *Taksim.*

This charming old quarter of Beyoğlu, radiating from a neighbourhood mosque on Çukurcuma Caddesi, has become an important centre

Suzani **textiles (see p212) on sale in Çukurcuma**

for Istanbul's furnishings and antiques trades. The old warehouses and houses in this district have been converted into shops and showrooms, where modern upholstery materials are piled up in carved marble basins and antique cabinets. It is worth browsing here to discover hidden treasures, ranging from valuable paintings and prints and 19th-century Ottoman embroidery to 1950s biscuit boxes.

Taksim **⑮**

Map 7 E3. 🚇 *Taksim.* 🚇 *Taksim.*
Taksim Art Gallery *Tel (0212) 245 20 68.* ⭕ *10am–7pm Mon–Sat.*

Centring on the vast, open Taksim Square (Taksim Meydanı), the Taksim area is the hub of activity in modern Beyoğlu. Taksim means "water distribution centre", and from the early 18th century it was from this site that water from the Belgrade Forest *(see p158)* was distributed throughout the city. The original stone reservoir, built in 1732 by Mahmut I, still stands at the top of İstiklâl Caddesi. In the southwest of the square is the 1928 Monument of Independence, by Italian artist Canonica. It shows Atatürk *(see pp30–31)* and the other founding fathers of the modern Turkish Republic.

Further up, on Cumhuriyet Caddesi, is the modern building of the **Taksim Art Gallery**. As well as temporary exhibitions, the gallery has a permanent display of Istanbul landscapes by some of Turkey's most important 20th-century painters.

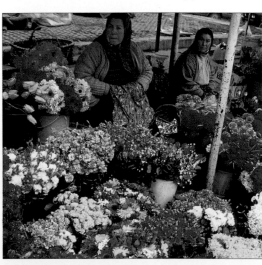

Flower sellers in Taksim Square

GREATER ISTANBUL

A way from the city centre there are many sights which repay the journey to visit them. Greater Istanbul has been divided into five areas shown on the map below; each also has its own map to help you get around. Closest to the centre are the mosques and churches of Fatih, Fener and Balat: most conspicuously the gigantic Fatih Mosque. Across the Golden Horn *(see p89)* from Balat are two sights worth seeing: Aynalı Kavak Palace and a fascinating industrial museum. The Theodosian Walls, stretching from the Golden Horn to the Sea of Marmara, are one of the city's most impressive monuments. Along these walls stand several ancient palaces and churches: particularly interesting is the Church of St Saviour in Chora, with its stunning Byzantine mosaics. Beyond the

Tiles depicting Mecca, Cezri Kasım Paşa Mosque, Eyüp

walls, up the Golden Horn, is Eyüp, a focus of pilgrimage to Muslims, where you can visit a number of fine mausoleums and walk up the hill to the historic café associated with the French writer Pierre Loti. Following the Bosphorus northwards past Beyoğlu *(see pp100–7)* brings you to the Dolmabahçe Palace, one of the top sights of Istanbul. This opulent fantasy created in the 19th century by Sultan Abdül Mecit I requires a lengthy visit. Beyond it is peaceful Yıldız Park containing yet more beautiful palaces and pavilions. Not all visitors to Istanbul make it to the Asian side, but if you have half a day to spare it is only a short ferry trip from Eminönü *(see pp 242–3)*. Its attractions include some splendid mosques, a handsome railway station and a small museum dedicated to Florence Nightingale.

KEY

☐ Central Istanbul	━ Motorway
☐ Greater Istanbul	━ Main road
⛴ Ferry boarding point	═ Other road
	━ City Walls

0 kilometres 1

0 miles 1

◁ **Fountain in the grounds of the sumptuous Dolmabahçe Palace**

Fatih, Fener and Balat

A visit to these neighbourhoods is a reminder that for centuries after the Muslim conquest *(see p26)*, Jews and Christians made up around 40 per cent of Istanbul's population. Balat was home to Greek-speaking Jews from the Byzantine era onwards; Sephardic Jews from Spain joined them in the 15th century. Fener became a Greek enclave in the early 16th century and many wealthy residents rose to positions of prominence in the Ottoman Empire. Hilltop Fatih is linked to the city's radical Islamic tradition and you will see far more devout Muslims here than anywhere else in Istanbul. All three areas are residential, their maze of streets the preserve of washing lines and children playing.

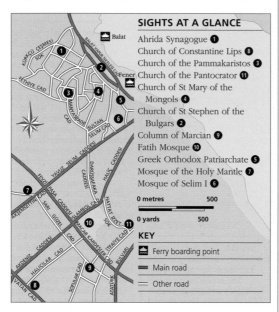

SIGHTS AT A GLANCE

Ahrida Synagogue ❶
Church of Constantine Lips ❽
Church of the Pammakaristos ❸
Church of the Pantocrator ⓫
Church of St Mary of the Mongols ❹
Church of St Stephen of the Bulgars ❷
Column of Marcian ❾
Fatih Mosque ❿
Greek Orthodox Patriarchate ❺
Mosque of the Holy Mantle ❼
Mosque of Selim I ❻

| 0 metres | 500 |
| 0 yards | 500 |

KEY

⛴ Ferry boarding point

━ Main road

═ Other road

Ahrida Synagogue ❶
Ahrida Sinagogu

Gevgili Sok, Balat. **Map** 1 C1. 🚌 55T, 99A. ⬤ *by appointment.* 📷

The name of Istanbul's oldest and most beautiful synagogue is a corruption of Ohrid, a town in Macedonia from which its early congregation came. It was founded before the Muslim conquest of the city in 1453 and, with a capacity for up to 500 worshippers, has been in constant use ever since. However, tourists can only visit by prior arrangement with a guided tour company *(see p228)*. The

synagogue's painted walls and ceilings, dating from the late 17th century, have been restored to their Baroque glory. Pride of place, however, goes to the central Holy Ark, covered in rich tapestries, which contains rare holy scrolls.

During an explosion of fervour that swept the city's Jewish population in the 17th century, the religious leader Shabbetai Zevi (1629–76), a self-proclaimed messiah, started preaching at this synagogue. He was banished from the city and later converted to Islam. However, a significant number of Jews held that Zevi's conversion was a subterfuge and his followers, the Sabbatians, exist to this day.

Church of St Stephen of the Bulgars ❷
Bulgar Kilisesi

Mürsel Paşa Cad 85, Balat. **Map** 1 C1. 🚌 55T, 99A. ⛴ *Balat.* ⬤ *9am–5pm daily.*

Astonishingly, this entire church was cast in iron, even the internal columns and galleries. It was created in Vienna in 1871, shipped all the way to the Golden Horn *(see p89)* and assembled on its shore. The church was needed for the Bulgarian community who had broken away from the authority of the Greek Orthodox Patriarchate just up the hill. Today, it is still used by this community, who keep the marble tombs of the first Bulgarian patriarchs permanently decorated with flowers. The church stands in a pretty little park that is dotted with trees and flowering shrubs and which runs down to the edge of the Golden Horn.

The Church of St Stephen of the Bulgars, wholly made of iron

Church of the Pammakaristos ❸
Fethiye Camii

Fethiye Cad, Draman. **Map** 1 C2. 🚌 90, 90B. ⬤ *prayer times only.* 📷

This Byzantine church is one of the hidden secrets of Istanbul. It is rarely visited despite the important role it has played in the history of the city and its breathtaking series of mosaics. For over

Byzantine façade of the Church of the Pammakaristos

100 years after the Ottoman conquest it housed the Greek Orthodox Patriarchate, but was converted into a mosque in the late 16th century by Murat III *(see p32)*. He named it the Mosque of Victory to commemorate his conquests of Georgia and Azerbaijan.

The charming exterior is obviously Byzantine, with its alternating stone and brick courses and finely carved marble details. The main body of the building is the working mosque, while the extraordinary mosaics are in a side chapel. This now operates as a museum and officially you need to get permission in advance from Haghia Sophia *(see pp72–5)* to see it. However, the caretaker, if around, may simply let you in.

Dating from the 14th century, the great Byzantine renaissance *(see p25)*, the mosaics show holy figures isolated in a sea of gold, a reflection of the heavens. From the centre of the main dome, Christ Pantocrator ("the All-Powerful"), surrounded by the Old Testament prophets, stares solemnly down. In the apse another figure of Christ, seated on a jewel-encrusted throne, gives his benediction. On either side are portraits of the Virgin Mary and John the Baptist beseeching Christ. They are overlooked by the four archangels, while the side apses are filled with other saintly figures.

Church of St Mary of the Mongols ❹
Kanlı Kilise

Tevkii Cafer Mektebi Sok, Fener. **Map** 1 C2. *Tel (0212) 521 71 39.* 55T, 99A. by appointment.

Consecrated in the late 13th century, the Church of St Mary of the Mongols is the only Greek Orthodox church in Istanbul to have remained continuously in the hands of the Greek community since the Byzantine era. Its immunity from conversion into a mosque was

Detail on Church of
St Mary of the Mongols

decreed in an order signed by Mehmet the Conqueror *(see p26)*. A copy of this is kept by the church to this day.

The church gets its name from the woman who founded it, Maria Palaeologina, an illegitimate Byzantine princess who was married off to a Mongol khan, Abagu, and lived piously with him in Persia for 15 years. On her husband's assassination, she returned to Constantinople, built this church and lived out her days in it as a nun.

A beautiful Byzantine mosaic which depicts Theotokos Pammakaristos ("the All-Joyous Mother of God") is the church's greatest treasure.

Greek Orthodox Patriarchate ❺
Ortodoks Patrikhanesi

Sadrazam Ali Paşa Cad 35, Fener. *Tel (0212) 525 54 16.* 55T, 99A. 9am–5pm daily.

This walled complex has been the seat of the patriarch of the Greek Orthodox Church since the early 17th century. Though nominally head of the whole church, the patriarch is now shepherd to a diminishing flock in and around Istanbul.

As you walk up the steps to enter the Patriarchate through a side door you will see that the main door has been welded shut. This was done in memory of Patriarch Gregory V, who was hanged here for treason in 1821 after encouraging the Greeks to overthrow Ottoman rule at the start of the Greek War of Independence (1821–32). Antagonism between the Turkish and Greek communities worsened with the Greek occupation of parts of Turkey in the 1920s *(see p31)*. There were anti-Greek riots in 1955, and in the mid-1960s many Greek residents were expelled. Today the clergy here is protected by a metal detector at the entrance.

The Patriarchate centres on the basilica-style Church of St George, which dates back to 1720. Yet the church contains much older relics and furniture. The patriarch's throne, the high structure to the right of the nave, is thought to be Byzantine, while the pulpit on the left is adorned with fine Middle Eastern wooden inlay and Orthodox icons.

The ornate, gilded interior of the Church of
St George in the Greek Orthodox Patriarchate

İznik tile panel capping a window in the Mosque of Selim I

Mosque of Selim I ❻

Selim I Camii

Yavuz Selim Cad, Fener. **Map** 1 C2.
🚌 55T, 90, 90B, 99A. ⬜ daily.

This much-admired mosque is also known locally as Yavuz Sultan Mosque: Yavuz, "the Grim", being the nickname the infamous Selim acquired (see p26). It is idyllic in a rather off-beat way, which seems at odds with the barbaric reputation of the sultan.

The mosque, built in 1522, sits alone on a hill beside a vast sunken parking lot, once the Byzantine Cistern of Aspar. Sadly it is rarely visited and has an air of neglect, yet the mosque's intimate courtyard gives an insight into concept of paradise in Islam. At the centre of this lovely garden is an octagonal, domed fountain, surrounded by trees filled with chirruping birds.

The windows set into the porticoes in the courtyard are capped by early İznik tiles (see p161). These were made by the cuerda seca technique, in which each colour is separated during the firing process, thus affording the patterns greater definition.

Similar tiles lend decorative effect to the simple prayer hall, with its fine mosque furniture (see pp38–9) and original painted woodwork.

Mosque of the Holy Mantle ❼

Hırka-i Şerif Camii

Keçeciler Cad, Karagümrük. **Map** 1 B3.
🚌 28, 87, 90, 91. ⬜ daily.

Built in the Empire Style in 1851, this mosque was designed to house a cloak (hırka) in the imperial collection which once belonged to and was worn by the Prophet Mohammed. This resides in a sanctuary directly behind the mihrab. The mosque's minarets are in the form of Classical columns, and its balconies styled like Corinthian capitals. The interior of the octagonal prayer hall, meanwhile, has a plethora of decorative marble. Abdül Mecit I, the mosque's patron, was jointly responsible for the design of its calligraphic frieze.

Knocker, Mosque of the Holy Mantle

Church of Constantine Lips ❽

Fenari İsa Camii

Vatan Cad, Fatih. **Map** 1 B4.
🚌 90B. ⬜ daily.

This 10th-century monastic church, dedicated to the Immaculate Mother of God, was founded by Constantine Lips Dungarios, a commander of the Byzantine fleet. Following the Byzantine reconquest

Byzantine brickwork exterior of the Church of Constantine Lips

of the city in 1261 (see p24), Empress Theodora, wife of Michael VIII Palaeologus (see pp24–5), added a second church. She also commissioned a funerary chapel, where she and her sons were buried.

This unusual history has given the structure its present rambling appearance. In an idiosyncratic touch, there are also four tiny chapels perched on the roof around the main dome. Another highlight is the building's eastern exterior wall. This is decorated with a tour de force of brick friezes, of the kind that are a hallmark of Byzantine churches of this period. When the church was converted into a mosque in 1496, it adopted the name Fenari İsa, or the Lamp of Jesus. This was in honour of İsa (Turkish for Jesus), the leader of a Sufi brotherhood (see p104) who worshipped here at that time. Inside the mosque, which is still in use today, there are some well-restored capitals and decorated cornices.

Column of Marcian ❾

Kız Taşı

Kıztaşı Cad, Saraçhane. **Map** 1 C4 (2 A3). 🚌 28, 87, 90, 91.

Standing in a little square, this 5th-century Byzantine column was once surmounted by a statue of the Emperor Marcian (AD 450–57). On its base you can still see a pair of Nikes, Greek winged goddesses of victory, holding an inscribed medallion.

Interestingly, the column's Turkish name translates as the Maiden's Column, suggesting that it was mistaken for the famous Column of Venus. According to legend, this column was said to sway at the passing of an impure maid. It originally stood nearby and is thought to have been employed as one of the largest columns in the Süleymaniye Mosque (see pp90–91).

Chandelier hanging in the light and airy interior of Fatih Mosque

Fatih Mosque ⑩
Fatih Camii

Macar Kardeşler Cad, Fatih. **Map** 1 C3. 🚌 28, 87, 90, 91. ⬜ daily.

A spacious outer courtyard surrounds this vast Baroque mosque, which is the third major structure on this site. The first was the Church of the Holy Apostles (see p23), the burial place of most of the Byzantine emperors. When Mehmet the Conqueror (see p26) came to construct a mosque here, the church's crumbling remains provided a symbolic location. But the first Fatih Mosque collapsed in an earthquake in 1766, and most of what you see today was the work of Mehmet Tahir Ağa, the chief imperial architect under Mustafa III. Many of the buildings he constructed around the prayer hall, including eight Koranic colleges (medreses) and a hospice, still stand.

The only parts of Mehmet the Conqueror's mosque to have survived are the three porticoes of the courtyard, the ablutions fountain, the

main gate into the prayer hall and, inside, the mihrab. Two exquisite forms of 15th-century decoration can be seen over the windows in the porticoes: İznik tiles made using the *cuerda seca* technique and lunettes adorned with calligraphic marble inlay.

Inside the prayer hall, stencilled patterns decorate the domes, while the lower level of the walls is revetted with yet more tiles – although these are inferior to those used in the porticoes.

The tomb of Mehmet the Conqueror stands behind the prayer hall, near that of his consort Gülbahar. His sarcophagus and turban are both appropriately large. It is a place of enormous gravity, always busy with supplicants.

If you pay a visit to the mosque on a Wednesday, you will also see the weekly market (see p214) which turns the streets around it into a circus of commerce. From tables piled high with fruit and vegetables to lorries loaded with unspun wool, this is a real spectacle, even if you don't buy anything.

Church of the Pantocrator ⑪
Zeyrek Camii

İbadethane Sok, Küçükpazar. **Map** 2 B2. 🚌 28, 61B, 87. ⬜ prayer times daily. ♿

Empress Irene, the wife of John II Comnenus (see p19), founded the Church of the Pantocrator ("Christ the Almighty") during the 12th century. This hulk of Byzantine masonry was once the centrepiece of one of the city's most important religious foundations, the Monastery of the Pantocrator. As well as a monastery and church, the complex included a hospice for the elderly, an asylum and a hospital. In this respect it prefigured the social welfare system provided by the great imperial mosque complexes that the Ottomans later built in the city (see p38).

The church, now a mosque, boasts a magnificent figurative marble floor. It is composed of three interlinked chapels. The one with the highest dome was built by Empress Irene. Emperor John II added another as a mortuary chapel when Irene died in 1124, and he later filled the area between with a third apsed chapel. The rest of the Comnenus dynasty and many of the Palaeologus imperial family were interred within these chapels.

Shortly after the Muslim conquest in 1453 (see p26), the building was converted into a mosque. A caretaker may let you in outside prayer times in the afternoons.

Church of the Pantocrator, built by Empress Irene in the 12th century

Along the City Walls

Istanbul's land walls are one of the most impressive remains of the city's Byzantine past. Pierced by monumental gates and strengthened by towers, they encompass the city centre in a great arc, stretching all the way from Yedikule, on the Sea of Marmara, to Ayvansaray, on the Golden Horn *(see p89)*. The suburbs that lie adjacent to the walls, particularly Edirnekapı and Topkapı, are mainly working-class, residential districts, interspersed with areas of wasteland which are unsafe to explore alone. Dotted around these suburbs, however, are important remnants of the city's past, particularly the Byzantine period. The outstanding sight here is the Church of St Saviour in Chora *(see pp118–19)*, with its beautifully preserved mosaics and frescoes.

Silivrikapı, one of the gateways through the Theodosian Walls

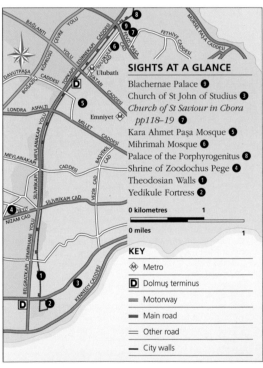

SIGHTS AT A GLANCE

Blachernae Palace **9**
Church of St John of Studius **3**
Church of St Saviour in Chora pp118–19 **7**
Kara Ahmet Paşa Mosque **5**
Mihrimah Mosque **6**
Palace of the Porphyrogenitus **8**
Shrine of Zoodochus Pege **4**
Theodosian Walls **1**
Yedikule Fortress **2**

| 0 kilometres | 1 |
| 0 miles | 1 |

KEY

Ⓜ	Metro
🅳	Dolmuş terminus
═══	Motorway
▬▬	Main road
═══	Other road
—	City walls

The walls were built between AD 412–22, during the reign of Theodosius II (408–50). In 447 an earthquake destroyed 54 of the towers but these were immediately rebuilt, under threat of the advancing Attila the Hun. Subsequently the walls resisted sieges by Arabs, Bulgarians, Russians and Turks. Even the determined armies of the Fourth Crusade *(see p24)* only managed to storm the ramparts along the Golden Horn, while the land walls stood firm.

Mehmet the Conqueror finally breached the walls in May 1453 *(see p26)*. Successive Ottoman sultans then kept the walls in good repair until the end of the 17th century.

Recently, large stretches of the walls, particularly around Belgratkapı (Belgrade Gate) have been rebuilt. Byzantine scholars have criticized the restoration for insensitive use of modern building materials, but the new sections do give you an idea of how the walls used to look. Many, although not all, of the gateways are still in good repair. Mehmet the Conqueror directed his heaviest cannon at the St Romanus and Charsius gates. Under the Ottomans, the former became known as Topkapı, the Gate

Theodosian Walls **1**

Teodos II Surları

From Yedikule to Ayvansaray.
Map 1 A1. 🚃 *Topkapı, Ulubatlı.*

With its 11 fortified gates and 192 towers, this great chain of double walls sealed Constantinople's landward side against invasion for more than a thousand years. Extending for a distance of 6.5 km (4 miles) from the Sea

of Marmara to the Golden Horn, the walls are built in layers of red tile alternating with limestone blocks. Different sections can be reached by metro, tram, train or bus; but to see their whole length you will need to take a taxi or dolmuş *(see p238)* along the main road that runs outside them.

Carving of the Byzantine eagle over Yedikule Gate

The moat prevented an enemy moving artillery within range of the main wall.

Engines to hurl "Greek Fire" *(see p19)* were placed on top of the towers.

Outer wall

The peribolos, a road, was used for troop movements.

Main or inner wall

The towers of the outer wall alternate with those of the inner wall to create a continuous line of defence.

Cross-Section Of the Theodosian Walls
The double walls, towers and moat managed to thwart attackers for almost 1,000 years.

of the Cannon (not to be confused with Topkapı Palace, *see pp54–9*). Unfortunately, a section of walls close to this gate was demolished in the 1950s to make way for a road, Millet Caddesi. The Charsius Gate (now called Edirnekapı), Silivrikapı, Yeni Mevlanakapı and other original gates still give access to the city. The Yedikule Gate (which stands beside the fortress of the same name) has an imperial Byzantine eagle *(see p25)* carved above its main archway.

Yedikule Fortress ❷
Yedikule Müzesi

Yedikule Meydanı Sok, Yedikule.
Tel (0212) 263 53 05. 🚌 *31, 80, 93T.*
🕐 *9am–4:30pm Thu–Tue.*

Yedikule, the "Fortress of the Seven Towers", is built on to the southern section of the Theodosian Walls. Its seven towers are connected by thick walls to make a five-sided fortification. One of the sides, with four towers spaced along it, is formed by a stretch of the land walls themselves.

The fortress as it is today incorporates both Byzantine and Ottoman features. The two stout, square marble towers built into the land walls once flanked the Golden Gate (now blocked up), the triumphal entrance into medieval Byzantium *(see p22)* built by Theodosius II. Imperial pro-

cessions would enter the city through this gate to mark the investiture of a new emperor or in celebration of a successful military campaign. When it was first built, the gate was covered in gold plate and the façade decorated with sculptures, including a statue of a winged Victory, four bronze elephants and an image of Emperor Theodosius himself.

In the 15th century, Mehmet the Conqueror added the three tall, round towers that are not part of the land walls, and the connecting curtain walls, to complete the fortress.

After viewing the castle from the outside, you can enter through a doorway in the northeastern wall. The tower immediately to your left as you enter is known as the *yazılı kule*, "the tower with inscriptions". This was used

as a prison for foreign envoys and others who fell foul of the sultan. These hapless individuals carved their names, dates and other details on the walls and some of these inscriptions are still visible.

Executions were carried out in Yedikule Castle, in the northern of the two towers flanking the Golden Gate. Among those executed here was the 17-year-old Osman II *(see p33)*. In 1622 he was dragged to Yedikule by his own Janissaries *(see p127)*, after four years of misrule, which included, it is alleged, using his own pages as targets for archery practice.

The walkway around the ramparts is accessible via a steep flight of stone steps. It offers good views of the land walls and nearby suburbs, and also of the cemeteries.

Aerial view of Yedikule Fortress with the Sea of Marmara behind

Church of St John of Studius ❸

İmrahor Camii

İmam Aşir Sok, Yedikule. 🚌 *80, 80B, 80T.* 🚆 *Yedikule.*

Istanbul's oldest surviving church, St John of Studius, is now a mere shell consisting only of its outer walls. However, you can still get an idea of the original beauty of what was once part of an important Byzantine institution.

The church was completed in AD 463 by Studius, a Roman patrician who served as consul during the reign of Emperor Marcian (450–57). Originally connected to the most powerful monastery in the Byzantine Empire, in the late 8th century it was a spiritual and intellectual centre under the rule of Abbot Theodore, who was buried in the church's garden. The abbot is venerated today in the Greek Orthodox Church as St Theodore.

Until its removal by the soldiers of the Fourth Crusade *(see p24),* the most sacred relic housed in the church was the head of St John the Baptist. The emperor would visit the church each year for the Beheading of the Baptist feast on 29 August.

In the 15th century the church housed a university and was converted into a mosque. The building was abandoned in 1894 when it was severely damaged by an earthquake.

The church is a perfect basilica, with a single apse at the east end, preceded by a narthex and a courtyard. It has a magnificent entrance portal, with carved Corinthian capitals and a sculpted architrave and cornice. Inside, it is empty, apart from a colonnade of six columns of verdigris.

Ruins of the Church of St John of Studius

The Shrine of Zoodochus Pege, founded on a sacred spring

Shrine of Zoodochus Pege ❹

Balıklı Kilise

Seyit Nizam Cad 3, Silivrikapı. **Tel** *(0212) 582 30 81.* 🚆 *Seyitnizam.* 🚌 *93T.* ⏰ *8am–4pm daily.*

The Fountain of Zoodochus Pege ("Life-Giving Spring") is built over Istanbul's most famous sacred spring, which is believed to have miraculous powers. The fish swimming in it are supposed to have arrived though a miracle which occurred shortly before the fall of Constantinople *(see p26).* They are said to have leapt into the spring from a monk's frying pan on hearing him declare that a Turkish invasion of Constantinople was as likely as fish coming back to life.

The spring was probably the site of an ancient sanctuary of Artemis. Later, with the arrival of Christianity, a church was built around it, which was dedicated to the Virgin Mary. The spring was popular throughout the Byzantine era, especially on Ascension Day, when the emperor would visit it. The church was destroyed and rebuilt many times over the years by various Byzantine emperors, but the present one dates from 1833. The inner courtyard is filled with tombs of bishops and patriarchs of the Greek Orthodox Church.

Kara Ahmet Paşa Mosque ❺

Kara Ahmet Paşa Camii

Undeğirmeni Sok, Fatma Sultan. ⏰ *Prayer times only.* 🚋 *Ulubatlı.* 🚆 *Topkapı.* 🚌 *93T.*

One of the most worthwhile detours along the city walls is the Kara Ahmet Paşa Mosque, also known as Gazi Ahmet Paşa. This lovely building, with its peaceful leafy courtyard and graceful proportions, is one of Sinan's *(see p91)* lesser known achievements. He built it in 1554 for Kara Ahmet Paşa, a grand vizier of Süleyman the Magnificent *(see p26).*

The courtyard is surrounded by the cells of a *medrese* and a *dershane,* or main classroom. Attractive apple-green and yellow İznik tiles *(see p161)* grace the porch, while blue-and-white ones are found on the east wall of the prayer hall. These tiles date from the mid-16th century.

Tilework over *medrese* doorway at Kara Ahmet Paşa Mosque

Of the three galleries, the wooden ceiling under the west one is elaborately painted in red, blue, gold and black.

Outside the city walls, nearby, is tiny Takkeci İbrahim Ağa Mosque, which dates from 1592. Wooden-domed, it has some particularly fine İznik tile panels.

Mihrimah Mosque ❻

Mihrimah Camii

Sulukule Cad, Edirnekapı. **Map** 1 A2 🚌 *28, 87, 91.* ⏰ *daily.*

An imposing monument located just inside the city walls, the Mihrimah Mosque complex was built by Sinan between 1562 and 1565. Mihrimah, the daughter of Süleyman the Magnificent (see p26), was then the recently widowed wife of Rüstem Paşa, a grand vizier who gave his name to the tiled mosque near the Spice Bazaar (see pp88–9).

This mosque rests on a platform, occupying the highest point in the city. Its profile is visible from far away on the Bosphorus and also when approaching Istanbul from Edirne (see pp154–7).

The building is square in shape, with four strong turrets at its corners, and is surmounted by a 37-m (121-ft) high dome. The single minaret is tall and slender, so much so that it has twice been destroyed by earthquakes. On the second occasion, in 1894, the minaret crashed through the roof of the mosque. The 20th-century stencilling on the inside of the prayer hall was added following this accident.

Stained-glass window in the Mihrimah Mosque

The interior is illuminated by numerous windows, some of which have stained glass. The supporting arches of the sultan's loge (see p39) have been skilfully painted to resemble green-and-white marble. The carved marble *minbar* is also impressive.

Church of St Saviour in Chora ❼

See pp118–19.

Palace of the Porphyrogenitus ❽
Tekfur Sarayı

Şişehane Cad, Edirnekapı. **Map** 1 B1.
87, 90, 126.

Only glimpses of the former grandeur of the Palace of the Porphyrogenitus (Sovereign) during its years as an imperial residence are discernible from the sketchy remains. Its one extant hall, now open to the elements, does, however, have an attractive three-storey façade in typically Byzantine style. This is decorated in red brick and white marble, with arched doorways at ground level and two rows of windows looking down on to a courtyard.

The palace dates from the late Byzantine era. Its exact age is debatable since the technique of alternating stone with three courses of brick is typical of the 10th century, whereas its geometrical designs were common in the 14th century. It was most likely constructed as an annexe of nearby Blachernae Palace. These two palaces became the principle residences of the imperial sovereigns during the last two centuries before the fall of Byzantium in 1453 (see p26).

During the reign of Ahmet III (1703–30, see p27) the last remaining İznik potters (see p161) moved to the palace and it became a centre for tile production. However, by this time their skills were in decline and the tiles made here never acquired the excellence of those created at the height of production in İznik. Yet, some strong colours, including a rich red, were used. Cezri Kasım Paşa Mosque (see p121) in Eyüp has some fine examples of these tiles.

Blachernae Palace ❾
Anemas Zindanları

İvaz Ağa Cad, Ayvansaray.
55T, 99A.

As the city walls approach the Golden Horn you come to the scant remains of Blachernae Palace. These consist of a tower in the city wall, known as the Prison of Anemas, a terrace to the east (the present site of the İvaz Efendi Mosque), and another tower to the south of the terrace, known as the Tower of Isaac Angelus.

The origins of the palace date as far back as AD 500, when it was an occasional residence for imperial visitors to the shrine of Blachernae. It was the great Comnenus emperors (see p21) who rebuilt the structure in the 12th century, transforming it into a magnificent palace.

The remains of the marble decoration and wall frescoes in the Anemas tower indicate that this was probably an imperial residence. Although you can walk around the site, you will be unable to gain access into the towers unless the caretaker is there.

Brick and marble façade in the Palace of the Porphyrogenitus

Church of St Saviour in Chora ❼
Kariye Camii

Scene from the Life of the Virgin

Some of the very finest Byzantine mosaics and frescoes can be found in the Church of St Saviour in Chora. Little is known of the early history of the church, although its name "in Chora", which means "in the country", suggests that the church originally stood in a rural setting. The present church dates from the 11th century. Between 1315–21 it was remodelled and the mosaics and frescoes added by Theodore Metochites, a theologian, philosopher and one of the elite Byzantine officials of his day.

View of St Saviour in Chora

THE GENEALOGY OF CHRIST

Theodore Metochites, who restored St Saviour, wrote that his mission was to relate how "the Lord himself became a mortal on our behalf". He takes the *Genealogy of Christ* as his starting point: the mosaics in the two domes of the inner narthex portray 66 of Christ's forebears.

The crown of the southern dome is occupied by a figure of Christ. In the dome's flutes are two rows of his ancestors: Adam to Jacob ranged above the 12 sons of Jacob. In the northern dome, there is a central image of the Virgin and Child with the kings of the House of David in the upper row and lesser ancestors of Christ in the lower row.

Mosaic showing Christ and his ancestors, in the southern dome of the inner narthex

THE LIFE OF THE VIRGIN

All but one of the 20 mosaics in the inner narthex depicting the *Life of the Virgin* are well preserved. This cycle is based mainly on the apocryphal Gospel of St James, written in the 2nd century, which gives an account of the Virgin's life. This was popular in the Middle Ages and was a rich source of material for ecclesiastical artists.

Among the events shown are the first seven steps of the Virgin, the Virgin entrusted to Joseph and the Virgin receiving bread from an angel.

THE INFANCY OF CHRIST

Scenes from the *Infancy of Christ*, based largely on the New Testament, occupy the semicircular panels of the outer narthex. They begin on

GUIDE TO THE MOSAICS AND FRESCOES

Outer narthex

Entrance

Inner narthex

Nave

Entrance to nave   Parecclesion

KEY

▧ The Genealogy of Christ	▢ Christ's Ministry
▧ The Life of the Virgin	▢ Other Mosaics
▧ The Infancy of Christ	▧ The Frescoes

Outer narthex looking east

Outer narthex looking west

...he north wall of the outer narthex with a scene of Joseph being visited by an angel in a dream. Subsequent panels include Mary and Joseph's *Journey to Bethlehem*, their *Enrolment for Taxation*, the *Nativity of Christ* and, finally, Herod ordering the *Massacre of the Innocents*.

The Enrolment for Taxation

CHRIST'S MINISTRY

While many of the mosaics in this series are badly damaged, some beautiful panels remain. The cycle occupies the vaults of the seven bays of the outer narthex and some of the south bay of the inner narthex. The most striking mosaic is the portrayal of Christ's temptation in the wilderness, in the second bay of the outer narthex.

Theodore Metochites presents St Saviour in Chora to Christ

OTHER MOSAICS

There are three panels in the nave of the church, one of which, above the main door from the inner narthex, illustrates the *Dormition of the Virgin*. This mosaic, protected by a marble frame, is the best preserved in the church. The Virgin is depicted laid out on a bier, watched over by the Apostles, with Christ seated behind. Other devotional panels in the two narthexes include one, on the east wall of the south bay of the inner narthex, of the *Deësis*, depicting Christ with the Virgin Mary and unusually, without St John. Another, in the inner narthex over the door into the nave, is of Theodore Metochites himself, shown wearing a large turban, and humbly presenting the restored church as an offering to Christ.

THE FRESCOES

The frescoes in the parecclesion are thought to have been painted just after the mosaics were completed, probably in around 1320. The

most engaging of the frescoes – which reflect the purpose of the parecclesion as a place of burial – is the *Anastasis*, in the semidome above the apse. In it, the central figure of Christ, the vanquisher of death, is shown dragging Adam and Eve out of their tombs. Under Christ's feet are the gates of hell, while Satan lies before him. The fresco in the vault overhead depicts *The Last Judgment*, with the souls of the saved on the right and those of the damned to the left.

Figure of Christ from the *Anastasis* fresco in the parecclesion

Inner narthex looking east

Parecclesion and outer narthex looking south

Inner narthex looking west

Parecclesion and outer narthex looking north

Eyüp

As the burial place of Eyüp Ensari, the standard bearer of the Prophet Mohammed, the village of Eyüp is a place of pilgrimage for Muslims from all over the world. Its sacrosanct status has kept it a peaceful place of contemplation, far removed from the squalid effects of industrialization elsewhere on the Golden Horn *(see p89)*. The wealthy elite established mosques and street fountains in the village but, above all, they chose Eyüp as a place of burial. Their grand mausoleums line the streets surrounding Eyüp Sultan Mosque, while the cypress groves in the hills above the village are filled with the gravestones of ordinary people.

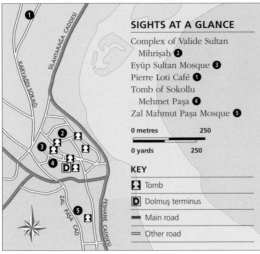

SIGHTS AT A GLANCE

Complex of Valide Sultan
Mihrişah ❷
Eyüp Sultan Mosque ❸
Pierre Loti Café ❶
Tomb of Sokollu
Mehmet Paşa ❹
Zal Mahmut Paşa Mosque ❺

0 metres	250
0 yards	250

KEY

🔳	Tomb
🅳	Dolmuş terminus
▬	Main road
═	Other road

Gateway to the Baroque Complex of Valide Sultan Mihrişah

Complex of Valide Sultan Mihrişah ❷

Mihrişah Valide Sultan Külliyesi

Seyit Reşat Cad. 🚌 39, 55T, 99A.
⏰ 9am–6pm Tue–Sun.

Most of the northern side of the street leading from Eyüp Mosque's northern gate is occupied by the largest Baroque *külliye (see p38)* in Istanbul, although unusually it is not centred on a mosque. Built for Mihrişah, mother of Selim III *(see p33)*, the *külliye* was completed in 1791.

The complex includes the ornate marble tomb of Mihrişah and a soup kitchen, which is still in use today. There is also a beautiful grilled fountain *(sebil)*, from which an attendant once served water and refreshing drinks of sweet sherbet to passers-by.

Pierre Loti Café ❶

Piyer Loti Kahvesi

Gümüşsuyu Karyağdı Sok 5, Eyüp.
Tel *(0212) 581 26 96.* 🚌 39, 55T, 99A. ⏰ 8:30am–midnight daily.

This famous café stands at the top of the hill in Eyüp Cemetery, about 20 minutes' walk or short funicular ride up Karyağdı Sokağı from Eyüp Mosque, from where it commands sweeping views down over the Golden Horn. It is named after the French novelist and Turkophile Pierre Loti, who frequented a café in Eyüp – claimed to be this one – during his stay here in 1876. Loti *(see p42)*, a French naval officer, fell in love with a married Turkish

woman and wrote an autobiographical novel, *Aziyade*, about their affair. The café is prettily decked out with 19th-century furniture and the waiters wear period clothing.

The path up to the café passes by a picturesque array of tombstones, most of which date from the Ottoman era. Just before the café on the right, a few tall, uninscribed tombstones mark the graves of executioners.

Period interior of the Pierre Loti Café

Eyüp Sultan Mosque ❸

Eyüp Sultan Camii

Cami-i Kebir Sok. **Tel** *(0212) 564 73 68.* 🚌 39, 55T, 99A. ⏰ daily.

Mehmet the Conqueror built the original mosque on this site in 1458, five years after his conquest of Istanbul *(see p26)*, in honour of Eyüp Ensari. That building fell into ruins, probably as a result of an earthquake, and the present mosque was completed in 1800, by Selim III *(see p33)*.

The mosque's delightful inner courtyard is a garden in which two huge plane trees grow on a platform. This plat-

'orm was the setting for the
Girding of the Sword of
Osman, part of a sultan's in-
auguration from the days of
Mehmet the Conqueror.

The mosque itself is pre-
dominantly covered in gleaming white marble.

Opposite the mosque is the
tomb of Eyüp Ensari himself,
believed to have been killed
during the first Arab siege of
Constantinople in the 7th
century *(see p21)*. The tomb
dates from the same period
as the mosque and most of its
decoration is in the Ottoman
Baroque style. Both the outer
wall of the tomb facing the
mosque, and most of its
interior, have an impressive
covering of tiles, some of
them from İznik *(see p160)*.

Zal Mahmut Paşa Mosque, as viewed from its tomb garden

Visitors at the tomb of Eyüp Ensari, Mohammed's standard bearer

Tomb of Sokollu Mehmet Paşa ❹
Sokollu Mehmet Paşa
Türbesi

Cami-i Kebir Sok. 🚌 *39, 55T, 99A.*
⏱ *9:30am–4:30pm Tue–Sun.*

Grand vizier *(see p29)*
Sokollu Mehmet Paşa
commissioned his tomb around
1574, five years before he was
assassinated by a madman in
Topkapı Palace *(see pp54–7)*.
Of Balkan royal blood, he
started his career as falconer
royal and steadily climbed the
social order until he became
grand vizier to Süleyman the
Magnificent *(see p26)* in 1565.
He held this position through
the reign of Selim II *(see p27)*
and into that of Murat III.
The architect Sinan *(see p91)*

built this elegantly proportioned octagonal tomb. It is
notable for its stained glass,
some of which is original.
A roofed colonnade connects
the tomb to what was formerly
a Koranic school.

Zal Mahmut Paşa Mosque ❺
Zal Mahmut Paşa Camii

Zal Paşa Cad. 🚌 *39, 55T, 99A.*
⏱ *daily.*

Heading south from the
centre of Eyüp, it is a short
walk to Zal Mahmut Paşa
Mosque. The complex was
built by Sinan for the man
who assassinated Mustafa, the

first-born heir of Süleyman
the Magnificent.

Probably erected some time
in the 1560s, the mosque is
notable for the lovely floral
tiles around its mihrab, and
for its carved marble *minbar*
and *müezzin mahfili (see
p38)*. Proceeding down some
stone steps to the north of the
mosque you will come to a
garden. In it stands the large
tomb of Zal Mahmut Paşa and
his wife, said to have both
died on the same day.

On the same street, Cezri
Kasım Paşa Mosque (1515) is
a small mosque with a pretty
portal and a tiled mihrab. Most
of the tiles were produced at
the Palace of the Porphyrogenitus *(see p117)* in the first
half of the 18th century.

OTTOMAN GRAVESTONES

The Ottoman graveyard was a garden
of the dead, where the living happily
strolled without morbid inhibitions. The
gravestones within it were often lavishly
symbolic: from their decoration you can
tell the sex, occupation, rank and even
the number of children of the deceased.
As the turban was banned in 1829 *(see
p30)*, only the fez appears on men's
gravestones erected after that date.

Women's *graves
have a flower for
each child.*

A turban's *size
reflected a gentle-
man's status.*

This hat *indicates
the grave of a mem-
ber of a Sufi order.*

A fez *was worn by
a paşa, or public
servant (see p28).*

Beyond Taksim

The area to the north of Taksim Square *(see p107)*
became fashionable in the 19th century, when
sultans built palaces along the Bosphorus and in the
wooded hills above it. The extravagant Dolmabahçe
Palace, built by Abdül Mecit I *(see p30)*, started the
trend. High-ranking court officials soon followed, and
the area achieved a glamour that it retains to this day.
Two other sights worth seeing are on the northern
shore of the Golden Horn. Aynalı Kavak Palace is the
last surviving trace of a grand palace built by Ahmet III
(see p27), while the Rahmi Koç Museum, in nearby
Hasköy, is an interesting industrial museum. Hasköy
became a royal park in the 15th century and later
supported fruit orchards, before dockyards brought
industrialization to the area in the 19th century.

Ortaköy's fashionable waterfront
square and ferry landing

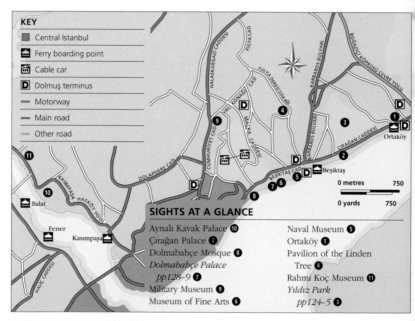

KEY

■	Central Istanbul
⛴	Ferry boarding point
🚠	Cable car
Ⓓ	Dolmuş terminus
—	Motorway
—	Main road
—	Other road

SIGHTS AT A GLANCE

Aynalı Kavak Palace ⑩
Çırağan Palace ②
Dolmabahçe Mosque ⑧
*Dolmabahçe Palace
pp128–9* ⑦
Military Museum ⑨
Museum of Fine Arts ⑥

Naval Museum ⑤
Ortaköy ①
Pavilion of the Linden
Tree ④
Rahmi Koç Museum ⑪
*Yıldız Park
pp124–5* ③

0 metres   750
0 yards   750

Cobbled Ortaköy side street lined
with cafés and shops

Ortaköy ①

Map 9 F3. 🚌 *25E, 40.*

Crouched at the foot of
Bosphorus Bridge *(see
p138)*, the suburb of Ortaköy
has retained a village feel. Life
centres on İskele Meydanı, the
quayside square, which was
until recently busy with fishermen unloading the day's catch.
Nowadays, though, Ortaköy
is better known for its lively
Sunday market *(see p215)*,
which crowds out the square
and surrounding streets, and
its shops selling the wares of
local artisans. It is also the

location for a thriving bar and
café scene, which in the summer especially is the hub of
Istanbul's nightlife *(see p221)*.

Mecidiye Mosque, Ortaköy's
most impressive landmark, is
located on the waterfront. It
was built in 1855 by Nikoğos
Balyan, who was responsible
for Dolmabahçe Palace *(see
pp128–9)*. A simple structure,
it has grace and originality,
with window-filled tympanum
arches and corner turrets.

Ortaköy also has a Greek
Orthodox church, Haghios
Phocas, and a synagogue, Etz
Ahayim. The origins of both
date from the Byzantine era.

Çırağan Palace ❷
Çırağan Sarayı

Çırağan Cad 32, Beşiktaş. **Map** 9 D3.
Tel *(0212) 258 33 77.* 🚌 *25E, 40.*
www.ciragan-palace.com

Sultan Abdül Mecit I started work on Çırağan Palace in 1864, but it was not completed until 1871, during the reign of Abdül Aziz *(see p30)*. It replaced an earlier wooden palace where torch-lit processions were held during the Tulip Period *(see p27)*.

The palace was designed by Nikogos Balyan. At the sultan's request he added Arabic touches from sketches of Moorish buildings such as the Alhambra at Granada in Spain. Externally this is evidenced in the honeycomb capitals over its windows. The sultan entered Çırağan Palace directly from the Bosphorus, through the ornate ceremonial gates along its shoreline.

Çırağan Palace had a sad, short history as an imperial residence. Abdül Aziz died here in 1876, supposedly committing suicide – although his friends believed he had been murdered. His successor, Murat V *(see p33)*, was imprisoned in the palace for a year after a brief reign of only three months. He died in the Malta Pavilion *(see p125)* 27 years later, still a prisoner. The palace was eventually destroyed by fire in 1910. It remained a

Baroque-style staircase at the Pavilion of the Linden Tree

burnt out shell for many years, before being restored in 1990 as the Çırağan Palace Kempinski *(see p190)*.

Yıldız Park ❸

See pp124–5.

Pavilion of the Linden Tree ❹
Ihlamur Kasrı

Ihlamur Teşvikiye Yolu, Beşiktaş.
Map 8 B2. **Tel** *(0212) 259 50 86.*
🚌 *26 (from Eminönü).* ◯ *9:30am–4pm Tue–Wed & Fri–Sun.* 🖼 ✔

This one-time residence of sultans, dating from the early 19th century, stands in beautiful, leafy gardens which are planted with magnolias and camellias, and decorated with ornamental fountains. Today, the gardens are a somewhat incongruous reminder of the city's Ottoman past, being situated in the midst of the modern suburbs of Teşvikiye and Ihlamur.

As the pavilion's name suggests, the area was once a grove of lime (linden) trees, and the gardens are all that remain of what was previously a vast wooded park. This park was a favourite retreat and hunting ground of the Ottoman

Çırağan Palace, notable for the Moorish-style embellishments above its windows

sultans. In the early 19th century, Abdül Mecit I *(see p30)* often came here and stayed in the original pavilion on this site. That building was so unassuming that the French poet Alphonse de Lamartine (1790–1869) expressed great surprise that a sultan should have entertained him in a humble cottage, with a gardener working in plain view through the windows.

In 1857 Abdül Mecit chose Nikogos Balyan, who had by then finished Dolmabahçe Palace with his father, to design another residence here. Two separate pavilions were built, the grander of which is the Ceremonial Pavilion, or Mabeyn Köşkü, used by the sultan and his guests. The Entourage Pavilion, or Maiyet Köşkü, a short distance away, was reserved for the sultan's retinue, including the women of the harem. Both buildings are open to visitors – the Entourage Pavilion is currently a café and bookshop.

The pavilions are constructed mainly of sandstone and marble. Their façades are in the Baroque style, with double stairways, many decorative embellishments and hardly a single straight line to be seen. The ornate interiors of the buildings reflect 19th-century Ottoman taste, incorporating a mixture of European styles. With their mirrors, lavish furnishings and gilded details, they are similar to but less ostentatious than those of Dolmabahçe Palace.

Yıldız Park **❸**
Yıldız Parkı

Yıldiz Park was originally laid out as the garden of the first Çırağan Palace *(see p123)*. It later formed the grounds of Yıldız Palace, an assortment of buildings from different eras now enclosed behind a wall and entered separately from Ihlamur-Yıldız Caddesi. Further pavilions dot Yıldız Park, which, with its many ancient trees

Fountain, Yıldız Palace Theatre

and exotic shrubs, is a favourite spot for family picnics. The whole park is situated on a steep hill and, as it is a fairly long climb, you may prefer to take a taxi up to the Şale Pavilion and walk back down past the other sights.

Bridge over the lake in the grounds of Yıldız Palace

Yıldız Palace

The palace is a collection of pavilions and villas built in the 19th and 20th centuries. Many of them are the work of the eccentric Sultan Abdül Hamit II (1876–1909, *see p33*), who made it his principal residence as he feared a sea-borne attack on Dolmabahçe Palace *(see pp128–9)*.

The main building in the entrance courtyard is the **State Apartments** (Büyük Mabeyn), dating from the reign of Sultan Selim III (1789–1807, *see p33*), but not presently open to the public. Around the corner, the **City Museum** (Şehir Müzesi) has a display of Yıldız porcelain. The Italianate building opposite it is the former armoury, or Silahhane. Next door to the City Museum is the **Yıldız Palace Museum**, housed in what was once the Marangozhane, Abdül Hamit's carpentry workshop. This has a changing collection of art and objects from the palace.

A monumental arch leads from the first courtyard to the harem section of the palace.

The Italianate Silahhane, the former armoury of Yıldız Palace

On the left beside the arch is a pretty greenhouse, the Limonluk Serası (Lemon House).

Further on, **Yıldız Palace Theatre** is now a museum. It was completed in 1889 by Abdül Hamit, who encouraged all forms of Western art. The decor of the theatre's restored interior is mainly blue and gold. The stars on the domed ceiling are a reference to the name of the palace: *yıldız* means "star" in Turkish.

Abdül Hamit sat alone in a box over the entrance. Since no one was allowed to sit with his back to the sultan, the stalls were not used. Backstage, the former dressing rooms are given over to displays on the theatre, including costumes and playbills.

The lake in the palace grounds is shaped like Abdül Hamit's *tuğra (see p95)*. A menagerie was kept on the islands in the lake where 30 keepers tended tigers, lions, giraffes and zebras.

Salon in the lavish Şale Pavilion

Şale Pavilion

The single most impressive building in the park, the Şale Pavilion (Şale Köşkü) was among those erected by Abdül Hamit II. Although its façade appears as a whole, it was in fact built in three stages.

The first, left-hand section of the buildling was designed to resemble a Swiss chalet. It probably dates from the 1870s. Winston Churchill, Charles de Gaulle and Nicolae Ceauşescu have all stayed in its rooms.

The second section was added in 1889, to accommodate Kaiser Wilhelm II on the first ever state visit of a foreign monarch to the Ottoman capital. The 14-room suite includes a dining room known as the Mother-of-Pearl Salon (Sedefli Salon) after the delicate inlay that covers almost all of its surfaces.

The third section was also built for a visit by Kaiser Wilhelm II, this time in 1898. Its reception chamber is the grandest room in the whole pavilion. The vast silk Hereke carpet *(see p218)* covering its floor was painstakingly hand-knotted by 60 weavers.

Malta and Çadır Pavilions

These two lovely pavilions were built in the reign of Abdül Aziz (1861–76, *see p30*). Both formerly served as prisons but are now open as cafés. Malta Pavilion, also a

restaurant, has a superb view and on Sunday is a haunt for locals wanting to relax and read the newspapers.

Midhat Paşa, reformist and architect of the constitution, was among those imprisoned in Çadır Pavilion, for instigating the murder of Abdül Aziz. Meanwhile, Murat V and his mother were locked away in Malta Pavilion for 27 years after a brief incarceration in Çırağan Palace *(see p123)*.

Façade of Çadır Pavilion, which has now been refurbished as a café

Imperial Porcelain Factory

In 1895 this factory opened to feed the demand of the upper classes for European-style ceramics to decorate their homes. The unusual building was designed to look like a stylized European medieval castle, complete with turrets and portcullis windows.

The original sugar bowls, vases and plates produced here depict idealized scenes of the Bosphorus and other local beauty spots; they can be seen in museums and palaces all over Istanbul. The factory is normally not open to visitors but the mass-produced china of today is on sale in its shop.

Park entrance

PALANGA CADDESI

ial Porcelain
Factory

ÇIRAĞAN CADDESI

0 metres	250
0 yards	250

KEY

▢ Buildings of palace

— Park wall/Palace wall

🅿 Parking

Naval Museum ❺
Deniz Müzesi

Hayrettin Paşa İskelesi Sok, Beşiktaş.
Map 8 B4. *Tel (0212) 327 43 45.* 🚌
25E, 28, 40, 56. ◯ *9am–12:30pm,
1:30–5:30pm Wed–Sun.* 🖼️ 🎫

This museum, located next to
the ferry landing in Beşiktaş,
is undergoing major
renovations and will be
closed until 2008. One
building, the Caïques Gallery,
is devoted to huge imperial
rowing boats, or caïques
(some of them manned by
replica oarsmen), dating from
the 17th century. The largest
of these, at 40 m (130 ft), was
used by Mehmet IV and powered by 144 oars-
men. The
rowing boats
used by
Atatürk *(see
p30)* look
tiny in
comparison:
it is remarkable
to think that he
entertained
heads of state in
them. The
exhibits in the
neighbouring main museum
include oil paintings of
various military scenes, ship
figureheads, naval uniforms
and objects from Atatürk's
yacht, the *Savarona*.

**Rowing boat
used by
Atatürk**

Museum of Fine Arts ❻
Resim ve Heykel Müzesi

Hayrettin Paşa İskelesi Sok, Beşiktaş.
Map 8 B4. *Tel (0212) 261 42 98.*
🚌 *25E, 28, 40, 56.* ◯ *10am–
4:30pm Wed–Sat.*

Formerly the Crown Prince
Pavilion, this building, adjacent to Dolmabahçe Palace
(see pp128–9), houses a fine
collection of 19th- and 20th-
century paintings and sculpture. In the 19th century, the
westernization of the Ottoman
Empire *(see pp30–31)* led
artists such as Osman Hamdi
Bey (1842–1910, *see p62)* to
experiment with Western-
style painting. While their
styles rely heavily on European art forms, the subject
matter of their work gives a

**Woman with Mimosas by Osman
Hamdi Bey, Museum of Fine Arts**

glimpse into the oriental
history of the city. Look out
for *Woman with Mimosas,
Portrait of a Young Girl* and
Man with a Yellow Robe, all
by Osman Hamdi Bey, *Sultan
Ahmet Mosque* by Ahmet Ziya
Akbulut (1869–1938) and
Âşık, a statue of a poet by
İsa Behzat (1867–1944).

Dolmabahçe Palace ❼

See pp128–9.

Dolmabahçe Mosque ❽
Dolmabahçe Camii

Meclis-i Mebusan Cad, Kabataş.
Map 8 A5. 🚊 Kabataş. 🚌 *25E, 40.*
◯ *daily*

Completed at the same time
as Dolmabahçe Palace in
1853, the mosque standing
beside it was also built by the
wealthy Balyan family. Its

slim minarets were constructec
in the form of Corinthian
columns, while great arching
windows lighten the interior.
Inside, the decoration includes
fake marbling and trompe
l'oeil, two fashionable effects
in the mid-19th century.

Military Museum ❾
Askeri Müzesi

Vali Konağı Cad, Harbiye. **Map** 7 F1.
Tel (0212) 233 27 20. 🚌 *46H.* Ⓜ
Osmanbey. ◯ *9am–5pm Wed–Sun.*
Mehter Band performances *3–
4pm Wed–Sun.* 🖼️ 🎫

One of Istanbul's most
impressive museums, the
Military Museum traces the
history of the country's con-
flicts from the conquest of
Constantinople in 1453 *(see
p26)* through to modern warfare. The building used to be
the military academy where
Atatürk studied from 1899–
1905. His classroom has been
preserved as it was then.
 The museum is also the
main location for performances
by the Mehter Band, which
was first formed in the 14th-
century during the reign of
Osman I *(see p25)*. From then
until the 19th century, the
band's members were Janissaries, who would accompany
the sultan into battle and perform songs about Ottoman
hero-ancestors and battle
victories. The band had much
influence in Europe, and is
thought to have inspired both
Mozart and Beethoven.
 Some of the most striking
weapons on display on the
ground floor are the curved

Dolmabahçe Mosque, a landmark on the Bosphorus shoreline

Cembiyes – Ottoman curved daggers – on display in the Military Museum

daggers *(cembiyes)* carried at the waist by foot soldiers in the 15th century. These are ornamented with plant, flower and geometric motifs in relief and silver filigree. Other exhibits include 17th-century copper head armour for horses and Ottoman shields made from cane and willow covered in silk thread.

A moving portrayal of trench warfare, commissioned in 1995, is included in the section concerned with the ANZAC landings of 1915 at Chunuk Bair on the Gallipoli peninsula *(see p30)*.

Upstairs, the most spectacular of all the exhibits are the tents used by sultans on their campaigns. They are made of silk and wool with embroidered decoration.

Not far from the museum, from the station on Taşkışla Caddesi, you can take the cable car across Maçka Park to Abdi İpekçi Caddesi in Teşvikiye. Also, some of the city's best designer clothes, jewellery, furniture and art shops are to be found in this area *(see pp212–13)*.

Aynalı Kavak Palace ⑩
Aynalı Kavak Kasrı

Kasımpaşa Cad, Hasköy. **Map** 6 A3. *Tel (0212) 250 40 94.* 🚌 47, 54. ⬜ 9am–5pm Tue, Wed, Fri–Sun. 📷

Aynali Kavak palace is the last vestige of a large Ottoman palace complex on the once lovely Golden Horn *(see p89)*. Originally it stood in extensive gardens covering an area of 7,000 sq m (75,300 sq ft). Inscriptions dated 1791 can be found all over the palace, but it is thought to have been built earlier by Ahmet III during the Tulip Period *(see p27)*, because of traces around the building of an older style of architecture.

The palace is built on a hill and as a result has two storeys on the southwest side and a single storey to the northeast. It retains some beautiful Ottoman features. These include the upper windows on the southwest façade, which are decorated with stained glass set in curvilinear stucco tracery. Particularly

striking is the composition room, which Sultan Selim III (1789–1807) is thought to have used for writing music.

The audience chamber is adorned with an inscription in gold on blue which describes the activities of Selim III while he stayed at the palace.

Restoration of Aynalı Kavak in 1984 has enabled it to be opened to the public. There is also a superb exhibition of archaic Turkish musical instruments permanently on show, in honour of Selim III, who contributed a great deal to Turkish classical music.

Audience chamber of Aynalı Kavak Palace on the Golden Horn

Rahmi Koç Museum ⑪
Rahmi Koç Müzesi

Hasköy Cad, Hasköy. *Tel (0212) 256 71 53.* 🚌 47. ⬜ 10am–5pm Tue–Sun. 📷

Situated in Hasköy, this old 19th-century factory, which once produced anchors and chains, now houses an eclectic collection named after its industrialist founder, Rahmi Koç. The building itself, with its four small domes, vaulted passageways and original wooden fittings is one of the museum's highlights.

The theme of the industrial age loosely connects exhibitions on aviation, transport, steam engines and scientific instruments. Exhibits range from mechanical toys and scale models of machinery to an entire recreated ship's bridge. Two fine restaurants are located on the premises.

JANISSARIES

The Janissary (New Army) corps was formed in the 14th century to serve as the sultan's elite fighting force. Its ranks were filled by *devşirme*, the levy of Christian youths brought to Istanbul to serve the sultan. A highly professional and strong army, it was instrumental in the early expansion of the Ottoman Empire and, as well as a fighting force, it acted as the sultan's personal guard. However, discipline eventually began to weaken, and by 1800 the Janissaries had become a destabilizing element in society. They mutinied and overthrew many sultans until their final demise under Mahmut II in 1826 *(see p30)*.

Janissaries depicted in a 16th-century miniature

Dolmabahçe Palace ❼

Dolmabahçe Sarayı

Sultan Abdül Mecıt *(see p33)* built Dolmabahçe Palace in 1856. As its designers he employed Karabet Balyan and his son Nikogos, members of the great family of Armenian architects who lined the Bosphorus *(see pp137–49)* with many of their creations in the 19th century. The extravagant opulence of the Dolmabahçe belies the fact that it was built when the Ottoman Empire was in decline.

Sèvres vase at the foot of the Crystal Staircase

The sultan financed his great palace with loans from foreign banks. The palace can only be visited on a guided tour, of which two are on offer. The best tour takes you through the Selamlık (or Mabeyn-i Hümayun), the part of the palace that was reserved for men and which contains the state rooms and the enormous Ceremonial Hall. The other tour goes through the Harem, the living quarters of the sultan and his entourage. If you only want to go on one tour, visit the Selamlık.

★ Crystal Staircase
The apparent fragility of this glass staircase stunned observers when it was built. In the shape of a double horseshoe, it is made from Baccarat crystal and brass, and has a polished mahogany rail.

The Süfera Salon, where ambassadors waited for an audience with the sultan, is one of the most luxurious rooms in the palace.

Entrance

Imperial Gate
Once used only by the sultan and his ministers, this gate is now the main entrance to the palace. The Mehter, or Janissary, Band (see pp126–7) performs in front of the gate every Tuesday afternoon throughout the summer.

Swan Fountain
This fountain stands in the Imperial Garden. The original 16th-century garden here was created from recovered land, hence the palace's name, Dolmabahçe, meaning "Filled-in Garden".

Selamlık

The Red Room was used by the sultan to receive ambassadors.

★ Ceremonial Hall
This magnificent domed hall was designed to hold 2,500 people. Its chandelier, reputedly the heaviest in the world, was bought in England.

VISITORS' CHECKLIST

Dolmabahçe Cad, Beşiktaş.
Map 8 B4. *Tel* (0212) 236 90 00.
25E, 40. 9am–4pm
(last adm) Tue, Wed & Fri–Sun
(Oct–Feb: last adm 3pm).
the first day of religious festivals.

Blue Salon
On religious feast days the sultan's mother would receive his wives and favourites in the Harem's principal room.

The Zülvecheyn, or Panorama Room

Harem

The Rose-coloured salon was the assembly room of the Harem.

Reception room of the sultan's mother

Atatürk's Bedroom
Atatürk (see pp30–31) died in this room at 9:05am on 10 November 1938. All the clocks in the palace, such as this one near the crystal staircase, are stopped at this time.

Main shore gate

Sultan Abdül Aziz's bedroom had to accommodate a huge bed built especially for the 150-kg (23-stone) amateur wrestler.

★ Main Bathroom
The walls of this bathroom are revetted in finest Egyptian alabaster, while the taps are solid silver. The brass-framed bathroom windows afford stunning views across the Bosphorus.

STAR FEATURES

★ Crystal Staircase

★ Ceremonial Hall

★ Main Bathroom

The Asian Side

The Asian side of Istanbul comprises the two major suburbs of Üsküdar and Kadıköy, which date from the 7th century BC *(see p19)*. Üsküdar (once known as Scutari after the 12th-century Scutarion Palace which was located opposite Leander's Tower) was the starting point of Byzantine trade routes through Asia. It retained its importance in the Ottoman period and today is renowned for its many classical mosques.

A number of residential districts radiate from Üsküdar and Kadıköy. Moda is a pleasant leafy suburb famous for its ice cream, while there is a lighthouse and an attractive park at Fenerbahçe. From there it is a short walk up to Bağdat Caddesi, one of Istanbul's best-known shopping streets *(see p204)*.

Leander's Tower, on its own small island

SIGHTS AT A GLANCE

Atik Valide Mosque **5**
Big Pine Hill **10**
Haydarpaşa Station **9**
İskele Mosque **3**
Karaca Ahmet Cemetery **7**
Leander's Tower **1**
Selimiye Barracks **8**
Şemsi Paşa Mosque **2**
Tiled Mosque **6**
Yeni Valide Mosque **4**

0 kilometres   1

0 miles   1

KEY

📧 Ferry boarding point

🚉 Railway station

D Dolmuş terminus

═══ Motorway

▬▬ Main road

═══ Other road

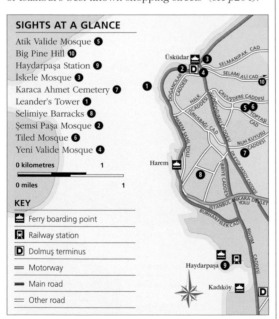

Leander's Tower **1**

Kız Kulesi

Üsküdar. **Map** 10 A3. **Tel** (0216) 342 47 47. 📧 *Üsküdar.*
www.kizkulesi.com.tr

Located offshore from Üsküdar, the tiny, white Leander's Tower is a well-known Bosphorus landmark. The islet on which this 18th-century tower stands was the site of a 12th-century Byzantine fortress built by Manuel I Comnenus. The tower has served as a quarantine centre during a cholera outbreak, a

lighthouse, a customs control point and a maritime toll gate. It is now a restaurant and nightclub *(see p206)*.

The tower is known in Turkish as the "Maiden's Tower" after a legendary princess, said to have been confined here after a prophet foretold that she would die from a snakebite. The snake duly appeared from a basket of figs and struck the fatal blow. The English name of the tower derives from the Greek myth of Leander, who swam the Hellespont (the modern-day Dardanelles, *see p170*) to see his lover Hero.

Şemsi Paşa Mosque **2**

Şemsi Paşa Camii

Sahil Yolu, Üsküdar. **Map** 10 A2.
📧 *Üsküdar.* 🔘 *daily.*

This is one of the smallest mosques to be commissioned by a grand vizier *(see p29)*. Its miniature dimensions combined with its picturesque waterfront location make it one of the most attractive mosques in the city.

Şemsi Ahmet Paşa succeeded Sokollu Mehmet Paşa *(see p82)* as grand vizier, and may have been involved in his murder. Sinan *(see p91)* built this mosque for him in 1580.

The garden, which overlooks the Bosphorus, is surrounded on two sides by the *medrese (see p38)*, with the mosque on the third side and the sea wall on the fourth. The mosque itself is unusual in that the tomb of Şemsi Ahmet is joined to the main building, divided from the interior by a grille.

Şemsi Paşa Mosque, built by Sinan for Grand Vizier Şemsi Ahmet Paşa

İskele Mosque ❸
İskele Camii

Hakimiyeti Milliye Cad, Üsküdar.
Map 10 B2. 🚇 Üsküdar. 🔲 daily.

One of Üsküdar's most
prominent landmarks, the
İskele Mosque (also known
as Mihrimah Sultan Mosque),
takes its name from the ferry
landing where it stands. A
massive structure on a raised
platform, it was built by Sinan
between 1547 and 1548 for
Mihrimah Sultan, favourite
daughter of Süleyman the
Magnificent and wife of Grand
Vizier Rüstem Paşa *(see p88)*.

Without space to build a
courtyard, Sinan constructed a
large protruding roof which
extends to cover the *şadırvan*
(ablutions fountain) in front
of the mosque. The porch
and interior are rather gloomy
as a result. This raised portico
is an excellent place from
which to look down on the
main square below, in which
stands the Baroque Fountain
of Ahmet III, built in 1726.

Fountain set into the platform
below the İskele Mosque

Yeni Valide Mosque ❹
Yeni Valide Camii

Hakimiyeti Milliye Cad, Üsküdar.
Map 10 B2. 🚇 Üsküdar. 🔲 daily.

Across the main square
from İskele Mosque, the
Yeni Valide Mosque, or New
Mosque of the Sultan's Mother,
was built by Ahmet III between 1708 and 1710 to

The *mektep* (Koranic school) over the gate of Yeni Valide Mosque

honour his mother, Gülnuş
Emetullah. The complex is
entered through a large gateway, with the *mektep* (Koranic
school) built above it. This
leads into a spacious courtyard. The buildings in the
complex date from an important turning point in Ottoman
architecture. The mosque is in
the classical style, yet there are
Baroque embellishments on
the tomb of the Valide Sultan,
the neighbouring *sebil* (kiosk
from which drinks were
served) and the *şadırvan*.

Atik Valide Mosque ❺
Atik Valide Camii

Çinili Camii Sok, Üsküdar. **Map** 10
C3. 🚌 12C (from Üsküdar). 🔲
prayer times only.

The Atik Valide Mosque,
set on the hill above
Üsküdar, was one of
the most extensive
mosque complex-
es in Istanbul.
The name trans-
lates as the Old
Mosque of the
Sultan's Mother,
as the mosque was
built for Nur Banu,
the Venetian-born
wife of Selim II
("the Sot") and the
mother of Murat III. She was
the first of the sultans' mothers
to rule the Ottoman Empire
from the harem *(see p27)*.

**Dome in the entrance
to Atik Valide Mosque**

Sinan completed the mosque,
which was his last major
work, in 1583. It has a wide
shallow dome which rests on
five semidomes, with a flat
arch over the entrance portal.

The interior is surrounded
on three sides by galleries, the
undersides of which retain
the rich black, red and gold
stencilling typical of the period.
The *mihrab* apse is almost
completely covered with
panels of fine İznik tiles *(see
p161)*, while the mihrab itself
and the *minbar* are both made
of beautifully carved marble.
Side aisles were added to the
north and south in the 17th
century, while the grilles and
architectural trompe l'oeil
paintings on the royal loge
in the western gallery date
from the 18th century.

Outside, a door in the north
wall of the courtyard leads
down a flight of stairs to the
medrese, where the
dershane (classroom)
projects out over
the narrow street
below, support-
ed by an arch.
Of the other
buildings in the
complex, the *şifa-
hane* (hospital) is
the only one which
has been restored
and is open to the
public. Located just
to the east of the mosque, it
consists of 40 cells around a
courtyard and was in use
well into the 20th century.

Women attending an Islamic class in the Tiled Mosque

Tiled Mosque 6
Çinili Camii

Çinili Camii Sok, Üsküdar. **Map** 10 C3. 🚇 Üsküdar, then 20 mins walk. ⏱ prayer times only.

This pretty little mosque is best known for the fine tiles from which it takes its name. It dates from 1640 and is noticeably smaller than other royal foundations of the 17th century. This is partly because by the middle of the century much of Istanbul's prime land had already been built on, and the size of the plot did not allow for a larger building. There was also a trend away from endowing yet more enormous mosque complexes in the city.

The mosque was founded by Mahpeyker Kösem Sultan. As the wife of Sultan Ahmet I (see p33), and mother of sultans Murat IV and İbrahim the Mad, she wielded great influence. Indeed, she was one of the last of the powerful harem women (see p27).

In the courtyard is a massive, roofed ablutions fountain. The adjacent medrese (see p38), however, is tiny. The façade and interior of the mosque are covered with İznik tiles (see p161) in turquoise, white, grey and a range of blues. There are none of the red and green pigments associated with the heyday of İznik tile production, but the designs are still exquisite. Even the conical cap of the marble minbar is tiled, and the carving on the minbar itself is picked out in green, red and gold paint.

The mosque's Turkish bath is on Çinili Hamam Sokağı. It has been renovated and is used by local residents.

Karaca Ahmet Cemetery 7
Karaca Ahmet Mezarlığı

Nuh Kuyusu Cad, Selimiye. **Map** 10 C4. 🚇 12. ⏱ 9:30am–5:30pm. **Tomb** ⏱ 9:30am–4:30pm daily.

Sprawling over a large area, this cemetery is a pleasant place in which to stroll among old cypress trees and look at ancient tombstones. The earliest dated stone is from 1521, although the cemetery itself, one of the largest in Turkey, is thought to date from 1338.

The carvings on each tombstone tell a story (see p121). A man's tomb is indicated by a fez or a turban. The style of the turban denotes the status of the deceased. Women's stones are adorned with carved flowers, hats and shawls.

Crimean War memorial in the British War Cemetery

Standing on the corner of Gündoğumu Caddesi and Nuh Kuyusu Caddesi is the tomb of Karaca Ahmet himself. This warrior died fighting in the Turkish conquest of the Byzantine towns of Chrysopolis and Chalcedon (Üsküdar and Kadıköy) in the mid-14th century. The tomb and monument to his favourite horse date from the 19th century.

Selimiye Barracks 8
Selimiye Kışlası

Çeşme-i Kebir Cad, Selimiye. **Map** 10 B5. **Tel** (0216) 556 80 00. 🚇 Harem. 🚇 12. ⏱ 9am–5pm Sat, Sun.

The Selimiye Barracks were originally built by Selim III in 1799 to house his New Army, with which he hoped to replace the Janissaries (see p127). He failed in his attempt and was deposed and killed in a Janissary insurrection in 1807–8 (see p30). The barracks burnt down shortly afterwards. The present building, which dominates the skyline of the Asian shore, was started by Mahmut II in 1828, after he had finally disbanded the Janissary corps. Abdül Mecit I added three more wings between 1842 and 1853.

The barracks were used as a military hospital during the Crimean War (1853–6). They became famously associated with Florence Nightingale, who lived and worked in the northeast tower from 1854. The rooms she occupied are now a museum, and are the only part of the barracks open to the public. They contain their original furniture and the lamp from which she gained the epitaph "Lady of the Lamp". Visits must be arranged in advance by faxing 0216 310 79 29.

Visitor praying at the tomb of the warrior Karaca Ahmet

Haydarpaşa Station, terminus for trains arriving from Anatolia

Two other sites near the barracks – the Selimiye Mosque and the British War Cemetery – are both worth seeing. Built in 1804, the mosque is in a peaceful, if somewhat neglected, garden courtyard. The interior is filled with light from tiers of windows set in high arches. It is simply decorated with a classically painted dome and grey marble *minbar*. The royal pavilion in the northwest corner of the compound is flanked by graceful arches.

The British War Cemetery is a short walk south, on Burhan Felek Caddesi. It contains the graves of men who died in the Crimean War, in World War I at Gallipoli (*see p170*) and in World War II in the Middle East. There is no sign outside and opening hours vary, but the caretaker will usually be there to let you in.

Haydarpaşa Station �«9»
Haydarpaşa Garı

Haydarpaşa İstasyon Cad, Haydarpaşa.
Tel (0216) 336 04 75 or 336 20 63.
Haydarpaşa or Kadıköy. ⬜ daily.

The waterfront location and grandeur of Haydarpaşa Station, together with the neighbouring tiled jetty, make it an impressive point of arrival or departure in Istanbul. The first Anatolian railway line, which was built in 1873, ran from here to İznik (*see p160*). The extension of this railway was a major part of Abdül Hamit II's drive to modernize

the Ottoman Empire. Lacking sufficient funds to continue the project, he applied for help to his German ally, Kaiser Wilhelm II. The Deutsche Bank agreed to invest in the construction and operation of the railway. In 1898 German engineers were contracted to build the new railway lines running across Anatolia and beyond into the far reaches of the Ottoman Empire. At the same time a number of stations were built. Haydarpaşa, the grandest of these, was completed in 1908. Trains run from Haydarpaşa into the rest of Asia.

Big Pine Hill 🟤«10»
Büyük Çamlıca

Çamlıca. 🚌 11F, KÇ1; then 30 mins walk. **Park** ⬜ 9am–midnight daily.

On a clear day the view from the top of this hill takes in the Princes' Islands, the Sea of Marmara, the Golden Horn and Beyoğlu, and the Bosphorus as far as the Black Sea. It is even possible to see snow-capped Mount Uludağ near Bursa (*see p169*) to the south. Big Pine Hill, 4 km (2.5 miles) east of Üsküdar, is the highest point in Istanbul, at 261 m (856 ft) above sea level. Even the forest of radio and TV masts further down the slopes of the hill does not obscure the view.

The park at the summit, which was created by the Turkish Touring and Automobile Club (*see p181*) in 1980, is laid out with gardens, marble kiosks and two 18th-century-style cafés.

Neighbouring Küçük Çamlıca (Little Pine Hill), located to the south, is rather less cultivated and consequently attracts fewer tourists to its little tea garden. It is another lovely place for a stroll, again with beautiful views.

FLORENCE NIGHTINGALE

A 19th-century painting of Florence Nightingale in Selimiye Barracks

The British nurse Florence Nightingale (1820–1910) was a tireless campaigner for hospital, military and social reform. During the Crimean War, in which Britain and France fought on the Ottoman side against the Russian Empire, she organized a party of 38 British nurses. They took charge of medical services at the Selimiye Barracks in Scutari (Üsküdar) in 1854. By the time she returned to Britain in 1856, at the end of the war, the mortality rate in the barracks had decreased from 20 to 2 percent, and the fundamental principles of modern nursing had been established. On her return home, Florence Nightingale opened a training school for nurses.

BEYOND
ISTANBUL

THE BOSPHORUS

If the noise and bustle of the city get too much, nothing can beat a trip up the Bosphorus (*see pp144–9*), the straits separating Europe and Asia, which join the Black Sea and the Sea of Marmara. The easiest way to travel is by boat. An alternative is to explore the sights along the shores at your own pace. For much of their length the shores are lined with handsome build-

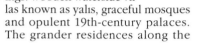

Faik and Bekir Bey Yalı, Yeniköy

ings: wooden waterside villas known as yalıs, graceful mosques and opulent 19th-century palaces. The grander residences along the Bosphorus have waterfront entrances. These date from the days when wooden caïques, boats powered by a strong team of oarsmen, were a popular form of transport along the straits among the city's wealthier inhabitants. Interspersed between the monumental architecture are former fishing villages, where you will find some of Istanbul's finest clubs and restaurants.

The Bosphorus is especially popular in summer, when the cool breezes off the water provide welcome relief from the heat of the city.

SIGHTS AT A GLANCE

Museums and Palaces
Aşiyan Museum ❺
Beylerbeyi Palace ❷
Khedive's Palace ⓫
Küçüksu Palace ❹
Maslak Pavilion ❿
Sadberk Hanım Museum ⓭
Sakıp Sabancı Museum ❾

Towns and Villages
Bebek ❸
Beykoz ⓬
Kanlıca ❼
Rumeli Kavağı ⓮

Historic Buildings
Bosphorus Bridge ❶
Fortress of Europe ❻

Parks
Emirgan Park ❽

KEY

⬛ Central Istanbul

⬜ Greater Istanbul

⛴ Ferry stops on Bosphorus trip

═ Motorway

▬ Main road

0 kilometres   5

0 miles   5

THE BOSPHORUS TRIP

This vital navigational channel is 33 km (20 miles) long and varies between 700 m (2,300 ft) and 3.6 km (2 miles) wide. The trip has been divided into three stages, indicated by the boxes on this map.

◁ **Anadolu Hisarı, the Fortress of Asia, on the Asian shore of the Bosphorus**

The Bosphorus suspension bridge between Ortaköy and Beylerbeyi

Bosphorus Bridge ❶
Boğaziçi Köprüsü

Ortaköy and Beylerbeyi. **Map** 9 F2.
🚌 40, 200, 202 (double deckers
from Taksim).

Spanning the Bosphorus
between the districts of
Ortaköy and Beylerbeyi, this
was the first bridge to be built
across the straits that divide
Istanbul. Known also as
Atatürk Bridge, it was finished
on 29 October 1973, the 50th
anniversary of the inauguration of the Turkish Republic
(see p31). It is the world's
ninth longest suspension
bridge, at a length of 1,074 m
(3,524 ft), and it reaches 64 m
(210 ft) above water level.

Beylerbeyi
Palace ❷
Beylerbeyi Sarayı

Çayırbaşı Cad, Asian side.
Tel (0216) 321 93 20. 🚌 15 (from
Üsküdar). 🚇 from Üsküdar.
🕐 9:30am–5pm Tue, Wed &
Fri–Sun (Oct–Apr until 4pm). 🖼 🎫

Designed in the Baroque
style by Sarkis Balyan,
Beylerbeyi Palace seems fairly
restrained compared to the
excesses of the earlier Dolmabahçe (see pp128–9) or
Küçüksu (see p140) palaces.
It was built for Sultan Abdül
Aziz (see p30) in 1861 as
a summer residence and a
place to entertain visiting heads
of state. Empress Eugénie of
France visited Beylerbeyi on
her way to the opening of the
Suez Canal in 1869 and had

her face slapped by the sultan's
mother for daring to enter the
palace on the arm of Abdül
Aziz. Other regal visitors to
the palace included the Duke
and Duchess of Windsor.
   The palace looks its most
attractive from the
Bosphorus, from
where its two
bathing pavilions
– one for the
harem and the
other for the
selamlık (the
men's quarters) –
can best be seen.
   The most attrac-
tive room is the
reception hall, which has a
pool and fountain. Running
water was popular in Ottoman
houses for its pleasant sound
and cooling effect in the heat.
   Egyptian straw matting is
used on the floor as a form of
insulation. The crystal chandeliers are mostly Bohemian
and the carpets (see pp218–19)

**Detail of the gate of the
Egyptian Consulate, Bebek**

**Ornate landing at the top of the stairs
in Beylerbeyi Palace**

are from Hereke. Despite her
initial reception, Empress
Eugénie of France was so de-
lighted by the elegance of the
palace that she had a copy of
the window in the guest
room made for her bedroom
in Tuileries Palace, in Paris.

Bebek ❸

European side. 🚌 25E, 40.

Bebek is one of the most
fashionable villages along
the Bosphorus. It is famous
for its marzipan (badem
ezmesi, see p213), and for
the cafés which line its waterfront. It was once a favourite
location for summer residences
and palaces of Ottoman aristocrats, and at the end of the
19th century, caïques (see
p126) of merry-
makers would
set off on moonlit
cruises from the
bay, accompanied
by a boat of mus-
icians. The women
in the party would
trail pieces of vel-
vet or satin edged
with silver fishes
in the water be-
hind them while the musicians
played to the revellers.
   One of the hosts of these
parties was the mother of
the last Khedive of Egypt
(see p29), Abbas Hilmi II. Built
in the late 19th century, the
only remaining monumental
architecture in Bebek is the
Egyptian Consulate, which,
like the Khedive's Palace
(see p142), was commis-
sioned by Abbas Hilmi II.
The steep, mansard roof
of this yalı is reminiscent
of 19th-century northern
French architecture. There
are lighter Art Nouveau
touches including the railings draped in wrought-
iron vines and a rising sun
between the two turrets,
symbolizing the beginning
of the new century.
   The khedive used the
yalı as a summer palace
until he was deposed by
the British in 1914. From
then on to the present
day it has been used as
the Egyptian Consulate.

Yalıs on the Bosphorus

At the end of the 17th century, *paşas*, grand viziers and other distinguished citizens of Ottoman Istanbul began to build themselves elegant villas – yalıs – along the shores of the Bosphorus. These served as summer residences, and the styles employed reflected their owners' prestige. Since then, the yalıs that have been built have become larger and more elaborate, adopting Baroque, Art Nouveau and modern styles of architecture. Most of them still conform to a traditional plan, making maximum use of the waterfront and, inside, having a large sitting room surrounded by bedrooms.

Old yalı at Kandilli, Asian side

Köprülü Amcazade Hüseyin Paşa Yalı (see p147), *near Anadolu Hisarı, was built in 1699 and is the oldest building on the shores of the Bosphorus. Early yalıs, like this one, were built at the water's edge, but in later years they were constructed a little way inland.*

A cumba, or bay window, projects over the water.

Traditional wooden yalıs were normally painted rust red, a colour known as "Ottoman rose".

Later yalıs, built from the 18th century, were painted in pastel shades.

A bracket supports the projecting upstairs rooms.

Fethi Ahmet Paşa Yalı (see p145), *or Mocan Yalı, at Kuzguncuk, was built in the late 18th century. Among visitors were the composer Franz Liszt and the architect Le Corbusier. Famous as the "Pink Yalı", after its boldly decorated exterior, the house is almost invisible from the land.*

Ethem Pertev Yalı (see p147), *at Kanlıca, is a prime example of the so-called "cosmopolitan period" of yalı building, between 1867 and 1908. It has a boat house below and combines intricate wood carving, a later development, with the more traditional features of a yalı.*

Baroque influence is clearly visible in the ornately carved balcony.

Boat house under the yali

The Egyptian Consulate (see p146) *at Bebek clearly shows the influence of Art Nouveau, with its wrought iron railings worked into a leaf design. It was commissioned by the Khedive of Egypt (see p138) in around 1900.*

French-style mansard roof

Ornamental details were inspired by Austrian Art Nouveau designs.

A narrow quay often separates 19th-century yalıs from the shore.

Küçüksu Palace ❹
Küçüksu Kasrı

Küçüksu Cad, Asian side. **Tel** *(0216)*
332 02 37. 🚌 *15 (from Üsküdar) or*
101 (from Beşiktaş). ⏲ *9:30am–5pm*
Tue, Wed, Fri–Sun (Oct–Apr until 4pm).

Küçüksu Palace, an ornate Bosphorus residence built in 1856

Marble-fronted Küçüksu
Palace has one of the
prettiest façades on the shores
of the Bosphorus. Particularly
attractive is the curving double
staircase which leads up to its
main waterside entrance.

Sultan Abdül Mecit I *(see
p30)* employed court architect
Nikogos Balyan *(see p128)* to
build this palace to accommodate his entourage on their
visits to the Sweet Waters of
Asia. This was the romantic
name European visitors gave
to the Küçüksu and Göksu
rivers. For centuries the Ottoman nobility liked to indulge
in picnics in the meadows
between the streams.

On the completion of
Küçüksu Palace in 1856, the
sultan complained that it was
too plain and demanded more
ornamentation, including his
monogram engraved on the
façade. Later, in the reign
of Abdül Aziz *(see p30)*, the
façade was further embel-
lished, with the result that
it is hard to follow the lines
of the original architecture.

The room arrangement is
typically Ottoman, with a
large central salon opening
on to four corner rooms on
each floor. The interior decor
was carried out by Séchan,
the decorator of the Paris
Opera, soon after the palace
was finished. The carpets are
fine examples from Hereke
(see pp218–19) and the chandeliers Bohemian crystal.
On the shore near Küçüksu

Palace is the picturesque,
turreted Fountain of the Valide
Sultan Mihrişah. Dating from
1796, it is in the Baroque style.

Kıbrıslı Yalı, just south of
the palace, was built in 1760.
At over 60 m (200 ft), its
brilliant white façade is the
longest of any yalı *(see p139)*
along the Bosphorus. A little
further south again is Kırmızı
Yalı, the Red Yalı, which is
so called for its distinctive
crimson colour. This yalı
was constructed for one of
Sultan Mahmut II's gardens
in the 1830s.

Aşiyan Museum ❺
Aşiyan Müzesi

Aşiyan Yolu, Asian side.
Tel *(0212) 263 69 82.* 🚌 *25E, 40.*
⏲ *9am–4:30pm Tue–Sat.*

Aşiyan, or bird's nest, is the
former home of Tevfik
Fikret (1867–1915), a teacher,
utopian visionary and one of
Turkey's leading poets. The
wooden mansion, built by
Fikret himself in 1906, is an
attractive example of Turkish
vernacular architecture. The
views from its upper-storey
balcony are stunning.

On show are the poet's
possessions and *Sis* (Fog),
a painting by Caliph Abdül
Mecit (1922–24), inspired by
Fikret's poem of that name.

Fortress of Europe ❻
Rumeli Hisarı

Yahya Kemal Cad, European side.
Tel *(0212) 263 53 05.* 🚌 *25E, 40.*
⏲ *9am–4:30pm Thu–Tue.* ♿

This fortress was built by
Mehmet the Conqueror
in 1452 as his first step in the
conquest of Constantinople
(see p26). Situated at the
narrowest point of the Bosphorus, the fortress controlled a major Byzantine supply
route. Across the straits is
Anadolu Hisarı, or the Fortress
of Asia, which was built in the
14th century by Beyazıt I.

The Fortress of Europe's layout was planned by Mehmet
himself. While his grand vizier
(see p29) and two other
viziers were each responsible
for the building of one of the
three great towers, the sultan
took charge of the walls. In
the spirit of competition which
evolved, the fortress was
completed in four months.

The Fortress of Europe, built by Mehmet the Conqueror to enable him to capture Constantinople

The new fortress was soon nicknamed Boğazkesen – meaning "Throat-cutter" or "Strait-cutter". It was garrisoned by a force of Janissaries *(see p127)*. These troops trained their cannons on the straits to prevent the passage of foreign ships. After they had sunk a Venetian vessel, this approach to Constantinople was cut off. Following the conquest of the city, the fortress lost its importance as a military base and was used as a prison, particularly for out-of-favour foreign envoys and prisoners-of-war.

The structure was restored in 1953. Open-air theatre performances are now staged here during the Istanbul Music and Dance Festival *(see p45)*.

Café serving the yoghurt for which Kanlıca is famous

Kanlıca ❼

Asian side. 🚌 *15, 101.*

A delicious, creamy type of yoghurt is Kanlıca's best known asset. The İskender Paşa Mosque, overlooking the village square, is a minor work by Sinan *(see p91)*, built for Sultan Süleyman's vizier İskender Paşa in 1559–60. There have been changes to the original building: the wooden dome has been replaced by a flat roof, and the porch was added later.

There are a number of yalis in and around Kanlıca, including the Köprülü Amcazade Hüseyin Paşa Yalı *(see p139)*, the oldest surviving Bosphorus yalı, just south of the village. This was built in 1698 by Mustafa II's grand vizier Hüseyin Paşa, the fourth grand vizier from the Köprülü family. The Treaty of

Karlowitz, in which the Ottomans acknowledged the loss of territory to Austria, Venice, Poland and Russia, was signed here in 1699 *(see p27)*. All that remains of the yalı, which is not open to visitors, is a T-shaped salon, its dome only saved by wooden props.

Emirgan Park ❽
Emirgan Parkı

Emirgan Sahil Yolu, European side. *Tel* (0212) 277 57 82. 🚌 *25E, 40.* ⭘ *7am–10:30pm daily.* 🚗 *for vehicles.*

Emirgan Park is the location of some famous tulip gardens, which are at their finest for the annual Tulip Festival in April *(see p44)*. Tulips originally grew wild on the Asian steppes and were first propagated in large quantities in Holland. They were later reintroduced to Turkey by Mehmet IV (1648–87). The reign of his son Ahmet III is known as the Tulip Period *(see p27)* because of his fascination with the flowers.

In the late 19th century Sultan Abdül Aziz gave the park to the Egyptian Khedive *(see p29)*, İsmail Paşa, and its three pavilions date from that era. They are known by their colours. The Sarı Köşk (Yellow Pavilion), built in the style of a Swiss chalet, suffered fire damage in 1954 and was rebuilt in concrete with a façade resembling the original. The Beyaz Köşk (White Pavilion) is a Neo-Classical style mansion, while the Pembe Köşk

Pembe Köşk in Emirgan Park

(Pink Pavilion) is in the style of a traditional Ottoman house. All three are now cafés.

Sakıp Sabancı Museum ❾
Sakıp Sabancı Müzesi

İstinye Cad 22, Emirgab 34467. *Tel* (0212) 277 22 00. 🚌 *40, 41 from Taksim Sq; any bus to İstinye or Sarıyer.* ⭘ *10am–6pm Tue, Thu, Fri, Sun; 10am–10pm Wed, Sat.* 🌑 *1 Jan, 1st day of religious hols.* 🎫 🖼 ⮑ ▯
🖥 www.muze.sabanciuniv.edu

With a superb view over the Bosphorus, the Sakıp Sabancı Museum, founded in 2005, is also known as the Horse Mansion (Altı Kösk). Exhibitions comprise over 400 years of Ottoman calligraphy and other Koranic and secular art treasures. The collection of paintings is exquisite, with works by Ottoman court painters and European artists enthralled with Turkey.

BIRDS OF THE BOSPHORUS

In September and October, thousands of white storks and birds of prey fly over the Bosphorus on their way from their breeding grounds in eastern Europe to wintering regions in Africa. Large birds usually prefer to cross narrow straits like the Bosphorus rather than fly over an expanse of open water such as the Mediterranean. Among birds of prey on this route you can see the lesser spotted eagle and the honey buzzard. The birds also cross the straits in spring on their way to Europe but, before the breeding season, they are fewer in number.

The white stork, which migrates over the straits

Hot-house plants in the conservatory at Maslak Pavilions

Maslak Pavilions ⑩
Maslak Kasırları

Büyükdere Cad, Maslak. **Tel** (0212) 276 10 22. ▦ 40S (from Taksim). ◯ 9am–6pm Tue, Wed & Fri–Sun (Oct–Mar until 3pm).

This small group of buildings was a royal hunting lodge and country residence, much prized for its glorious views. The pavilions were built in the early and mid-19th century, when the focus of Istanbul court life moved away from Topkapı Palace (see pp54–9), in the centre of the city, to the sultans' lavish estates along the shore of the Bosphorus. The buildings are thought to date mainly from the reign of Abdül Aziz (1861–76). He gave Maslak to his son Abdül Hamit in the hope that the crown prince would then stop sailing at Tarabya (see p148), which his father regarded as unsafe.

The four main buildings are less ornate than other 19th-century pavilions in Istanbul. This is possibly due to the austere character of Abdül Hamit. He personally crafted the balustrades of the beautiful central staircase in the Kasr-ı Hümayun (the Pavilion of the Sultan) during his stay here. His initials in Western script – AH – can also be seen in the headpieces over the mirrors. The pavilion's lounge retains an Oriental feel, with a low sofa and a central coal-burning brazier.

Behind the small but elegant Mabeyn-i Hümayun (the Private Apartments) is a large conservatory full of camellias, ferns and banana plants. Nearby, at the edge of the forest stands a tiny octagonal folly with an ornate balcony called the Çadır Köşkü, or Tent Pavilion, which now serves as a bookshop. The Paşalar Dairesi (the Apartments of the Paşa) are located at the other side of the complex.

Khedive's Palace ⑪
Hıdiv Kasrı

Hıdiv Kasrı Yolu 32, Çubuklu. **Tel** (0216) 425 06 03. ▦ 15, 15A, 15P (from Üsküdar) or 221 (from Taksim), then 5 mins' walk from Kanlica. ◯ 9am–11pm daily (May–Oct 9am–10:30pm). ▣

Built in 1907 by the last khedive (the hereditary viceroy of Egypt, see p29), Abbas Hilmi II, this summer palace is one of the most striking buildings of its era in Istanbul. Its tower is an imposing landmark for those travelling up the Bosphorus.

The Italian architect Delfo Seminati based the design of the palace on an Italianate villa, throwing in Art Nouveau and Ottoman elements. Most impressive of all is the round entrance hall. This is entered through Art Nouveau glass doors and features a stained-glass skylight above a central fountain surrounded by eight pairs of elegant columns.

Renovated by the Turkish Touring Club (TTOK, see p245), the palace is now open to visitors as a luxury restaurant (see p206).

Beykoz ⑫

Asian shore. ▦ 15 (from Üsküdar) or 221 (from Taksim).

Beykoz is famous for its walnuts (beykoz means "prince's walnut") and for the glass produced here in the 19th century. The distinctive, mainly opaque, Beykoz glass (see p213), with its rich colour

JASON AND THE SYMPLEGADES

The upper Bosphorus features in the Greek myth of Jason's search for the Golden Fleece. The Argonauts, Jason's crew, helped a local king, Phineus, by ridding him of the harpies (female demons) sent by Zeus to torment him. In return, the king advised them on how to tackle the Symplegades, two rocks at the mouth of the Bosphorus which were reputed to clash together, making passage impossible. His advice was to send a dove in advance of the ship; if it went through safely, so would the ship. This the Argonauts duly did, and the rocks clipped the dove's tail feathers. The Argo then went through with only some damage to its stern.

Jason and the Argonauts making their way through the Symplegades

Fountain in the village square at Beykoz

nd graceful designs, can be seen in museums all over Turkey. Nowadays, the village's main attraction is its fish restaurants, which serve excellent turbot.

A fine 18th-century fountain stands in the central square. Built on the orders of Sultan Mahmut I *(see p33)*, it is called the İshak Ağa Çeşmesi, after the customs inspector who commissioned it in 1780. It has a large domed and colonnaded loggia, and 10 conduits spouting a constant stream of water.

Industrialization, mainly bottling and leather factories, has taken its toll and only a few buildings hint at the village's former splendour. The attractive 19th-century waterside mansion, Halil Ethem Yalı, is an interesting mixture of Neo-Classical and Neo-Baroque styles. It stands on İbrahim Kelle Caddesi,

Attic vase, Sadberk Hanım Museum

Sadberk Hanım Museum ⓭
Sadberk Hanım Müzesi

Piyasa Cad 27–29, Büyükdere, **Tel** *(0212) 242 38 13.* 🚌 *25E.* 🕙 *10:30am–6pm (Oct–Mar 9am–5pm).* ● *Wed.* 🎫 📷
www.sadberkhanimmuzesi.org.tr

Occupying two archetypal wooden Bosphorus yalıs *(see p139)*, the Sadberk Hanım Museum was the first private museum to open in Turkey, in 1981. The larger of these yalıs, the Azaryan Yalı, is the former summer house of the wealthy Koç family. A four-storey mansion, it was built in 1911 and, like many buildings of the time, was inspired by European architecture. The distinctive criss-crossed wooden slats on its façade distinguish it from the neighbouring buildings. It contains some fine ethnographic artifacts collected by Sadberk Hanım, wife of the industrialist Vehbi Koç, to whom the museum is dedicated. She found many of them in the Grand Bazaar *(see pp98–9)* and in Istanbul's other markets. A number of exhibits are laid out in tableaux depicting 19th-century Ottoman society. These include a henna party, at which the groom's female relatives would apply henna to the hands of his bride; and a circumcision bed, with a young boy dressed in traditional costume. Also worth seeking out in this section is a display of infinitely delicate *oya*, Turkish embroideries. These remarkably life-like pieces imitate garlands of flowers, such as carnations, roses, hyacinths and lilies and were used to fringe scarves and petticoats. Some of the examples on show were made in palace

harems in the 18th century. The neighbouring building is called the Sevgi Gönül Wing. Also dating from the early 20th century, it was bought to house the archaeological collection of Hüseyin Kocabaş, a friend of the Koç family. Displays are ordered chronologically, ranging from the late Neolithic period (5400 BC) to the Ottoman era. Exhibits are changed from time to time, but typically include Assyrian cuneiform tablets dating from the second millennium BC, Phrygian metalwork and Greek pottery from the late Geometric Period (750–680 BC). Among other items are Byzantine reliquary and pendent crosses, and a selection of Roman gold jewellery.

Rumeli Kavağı ⓮

European shore. 🚌 *25A (from Beşiktaş).* 🚢 Rumeli Kavağı.

This pretty village has a broad selection of restaurants specializing in fish and fried mussels. They are clustered around the harbour from where there are views of the wild, rocky shores on the approach to the Black Sea. On the hill above Rumeli Kavağı are the scant remains of a castle, İmros Kalesi, built by Manuel I Comnenus *(see p21)* in the 12th century to guard his customs point.

Further up the Bosphorus, the shore road leads from Rumeli Kavağı to Altın Kum beach. This small strip of sand backed by restaurants is popular with local people.

The fishing village of Rumeli Kavağı, on the upper Bosphorus

The Bosphorus Trip

Ceremonial gate, Çırağan Palace

One of the great pleasures of a visit to Istanbul is a cruise up the Bosphorus. You can go on a pre-arranged guided tour or take one of the small boats that tout for passengers at Eminönü. But there is no better way to travel than on the official trip run by Turkish Maritime Lines (TDİ, *see pp242–3*), which is described on the following pages. Laden with sightseers, the TDİ ferry makes a round-trip to the upper Bosphorus two or three times daily, stopping at six piers along the way, including a leisurely stop at Anadolu Kavağı for lunch. You can return to Eminönü on the same boat or make your way back to the city by bus, dolmuş or taxi.

LOCATOR MAP

Dolmabahçe Palace
This opulent 19th-century palace (see pp128–9) has a series of ornate gates along the waterfront. These were used by the sultan to enter the palace from his imperial barge.

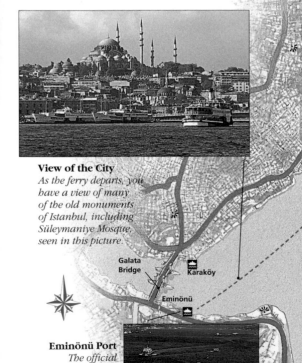

View of the City
As the ferry departs, you have a view of many of the old monuments of Istanbul, including Süleymaniye Mosque, seen in this picture.

Naval Museum *(see p126)*

Barbaros Hayrettin Paşa

İnönü Stadium

Kabataş

Museum Fine Art *(see p126)*

Dolmabahçe Mosque was completed in at the same time as the palace *(see p126).*

Galata Bridge

Karaköy

Eminönü

Eminönü Port
The official Bosphorus ferry departs from Istanbul's busiest ferry terminal.

Leander's Tower
One the landmarks of the city, this white tower stands prominently in mid-channel, a short way off the Asian shore (see p130).

145

VISITORS' CHECKLIST

Eminönü Pier 3 (Boğaz Hattı).
Map 3 D2. **Tel** (0212) 522 00
45. 🚇 Eminönü. 🚢 daily: May–
Sep, 10:30am & 1:30pm; Oct–
Apr, 10:30am. Round trip takes 6
hours. 🎟 Bookings are accepted
online and 1 hour before
departure. 🖥 www.ido.com.tr

**Kuleli Military
School** has a
pretty wooden
mosque
beside it.

Arnavutköy

Mecidiye Mosque
*Sultan Abdül
Mecit I ordered the
construction of this
Baroque mosque
on a promontory
near the ferry
pier at Ortaköy*
(see p122).

**Galatasaray
Island** is a
private sports
complex.

Çengelköy

Sadullah Paşa Yalı, built
in the 1783, is painted
red-brown, as are
many old yalıs
(see p139).

Ortaköy
(see p122)

Beylerbeyi

Yıldız Park
(see pp124–5)

**Bosphorus
Bridge**
(see p138)

**Fethi Ahmet
Paşa Yalı**
(see p139)

Çırağan Palace dates
from 1874, but had to
be rebuilt after a dev-
astating fire in 1910.
It is now a luxury
hotel (see p123).

Kuzguncuk

İskele Mosque
(see p131)

Üsküdar

Beylerbeyi Palace
*The palace grounds contain two
shore-side bathing pavilions: one
for men and the other for the women
of the harem (see p138).*

0 metres		750
0 yards		750

KEY

▬	Motorway
▬	Main road
	Other road
🏙	Built-up area
🚢	Ferry boarding point
– –	Route of Bosphorus trip
🕌	Yalı (see p139)
🌼	Viewpoint

Şemsi Paşa Mosque
*The circular windows of this 16th-
century mosque by Sinan (see p130)
are an allusion to Şemsi Paşa, whose
name derives from the word "shams",
meaning "sun" in Arabic.*

See pages
146–7

The Middle Bosphorus

North of Arnavutköy, the outskirts of Istanbul give way to attractive towns and villages, such as Bebek with its popular bars and cafés. The Bosphorus flows fast and deep as the channel reaches its narrowest point – 700 m (2,300 ft) across – on the approach to the Fatih Sultan Mehmet suspension bridge. It was at this point that the Persian emperor Darius and his army crossed the Bosphorus on a pontoon bridge in 512 BC, on their way to fight the Greeks. Two famous old fortresses face each other across the water near here. Several elegant yalıs are also found in this part of the strait, particularly in the region known to Europeans as the Sweet Waters of Asia.

Paşabahçe glass vase

Black Sea

EUROPE

ASIA

ISTANBUL

LOCATOR MAP

İstinye Bay
This huge natural bay, the largest inlet on the Bosphorus, has been used as a dock for centuries. There is a fish market along the quay every morning.

Emirgan Park
Situated above the pretty village of Emirgan, this park is famous for its tulips in spring (see p44). The grounds contain pleasant cafés and pavilions (see p141).

The Bosphorus University, one of the most prestigious in Turkey, enjoys spectacular views. Almost all teaching here is in English.

Fortress of Europe
Situated at the narrowest point on the Bosphorus, this fortress (see p140) was built by Mehmet II in 1452, as a prelude to his invasion of Constantinople (see p26).

Bebek
(see p138)

Egyptian
Consulate
(see p138)

K

Arnavutköy

See pages
144–5

See pages 148–9

Yeniköy
Handsome 19th-century villas define the waterfront of this village dating from Byzantine times.

Yeniköy

Paşabahçe

Sait Halim Paşa Yalı

The Paşabahçe Glass Works produce Turkey's finest glassware *(see p213)*.

stinye

Kanlıca is a pretty village *(see p141)* with a mosque built by Sinan *(see p91)*. It is also known for its delicious yoghurt.

Çubuklu

Khedive's Palace
Above çubuklu stands the palace built by the last viceroy of Egypt (see p29), Abbas Hilmi Paşa, in around 1900. It is now a hotel and restaurant (see p142).

Kanlıca

Ethem Pertev Yalı *(see p139)*

Sultan et

ade antinople 1)

Fortress of Asia
Fifty years older than the Fortress of Europe, this fortress was built by Beyazıt I just before the failed Ottoman siege of Constantinople in 1396–7.

nadolu lisarı

u 40)

Göksu River
This pretty little river and the Küçüksu River south of it are together known as the Sweet Waters of Asia (see p140).

KEY

▬	Motorway
▬	Main road
▬	Other road
▨	Built-up area
⚓	Ferry boarding point
- -	Route of Bosphorus trip
⌂	Yalı *(see p139)*
⚘	Viewpoint

0 metres 750
0 yards 750

The Upper Bosphorus

Black Sea mussels

In the 19th century ambassadors to Turkey built their summer retreats between Tarabya and Büyükdere, on the European side of the Bosphorus. As the hills fall more steeply towards the shore along the upper reaches of the straits, the built-up area peters out. The public ferry pauses for lunch at Anadolu Kavağı on the Asian side before heading back to Istanbul. You can also catch a bus or dolmuş back to the city. The Bosphorus itself continues for another 8 km (5 miles) or so to meet the Black Sea, but the land on both sides of this stretch is now under military control.

LOCATOR MAP

Sadberk Hanım Museum
This museum, housed in two wooden yalıs, has variety of interesting exhibits. These include antiquities from Greece and Rome, and Ottoman craftwork (see p143).

Sarıyer

Büyükdere

Tarabya Bay
The small village set within a lovely bay first attracted wealthy Greeks in the 18th century. The bay still thrives as an exclusive resort with up-market fish restaurants.

Huber Kö
is a 19
centur
yalı ov
by the go
ment.

FISHING ON THE BOSPHORUS

A multitude of fishing vessels ply the waters of the Bosphorus, ranging from large trawlers returning from the Black Sea to tiny rowing boats from which a line is cast into the water. On a trip up the Bosphorus you often see seine nets spread out in circles, suspended from floats on the surface. The

Fishing boats at Sarıyer, the main fishing port on the Bosphorus

main types of fish caught are mackerel, mullet, *hamsi* (similar to anchovy, *see p194*) and sardine. Much of the fish caught is sold at Istanbul's principal fish market in Kumkapı.

Rumeli Kavağı
This village is the most northerly ferry stop on the European side (see p143). From here the Bosphorus widens out to meet the Black Sea.

Anadolu Kavağı
A short climb from this village – the last stop on the trip – brings you to a ruined 14th-century Byzantine fortress, the Genoese Castle, from which there are great views over the straits.

Beykoz
Beykoz is the largest fishing village along the Asian shore. Close to its village square, which has this fountain dating from 1746, are several fish restaurants which are very popular in summer (see p142).

Beykoz

Halil Ethem Yalı *(see p143)*

0 metres 750
0 yards 750

See pages 146–7

KEY	
◼	Main road
	Other road
▨	Built-up area
⚓	Ferry boarding point
- -	Route of Bosphorus trip
⌂	Yalı *(see p139)*
☀	Viewpoint

EXCURSIONS FROM ISTANBUL

*S*tanding at a natural crossroads, Istanbul makes a good base
for excursions into the neighbouring areas of Thrace and
Anatolia – European and Asian Turkey respectively. Whether
you want to see great Islamic architecture, immerse yourself in a busy
bazaar, relax on an island or catch a glimpse of Turkey's rich birdlife,
you will find a choice of destinations within easy reach of the city.

On public holidays and weekends nearby resorts become
crowded with Istanbul residents taking a break from
the noisy city. For longer
breaks, they head for the
Mediterranean or Aegean, so
summer is a good time to
explore the Marmara and
western Black Sea regions
while they are quiet.

The country around Istanbul
varies immensely from lush
forests to open plains and,
beyond them, impressive
mountains. The Belgrade
Forest is one of the closest
green areas to the city if you want a
short break. The Princes' Islands,
where the pine forests and monasteries can be toured by a pleasant ride in
a horse-and-carriage, are also just a
short boat trip away from the city.

**Window, Selimiye
Mosque, Edirne**

Further away, through rolling
fields of bright yellow sunflowers, is Edirne, the former
Ottoman capital. The town
stands on a site first settled in
the 7th century BC. It is visited
today for its fine mosques,
especially the Selimiye.

South of the Sea of Marmara
is the pretty spa town of Bursa,
originally a Greek city which
was founded in 183 BC.
The first Ottoman capital, it
has some fine architecture.

Near the mouth of the straits
of the Dardanelles (which
link the Sea of Marmara to the
Aegean) lie the ruins of the legendary
city of Troy, dating from as early as
3600 BC. North of the Dardanelles are
cemeteries commemorating the battles
which were fought over the Gallipoli
peninsula during World War I.

Boats in Burgaz Harbour on the Princes' Islands, a short ferry ride from Istanbul

◁ **The Green Tomb of Mehmet I in Bursa, one of the city's best-known landmarks**

Exploring Beyond Istanbul

Within a radius of 250 km (150 miles) of Istanbul there are many destinations worth visiting. To the northwest is Edirne, an attractive riverside town and the location of several fine mosques. South of Istanbul is Bursa, which lies at the foot of Uludağ, a mountain famed for its skiing. Closer to Istanbul are the Black Sea resorts of Şile and Kilyos, and the Princes' Islands, popular in summer, which are easily reached by ferry. The war cemeteries of the Dardanelles and the site of ancient Troy require a longer trip.

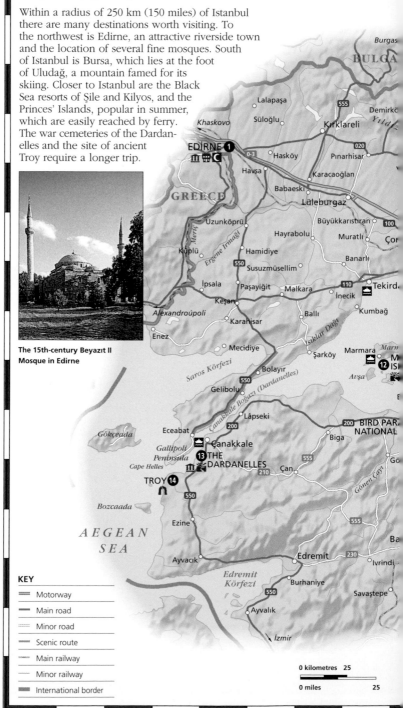

The 15th-century Beyazıt II Mosque in Edirne

Burgas

BULGA

Lalapaşa

Khaskovo   Süloğlu   Kırklareli   Demirkö

555   Yıldı

EDİRNE ❶   Haşköy   Pınarhisar   020

🏛 🕌 C   0-3   Havsa   Karacaoğlan

Babaeski   Lüleburgaz

GREECE

Uzunköprü   Büyükkarıştıran   100

Hayrabolu   Muratlı   Çor

Merik

Küplü   Ergene Irmağı   Hamidiye   Banarlı

550   Susuzmüsellim

İpsala   Paşayiğit   Malkara   110   Tekird

Keşan   İnecik

Alexandroúpoli   Karahisar   Ballı   Kumbağ

Enez   Işıklar Dağı

Mecidiye   Şarköy   Marmara   Marn

❶❷   M

Saros Körfezi   Bolayır   Avşa   IS

550

Gelibolu   BIRD PAR.

Çanakkale Boğazı (Dardanelles)   200   NATIONAL

Lâpseki   Biga

Gökçeada   Eceabat   200   Gö

Çanakkale   555

Gallipoli   ❶❸ THE   Gönen Çayı

Peninsula   🏛 DARDANELLES   Çan   210

Cape Helles

TROY ❶❹

550   Bozcaada

Ezine   555

AEGEAN   Edremit   230   Ba

SEA   Ayvacık   İvrindi

Edremit   Burhaniye   Savaştepe

Körfezi   550

Ayvalık

İzmir

KEY

▬▬▬	Motorway
▬▬▬	Main road
▬▬▬	Minor road
▬▬▬	Scenic route
▬▬▬	Main railway
▬▬▬	Minor railway
▬▬▬	International border

0 kilometres 25

0 miles 25

For additional map symbols *see back flap*

SIGHTS AT A GLANCE

Belgrade Forest **3**
Bird Paradise National Park **11**
Bursa pp162–8 **9**
The Dardanelles **13**
Edirne pp154–7 **1**
İznik **8**
Kilyos **2**
Marmara Islands **12**
Polonezköy **5**
Princes' Islands **6**
Şile **4**
Termal **7**
Troy **14**
Uludağ National Park **10**

View over the picturesque city of Bursa

One of the main ski runs in Uludağ National Park

‌TING AROUND

‌road network around
‌bul is steadily improving,
‌modern, cheap and efficient
‌ies *(see p244)* will get you to
‌places. Ferries and sea buses
‌244) cross the Sea of
‌nara to ports on its southern
‌e and reach both the Princes'
‌Marmara Islands.

Edirne ❶

Standing on the river Tunca near the border with Greece, Edirne is a provincial university town which is home to one of Turkey's star attractions, the Selimiye Mosque *(see pp156–7)*. As this huge monument attests, Edirne was historically of great importance. It dates back to AD 125, when the Roman Emperor Hadrian joined two small towns to form Hadrianopolis, or Adrianople. For nearly a century, from when Murat I *(see p25)* took the city in 1361 until Constantinople was conquered in 1453 *(see p26)*, Edirne was the Ottoman capital. The town has one other claim to fame – the annual grease wrestling championships in June.

Entrance arch, Mosque of the Three Balconies

of the commonest afflictions. The colonnaded inner mosque courtyard, unlike most later examples, covers three times the area of the mosque itself. Inside, the weight of the impressive dome is supported on sweeping pendentives.

◯ Mosque of the Three Balconies
Üç Şerefeli Camii
Hükümet Cad. ◯ *daily.* ✹
Until the fall of Constantinople, this was the grandest building in the early Ottoman state. It was finished in 1447 and takes its name from the three balconies adorning its southeast minaret, at the time the tallest in existence. In an unusual touch, the other three minarets of the mosque are each of a different design and height. Unlike its predecessors in

Bursa *(see pp162–8)*, the mosque has an open courtyard, setting a precedent for the great imperial mosques of Istanbul. The plan of its interior was also innovative. With minimal obstructions, the mihrab and *minbar* can both be seen from almost every corner of the prayer hall. Like the minarets, the dome, too, was the largest of its time.

◯ Old Mosque
Eski Cami
Talat Paşa Asfaltı. ◯ *daily.* ✹
The oldest of Edirne's major mosques, this is a smaller version of the Great Mosque in Bursa *(see p164)*. The eldest son of Beyazıt I *(see p32)*, Süleyman, began the mosque in 1403, but it was his youngest son, Mehmet I, who completed it in 1414.

A perfect square, the mosque is divided by four massive piers into nine domed sections. On either side of the prayer hall entrance there are massive Arabic inscriptions proclaiming "Allah" and "Mohammed".

Entrance to Beyazıt II Mosque viewed from its inner courtyard

◯ Beyazıt II Mosque
Beyazıt II Külliyesi
Yeni Maharet Cad. ◯ *daily.*
Health Museum
Tel (0284) 212 09 22. ◯ 9:30am–5:30pm daily. 📷 ♿
Beyazıt II Mosque stands in a peaceful location on the northern bank of the Tunca River, 1.5 km (1 mile) from the town centre. It was built in 1484–8, soon after Beyazıt II *(see p32)* succeeded Mehmet the Conqueror *(see p26)* as sultan.

The mosque and its courtyards are open to the public. Of the surrounding buildings in the complex, the old hospital, which incorporated an asylum, has been converted into the **Health Museum**. Disturbed patients were treated in the asylum – a model of its time – with water, colour and flower therapies. The Turkish writer Evliya Çelebi (1611–84) reported that singers and instrumentalists would play soothing music here three times a week. Overuse of hashish was one

GREASE WRESTLING

The Kırkpınar Grease Wrestling Championships take place annually in July, on the island of Sarayiçi in the Tunca River. The event is famed throughout Turkey and accompanied by a week-long carnival. Before competing, the wrestlers dress in knee-length leather shorts *(kispet)* and grease themselves from head to foot in diluted olive oil. The master of ceremonies, the *cazgır*, then invites the competitors to take part in a high-stepping, arm-flinging parade across the field, accompanied by music played on a deep-toned drum *(davul)* and a single-reed oboe *(zurna)*. Wrestling bouts can last up to two hours and involve long periods of frozen, silent concentration interspersed by attempts to throw down the opponent.

Grease wrestlers parading before they fight

🏛 Rüstem Paşa Caravanserai

Rüstem Paşa Kervansarayı
İki Kapılı Han Cad 57.
Tel *(0284) 215 24 89.*
Sinan *(see p91)* designed this caravanserai for Süleyman's most powerful grand vizier, Rüstem Paşa *(see p88)*, in 1560–61. It was constructed in two distinct parts. The larger courtyard, or han *(see p96)*, which is now the Rüstem Paşa Kervansaray Hotel *(see p191)*, was built for the merchants of Edirne, while the smaller courtyard, now a student hostel, was an inn for other travellers.

A short walk away, on the other side of Saraçlar Caddesi, is the Semiz Ali Paşa Bazaar, where Edirne's merchants still sell their wares. This is another work of Sinan, dating from 1589. It consists of a long, narrow street of vaulted shops.

🏛 Museum of Turkish and Islamic Arts

Türk ve İslam Eserleri Müzesi
Kadir Paşa Mektep Sok. **Tel** *(0284) 225 11 20.* ⬜ *9am–noon, 1:30–5:30pm Tue–Sun.* 📷
Edirne's small collection of Turkish and Islamic works of art is attractively located in the *medrese* of the Selimiye Mosque *(see pp156–7)*.

The museum's first room is devoted to the local sport of grease wrestling. It includes enlarged reproductions of miniatures depicting 600 years of the sport. These show the wrestling stars resplendent in their leather shorts, their skin glistening with olive oil.

Other objects on display include the original doors of the Beyazıt II Mosque. There are also military exhibits. Among them are some beautiful 18th-century Ottoman shields, with woven silk exteriors, and paintings of military subjects.

The tranquil 15th-century Muradiye Mosque

🔶 Muradiye Mosque

Muradiye Camii
Küçükpazar Cad. ⬜ *prayer times only.* 📷
This mosque was built as a *zaviye* (dervish hospice) in 1421 by Murat II *(see p32)*, who dreamt that the great dervish leader Jelaleddin Rumi *(see p104)* asked him to build one in Edirne. Only later was it converted into a mosque. Its interior is notable for its massive inscriptions, similar to those in the Old Mosque, and for some fine early 15th-century İznik tiles *(see p161)*.

EDİRNE CITY CENTRE

0 metres   750
0 yards   750

Bus Station
2 km (1.25 miles)

Train Station
3 km (2 miles)

Key to symbols *see back flap*

Edirne: Selimiye Mosque
Selimiye Camii

The Selimiye is the greatest of all the Ottoman mosque complexes, the apogee of an art form and the culmination of a lifetime's ambition for its architect, Sinan *(see p91)*. Built on a slight hill, the mosque is a prominent landmark. Its complex includes a *medrese (see p38)*, now housing the Museum of Turkish and Islamic Arts *(see p155)*, a school and the Kavaflar Arasta, a covered bazaar.

Selim II *(see p27)* commissioned the mosque. It was begun in 1569 and completed in 1575, a year after his death. The dome was Sinan's proudest achievement. In his memoirs, he wrote: "With the help of Allah and the favour of Sultan Selim Khan, I have succeeded in building a cupola six cubits wider and four cubits deeper than that of Haghia Sophia". In fact, the dome is of a diameter comparable to and slightly shallower than that of the building *(see pp72–5)* Sinan had so longed to surpass.

★ Minarets
The mosque's four slender minarets tower to a height of 84 m (275 ft). Each one has three balconies. The two northern minarets contain three intertwining staircases, each one leading to a different balcony.

Ablutions Fountain
Intricate, pierced carving decorates the top of the 16-sided open şadırvan (ablutions fountain), which stands in the centre of the courtyard. The absence of a canopy helps to retain the uncluttered aspect of the courtyard.

STAR FEATURES

★ Minarets

★ Dome

★ Minbar

The columns supporting the arches of the courtyard are made of old marble, plundered from Byzantine architecture.

Courtyard Portals
Alternating red and honey-coloured slabs of stone were used to build the striking arches above the courtyard portals. This echoes the decoration of the magnificent arches running around the mosque courtyard itself.

★ Dome
The dome masterfully dominates the entire interior of the mosque. Not even the florid paintwork – the original 16th-century decoration underwent restoration in the 19th century – detracts from its effect.

★ Minbar
Many experts claim that the Selimiye's minbar, with its conical tiled cap, is the finest in Turkey. Its lace-like side panels are exquisitely carved.

Mihrab, cut from Marmara marble

VISITORS' CHECKLIST

Mimar Sinan Cad, Edirne.
***Tel** (0284) 213 97 35.*
⬜ *daily.* ⬤ *prayer times.*

The Interior
The mosque is the supreme achievement of Islamic architecture. Its octagonal plan allows for a reduction in the size of the buttresses supporting the dome. This permitted extra windows to be incorporated, making the mosque exceptionally light inside.

The müezzin mahfili
(see p38) still retains original, intricate 16th-century paintwork on its underside. Beneath it is a small fountain.

Entrance from Kavaflar Arasta

Sultan's Loge
The imperial loge is supported on green marble columns. They are connected by pointed arches, whose surrounds are adorned with floral İznik tiles (see p161). Unusually, its ornately decorated mihrab contains a shuttered window, which opened on to countryside when the mosque was first built.

Main entrance

Kilyos ❷

27 km (17 miles) N of Istanbul.
🚏 *1,665.* 🅓 *from Sarıyer.*

Kilyos, on the shore of the Black Sea, is the closest seaside resort to Istanbul and very popular. It has a long, sandy beach and temptingly clear water, but visitors should not swim here in the absence of a lifeguard because there are dangerous currents beneath the calm surface.

A 14th-century Genoese castle perches on a cliff top overlooking the town but it is not open to visitors. The three ruined towers on the left of the main approach road into the village were formerly water control towers. They were part of the system that once brought water here from the Belgrade Forest.

Belgrade Forest ❸
Belgrad Ormanı

20 km (12 miles) N of Istanbul.
🚌 *42, 40S from Taksim to Çayırbaşı, then 42 to Bahçeköy.*
Park Tel *(0212) 226 23 35.* ◯
May–Sep 6am–9pm daily; Oct–Apr 7am–7:30pm. 🏞 ♿

One of the most popular escapes from the city, the Belgrade Forest is the only sizeable piece of woodland in the immediate vicinity of Istanbul. The forest is made up of pines, oaks, beeches, chestnuts and poplars, beneath which a profusion of wild flowers grow in spring. Within it is a huge woodland park, best visited during the week, since it attracts hordes of picnickers at weekends. The main entrance to the park is near the village of Bahçeköy and the popular Neşetsuyu picnic area is a half-hour stroll from this gate.

The park's other attractions are the relics of the dams, reservoirs and aqueducts used for over 1,000 years to transport spring water in to Istanbul. The

Büyük Bent, a Byzantine dam and reservoir in the Belgrade Forest

oldest structure, Büyük Bent (Great Reservoir), dates back to the early Byzantine era. It is a pleasant half-hour walk from Neşetsuyu picnic area. Meanwhile, the Sultan Mahmut Dam, outside the park's gate, is a fine curve of marble which dates from 1839.

Eğri Kemer (Crooked Aqueduct) and Uzun Kemer (Long Aqueduct) are on the 016 road between Levent and Kısırmandıra and are best reached by taxi. Both have impressive rows of arches. The former probably dates from the 12th century, while Sinan *(see p91)* built the latter for Süleyman the Magnificent *(see p26)*.

Şile ❹

72 km (45 miles) NE of Istanbul.
🚏 *25,372.* 🚌 *from Üsküdar.*

The quintessential Black Sea holiday village of Şile has a number of fine, sandy beaches and a black-and-white striped cliff-top light-

The village of Şile, a holiday resort and centre for cotton production

house. In antiquity, the village then known as Kalpe, was a port used by ships sailing east from the Bosphorus.

Şile's lighthouse, the largest in Turkey, was built by the French for Sultan Abdül Aziz *(see p30)* in 1858–9; it can be visited after dusk. Apart from tourism, the main industry is now the production of a coarse cotton which is made into clothing and sold in shops along Üsküdar Caddesi.

Polonezköy ❺

25 km (16 miles) NE of Istanbul.
🚏 *500.* 🚌 *221 from Taksim to Beykoz, then dolmuş.*

Polonezköy was originally called Adampol, after the Polish Prince Adam Czartoryski who bought prime arable land here in 1842 for Polish emigrants settling in Turkey. Soon after, in 1853, the Poles formed a band of Cossack soldiers to fight for Abdül Mecit I *(see p30)* in the Crimea. After this he granted them the land as a tax-free haven.

Polonezköy's rustic charm is now big business, and a number of health spas and villas have sprung up. A couple of restaurants *(see p207)* still serve the pork for which the town was once famous.

The surrounding beech forest, which offers pleasant walks, has now been protected from further development. As part of this scheme, the locals have even waived their rights to collect firewood.

Princes' Islands ❻
Kızıl Adalar

12 km (7 miles) SE of Istanbul. 🏛
16,171. 🚢 2pm from Sirkeci (sea
bus). 🛈 (0216) 382 70 71.

The pine-forested Princes'
Islands provide a welcome
break from the bustle of the
city and are just a short ferry
ride southeast from Istanbul.
Most ferries call in turn at the
four largest of the nine islands:
Kınalıada, Burgazada, Heybeliada and finally Büyükada.

Easily visited on a day trip,
the islands take their name
from a royal palace built
by Justin II on Büyük-
ada, then known as
Prinkipo (Island of the
Prince) in 569. During
the Byzantine era the
islands became infa-
mous as a place of
exile. Members of the
royal family and public
figures were often
banished to the mon-
asteries here.

In the latter half of
the 19th century, with
the inauguration of
a steamboat service from
Istanbul, several wealthy ex-
patriates settled on the islands.
Among the foreign exiles to
live here was Leon Trotsky.
From 1929–33 he lived at 55
Çankaya Caddesi, one of the
finest mansions on Büyükada.

Büyükada is the largest
island and attracts the most
visitors with its sandy beaches,
ice creams and *fin-de-siècle*
elegance. Its 19th-century
atmosphere is enhanced by

Door to the Monastery of St George

the omnipresence of horse-
drawn phaetons. These quaint
carriages are in fact the only
form of public transport on
Büyükada (and Heybeliada)
since motorized transport is
banned. At the top of Büyükada's wooded southern hill,
in a clearing, stands the
Monastery of St George. It is
a 20th-century structure, built
on Byzantine foundations.

To the left of the ferry pier
on Heybeliada, the second
largest island, is the imposing
former Naval High School
(Deniz Harp Okulu), built
in 1942. The island's
northern hill is the
stunning location of
the Greek Orthodox
School of Theology
(built in 1841). The
school is now closed
but its library, famous
among Orthodox
scholars, is still open.
The island also has a
pleasant beach on its
south coast at Çam
Limanı Köyü.

The smaller islands
of Kınalıada and
Burgazada are less
developed and are peaceful
places to stop off for a meal.

Termal ❼

38 km (24 miles) SE of Istanbul. 🏛
5,018. 🚢 from Kabataş to Yalova. 🛈
Yalı Cad, Varol İşhanı, (0226) 813 85 07.

This small spa buried deep
in a wooded valley has been
patronized by ruling elites
since the Roman era. Termal is

Ornamental fountain at Atatürk's former house at Termal

12 km (7 miles) from the port
of Yalova. Its popularity was
revived by Sultan Abdül Hamit
II (*see p33*) in the early 20th
century, when he refurbished
the **Yalova Termal Baths**, now
part of the Turban Termal
complex of four baths and a
couple of hotels. Facilities
include Turkish baths (*see p67*),
a sauna and a swimming pool.

Atatürk enjoyed taking the
waters here. The small chalet-
style house he built at the
bottom of the valley, now the
Atatürk Museum, preserves
some of his possessions.

� Yalova Termal Baths
Termal. **Tel** (0226) 675 74 00.
⬤ 8am–10pm daily.

🏛 Atatürk Museum
Atatürk Köşkü, Termal. **Tel** (0226) 675
70 28. ⬤ May–Oct 9am–5pm Tue,
Wed, Fri–Sun; Nov–Apr 9:30am–4pm.

The harbour of Burgazada, one of the relaxed and picturesque Princes' Islands near Istanbul

İznik ⑧

87 km (54 miles) SE of Istanbul.
🕍 20,100. 🚌 Yeni Mahalle,
Yakup Sok, (0224) 757 25 83.
ℹ Belediye Hizmet Binasi,
Kılıçaslan Cad 97, (0224) 757 19
33. 🛒 Wed. 🎪 İznik Fair (5–10
Oct); Liberation Day (28 Nov).

A charming lakeside town,
İznik gives little clue
now of its former glory as, at
one point, the capital of the
Byzantine Empire. Its most important legacy dates, however,
from the 16th century, when
its kilns produced the finest
ceramics ever to be made in
the Ottoman world.

Grand domed portico fronting the Archaeological Museum

The town first reached
prominence in AD 325, when
it was known as Nicaea. In
that year Constantine (see
p20) chose it as the location
of the first Ecumenical Council
of the Christian Church. At
this meeting, the Nicene Creed,
a statement of doctrine on the
nature of Christ in relation to
God, was formulated.

The Seljuks (see p21) took
Nicaea in 1081 and renamed
it İznik. It was wrested back
from them in 1097 by the First
Crusade on behalf of Emperor
Alexius I Comnenus. After the
capture of
Constantinople in
1204 (see p26), the
city was capital of
the 'Empire of
Nicaea', a remaining fragment of
the Byzantine
Empire, for half
a century. In
1331, Orhan
Gazi (see p32)
captured İznik

and incorporated it into the
Ottoman Empire. İznik still
retains its original layout.
Surrounded by the **city walls**,
its two main streets are in the
form of a cross, with minor
streets running out from them
on a grid plan. The walls still
more or less delineate the
town's boundaries. They were
built by the Greek Lysimachus,
then ruler of the
town, in 300
BC, but they
were frequently
repaired by
both the
Byzantines
and later the
Ottomans. They
cover a total of
3 km (2 miles)
in circumference
and are punctuated by huge gateways. The
main one of these, Istanbul
Gate (İstanbul Kapısı), is at
the city's northern limit. It is
decorated with a carved relief
of fighting horsemen and is
flanked by Byzantine towers.

One of the town's oldest
surviving monuments, the
ruined church of **Haghia
Sophia**, stands at the inter-

**Istanbul Gate from within
the city walls**

section of the main streets,
Atatürk Caddesi and
Kılıçaslan Caddesi. The
current building was erected
after an earthquake in 1065.
The remains of a fine mosaic
floor, and also of a Deësis, a
fresco that depicts Christ, the
Virgin and John the Baptist,
are protected from damage
behind glass screens. Just off
the eastern end
of Kılıçaslan Caddesi, the 14th-
century **Green
Mosque** (Yeşil
Cami) is named
after the tiles
covering its
minaret. Unfortunately, the
originals have
been replaced
by modern
copies of an inferior quality.

Opposite the mosque, the
Kitchen of Lady Nilüfer
(Nilüfer Hatun İmareti), one
of İznik's loveliest buildings,
now houses the town's
Archaeological Museum.
This imaret was set up in 1388
by Nilüfer Hatun, wife of
Orhan Gazi, and also served
as a hospice for wandering
dervishes. Entered through a
spacious five-domed portico,
the central domed area is
flanked by two further domed
rooms. The museum has displays of Roman antiquities and
glass as well as some recently
discovered examples of Seljuk
and Ottoman tiles.

🕌 **Haghia Sophia**
Atatürk Cad. **Tel** (0224) 757 10 27.
🔵 by appointment. 📷

🟢 **Green Mosque**
Müze Sok. 🔵 daily (after prayer).

🏛 **Archaeological Museum**
Müze Sok. **Tel** (0224) 757 10 27.
🔵 by appointment. 📷

Green Mosque, İznik, named after the green tiles adorning its minaret

İznik Ceramics

Towards the end of the 15th century, the town of İznik began to produce large quantities of ceramic bowls, jars and, later, tiles for the many palaces and mosques of Istanbul. Drawing on local deposits of fine clay and inspired by imported Chinese ceramics, the work of the craftsmen of İznik soon excelled both technically and aesthetically. İznik pottery is made from hard, white "fritware", which is

16th-century İznik mosque lamp

akin to porcelain. This style of pottery was invented in Egypt in around the 12th century. It is covered by a bright, white slip (a creamy mixture of clay and water) and a transparent glaze. Early İznik pottery is brilliant blue and white. Later, other colours, especially a vivid red, were added. The potteries of İznik reached their height in the late 16th and early 17th centuries but shortly after fell into decline.

Chinese porcelain, *which was imported into Turkey from the 14th century and of which there is a large collection in Topkapı Palace (see pp54–9), often inspired the designs used for İznik pottery. During the 16th century, İznik potters produced imitations of pieces of Chinese porcelain such as this copy of a Ming dish.*

Rock and wave border pattern

Cobalt blue and white *was the striking combination of colours used in early İznik pottery (produced between c.1470–1520). The designs used were a mixture of Chinese and Arabesque, as seen on this tiled panel on the wall of the Circumcision Chamber in Topkapı Palace. Floral patterns and animal motifs were both popular at this time.*

Damascus ware *was the name erroneously given to ceramics produced at İznik during the first half of the 16th century. They had fantastic floral designs in the new colours of turquoise, sage green and manganese. When such tiles were discovered at Damascus, the similar İznik pots were wrongly assumed to have been made there.*

Armenian bole, *an iron-rich red colour, began to be used in around 1550, as seen in this 16th-century tankard. New, realistic tulip and other floral designs were also introduced, and İznik ware enjoyed its heyday, which lasted until around 1630.*

Wall tiles *were not made in any quantity until the reign of Süleyman the Magnificent (1520–66). Süleyman used İznik tiles to refurbish the Dome of the Rock in Jerusalem.*

Some of the best examples are seen in Istanbul's mosques, notably in the Süleymaniye (see pp90–91), Rüstem Paşa Mosque (pp88–9) and, here, in this example from the Blue Mosque (pp78–9).

Miniature depicting potters

Bursa ⑨

Basin, Museum of Turkish and Islamic Arts

Bursa extends in a swathe along the northern foothills of Mount Uludağ *(see p169)*. A settlement known as Prusa was reputedly established here in the 3rd century BC by Prusias I of Bithynia. However, it was the Romans who first spotted the potential of Bursa's mineral springs: today there are an estimated 3,000 baths in the city. In 1326 Bursa became the first capital of the Ottoman Empire, following its capture by Osman Gazi *(see p25)*.

View over the rooftops of the city of Bursa

Today Bursa is a provincial capital whose status as one of Turkey's foremost centres of commerce and industry is evident in its broad boulevards and busy shops and bazaars. Apart from the central market area *(see pp164–5)*, the most frequented sightseeing area is Yeşil, on the eastern side of the Gök River, where the Green Mosque and Green Tomb are the main attractions.

🄲 Yıldırım Beyazıt Mosque
Yıldırım Beyazıt Camii
Yıldırım Cad. ⬭ daily.
This mosque is named after Beyazıt I *(see p32)*, whose nickname was "Yıldırım", meaning "thunderbolt". This referred to the speed with which he reacted to his enemies. Built in 1389, just after Beyazıt became sultan, the mosque at first doubled as a lodge for Sufi dervishes *(see p104)*. It has a lovely portico with five domed bays.

Inside, the interior court (a covered "courtyard" in Bursa mosques, which prefigures the open courtyards preferred by later Ottoman architects) and prayer hall are divided by an impressive arch. This rises from two mihrab-like niches. The walls of the prayer hall itself are adorned with several bold and attractive pieces of calligraphic design *(see p95)*.

🄴 Green Tomb
Yeşil Türbe
Yeşil Cad. ⬭ daily. 🖾 donation.
The tomb of Mehmet I *(see p30)*, which stands elevated above the mosque among tall cypress trees, is one of the city's most prominent landmarks. It was built between 1414 and 1421. The tomb is much closer to the Seljuk *(see p21)* style of architecture than Classical Ottoman. Its exterior is covered in green tiles, although these are mainly 19th-century replacements for the original faïence. However, a few older tiles survive around the entrance portal.

The interior, entered through a pair of superbly carved wooden doors, is simply dazzling. The space is small and the ornamentation, covering a relatively large surface area, is breathtaking in its depth of colour and detail. The mihrab has especially intricate tile panels, including a representation of a mosque lamp hanging from a gold chain between two candles.

The sultan's magnificent sarcophagus is covered in exquisite tiles and adorned by a long Koranic inscription. Nearby sarcophagi contain the remains of his sons, daughters and nursemaid.

🄲 Green Mosque
Yeşil Cami
Yeşil Cad. ⬭ daily.
Bursa's most famous monument was commissioned by Mehmet I in 1412, but it remained unfinished at his death in 1421 and still lacks a portico. Nevertheless, it is the finest Ottoman mosque built before the conquest of Constantinople *(see p26)*.

The main portal is tall and elegant, with an intricately carved canopy. It opens into the entrance hall. Beyond this is an interior court, with a carved fountain at its centre. A flight of three steps leads up from here into the prayer hall. On either side of the steps are niches where worshippers once left their shoes *(see p39)*. Above the entrance to the court is the sultan's loge, resplendent in richly patterned tiles created using the *cuerda seca* technique. They are in beautiful greens, blues and yellows, with threads of gold which were added after firing.

The Green Tomb and Green Mosque, Bursa's most distinctive monuments

The tiling of the prayer hall was carried out by Ali Íbn Ilyas Ali, who learnt his art in Samarkand. It was the first time that tiles were used extensively in an Ottoman mosque and set a precedent for the later widespread use of Íznik tiles *(see p161)*. The tiles covering the walls of the prayer hall, which is well lit by floor-level windows, are simple, green and hexagonal. Against this plain backdrop, the effect of the mihrab is especially glorious. Predominantly turquoise, deep blue

and white, with touches of gold, the mihrab's tiles depict flowers, leaves, arabesques and geometric patterns. The mosque's exterior was also once clad in tiles, but they have since disappeared.

🏛 Museum of Turkish and Islamic Arts

Türk ve Islam Eserleri Müzesi Yeşil Cad. **Tel** (0224) 327 76 79. ◯ 9am–noon, 1–4:30pm Mon–Fri. 🖼
This museum is housed in a fine Ottoman building, the former *medrese (see p38)* of the Green Mosque. A colon-

VISITORS' CHECKLIST

90 km (60 miles) S of Istanbul.
🚉 1,995,000. ✈ 20 km (12 miles) NW. 🚌 Kıbrıs Şehitler Cad, (0224) 261 54 00. 🚎 Atatürk Cad; Osman Gazi Cad.
🛈 Ulucami Parkı, Orhangazi Altgeçidi, No. 1 (0224) 220 18 48. 🎭 Textiles Fair (mid-Apr); Bursa Festival (12 Jun–12 Jul).

nade surrounds its courtyard on three sides and the cells leading off from it, formerly used by the students, are now exhibition galleries. At the far end of the courtyard is the large, domed hall which was originally the main classroom.

Exhibits dating from the 12th–20th centuries include Seljuk and Ottoman ceramics, elaborately decorated Korans and costumes ranging from linen dervish robes to ornate wedding gowns. A display on Turkish baths *(see p67)* features embroidered towels and exotic high-heeled silver bath clogs. There is also a recreated setting of a traditional circumcision room, complete with a four-poster bed.

façade of the **Museum of Turkish and Islamic Arts**

BURSA CITY CENTRE

Alaeddin Mosque ⑦
Archaeological Museum ⑩
Green Mosque ③
Green Tomb ②
Hüsnü Züber House ⑨

Muradiye Mosque ⑧
Museum of Turkish
and Islamic Arts ④
Osman Gazi Tomb ⑥
Tophane Citadel ⑤
Yıldırım Beyazıt Mosque ①

KEY

🟦 Street-by-Street area
See pp164–5

ANKARA CAD
KIBRIS ŞEHITLER CAD

⑩ Archeological Museum
Kültür Parkı

0 metres 750
0 yards 750

Airport 🛫
20 km (12 miles)

ANKARA
ISTANBUL

Hüsnü Züber ⑨ House
⑧ Muradiye Mosque
ALTIPARMAK CAD
SAKARYA CAD

MURADIYE

HAŞIM IŞCAN CAD

HAŞIM IŞCAN CAD

① Yıldırım Beyazıt Mosque

⑥ Osman Gazi Tomb
⑤ Tophane Citadel
CUMHURIYET CAD

HASTALARYURDU CAD
ORTAPAZAR CAD

TOPHANE 🅳

UZUN ÇARŞI CAD

Museum of Turkish and Islamic Art

INCIRLI CAD

Alaeddin ⑦ Mosque
Çakir Ağa Hamamı

ATATÜRK CAD

④ ③ Green Mosque

② Green Tomb

YEŞIL

Key to Symbols *see back flap*

Bursa: The Market Area

Bursa's central market area is a warren of streets and ancient Ottoman courtyards (hans). The area is still central to Bursa's commercial activity and is a good place to experience the life of the city. Here too you can buy the local fabrics for which the town is famous, particularly handmade lace, towelling and silk. The silkworm was introduced to the Byzantine Empire in the 6th century and there is still a brisk trade in silk cocoons carried out in Koza Han all year round. Among the many other items on sale today are the lovely hand-painted, camel-skin Karagöz puppets (see p168).

★ **Covered Bazaar**
The great bazaar, built by Mehmet I in the 15th century, consists of a long hall with domed bays, adjoining by a high, vaulted hall. The Bedesten is home to jewellers' shops.

★ **The Great Mosque**
A three-tiered ablutions fountain stands beneath the central dome of this monumental mosque, which was erected in 1396–9.

Şengül Hamamı Turkish baths

FEVZI ÇAKMAK CAD

Bey Han (also called Emir Han) was built as part of the Orhan Gazi Mosque complex, to provide revenue for the mosque's upkeep.

Cafés

KOZA PAR

ATATÜRK CA

The Bey Hamamı (1339) is the oldest Turkish baths building in the world. It now houses workshops.

Koza Park
The gardens in front of Koza Han, with their fountains, benches and shaded café tables, are a popular meeting place for locals and visitors throughout the day.

★ Koza Han
This is the most attractive and fascinating building in the market area. Since it was built in 1491 by Beyazıt II, it has been central to the silk trade.

Geyve Han is also known as İvaz Paşa Han.

Fidan Han dates from around 1470, when it was built by a grand vizier of Mehmet the Conqueror.

İçkoza Han

Flower Market
The numerous bunches of flowers for sale in the streets around the town hall make a picturesque sight in the midst of Bursa's bustling market area.

0 metres	40
0 yards	40

RSA SOK

UZUN ÇARŞI CAD

ÇÖMLEK SOK

BELEDIYE CAD

STAR SIGHTS

★ Great Mosque

★ Covered Bazaar

★ Koza Han

The Belediye, Bursa's town hall, is a Swiss chalet-style, half-timbered building that forms a surprising landmark in the centre of the town.

Tourist information

KEY

– – – Suggested route

Orhan Gazi Mosque
Built in 1339, just 13 years after the Ottoman conquest of Bursa, this mosque is the oldest of the city's imperial mosques.

Bursa: Tophane and Muradiye

The clocktower in Tophane

Tophane, the most ancient part of Bursa, is distinguished by its clocktower which stands on top of a hill. This area was formerly the site of the citadel and is bounded by what remains of the original Byzantine walls. It is also known as Hisar, which means "fortress" in Turkish. If you continue westwards for 2 km (1mile), crossing the Cılımboz River, you come to the historic district of Muradiye. The 15th-century Muradiye Mosque, from which this suburb takes its name, is one of the most impressive royal mosque and tomb complexes in the city.

Exploring Tophane

Tophane's northern limit is marked by the best preserved section of the citadel walls, built on to an outcrop of rock. At the top is a pleasant park filled with cafés, which also contains the imposing clocktower and the tombs of the founders of the Ottoman dynasty. From here you can look down on the lower part of Tophane, where archetypal Ottoman houses still line many of the twisting streets. Pınarbaşı Kapısı, at Tophane's southern point, is the gate through which Orhan Gazi entered Bursa in 1326 *(see p25)*.

▣ Tophane Citadel
Hisar
Osman Gazi Cad. ◯ *daily.* ♿
The citadel walls can be viewed from a set of steps which lead uphill from the intersection of Cemal Nadir Caddesi and Atatürk Caddesi. These steps end at the tea gardens above. The citadel fell into Turkish hands when

Orhan Gazi's troops broke through its walls. Later, he built a wooden palace inside the citadel and had the old Byzantine ramparts refortified. The walls had until this era delimited the entire circumference of the ancient city. However, Orhan began to encourage Bursa's expansion and developed the present-day commercial heart of the city further to the east.

South of Hastalaryurdu Caddesi is an area notable for its old Ottoman houses *(see p61)*. Most of these have overhanging upper storeys. They consist of a timber frame filled in with adobe and plastered over, then painted in bright colours. Kaleiçi Sokağı, which can be reached down Karadut Sokağı from Hastalaryurdu Caddesi, is one of the best streets of such houses.

▣ Tombs of Osman and Orhan Gazi
Osman & Orhan Gazi Türbeleri
Ulu Cami Cad. ◯ *daily.* 📷 *donation.*
Osman Gazi began the process of Ottoman expansion in the 13th century *(see p25)* and attempted to capture Bursa. But it was his son, Orhan, who took the city just before his father died. Orhan brought his father's body to be buried in the baptistry of a converted church and he himself was later buried in the nave. The tombs that can be seen to-day date from 1868. They were rebuilt after the destruction of the church and the original tombs in an earthquake in 1855. Fragments of the church's mosaic floor survive inside the tomb of Orhan Gazi.

Tomb of Osman Gazi, the first great Ottoman leader

▣ Alaeddin Mosque
Alaeddin Camii
Alaeddin Mahallesi. ◯ *prayer times only.* 🚫
Further exploration in the Tophane area reveals the Alaeddin Mosque, the oldest in Bursa, built within 10 years of the city's conquest. It is in the form of a simple domed square, fronted by a portico of four Byzantine columns with capitals. The mosque was commissioned by Alaeddin Bey, brother of and vizier *(see p39)* to Orhan Gazi.

Exploring Muradiye
Muradiye is a leafy, largely residential district. Close to the Muradiye Mosque are the Hüsnü Züber House and the Ottoman House, two fine examples of traditional Turkish homes. To the north is a park, among the attractions of which are a boating lake and the Archaeological Museum.

▣ Muradiye Mosque
Muradiye Külliyesi
Murat II Cad. ◯ *daily.* 📷 *donation.*
This mosque complex was built by Murat II, father of Mehmet the Conqueror *(see p26)*, in the early 15th century. The mosque itself is preceded by a graceful domed portico.

Popular café in the park above the ancient citadel walls in Tophane

Octagonal tomb of Mustafa in the grounds of Muradiye Mosque

Its wooden door is finely carved and the interior decorated with early İznik tiles *(see p161)*. The *medrese*, beside the mosque, now serves as a dispensary. It is a perfectly square building, with cells surrounding a central garden courtyard. Its *dershane*, or main classroom, is richly tiled and adorned with an ornate brickwork façade.

The mosque garden, with its cypresses, well-tended flower beds and fountains, is one of Bursa's most tranquil retreats. Murat II was the last Ottoman sultan to be buried in Bursa and his mausoleum, standing in the garden beside the mosque and *medrese*, was completed in 1437. His earth-filled sarcophagus lies beneath an opening in the roof. The eaves above the tomb's 16th-century porch still retain their original painted decoration.

Muradiye Mosque, constructed by Murat II

There are 11 other tombs in the garden, several of which were built for murdered princes. One such is the tomb of Mustafa, a son of Süleyman the Magnificent, who was disposed of to clear the way for his younger brother, Selim II, "the Sot" *(see p76)*. According to an inscription, Selim had the octagonal mausoleum built for his brother. The interior is decorated with some particularly beautiful İznik tile panels depicting carnations, tulips and hyacinths. The tiles date from the best İznik period, the late 16th century.

Hüsnü Züber House

Hüsnü Züber Evi, Yaşayan Müze
Uzunyol Sok 3, Muradiye. **Tel** *(0224)*
221 35 42. ◻ *10am–midday, 1–5pm
Tue–Sun.* **Ottoman House**
temporarily closed.

Among the numerous well-preserved houses in the Muradiye district is the Hüsnü Züber House. This 150-year-old mansion has been opened as a museum by its present owner, the artist Hüsnü Züber. It was originally a guest house for visiting dignitaries, later becoming the Russian Consulate and, most recently, a private residence.

The house is an interesting example of vernacular architecture. The upper storey projects over the street in the traditional manner of Ottoman houses *(see p63)*. Overlooking the interior courtyard, which has rooms arranged around it on three sides, there is a loggia. Originally this would have been open, but it is now glazed. Meanwhile, inside the house, the decorative wooden ceilings (some with hand-painted borders) are particularly attractive.

Hüsnü Züber's private collection of carved wooden objects is now displayed here. These include spoons, musical instruments and even farming utensils. They are all decorated with Anatolian motifs by a unique technique of engraving by burning known as pyrogravure.

The 18th-century **Ottoman House** (Osmanlı Evi) stands on the square in front of the Muradiye Mosque. It is another fine house, but is closed to the public at present. The upper storey is adorned with elaborately patterned brickwork. Shutters and grilles hide the windows.

Hüsnü Züber House, dating from the mid-19th century

Archaeological Museum

Arkeoloji Müzesi
Kültür Parkı. **Tel** *(0224) 234 49 18.*
◻ *8am–midday, 1–5pm Tue–Sun.*
Finds dating from the third millennium BC up to the Ottoman conquest of Bursa are collected in this museum. In the first hall there are clasps, vessels and an inscription from the Phrygian period. Other exhibits include Roman and Hellenistic jewellery and ceramics, a number of Roman statues of Cybele, goddess of nature, and a Roman bronze of the god Apollo with strange, lifelike eyes. There are also displays of Byzantine religious objects and coins.

Bursa: Çekirge

With a name which translates literally as "Realm of the Crickets", Çekirge still earns Bursa the tag of yeşil, or "green", by which it is known in Turkey. This leafy western spa suburb of the city has attracted visitors to its mineral springs since Roman times. In the 6th century the Emperor Justinian (see p20) built a bathhouse here and his wife Theodora later arrived with a retinue of 4,000. Çekirge is also the location of most of the city's finest hotels and the area's hillside setting affords some spectacular views.

Çekirge's Old Spa, dating back to the 14th-century reign of Murat I

🅝 New Spa

Yeni Kaplıca
Mudanya Yolu 6. **Tel** (0224) 236 69 68. ◯ daily 5am–midnight.
Despite their name, the New Spa baths have a substantial pedigree. They were rebuilt in 1522 by Rüstem Paşa, grand vizier (see p29) to Süleyman the Magnificent (see p26). The sultan is said to have ordered their rebuilding in gratitude after his recovery from gout when bathing in the Byzantine baths that stood on this site.

The central pool is surrounded with bays adorned with beautiful but damaged İznik tiles (see p161). They are not open to women. Within the same complex, however, there are two other baths: the modern Kaynarca baths which is for women and the Karamustafa baths for couples.

🎏 Çelik Palas Hotel

Çelik Palas Otel
Çekirge Cad 79.
Tel (0224) 233 38 00.
This five-star hotel (see p191) stands on one of Bursa's main thoroughfares. Built in 1933, it is the city's oldest, most prestigious spa hotel. Atatürk (see pp30–31) frequented its baths. Open to both sexes, their centrepiece is an attractive circular pool in a domed marble room.

🅞 Old Spa

Eski Kaplıca
Hotel Kervansaray, Çekirge Meydanı, Kervansaray. **Tel** (0224) 233 93 00. ◯ 8am–10:30pm daily.
The Old Spa baths were established by Murat I in the late 14th century and renovated in 1512, during the reign of Beyazıt II. Remnants of an earlier building, said to date from the reign of Emperor Justinian (see p20), are also visible. These include some Byzantine columns and capitals in the hararet (steam room) of the men's section (see p67). You enter the baths through the new Kervansaray Termal Hotel. Spring water, said to cure skin diseases and rheumatism, bubbles into the central pool of both the men's and women's sections at 45 °C (113 °F). The women's baths are not as old or grand, but are still the most attractive women-only ones in Bursa.

🅒 Murat I Hüdavendigar Mosque

Murat I Hüdavendigar Camii
I. Murat Cad, Çekirge. ◯ daily.
Bursa's most unusual mosque was built for Murat I, self-styled Hüdavendigar, meaning "Creator of the Universe", in 1385. It is unlike any other mosque in the Ottoman world: its prayer hall is on the ground floor, with the medrese built around a second storey.

The façade looks more like that of a palace than a mosque, with a five-arched portico surmounted by a colonnade. This colonnade in turn has five sets of double-arched windows divided by Byzantine columns. Inside, the domed court and prayer hall rise through both storeys. The upper storey colonnade leads to the cells of the medrese. On this level, passageways lead around both sides of the mosque to a mysterious room, located over the mihrab, whose original purpose is unknown.

KARAGÖZ SHADOW PUPPETS

Suspended above Çekirge Caddesi is an imposing monument to the town's two famous scapegoats, Karagöz and Hacıvat. According to legend, these local clowns were executed in the 14th century for distracting their fellow workers while building the Orhan Gazi Mosque (see p165). It is said that Sultan Orhan (see p32) created a shadow play about them in remorse.

In fact, shadow puppet theatre arrived in Turkey later and is thought to have originated in Southeast Asia. Selim I is reported to have brought it back to Istanbul after his Egyptian campaign in 1517. The camel-skin puppets are 35–40 cm (14–16 in) high, brightly dyed and oiled to aid translucency. They are still made today and can be purchased in an antique shop in the Bedesten run by Şinasi Çelikkol, who also occasionally puts on shows.

Cadi, a witch in the Karagöz puppet shows

Uludağ National Park, a popular ski resort in winter

Uludağ National Park

Uludağ Milli Parkı

100 km (60 miles) S of Istanbul.
Tel (0224) 283 21 97. 🚠 *Teleferik to Sarıalan, then dolmuş.* ⬤ *daily.* 🅿 *only for vehicles.*

One of a number of Turkish mountains to claim the title of Mount Olympus, Uludağ was believed by the Bithynians (of northwest Asia Minor) to be the home of the gods. In the Byzantine era, it was home to several monastic orders. After the Ottoman conquest of Bursa, Muslim dervishes *(see p104)* moved into their abandoned monasteries. Nowadays, however, no traces of Uludağ's former religious communities remain.

A visit to Uludağ National Park is especially enjoyable in spring or summer, when its alpine heights are relatively cool and it becomes a popular picnic area. The park includes 27,000 acres (67,000 hectares) of woodland. As you ascend, the deciduous beech, oak and hazel gradually give way to juniper and aspen, and finally to dwarf junipers. In spring, hyacinths and crocuses blanket the wooded slopes.

In winter, Uludağ is transformed into Turkey's most fashionable ski resort. The industry centres on the Oteller region, which has good alpine-style hotels.

Osman Gazi *(see p25)* is supposed to have founded seven villages for his seven sons and their brides in the Bursa region. **Cumalıkızık**, on the lower slopes of Uludağ, is the most perfectly preserved of the five surviving villages and is now registered as a national monument. Among its houses are many 750-year-old semi-timbered buildings. The village can be reached by minibus from Bursa.

Bird Paradise National Park

Kuşcenneti Milli Parkı

115 km (70 miles) SW of Istanbul.
Tel (0266) 735 54 22. 🅳 *from Bandırma.* ⬤ *8am–8pm daily.* ♿

An estimated 255 species of birds visit Bird Paradise National Park at the edge of Kuş Gölü, the lake formerly known as Manyas Gölü. Located on the great migratory paths between Europe and Asia, the park is a happy combination of plant cover, reed beds and a lake that supports at least 20 species of fish.

At the entrance to the park, there is a small museum with displays about various birds.

Spoonbill wading in the lake at Bird Paradise National Park

Binoculars are provided at the desk and visitors make their way to an observation tower.

Two main groups of birds visit the lake: those that come here to breed (March–July), and those which pass by during migration, either heading south (November) or north (April–May). Among the numerous different birds that breed around the lake are the endangered Dalmatian pelican, the great crested grebe, cormorants, herons, bitterns and spoonbills. The migratory birds, which can be seen in spring and autumn, include storks, cranes, pelicans and birds of prey such as sparrowhawks and spotted eagles.

Sandy beach on Avşa, the most popular of the Marmara Islands

Marmara Islands

Marmara Adaları

120 km (75 miles) SW of Istanbul.
🚢 *from Yenikapı.* 🛈 *Neyire Sıtkı Cad 31/3, Erdek, (0266) 835 11 69.*

This beautiful archipelago in the Sea of Marmara is a popular destination with Turkish holiday-makers, particularly with residents of Istanbul.

The loveliest of the islands is Avşa, whose sandy beaches and regular summer ferry service make it popular with Turks and, increasingly, foreign tourists. The ferry arrives at Türkeli on the west coast. Transport to the most popular beach, at Maviköy, is by a tractor-pulled train.

Marmara, the largest island, has one beach, north of Marmara village at Çınarlı. It is famous for producing the prized Proconnesian marble.

The Dardanelles ⓫

Çanakkale Boğazı

200 km (125 miles) SW of Istanbul.
🚗 *Çanakkale–Eceabat car ferry.*
🚌 *Çanakkale.* ℹ️ *Çanakkale İskele Meydanı 27, (0286) 217 11 87.*

LOCATOR MAP

Anzac Cove ③
Çanakkale ⑥
Cape Helles ⑦
Chunuk Bair ②
Kabatepe Visitors'
  Centre ④
National Park Information
  Centre ⑤
Suvla Bay ①

KEY

☐   Area of war memorials

▬   Road

---   Ferry route

Named after Dardanus, an ancient king of Çanakkale, the Dardanelles are the straits that link the Aegean Sea to the Sea of Marmara, and which separate European Turkey from Asia. Some 40 km (25 miles) long and narrowing to little more than a kilometre (half a mile) wide, they are steeped in legend and have been of strategic importance for thousands of years. In modern times they are probably best known as the setting for a disastrous Allied campaign during World War I.

The classical name for this channel of water was the Hellespont. According to legend, the Greek goddess Helle fell into the straits from the back of a golden winged ram. In another tale, the lovelorn Leander swam nightly across the Hellespont to meet his lover, Hero, until one night he drowned. The English Romantic poet Byron swam across the straits in 1810, in emulation of Leander, and remarked on the hazardous nature of the currents.

Çanakkale, the old town at the mouth of the Dardanelles, has two museums. The **Military and Naval Museum** is a short walk from the ferry docks. Its collection includes a pocket watch that saved the

The Çanakkale Şehitleri Memorial, honouring the Turkish dead

life of Atatürk *(see pp30–31)* when he was hit by shrapnel. The **Archaeological Museum**, south of the town centre, has exhibits from ancient Troy.

To the west is the beautiful **Gallipoli** (Gelibolu) **Peninsula**. Part of this land is a national park, with an information centre near Eceabat. The peninsula, which is now quite tranquil, was the scene of horrific battles that took place in 1915. The objectives of the Allied forces' invasion of Gallipoli were to capture Istanbul, force Turkey into submission and open a strategic supply route to Russia. The campaign began on 25 April 1915 with the landings of British and French troops at **Cape Helles**, and the Anzacs (Australian and New Zealand forces) at what they thought was the beach at Kabatepe. But currents had swept the Anzac force about 1.5 km (1mile) to the north, to a place now known as **Anzac Cove**, near Arı Burnu. Here they were faced with unknown and tough terrain, including a cliff.

The Turks managed to retain the high ground of **Chunuk Bair**. The battle here lasted three days, during which 28,000 men were

killed. When the Allied forces failed to make headway, more British troops landed at **Suvla Bay** on 6 August. This new offensive might have been successful, but Allied intelligence continually underestimated the Turks and the difficult ground. The terrible slaughter of deadlocked trench warfare continued until the Allies were finally evacuated on 19 December. More than 500,000 Allied and Turkish troops lost their lives and the whole peninsula is scattered with battlefield sites and war memorials.

Mehmetcik Memorial near Anzac Cove

The best place to begin a tour of the war memorials and cemeteries is at the **Kabatepe Visitors' Centre**, which houses a small collection of memorabilia including weapons, uniforms and soldiers' poignant letters home. North of here, near Anzac Cove, are several cemeteries and monuments. Chunuk Bair, now a peaceful pine grove above the beaches, has a memorial to the New Zealanders who died and some reconstructed Turkish trenches. The British Memorial is at Cape Helles, on the peninsula's tip. Further east along the coast stand both the French Memorial and the vast Çanakkale Şehitleri Memorial to the Turks who died defending Gallipoli.

🏛 **Military Museum**
Çimenlik Kalesi, Çanakkale. *Tel (0286) 217 24 60.* ◻ *9am–noon, 1:30–5:30pm Tue, Wed & Fri–Sun.* 📷

🏛 **Archaeological Museum**
Atatürk Cad, Çanakkale. *Tel (0286) 217 67 40.* ◻ *call for opening times.* 📷

🅷 **National Park Information Centre**
Near Eceabat. *Tel (0286) 814 11 28.* ◻ *9am–6pm Mon–Fri.* ***Park*** ◻ *daily.* 📷

🅷 **Kabatepe Visitors' Centre**
Near Kabatepe. *Tel (0286) 814 12 97.* ◻ *9am–6pm daily.* 📷

Troy ⑭
Truva

350 km (220 miles) SW of Istanbul. 🚌 *from Çanakkale.* 🅷 *Çanakkale İskele Meydanı 27, (0286) 217 11 87.* ◻ *8am–7pm daily (Nov–Apr: until 5pm).* 📷

Model of the legendary wooden horse at Troy

In Homer's epic poem, the *Iliad*, the city of Troy is besieged by the Greeks for ten years. For centuries Troy was assumed by many to be as mythical as Achilles, Hector and the other heroes in the tale. But a handful of 19th-century archaeologists were convinced that Homer had based his story on the events that happened to a real city and that traces of it could be found by searching near the Dardanelles. In 1865 British Consul Frank Calvert began investigating some ruins in Hisarlık. This interested the German archaeologist Heinrich Schliemann who soon found evidence of an ancient city resembling the layout of Homer's Troy. Over the last hundred years most historians have come to accept that this city must at least have inspired Homer, and was possibly even called Troy and besieged at the time specified in the story.

The settlement mound in fact has nine distinct levels (labelled Troy I–IX) representing 3,000 years of habitation. Sadly, the remains are sparse, and it takes some imagination to evoke an image of a city. Many structures were made of mud bricks and obviously levelled before new settlements were built on top.

The city Homer refers to is probably Troy VI (1800–1250 BC), while the Greek and Roman levels, when the city was known as Ilion, are Troy VIII (700–300 BC) and Troy IX (300 BC–AD 1) respectively.

What has survived includes a defence wall, palaces and houses from various periods, two sanctuaries (probably 8th century BC) and a Roman theatre. The grandest dwelling is the Pillar House, near the southern gate. Some believe this is the Palace of King Priam mentioned in the *Iliad*.

More conspicuous is a re-creation of the wooden horse, inside which a small group of the Greeks supposedly hid. There is also a visitors' centre with a video and a scale model of the site.

SCHLIEMANN'S SEARCH FOR ANCIENT TROY

Heinrich Schliemann used a fortune amassed in business to realize his life-long dream of discovering ancient Troy. He began excavating some likely sites in the 1860s and started

Schliemann's wife wearing some of the excavated treasure

on the ruins at Hisarlık in 1870. An amateur, Schliemann drove a great trench through the mound, destroying some walls in his haste. He soon claimed to have found Troy, though he knew not all his findings pointed to this. His greatest find – a hoard of gold and silver jewellery that he smuggled to Germany, calling it "Priam's Treasure" *(see p64)* – pre-dates Homer's Troy by 1,000 years. Some of the treasure disappeared after World War II only to reappear spectacularly in Moscow in August 1994.

THREE GUIDED WALKS

With its frenetic atmosphere, traditional cafés at almost every corner and historic sights from centuries of different rulers, Istanbul is a wonderful city for walkers.

On the following five pages are routes for three walks that take you through three different areas of Istanbul. They will take you past many of the most interesting sights. The areas covered range from the old Greek and Jewish neighbourhoods of Balat and Fener, where historic synagogues can still be seen amid traditional tripe shops, to the wonderful aromas of coffee, spices and fresh fish permeating

Istanbul Modern Art Museum sign

the air in the Galata region of the city. For a little more elegance, a stroll along İstiklâl Caddesi will confirm why this area of Istanbul has the reputation for celebrating its European side, rather than Asian, while the Istanbul Modern Art Museum *(see p107)* is the finest venue in the city for contemporary art. All the walks are intended to be done at a leisurely pace, and there are plenty of suggestions for refreshment stops along each route. In addition to these walks, each of the four areas of Istanbul described in the *Area-by-Area* section of this book has a walk on its *Street-by-Street* map.

CHOOSING A WALK

Spices from the Grand Bazaar in Galata
(see pp98–9)

The Three Walks
This map shows the location of the three guided walks in relation to the main sightseeing areas of Istanbul.

The Beyoğlu district seen from the Golden Horn
(see p100–107)

Beyoğlu

Taksim to the Istanbul Modern
(pp176–7)

Balat and Fener
(p173)

Beyazit to Galata
(pp174–5)

Seraglio Point

The Bazaar Quarter

Sultanahmet

0 kilometres   1

0 miles   1

KEY

•••••• Walk route

A 45-Minute Walk in Balat and Fener

The Balat and Fener neighbourhoods epitomize the cultural diversity and tolerance that was the hallmark of the Ottomans. Fener was predominantly a Greek area, while Balat was Jewish, and this walk guides you around the ancient churches, synagogues, Turkish baths and mosques in the atmospheric back streets. They may have seen better days, but a rejuvenation scheme is putting life back into this picturesque locality.

TIPS FOR WALKERS

Starting point: *Ahrida Synagogue.*
Length: *1.5 km (1 mile)*
Getting there: *From Eminönü bus terminus, take No 99 or any bus displaying Eyüp or Ayvansaray. Ask the driver to let you off at Balat. There are also ferry points at Fener and Balat.*
Stopping-off points: *Hotel Daphnis* ⑬ *is a good spot to stop for a meal.*

Hotel Daphnis ⑬

This walk starts in the heart of Balat at the Ahrida Synagogue ① *(see p110)*, founded before the Ottoman conquest in 1453. It has been restored many times, most recently in 1992. The 19th-century Yanbol synagogue ②, however, is now boarded up but its position indicates its former significance. The Church of Holy Angels ③ dates from Byzantine times. Below it flows a sacred spring and every 14 September supplicants of all religions gather here to pray for cures from their ailments.

Walk to Leblebiciler Sokak and on the right at No. 51 is Merkez şekerci ④, a sweet shop since the 1870s. Further along is Agora ⑤, Istanbul's oldest tavern *(meyhane).* Turn left on Hızır Çavuş Köprü Sokak and continue down this road until you reach

KEY

• • • Walk route

⚓ Ferry boarding point

0 metres 250
0 yards 250

Köfteci Arnavut ⑥. This traditional meatball restaurant has been serving its loyal customers since 1947.

Turn right and then left on to Vodina Caddesi and on your right is Tahtalı Minare Hamam ⑦, one of the oldest Turkish baths in the city, dating from the 1500s. Note the boiler room chimney on the roof. A short distance further on your right is Tahtalı Minare Mosque ⑧, built by Fatih Sultan Mehmet II in 1458. Next door is the Tomb

of Hazreti Hüseyin Sadık ⑨, who was buried as a *gazi* (warrior of the faith) in the 1450s. Continue down the road and you will be able to see the cross of Aya Yorgi Metokhi Church ⑩ (no public access) above its high wall.

At the end of the road turn left and on the right is the Greek Orthodox Patriarchate ⑪ *(see p111)*, seat of the Greek church since 1601. Look at the red-brick building on the ramparts above. This is the Fener Greek Boys High School ⑫, established in Byzantine times. On the left is the Hotel Daphnis ⑬. Turn left onto Abdülezel Paşa Caddesi and the stone building on your right is the Women's Library ⑭, the city's sole female-only information centre. Further up is the Church of St Stephen of the Bulgars ⑮ *(see p110)*. From here the Fener ferry point will take you back to the city centre.

Back streets of the Balat district

A 90-Minute Walk from Taksim Square to the Istanbul Modern Art Museum

It was in the Pera district that Constantinople's cosmopolitan population lived and worked in the 19th century, where the embassies and palatial residences mirrored the lifestyle of Topkapı Palace, on the opposite side of the Golden Horn. Once known as the "Paris of the East", life centred on the main street of Pera, today's İstiklâl Caddesi. Even today the Avrupa Pasajı and Balık Pazar markets seem wistfully unchanged, especially when contrasted with the remarkable Pera Museum and the sophisticated Istanbul Modern Art Museum.

A Çiçek Pasajı restaurant ④

Avrupa Pasajı bazaar ⑥

Along İstiklâl Caddesi

Begin the walk in Taksim Square ① at the Independence Monument, completed by Pietro Canonica in 1928, that depicts Atatürk with his political contemporaries. Before following the vintage tram line down İstiklâl Caddesi, have a look at the octagonal stone tower, known as the Maksem ②, on the corner of Taksim Caddesi. Dating from 1832, it was once used as a reservoir – you can still see carved bird houses and remains of a fountain. On your right is the French Cultural Centre, while on the left, further down at No. 127 is a traditional sweet shop, Hacı Bekir, dating from 1777. Saray Muhallebicisi ③ is perfect for a coffee break and a chance to sample one of the renowned pastries.

Market shopping

Pass Yeşilçam Sokak, the home of Turkish cinema, and at Şarabi Wine House, turn into the former flower market, Çiçek Pasajı ④, built by Italian architect Michel Capello in 1856, and now filled with restaurants. At Stop Restaurant, veer left then right on Şahne Sokak, which forms the backbone of the Fish Market, or Balık Pazar ⑤.

Return along Sahne Sokak and stroll down the arcaded Hall of Mirrors, or Avrupa Pasajı ⑥ on the right. The Neo-Renaissance interior, with marble floors and classical statues, was once lit by gas lamps and mirrors amplified the light.

Turn right and then left onto Meşrutiyet Caddesi and follow the road around to the left with the British Consulate General ⑦ on your right. Follow this street down, past TRT (Turkish Radio and Television) and the celebrated but now faded Grand Hotel de Londres until

you reach the exquisite Pera Museum ⑧ (once the Bristol Hotel), where the philanthropic Koç family exhibits their art collection and Turkish tiles.

Dome of the Kılıç Ali Pasa Mosque ⑮

Historic buildings

Walk through the Odakule Arkade and turn left on to İstiklâl Caddesi. Opposite the Galatasaray High School is the Old Beyoğlu Post Office ⑨. A campaign to keep it open was unsuccessful and the Baroque marble building was closed in 1998. Originally a wealthy merchant's residence, it still has an ornamental fountain in the penthouse.

Take the second right onto Tornacıbaşı Sokak,

Istanbul Modern Art Museum ⑳

which takes you past the Greek Orthodox school, Zografyon ⑩ on the left. In front of you is Galatasaray Hamamı ⑪, Turkish baths built in 1481 and in use ever since.

Take the steep cobbled street that descends beside the Turkish baths, Çapanoğlu Sokak, which becomes a staircase at the bottom. Turn right onto Harbiye Sokak and you will reach French Street, or Fransız Sokağı ⑫ on the left, where an elegant French ambience meets classy Beyoğlu. Enjoy lunch or a glass of wine at one of the French-style cafés.

Refreshed, continue along French Street and at the end turn right onto Boğazkesen Caddesi and continue left down the hill until you reach Tomtom Kaptan Mosque ⑬. The 17th-century fountain here, which was once a grand landmark, is now sadly neglected.

Interior of the Tophane foundry ⑮

TIPS FOR WALKERS

Starting point: Taksim Square
Length: 2.5 km (1.5 miles)
Getting there: From Sultanahmet, a city bus goes regularly from outside Haghia Sophia direct to Taksim Square. Or take the Tünel funicular train up the hill from Karaköy, then travel up İstiklâl Caddesi by nostalgic tram to Taksim Square.
Stopping-off points: The fish market on Sahne Sokak has lots of cheerful eateries. French Street is ideal for an elegant drink.

Shopping and museums

Çukurcuma Caddesi and Tomtom Kaptan Sokak intersect here and both have curio shops such as Tüterler ⑭ at No. 186. At the bottom of this street on the corner of Defterdar Yokuşu is the Tophane ⑮, once an Ottoman cannon foundry.

Cross Necatibey Caddesi over the tramline to the 16th-century Kılıç Ali Paşa Mosque ⑯ *(see p106)*, one of the last masterpieces of architect Mimar Sinan. Opposite is the Tophane fountain ⑰ *(see p106)* built in 1732, which now bestows locally bottled drinking water. From here you can also see the Baroque Clock Tower ⑱.

Continue left along Salı Pazarı ⑲ with its shops, restaurants and *narghile* (pipe) smokers. A sign directs you to the Istanbul Modern Art Museum ⑳ *(see p107)*, with its collection of contemporary Turkish art.

To get back to the city centre, catch the west-bound tram which takes you directly back to Sultanahmet over the Galata Bridge.

Pera Museum ⑧

A 90-Minute Walk from Beyazit to Galata

Istanbul is a seductive mix of ancient and modern, religious and secular, and this walk will give you a flavour of both. Starting at Beyazit Tower in the city's historic quarter, the route takes you through narrow shopping streets brimming with energy, over the Galata Bridge with its stunning views of the Bosphorus, to the Beyoğlu district and trendy Tünel area, where the shops, bars and cafés lend Istanbul its chic reputation.

Striking façade of Sülemaniye Mosque

Mimar Sinan architecture

Start at Sami Onar Cadessi, from where you can see the striking Beyazit Tower ①, also visible from much of the surrounding area. It was built in 1828 as a fire watch and stands in the grounds of Istanbul University ②, which once served as the Ministry of War and whose huge, ornamental gates are a worthy photographic subject in

TIPS FOR WALKERS

Starting point: *Beyazit Tower,*
Length: *1 km (0.5 miles)*
Getting there: *Get off at Beyazit on the tramway that runs from Zeytinburnu near the airport to Eminönü, or take either the T4 or 61B bus, both of which run from Taksim to Sultanahmet.*
Stopping off points: *You are never far from a café or bar in Istanbul, but the obvious halfway stopping off point is at one of the numerous cafés or bars on Galata Bridge. The Tünel district also has plenty of elegant taverns (meyhanes) and restaurants if you want to end your walk with a leisurely lunch or dinner or ponder over a glass of wine.*

themselves. Take a right up Prof Siddik Sokak past the stunning Sülemaniye Mosque ③ *(see pp90–91)*. This breathtaking structure was completed in 1557 by the architect Mimar Sinan *(see p91)*. Keep going until you reach Sifahane Sokak. Turn right into the street and, if you are feeling peckish or thirsty, you can make a pit stop at historic Dârüzziyafe restaurant ④, with its 16th-century detailing, housed in the former soup kitchens of the Sülemaniye Mosque *(see p201)*.

Turn right on to Mimar Sinan Caddesi and at the bottom of the street, on the corner in front of you, is the tomb of the architect Mimar Sinan ⑤ – a poignant tribute to the great man even if its design is a little humble compared to his own creations.

Coffee and spices

Turn left onto Ismetiye Caddesi and then left again on to Uzunçarsi Caddesi. Walk to the end of the street until you reach bustling Tahtakale Caddesi, where you can jostle with the locals who come here to shop for bargains on everything from electronic goods to clothing. On the right is the Tahtakale Hamami Çarsisi ⑥, a 500-year-old Turkish bathhouse that has been renovated and turned into a shopping centre. There is also a lovely café under the domed roof where you can stop to refuel.

Turn down any of the side streets to the left and you will come to Hasircilar Caddesi ⑦ famed for its spice shops, coffee stalls and delis. Walk towards the end of the street, turn left on to Tahmis Caddes

and you will reach Kurukahreci Mehmet Efendi ⑧, a traditional coffee shop, opened in 1871, famous for its range of blends.

Galata Bridge

Walk to Galata Bridge ⑨ for fantastic views of the city. You can either stroll across the top and watch the many amateur fishermen suspending their rods into

Fishermen hoping for a catch on Galata Bridge

Coffee machine, Kurukahveci Mehmet Efendi ⑧

KEY

•• Walk route

▦ Funicular stop

meters   250

yards   250

he water below in hope of a catch, or go down the steps and walk along the lower deck, where there are a number of cafés, bars and restaurants. After a leisurely moment spent taking in the breathtaking views of the Bosphorus below, continue to the bustling and aromatic Karaköy fish market ⑩, where you can buy some of the freshest, cheapest fish Istanbul has to offer.

Judaism to Islam

Walk up Harraççi Ali Sokak until you reach the Jewish Museum ⑪ on Karaköy Meydani. This 17th-century museum, once a synagogue, now contains a fascinating collection of old photographs, documents and religious objects relating to the city's Jewish population.

From here, walk up Camekan Sokak to the Gothic-looking Beyoğlu Hospital ⑫, built in 1904 as a British naval hospital. Continue until you come to the Galata Tower ⑬ *(see p105)* in Galata Square, the focal point of the district. The 360° viewing deck at the top of the tower gives the perfect vantage point from which to see almost the entire city laid out before you.

Now turn right and left on to Yüsek Kaldirim Caddesi ⑭, a steep cobblestone street lined with music shops selling just about every conceivable musical instrument you can think of,

both traditional and hi-tech. Tucked away off to the right on Galip Dede Caddesi is the Mevlevi Monastery ⑮ *(see p104)*, once home to the Whirling Dervishes.

Chic Tünel

At the top of the street, at Tünel Square, you have the option to catch the underground funicular ⑯ back down to Karaköy. The one-stop subway was opened in 1876 and is the third-oldest underground system in the world after London and New York. However do not miss the opportunity to experience this fashionable neighbourhood. Just opposite the funicular is Tünel Gecedi, an open-air passage lined with Ottoman buildings, most of which have now been turned into apartments with shops and cafés at ground level. For a refreshing iced coffee in sumptuous Viennese-style surroundings, pop into the KV restaurant ⑰, before making your way to ARtrium ⑱ to pick up a high-class antique.

To get back to the city centre, from Tünel square you can catch buses 46H and 47 across the Golden Horn to the Sultanahmet district. Alternatively you can head to the ferry port of Kasımpaşa and take a ferry to the Haliç Hatti stop across the water.

Fresh fish at the Karaköy fish market

TRAVELLERS' NEEDS

WHERE TO STAY

Whether you feel like staying in an Ottoman palace, taking a room in a restored mansion or traditional wooden house, or even spending a night in a converted prison, you will find the hotel of your choice in Istanbul. Following a recent boom in tourism, the city's hotels and guesthouses now cater for every taste, as well as all budgets. Hotels tend to be clustered around Istanbul's main sightseeing areas. Sultanahmet contains many of the city's historic hotels, guesthouses and

Doorman at
Hilton *(p190)*

new boutique hotels. Beyoğlu, across the Golden Horn, is a good place to look for three- and four-star hotels, including the grand old hotels of the 19th century. The hotels listed on pages 184–91 have been chosen from the best the city can offer across all price ranges. Each hotel is given a brief description and details are provided about the facilities available. Also check the website www.istanbulhotels.com on the internet. Information on other types of accommodation is on page 183.

CHOOSING A HOTEL

Many hotels in Istanbul are rated by the Ministry of Culture and Tourism according to a star system. They range from comfortable but basic one-star hotels to five-star luxury hotels. Other types of accommodation licensed by the Ministry are the converted buildings known as Special Licence hotels. A further category is the accommodation licensed by the Greater Istanbul Municipality. These hotels provide perfectly reasonable facilities, but with less stringent standards.

Accommodation is available in most central areas of the city. The Sultanahmet district is conveniently situated within walking distance of most of the city's major sights. Many of the Special Licence hotels in this area are tucked away on residential side streets. There are guesthouses along Divan-

Lounge of the Ceylan Intercontinental Hotel in Taksim *(see p189)*

yolu Caddesi, the main through road, and on the slopes leading down to the Sea of Marmara. There are also middle-range hotels in central Sultanahmet.

A short tram ride west from Sultanahmet are the Beyazıt, Laleli and Aksaray districts, which are packed with one-, two- and three-star hotels. The cheaper hotels here are used mostly by Central Asian and Russian traders, while many of the three-star hotels cater for package tour groups.

Beyoğlu and Taksim, the old European centre of Istanbul, are within easy reach of the best sights in the city. Both have innumerable cheap hotels that are comfortable and dependable, as well as international chain hotels.

The Asian side of Istanbul is a mainly residential area but also contains some hotels. There are also hotels in Kadıköy, which are used more by Turks than foreigners and tourists.

The luxurious Four Seasons Hotel, formerly a prison *(see p187)*

LUXURY HOTELS

There has been a rapid growth in the number of luxury hotels in the city, and most international chains are now represented in Istanbul. Almost all five-star hotels boast spectacular Marmara or Bosphorus views, and between them they have some of the best international restaurants in the city. All the major hotels have swimming pools and health clubs. Many of them also have Turkish baths. Conference facilities are provided, and many hotels have extensive entertainment facilities. Most can also arrange tours of Istanbul and nearby places through local companies. Most of the hotels now have floors where smoking is forbidden. They also provide facilities for the disabled, arrange special activities for children *(see p182)* and have wireless internet in all rooms.

◁ Freshly fried fish sandwiches being prepared on a boat in Eminönü *(see p208)*

SPECIAL LICENCE HOTELS

In recent years, a number of old buildings have been renovated and transformed into hotels. However, due to the nature of the buildings in which they are housed, some of these hotels cannot provide facilities such as lifts. They belong to a separate category, the Special Licence hotel, and are under private management.

The Special Licence hotels constitute some of Istanbul's most interesting and attractive hotels. They are often located in the residential streets of historic areas, and range from small, modestly priced traditional wooden houses to luxury Ottoman mansions. Special Licence hotels, whether large or small, are generally of a high standard. The authentic period decor of

Latticed window of a Special Licence hotel

many of them gives even the larger ones a cosy atmosphere. A number of Special Licence hotels exist only as a result of the strenuous efforts of the Turkish Touring and Automobile Club (the TTOK, *see p245*). Led by its former crusading director, Çelik Gülersoy, it has successfully

Yeşil Ev *(see p186)*, a Special Licence hotel

preserved the Ottoman atmosphere of parts of the city by saving old buildings from demolition and restoring them. Its work can be seen particularly in the Special Licence hotels of Soğukçeşme Sokağı *(see p61)*. Increasingly, many of the city's newly opened boutique-style hotels are choosing not to apply for official ratings or stars. This does not, however, imply any lack of standards or amenities. In fact, these establishments are contributing to the continually rising standards of accommodation. All have their own websites where you can take a virtual tour and compare prices and facilities.

CHEAPER HOTELS

Istanbul has plenty of cheap, comfortable accommodation which meets the standards of the Turkish Ministry of Culture and Tourism. When choosing a cheaper hotel, however, do not base your decision on the façade or lobby, which may look brand new.

One-star hotels provide the most basic facilities, but often have rooms with a private shower and toilet. Two- and three-star hotels have more comfortable rooms and usually a café or bar. Many three-star hotels offer rooms with a TV and mini-bar.

Guesthouses vary in terms of facilities. Most provide bed-linen and towels, and the better ones will have rooms with ensuite bathrooms. All should have communal cooking

Hotel roof terrace overlooking Sultanahmet

facilities. While cheaper hotels usually have central heating they are unlikely to have air conditioning, but an electric fan may be provided. Some small hotels may not provide hot water 24 hours a day.

WHAT TO EXPECT

All hotels listed in this book are comfortable and welcoming. Front desk staff usually speak English, and will be able to give information on sights and travel.

Hotel rooms in Istanbul generally have two single beds, and enough space to add a third one if need be. If you want a double bed you should make this clear when book-ing or checking in.

Most hotels with three or more storeys will have a lift. There may not be a lift in a Special Licence hotel, however, because of the problems of installing one in an older building. Facilities for wheelchair users are increasingly found in hotels.

Noise can be a problem even in some smart hotels, so in busy areas choose a room that doesn't face on to a main street. If you are not satisfied with your room, you can always ask for another.

Breakfast *(see p194)* is included in the price of the room and typically consists of a generous open buffet, including cold meats, fruits, cereals and yoghurt. Many larger hotels have restaurants that serve à la carte meals. Upmarket hotels have at least one dining room serving evening meals, but some of the smaller, cheaper hotels do not. It is a good idea to check when booking and confirm by email or fax.

Reception desk at the Istanbul Hilton *(see p190)*

PRICES AND DISCOUNTS

Hotel prices are quoted in euros or New Turkish Lira (YTL) and sometimes in US dollars. Prices are per room not per person. All prices usually include breakfast, and tax. Apart from top-class hotels, which have standard prices that do not change throughout the year, tariffs differ according to the season. The busy season, when hotel prices tend to be at their highest, is from April to the end of October. During the brief Christmas and New Year period, the higher summer tariffs are applied. There are no single rooms, but all hotels offer a single room rate of slightly more than half the price of a double room.

Lounge area of the Empress Zoe *(see p185)*

It is always worth attempting to bargain with hotels, but do not expect to get a discount. For longer stays of a week or more you may be able to get a reduction. Some hotels also offer discounts for internet bookings, cash payments, or out-of-season stays. However, do not expect a room with any kind of view if you have got it at a discount.

BOOKING A ROOM

While you will always be able to find a room of a reasonable standard, it is advisable to book in advance for the best hotels or those of your choice during the busy season. You can book any hotel listed in this guide directly, by telephone, fax and e-mail. Many hotels also have their own website registration forms. You may be asked to give your credit card details, which will guarantee your reservation. If you cannot find a place in any of the hotels that fall in your preferred price range, try one of the established travel companies based in Istanbul, such as **Meptur**, **Plan Tours** *(see p228)* or **Vip Tourism**. If you arrive without having reserved a room, the tourist information offices *(see p229)* in the airport, Sirkeci Station, Sultanahmet Square or Karaköy International Maritime Terminal will help you find a hotel, but they will not make a reservation for you.

CHECKING OUT AND PAYING

Guests are expected to check out by midday, but hotels will usually keep luggage for collection later. All hotels accept the major credit cards, as well as Turkish lira and other currencies. VAT is always included in the room price although, leave a few dollars, or its equivalent, in the room for the cleaner, and give a tip to the receptionist to be divided among the staff. Phone calls and mini-bar drinks can add to the size of your bill.

CHILDREN

Children up to six years old are often not charged for rooms, and pay 50% until 12 years old. It is possible to negotiate a discount for older children who share a room with their parents. Most hotels also have cots for babies.

Some hotels arrange special entertainment for children. The Swissôtel *(see p190)* offers a weekend package.

HOSTELS

For those on a tight budget, Istanbul has a number of inexpensive hostels, mostly in the Sultanahmet area. The best known, which has been a firm favourite for several decades, is the **Yücelt Interyouth Hostel**. This hostel is right in the heart of the Sultanahmet district, on a peaceful, tree-lined street beside Haghia Sophia and literally next door to the Haghia Sophia Museum.

Double room in the Special Licence Kariye Hotel *(see p189)*

Guests in the Yücelt Interyouth Hostel

Yücelt was established in 1965 with the specific aim of providing accommodation for the younger and more independent travellers on a restricted budget. It was often the first choice of travellers on the hippy trail in the 1970s. It is still a popular and friendly hostel, offering 320 beds in dormitories, or in more expensive, but less-crowded, rooms (single, double and triple rooms are available). All rooms have heating. Yücelt is a member of the International Youth Hostel Federation (IYHF) and offers a discount for members. The hostel has a wealth of facilities, including hot-water showers, a laundry, a safe, a luggage room, an internet room, a cafeteria and even a bar and disco. Nearby, on Akbıyık Caddesi, the **Orient Guesthouse** is a modern youth hostel with excellent facilities, including a rooftop café, a bar and a safe.

The tour operator Gençtur (*see p229*) is also affiliated to the IYHF and can provide detailed information on additional hostels in the city.

CAMPING

Camping and caravanning in Turkey have steadily gained popularity in recent years. There is an ever-increasing variety of excellent camping places with self-catering facilities open in the summer season, which lasts from May until October. **Londra Kamping** is open throughout the year. It has washing and cooking facilities, a fast-food restaurant, bar, pool table and football pitch. As well as providing camping facilities, it also has two-room bungalows for rent. On the Black Sea

coast but situated to the east of the Bosphorus is another equally attractive and popular camp site, the **Kumbaba Moteli**, which is situated 1.2 miles (2 km) outside the resort of Şile (*see p158*). This site is open between May and September, and the amenities it has to offer include hot showers and cooking facilities.

For further details, contact the **Turkish Camping and Caravanning Association**, which is helpful and informative. The association also has a website with comprehensive listings of sites throughout the country.

View over Dolmabahçe Mosque from the Swissôtel (*see p190*)

SELF-CATERING

Istanbul has a number of apartment hotels located near various central business and residential districts, providing fully furnished apartments for those who prefer more homely surroundings. The **Akmerkez Residence Apart Hotel**, which is mostly used by business-men, is in the upmarket Akmerkez shopping mall in Etiler (*see p211*). Its luxuriously decorated flats have air-conditioning and all domestic appliances. The **Entes Apart Hotel** has compact modern apartments.

Global real estate franchises like **Century 21** and **Remax** can assist in finding long- or short-term rental accommodation.

DIRECTORY

TRAVEL AGENTS

Meptur
Tel (0212) 275 02 50.
Fax (0212) 275 40 09.

Vip Tourism
Tel (0212) 241 65 14. **Fax** *(0212) 230 66 76.* **www**.viptourism. com.tr

YOUTH HOSTELS

Orient Guesthouse
Akbıyık Cad 13, Sultanahmet.
Map 3 E5 (5 E5).
Tel (0212) 517 94 93. **Fax** *(0212) 518 38 94* **www**.hostels.com/ orienthostel

Yücelt Interyouth Hostel
Caferiye Sok 6/1, Sultanahmet.
Map 3 E4 (5 E3).
Tel (0212) 513 61 50. **Fax** *(0212) 512 76 28.* **www**.yucelthostel. com

CAMPING

Kumbaba Moteli
Şile. *Tel (0216) 711 50 38.*

Londra Kamping
Londra Asfaltı, Bakırköy.
Tel (0212) 560 42 00. **Fax** *(0212) 559 34 38.*

Turkish Camping and Caravanning Association
Feliz Sok, 52 Kartaltepe Mah, Bakırköy.
Tel (0212) 662 46 15. **Fax** *(0212) 662 46 14.* **www**.kampkaravan. org

SELF-CATERING

Akmerkez Residence
Akmerkez Shopping & Business Centre, Etiler.
Tel (0212) 282 01 20. **Fax** *(0212) 282 06 12.* **www**.akmerkez.com. tr

Century 21
www.century21.com.tr

Entes Apart Hotel
İpek Sok 19, Taksim.
Map 7 E4.
Tel (0212) 293 22 08. **Fax** *(0212) 293 15 98.*

Remax
www.remax.com.tr

Choosing a Hotel

The hotels in this guide have been selected across a wide range for their good value, facilities and location. These listings highlight some of the factors that may influence your choice. Hotels are listed by area, beginning with Seraglio Point. All the entries are alphabetical within each price category.

PRICE CATEGORIES
For a standard double room per night, inclusive of breakfast, service charges and any additional taxes.
$ under US$70
$$ US$70–$100
$$$ US$100–$150
$$$$ US$150–$200
$$$$$ Over US$200

SERAGLIO POINT

Apricot $
Akbıyık Caddesi 75, Sultanahmet, 34400 **Tel** *(0212) 638 16 58* **Fax** *(0212) 638 16 58* **Rooms** *18* **Map** *3 E5 (5 E5)*

This is such a pretty little hotel and it has been restored to a far better state than the original Ottoman building. It boasts comfortable beds, well-furnished rooms and polished hard-wood floors. Internet access and many other amenities are also available. Meals (except breakfast) are served by arrangement. **www.hotelapricot.com**

Ararat $$
Torun Sokak 3, Sultanahmet, 34400 **Tel** *(0212) 516 04 11* **Fax** *(0212) 518 52 41* **Rooms** *14*   **Map** *3 E5 (5 E5)*

An unusual and highly individualistic family-run hotel. Each room has its own theme with one-of-a-kind decor. The owner is always available to offer advice and to attend to details. The hotel is close to the Blue Mosque and has splendid views across the Sea of Marmara from the top floor terrace. **www.ararathotel.com**

Spectra Hotel $$
Şehit Mehmetpaşa Yok 2, Sultanahmet, 34400 **Tel** *(0212) 516 35 46* **Rooms** *19*   **Map** *3 D5 (5 D5)*

One of the assets of this hotel is the owner, a retired archaeologist, who is a source of wisdom on many aspects of local life. The rooms are comfortable and well-appointed. Breakfast is served on the terrace with grand views of the Blue Mosque. Guests have free internet access. The Spectra is handy to all central sights. **www.hotel spectra.com**

Ayasofya Evleri $$$
Soğukçeşme Sokak, Sultanahmet, 34122 **Tel** *(0212) 513 36 60* **Fax** *(0212) 513 36 69* **Rooms** *63* **Map** *3 E4 (5 F3)*

Nine restored wooden houses comprise this charming accommodation on the cobbled street behind Haghia Sophia. They have beautiful names such as Jasmine, Honeysuckle and Rose and are painted in pastel colours. The rooms are elegant and decorated with antiques. Booking is essential. **www.ayasofyapensions.com**

Kybele Hotel $$$
Yeribatan Caddesi 33–35, 34410 **Tel** *(0212) 511 77 66* **Fax** *(0212) 513 43 93* **Rooms** *16*   **Map** *3 E4 (5 E3)*

This tiny, multi-storied hotel is located in the heart of the tourist area. The antiques and craft items of every description create a homely and friendly atmosphere. A wonderful breakfast is served in the garden in summer and in one of the ornate rooms in winter. The Kybele is a firm favourite with many visitors. **www.kybelehotel.com**

Mavi Ev $$$
Dalbastı Sokak 14, Sultanahmet, 34400 **Tel** *(0212) 638 90 10* **Fax** *(0212) 638 90 17* **Rooms** *27*   **Map** *3 E5 (5 E5)*

Under the same polished management as the Pudding Shop , this is a distinctive Wedgwood blue *konak* (wooden mansion) restored in period style in the heart of Sultanahmet. It is peaceful and has a leafy garden and acclaimed rooftop restaurant. The views over the Sea of Marmara are magnificent. **www.bluehouse.com.tr**

Seven Hills $$$$
Tevkifhane Sokak 8/A, Sultanahmet, 34400 **Tel** *(0212) 516 94 97/98/99* **Rooms** *14*   **Map** *3 E5 (5 D5)*

This is a hotel that goes out of its way to ensure your stay exceeds expectations. Rooms are beautifully decorated and suites are spacious with private Jacuzzis and fitness facilities in each room. Incredible views along with a first-class restaurant (*see p198*) are found on the terrace. **www.hotelsevenhills.com**

SULTANAHMET

Antea $
Piyerloti Caddesi 21, Çemberlitaş, 34400 **Tel** *(0212) 638 11 21-25* **Rooms** *45*   **Map** *3 D4 (4 C4)*

The Antea is a peaceful hotel on a side street off the main tourist area of Sultanahmet. Like its neighbours, this is a restored building. Rooms are modern and attractively furnished. The restaurant serves Turkish and international dishes. A perfect place to relax after a day of sightseeing and shopping. **www.anteahotel.com**

Key to Symbols *see back cover flap*

Hotel Mina
☆🗏 ⑤

Piyerloti Caddesi, Dostluk Urdu Sokak 6, Sultanahmet, 34400 **Tel** *(0212) 458 28 00* **Rooms** *44* **Map** *3 D4 (4 C4)*

Hotel Mina is tucked away in the backstreets protected from the hustle of the main tourist area. The owners are very welcoming and friendly. Rooms are comfortable and well furnished, although they are not too ornate or fussy. This is a comfortable base within walking distance of all the main attractions of Sultanahmet. **www.minahotel.com.tr**

Hotel Sultanahmet
🔲 🍴 ☆🗏 ⑤

Divanyolu Caddesi 20, Sultanahmet, 34400 **Tel** *(0212) 527 02 39* **Rooms** *20* **Map** *3 D4 (5 D5)*

A well-located budget hotel close to all the sights. It has few frills but is clean and neat, and adequately furnished. There is a pretty terrace with a decent view and evening meals and snacks are served here. The hotel is well run and staff are always hospitable. **www.hotelsultanahmet.com**

Orient Guesthouse
🗐☆ ⑤

Akbıyık Caddesi 13, Sultanahmet, 34400 **Tel** *(0212) 517 94 93* **Fax** *(0212) 518 38 94* **Rooms** *15* **Map** *3 E5 (5 E5)*

This is the cheapest and most cheerful place to stay in Sultanahmet making it the proverbial backpackers' paradise. Rooms are sparse and many resemble a dormitory with three or four beds. Forget about chandeliers and en suite bathrooms, but there is always hot water and other weary, friendly wanderers. **www.orienthostel.com**

Şebnem
🗏 ⑤

Adliye Sokak 1, Sultanahmet, 34400 **Tel** *(0212) 517 66 23* **Fax** *(0212) 638 10 56* **Rooms** *23* **Map** *3 E4 (5 F4)*

This small but welcoming guesthouse, is more like a doll's house. It has pretty, colourful rooms and serviceable wooden furniture. There is a panoramic roof terrace where you can look out at the main buildings of Sultanahmet and across the Bosphorus and Sea of Marmara. **www.sebnemhotel.com**

Dersaadet
🔲☆🗏 P ⑤⑤

Küçük Ayasofya Caddesi, Kapıağası Sokak 5, 34400 **Tel** *(0212) 458 07 60/61* **Rooms** *17* **Map** *3 E5 (5 D5)*

This impeccable hotel is a local pioneer in renovation. It has been authentically designed and furnished by traditional artisans. Small details abound and the owner is always around to ensure your stay is memorable. The Sultan's Penthouse suite has recently been added. **www.hoteldersaadet.com**

Empress Zoe
🔲 🍴 ☆🗏 ⑤⑤

Akbıyık Caddesi, Adliye Sokak 10, 34400 **Tel** *(0212) 518 25 04* **Fax** *(0212) 518 56 99* **Rooms** *22* **Map** *3 E4 (5 F4)4*

It is claimed that Empress Zoe actually lived here. The two buildings have been restored to an exceptionally high standard of taste and design with an abundance of spacious suites. The garden is idyllic and contains the remains of a bath house built in 1483. There are some no-smoking rooms available. **www.emzoe.com**

Historia
☆🗏 ⑤⑤

Amiral Tafdil Sokak 23, 34400 **Tel** *(0212) 517 74 72* **Fax** *(0212) 516 81 69* **Rooms** *25* **Map** *3 E5 (5 F5)*

This attractive wooden hotel has wonderful sea views from the rooftop terrace. Most rooms tend to be quite basic, but they are well decorated and comfortable. Several also have balconies that overlook the back garden. The breakfast patio is secluded and shaded. **www.historiahotel.com**

Hotel Alp Guest House
🍴🗏☆ ⑤⑤

Akbıyık Caddesi, Adliye Sokak 4, Sultanahmet, 34400 **Tel** *(0212) 517 70 67* **Rooms** *14* **Map** *3 E4 (5 F4)*

There are wonderful views from the roof terrace of this hotel hidden away behind the Blue Mosque. It is known as a friendly place to stay with excellent service. The hotel has recently been extensively renovated to a high standard, with new traditional furnishings in the bedrooms. **www.alpguesthouse.com**

Hotel Nena
🔲🍴☆🗏 ⑤⑤

Binbirdirek Mahallesi, Klodfarer Caddesi 8–10, 34400 **Tel** *(0212) 516 52 64* **Rooms** *29* **Map** *3 D4 (5 D4)*

Hotel Nena has a Byzantine atmosphere and is richly decorated and very comfortable. Some rooms have balconies with classic sea and mosque vistas. The beautiful conservatory basks in sun and has wrought-iron and glass furniture as well as flourishing tropical greenery. **www.nenahotel.com**

Nomade
🍴☆🗏 ⑤⑤

Ticarethane Sokak 15, Çağaloğlu, 34400 **Tel** *(0212) 511 12 96* **Fax** *(0212) 513 24 04* **Rooms** *16* **Map** *3 E4 (5 D3)*

One of the oldest houses in this area, the Nomade has recently undergone a wonderful and extensive renovation. The owners have added appealing designer touches to the individually designed bedrooms and bathrooms. Meals and afternoon drinks are served on the rooftop terrace. **www.hotelnomade.com**

Sarı Konak
☆🗏 ⑤⑤

Mimar Mehmet Ağa Caddesi 42–46, Sultanahmet, 34400 **Tel** *(0212) 638 62 58* **Rooms** *17* **Map** *3 E5 (5 E5)*

Sarı means "yellow" in Turkish and this delightful wooden house is easily identifiable by its distinctive hue. It has a charming patio, marble fountain and latticed balconies. Rooms are tastefully decorated and the suites have high-speed internet access. **www.istanbulhotelsarikonak.com**

Sarnıç
☆🗏 P ⑤⑤

Küçük Ayasofya Caddesi 26, 34400 **Tel** *(0212) 518 23 23* **Fax** *(0212) 518 24 14* **Rooms** *16* **Map** *3 D5 (5 D5)*

Sarnıç is a clean and tidy place with a homely feel. It is painted a soft pink colour and the building is surrounded by others of the same history and heritage. It has well decorated rooms and a rooftop restaurant and bar area. Useful extras include a laundry service, baby-sitting and valet parking. **www.sarnichotel.com**

Side Hotel and Pension

🔲 ⑪ ⛲ 🍴 $$

Utangaç Sokak 20, Sultanahmet, 34400 **Tel** *(0212) 517 66 23* **Fax** *(0212) 638 10 56* **Rooms** *36*   **Map** *3 E4*

This family run establishment combines a pension for budget-conscious guests and also a ritzier hotel. Pension prices are cheaper and facilities are fewer, with no air conditioning in rooms. The hotel is comfortable and some rooms have private Jacuzzis available as an extra. **www.sidehotel.com**

Alzer

🔲 ⑪ ⛲ 🍴 $$$

At Meydanı 72, Sultanahmet, 34400 **Tel** *(0212) 516 62 62/63* **Fax** *(0212) 516 00 00* **Rooms** *21* **Map** *3 D4 (5 D4)*

This renovated town house with beautifully appointed and furnished rooms has plenty of definitive touches. In the summer tables are available at street level, but the greatest attraction is the roof restaurant. A cheerful bijou hotel with attentive service. **www.alzerhotel.com**

Avicenna

🔲 ⑪ ⛲ 🍴 $$$

Amiral Tafdil Sokak 31–33, 34400 **Tel** *(0212) 517 05 50-54* **Fax** *(0212) 516 65 55* **Rooms** *50*   **Map** *3 E5 (5 E5)*

Occupying two handsomely renovated Ottoman buildings, this conveniently located mid-range hotel has luxurious interior furnishings, including rich textiles, carpets and traditional wooden floors. Try to reserve rooms on the attic floors for panoramic sea views. **www.avicenna.com.tr**

Aziyade

⑪ 🏊 ⛲ 🍴 $$$

Piyerloti Caddesi 62, Çemberlitaş, 34490 **Tel** *(0212) 638 22 00* **Fax** *(0212) 518 50 65* **Rooms** *105* **Map** *3 D4 (4 B4)*

Aziyade has some lovely features that one might expect to find at a more luxurious level. The small swimming pool on the roof is unique in the area. Rooms are elegant and tastefully decorated. The café is remniscent of the Fruit Room in the Harem at Topkapı Palace *(see p58)*. **www.festivalhotels.com**

Citadel

⑪ ⛲ 🍴 $$$

Kennedy Caddesi, Sahil Yolu 32, Ahırkapı, 34400 **Tel** *(0212) 516 23 13* **Rooms** *31*   **Map** *3 E5 (5 F5)*

Now under the umbrella of the Best Western Group, the dusty pink Citadel Hotel occupies a large stone building under the city walls. Rooms are small but pleasantly furnished with all the essentials. No-smoking rooms are available and some rooms look directly onto the sea. **office@citadelhotel.com**

İbrahim Paşa

🔲 ⑪ ⛲ 🍴 $$$

Terzihane Sokak 5, Sultanahmet, 34400 **Tel** *(0212) 518 03 94* **Fax** *(0212) 518 44 57* **Rooms** *16* **Map** *3 D4 (5 D4)*

This charming stone-built hotel is located opposite the Museum of Turkish and Islamic Arts *(see p77)*. Rooms are individually furnished and, along with the rooftop terrace, are stylish and unique. The decor successfully blends Art Deco with traditional Turkish influences. **www.ibrahimpasha.com**

Pierre Loti

🔲 ⑪ ⛲ 🍴 $$$

Piyerloti Caddesi 5, Çemberlitaş, 34400 **Tel** *(0212) 518 57 00* **Fax** *(0212) 516 18 86* **Rooms** *38*   **Map** *3 D4 (4 C4)*

Named after a Romantic novelist who lived in Istanbul, this was one of the first hotels in the area to be renovated to a high standard. It is in the thick of things on the main road but the summer garden and glassed-in café give you a fine view of the world going by. Rooms are small but wonderfully comfortable. **www.pierreloti.com**

Valide Sultan Konağı

⑪ ⛲ 🍴 $$$

Kutlugün Sokak 1, Sultanahmet, 34400 **Tel** *(0212) 638 06 00* **Fax** *(0212) 638 07 05* **Rooms** *17*   **Map** *3 E4 (5 F4)*

A long-term favourite with visitors to Istanbul, the Valide Sultan's proximity to the Topkapı Palace is an advantage. It has kept up appearances, like its palatial neighbour. The rooms have been individually decorated and, although small, are comfortable. There is a glorious summer terrace with good views. **www.hotelvalidesultan.com**

Armada

🔲 ⑪ 🏊 ⛲ 🎵 🍴 🅿 $$$$

Ahır Kapı Sokak 24, Sultanahmet, 34400 **Tel** *(0212) 638 13 70* **Fax** *(0212) 518 50 60* **Rooms** *110* **Map** *3 E5 (5 F5)*

Possibly one of Istanbul's best kept secrets, this hotel is dignified and yet immensely friendly. The rooms are elegantly decorated in soothing colours and the restaurant is highly recommended. There is great live music and regular tango evenings are held here. **www.armadahotel.com.tr**

Sultanahmet Palace

🔲 ⑪ ⛲ 🍴 $$$$

Torun Sokak 19, Sultanahmet, 34400 **Tel** *(0212) 458 04 60* **Fax** *(0212) 518 62 24* **Rooms** *36*   **Map** *3 E5 (5 E5)*

This is the ideal place to spoil yourself. Less authentically refurbished than some other establishments, it is, nevertheless, a refined hotel that deserves its palace title. The domes of the Blue Mosque rise right beside you. The garden is perfect and the service is subtle and polished. **www.sultanahmetpalace.com**

Yeşil Ev

🔲 ⑪ ⛲ 🍴 $$$$

Kabasakal Sokak 5, Sultanahmet, 34400 **Tel** *(0212) 517 67 85* **Rooms** *19*   **Map** *3 E4 (5 E4)*

Yeşil Ev (Green House) is a local landmark that typifies the spirit of Ottoman luxury. Rooms are furnished with antiques, one even has its own Turkish bath, and the service is impeccable. There is a secluded garden and an outstanding restaurant. **www.istanbulyesilev.com**

Eresin Crown

🔲 ⑪ 🏊 ⛲ 🎵 🍴 🅿 $$$$$

Küçük Ayasofya Caddesi 40, Sultanahmet, 34400 **Tel** *(0212) 639 44 28* **Rooms** *60*   **Map** *3 D5 (5 D5)*

This highly rated, luxury hotel stands on the site of what was once the Great Palace *(see p82)*. Some of the extraordinary Byzantine treasures and heritage mosaics unearthed here are on display in the hotel's own museum. There are several bars and dining options. The Eresin Crown is in a class of its own. **www.eresincrown.com.tr**

Key to Price Guide *see p184* **Key to Symbols** *see back cover flap*

Four Seasons

🛌 🍴 🏊 🚻 📺 🍽️   ⑤⑤⑤⑤⑤

Tevkifhane Sokak 1, Sultanahmet, 34110 **Tel** *(0212) 638 82 00* **Fax** *(0212) 638 85 30* **Rooms** *65* **Map** *3 E4 (5 F4)*

Built as a prison for dissident writers in 1917, the Four Seasons has been restored to a Neo-Classical haven of luxury. Every room has a theme that blends Turkish traditions with contemporary comfort. It is ideally situated a short distance from the main Sultanahmet sights. **www.fshr.com**

Kalyon

🛌 🍴 🏊 🚻 📺 Ⓟ   ⑤⑤⑤⑤⑤

Sahil Yolu, Cankurtaran, 34122 **Tel** *(0212) 517 44 00* **Fax** *(0212) 638 11 11* **Rooms** *112*   **Map** *3 E5 (5 F5)*

The Kalyon is not just a tourist hotel; locals use it and it is a first-rate business hotel. Its position away from the centre of Sultanahmet means that it is quiet and it faces directly onto the Sea of Marmara. Rooms are beautifully furnished to a superb standard. The restaurant is one of the most underrated in the city. **www.kalyon.com**

THE BAZAAR QUARTER

Aspen

🛌 🍴 🚻 📺   ⑤

Aksaray Caddesi 27, Laleli, 34480 **Tel** *(0212) 518 53 61* **Fax** *(0212) 518 53 91* **Rooms** *80*   **Map** *2 A4*

Although there are no glorious views or extra luxuries, Aspen is still an excellent hotel for those on a budget who do not want to sacrifice a central location. The hotel is near all the main sights and adjacent to public transport in the busy Aksaray area. The service is cheerful. **www.aspenotel.com.tr**

Sidera

🚻 📺   ⑤

Dönüş Sokak 14, Kumkapı **Tel** *(0212) 638 34 60* **Fax** *(0212) 518 72 62* **Rooms** *18*   **Map** *3 D5 (4 B5)*

A converted 19th-century wooden house, the Sidera is painted a distinctive green and is more like a family home. Although small, it offers adequate facilities. Rooms can be a bit dark but the location, on a narrow street lined with other Ottoman-style wooden houses, is part of its nostalgic charm. **www.hotelsiderapalace.com**

Bulvar Palas

🛌 🍴 🏊 🚻 📺   ⑤⑤

Atatürk Bul 152, Saraçhane, 34470 **Tel** *(0212) 528 58 81* **Fax** *(0212) 528 60 81* **Rooms** *70*   **Map** *2 A3*

A makeover has given this cheerful hotel a pleasant atmosphere. The beauty treatment and fitness centre complement the hairdressing salon and Turkish bath. The decor is traditional, but it is an excellent hotel at a fair price. The large restaurant serves some good Turkish dishes. **www.hotelbulvarpalas.com**

Royal Hotel

🛌 🍴 🚻 📺   ⑤⑤

Aksaray Caddesi 16, Laleli, 34480 **Tel** *(0212) 518 51 51* **Fax** *(0212) 518 51 60* **Rooms** *128*   **Map** *2 A4*

Within walking distance of all the main sights and transport facilities, Royal Hotel is well recommended and popular with many visitors. It is very good value for the many services it provides, including a satellite TV and a minibar in all rooms. The Royal is comfortable, well furnished and meticulously maintained. **www.royalhotelistanbul.com**

President

🛌 🍴 🚻 📺   ⑤⑤⑤

Tiyatro Caddesi 25, Beyazıt, 34126 **Tel** *(0212) 516 69 80* **Fax** *(0212) 516 69 98* **Rooms** *204*   **Map** *2 C4 (4 A4)*

The first hotel in Istanbul to have an English pub, the President has an excellent reputation. It is located in the heart of the city with well appointed rooms and good service. Wireless internet is available in the the reception area and in many rooms. The Turkish nights and belly-dancing evenings are legendary. **www.thepresidenthotel.com**

Antik Hotel

🍴 🚻 📺   ⑤⑤⑤⑤

Ordu Caddesi, Sekbanbaşı Sokak 10, Beyazıt, 36420 **Tel** *(0212) 638 58 58* **Rooms** *96*   **Map** *2 B4*

This comfortable hotel built around a 1,500-year-old water cistern, has fine views over the Sea of Marmara. It also has an acclaimed pub, wine bar and unusual restaurant. The cistern itself has been converted into a subterranean night club. The Antik is a swinging and lively hotel that makes all ages feel at home. **www.antikhotel.com**

BEYOĞLU

Hotel the Pera Hill

🛌 🚻 📺   ⑤

Meşrutiyet Caddesi 95, Beyoğlu, 34430 **Tel** *(0212) 245 66 06* **Fax** *(0212) 245 66 42* **Rooms** *28*   **Map** *7 D4*

In the cultural heart of Beyoğlu and housed in a solid stone building this hotel was once the Libyan consulate. It is a modest but hugely comfortable establishment and well known as an ideally situated budget hotel. Rooms are plain but are kept meticulously clean. **www.hoteltheperahill.com**

Aygün

🛌 🍴 🚻 📺   ⑤⑤

Lamartin Caddesi 53-55, Taksim, 80090 **Tel** *(0212) 238 90 90* **Fax** *(0212) 235 47 47* **Rooms** *83*   **Map** *7 E3*

Tucked away in a tranquil corner of Taksim, the Aygün is well equipped as a home away from home. Rooms are beautifully designed and there is a Turkish bath and fitness centre, along with restaurants and a Vitamin Bar. This is an extremely comfortable hotel. **www.aygunhotels.com**

Gezi Hotel
🖥 🍴 ⚡ 🗏 ⑤⑤

Mete Caddesi 42, Taksim, 80090 **Tel** *(0212) 251 74 30* **Fax** *(0212) 251 74 73* **Rooms** *46* **Map** *7 F3*

The Gezi has been renovated and upgraded with well-equipped rooms awaiting guests. Some have spectacular view of the Bosphorus and bridges, others look out over Taksim Park. There is an excellent restaurant with a formal atmosphere and beautifully presented classic dishes. **www.hotelgezi.com**

Hotel La Villa
🖥 ⚡ 🗏 🅿 ⑤⑤

Topçu Caddesi 28, Taksim, 34437 **Tel** *(0212) 256 56 26/27* **Fax** *(0212) 297 53 28* **Rooms** *28* **Map** *7 E3*

La Villa is a small, low-cost but attractive hotel in the shadow of many prestigious, high-rise neighbours. It has all the things one would expect from a modern hotel, including internet access, no-smoking rooms and 24-hour room service. The hotel arranges day trips and Turkish evenings for guests. **www.hotellavilla.net**

Hotel Residence
🖥 ⚡ 🗏 ⑤⑤

İstiklâl Caddesi, Sadri Alışık Sokak 19, Taksim, 80090 **Tel** *(0212) 252 76 85/87* **Rooms** *30* **Map** *7 E4*

From the slick reception area to the beautifully fitted and furnished rooms, Residence Hotel offers outstanding value given its location in the middle of the city. The rooms have all the hallmarks of more upmarket hotels and there is also a fine restaurant with some inspired touches. **www.hotelresidence.com.tr**

Hotel Villa
🖥 🍴 ⚡ 🗏 ⑤⑤

Sıraselviler Caddesi 49, Taksim, 80090 **Tel** *(0212) 252 96 00* **Fax** *(0212) 249 70 77* **Rooms** *50* **Map** *7 E4*

With a great location near Taksim Square, this is a simple hotel without airs and graces. It is known for its pleasant atmosphere with lots of floral patterns and velvet throughout. There is a terrace restaurant and a café-bar for snacks as well as a plush lounge. There are many conveniences and a helpful staff. **www.hotelvillaist.com**

Seminal
🖥 ♒ ⚡ 📺 🗏 ⑤⑤

Şehit Muhtar Caddesi 23-25, Taksim, 80090 **Tel** *(0212) 297 34 34* **Fax** *(0212) 297 28 18* **Rooms** *88* **Map** *7 E3*

This is an agreeable place to stay with friendly staff, and sights and shops nearby. There is a small fitness room, a room for disabled guests and also a fine swimming pool. The ten rooms all have sea views. This is an established hotel with a good reputation. **www.seminalhotels.com**

Green Park
🖥 🍴 ⚡ 🗏 ⑤⑤⑤

Abdülhak Hamit Caddesi 50, Taksim, 34437 **Tel** *(0212) 238 05 05* **Fax** *(0212) 237 76 46* **Rooms** *81* **Map** *7 E3*

One of the first modern hotels to open in Taksim, the Green Park has comfortable, well-decorated rooms. The restaurant is spacious and serves up decent food and a wonderful open buffet breakfast. The staff can arrange tours of the city, car hire or Bosphorus cruises. **www.thegreenpark.com**

Lamartine
🖥 🍴 ⚡ 🗏 ⑤⑤⑤

Lamartin Caddesi 25, Taksim, 80090 **Tel** *(0212) 254 62 70* **Fax** *(0212) 256 27 76* **Rooms** *66* **Map** *7 E3*

Named after the French poet who once visited Istanbul, Lamartine is close to all the sights in Taksim, shopping outlets and a short walk to the lively cultural district of Beyoğlu. The hotel offers a consistently reliable standard of comfort at an affordable price. **www.lamartinehotel.com**

Taksim Select
🖥 🍴 ⚡ 🗏 🅿 ⑤⑤⑤

Topçu Caddesi 19, Taksim, 34437 **Tel** *(0212) 235 10 00* **Fax** *(0212) 254 75 95* **Rooms** *65* **Map** *7 E3*

This is one of the friendliest mid-range hotels in the crowded "hotel quarter" bordering Taksim Square. Well appointed rooms with all services and amenities are available. The hotel serves a fantastic breakfast with great coffee It is convenient for transport and shopping in Nişantaşı and Beyoğlu. **www.taksimselect.com**

Taxim Hill
🖥 🍴 ⚡ 📺 🗏 ⑤⑤⑤

Sıraselviler Caddesi 9, Taksim, 80090 **Tel** *(0212) 334 85 00* **Fax** *(0212) 334 85 98* **Rooms** *58* **Map** *7 E4*

A distinctive landmark on the corner of Taksim's main square, the Hill is a great place to stay with excellent business facilities, Jacuzzis and a well-equipped health club. Rooms are attractively decorated and comfortable, and some have a view over the Bosphorus. **www.taximhill.com**

Central Palace
🖥 🍴 ⚡ 📺 🗏 ⑤⑤⑤⑤

Lamartin Caddesi 18, Taksim, 34437 **Tel** *(0212) 313 40 40* **Fax** *(0212) 313 40 39* **Rooms** *54* **Map** *7 E3*

Late Ottoman style is combined with modern luxuries at this eminent hotel. The rooms are luxurious and supremely comfortable, and there is an excellent healthfood restaurant. No alcohol is sold or served but you can bring your ow to rooms. The Central Palace is highly recommended. **www.thecentralpalace.com**

Divan
🖥 🍴 ♒ ⚡ 📺 🗏 🅿 ⑤⑤⑤⑤

Cumhuriyet Caddesi 2, Elmadağ, 80090 **Tel** *(0212) 315 55 00* **Fax** *(0212) 315 55 15* **Rooms** *180* **Map** *7 F3*

It may look like a brutal hunk of concrete but there is no denying that this is one of the city's top hotels, with superb service and excellent attention to detail. The attached pub has terrific food, as does the sushi restaurant. Rooms are tastefully appointed. **www.divan.com.tr**

Germir Palas
🖥 🍴 ⚡ 🗏 ⑤⑤⑤⑤

Cumhuriyet Caddesi 17, Taksim, 34437 **Tel** *(0212) 361 11 10* **Fax** *(0212) 361 10 70* **Rooms** *49* **Map** *7 E3*

It is easy to miss the entrance to this mid-town gem on the main street. The lobby and bars are plush, and the rooms are well decorated with interesting textiles. The terrace restaurant is great in summer, with fine views over the Bosphorous. The street-level Vanilla Café is very stylish. **www.germirpalas.com**

Key to Price Guide *see p184* **Key to Symbols** *see back cover flap*

Ceylan Intercontinental

🖥 🔢 🏊 🏋 📺 🖩 🅿   ⑤⑤⑤⑤⑤

Asker Ocağı Caddesi 1, Taksim, 34435 **Tel** *(0212) 368 44 44* **Fax** *(0212) 368 44 99* **Rooms** *390*   **Map** *7 F3*

This is one of the top hotels in Istanbul with first-class facilities for groups, visitors and business travellers. High profile guests welcome the security barriers at the exit and entrance. The tea lounge is an afternoon tradition and harp music is played here. The lively City Lights bar is innovative. **www.interconti.com.tr**

Hyatt Regency

🖥 🔢 🏋 📺 🖩 🅿   ⑤⑤⑤⑤⑤

Taşkışla Caddesi, Taksim, 800990 **Tel** *(0212) 368 12 34* **Fax** *(0212) 368 10 00* **Rooms** *332*   **Map** *7 F3*

The Hyatt offers everything a traveller could wish for – lounge bars, three excellent restaurants including one of the best Japanese restaurants in town and many other amenities. All the rooms are richly furnished and decorated, and many have good views. There are fitness and spa facilities, and an indoor tennis court. **www.istanbul.hyatt.com**

Marmara Pera

🖥 🔢 🏊 🏋 📺 🖩 🅿   ⑤⑤⑤⑤⑤

Meşrutiyet Caddesi, Tepebaşı, 34437 **Tel** *(0212) 251 46 46* **Fax** *(0212) 249 80 33* **Rooms** *200*   **Map** *7 D5*

This is one of the most recent additions to Istanbul's luxury hotels, providing every service you could ever need and 360-degree views of the city. Excellent for business travellers, with wireless internet access available in every room. There is an interesting mural in the lobby, along with plenty of seating. **www.themarmarahotels.com**

Marmara Taksim

🖥 🔢 🏊 🏋 📺 🖩 🅿   ⑤⑤⑤⑤⑤

Taksim Meydanı, Tak-ı Zafer Caddesi, Taksim, 34430 **Tel** *(212) 251 46 96* **Rooms** *410*   **Map** *7 E4*

The rooms here are extremely comfortable and beautifully decorated. The staff are always helpful and happy. The panorama restaurant on the roof is a presitigious eating spot, while the trendy café on the ground floor is one of Istanbul's favourite meeting places. **www.themarmarahotels.com**

Pera Palas

🖥 🔢 🏋 📺 🅿   ⑤⑤⑤⑤⑤

Meşrutiyet Caddesi 98, Tepebaşı, 34430 **Tel** *(0212) 251 45 60* **Fax** *(0212) 251 40 89* **Rooms** *145*   **Map** *7 D5*

A legendary Istanbul landmark *(see p104)*, this hotel caters to the famous. Agatha Christie stayed here and her room has been maintained exactly as it was. Luxury can be found elsewhere but if mystery and history appeal, you will love the atmosphere and original trappings. An authentic sense of faded grandeur prevails. **www.perapalas.com**

Ritz Carlton

🖥 🔢 🏊 🏋 📺 🖩 🅿   ⑤⑤⑤⑤⑤

Süzer Plaza, Elmadağ, Şişli, 34367 **Tel** *(0212) 334 44 44* **Fax** *(0212) 334 44 55* **Rooms** *244*   **Map** *7 F3*

The Ritz Carlton easily stands out with its classy, contemporary style and practised elegance. Every amenity is on offer in this world of privilege with costumed Ottoman staff on hand. Highly recommended restaurants serve the best of Turkish food. The spa is one of the best in the city. **www.ritzcarlton.com**

GREATER ISTANBUL

Taşhan

🖥 🔢 🏋 📺 🅿   ⑤⑤

Taşhan Caddesi 57, Bakırköy, 34142 **Tel** *(0212) 543 65 75* **Fax** *(0212) 561 09 88* **Rooms** *40*

Once a mediocre hotel snuggled in a leafy residential area, the Taşhan is now a Best Western hotel. Refreshingly remote from city lights, it is a short walk from Ataköy Marina, the Galleria shopping centre *(see p220)*, and a ten-minute journey to the airport. This is a friendly, efficient hotel. **www.tashanhotel.com.tr**

Kariye

🔢 🏋 📺 🅿   ⑤⑤

Kariye Camii Sokak 18, Edirnekapı, 34240 **Tel** *(0212) 635 79 97/534 84 14* **Rooms** *24*   **Map** *1 B1*

Situated in the shadow of the Church of St Saviour in Chora *(see pp118–19)*, the Kariye is a wooden *konak* (mansion) renovated in the style of the early 1900s. The rooms feature polished wooden floors and latticed windows. The Asitane restaurant *(see p204)* is famous for its rare Ottoman recipes. **www.kariyeotel.com**

Village Park Country Resort

🖥 🔢 🏊 🏋 📺 🅿   ⑤⑤⑤

Ayazma Mahallesi 19, Ishaklı Köyü, Beykoz, Asian side, 81680 **Tel** *(0216) 434 59 99* **Rooms** *20*

This is a haven of peace and tranquility for those who do not want to be in the city. Weekend packages are available as well as country pursuits such as horse riding. Dogs are welcome and kennels are provided. A restaurant, several bars and a popular picnic area make this a sought-after retreat. **www.villagepark.com.tr**

Bentley Hotel

🖥 🔢 🏋 📺 🖩   ⑤⑤⑤⑤

Halaskargazi Caddesi 75, Harbiye, 80220 **Tel** *(0212) 291 77 30* **Fax** *(0212) 291 77 40* **Rooms** *50*   **Map** *7 F1*

The Bentley is a reliable provider of luxury and style in the heart of the city. Many beautifully furnished suites are available and the guest list of the glamorous and famous is impressive. The fusion cuisine restaurant and stylish bar have won accolades. **www.bentley-hotel.com**

Çınar

🖥 🔢 🏊 🏋 📺 🖩 🅿   ⑤⑤⑤⑤

Şevketiye Mahallesi, Fener Mevkii, Yeşilköy **Tel** *(0212) 663 29 00* **Fax** *(0212) 663 29 21* **Rooms** *220*

The Çınar borders the Sea of Marmara, so try to get a room facing the sea. It has wonderful restaurants and bars, and the outdoor pool area and terrace are great in summer. Guests can jog along the sea shore path with the locals. It is only five minutes from the airport. **www.cinarhotel.com.tr**

Güneş
🖥 ⏸ ♨ ⛷ 📺 🖥 🅿 $$$$
Nadide Caddesi, Günay Sokak 10, Merter, 34010 **Tel** *(0212) 483 30 30* **Fax** *(0212) 483 30 45* **Rooms** *130*

This hotel is situated in a quiet residential suburb, but it is only 10 km (6 miles) from the airport and is an established and popular executive hotel. The tramway to the central sights is a five-minute walk away. Book online for discounted prices. **www.guneshotel.com.tr**

Barceló Eresin Topkapı
🖥 ⏸ ♨ ⛷ 📺 🖥 🅿 $$$$$
Millet Caddesi 186, Topkapı, 34093 **Tel** *(0212) 631 12 12* **Fax** *(0212) 631 37 02* **Rooms** *231*

Not related to or near Topkapı Palace, the Barceló was once the Eresin Hotel. It is a huge stone edifice situated away from the main hotel quarter. It is run by a Spanish conglomerate and is efficiently grand, with an excellent restaurant. Public transport is convenient and most sights are a short distance away. **www.barcelo.com**

Hilton
🖥 ⏸ ♨ ⛷ 📺 🖥 🅿 $$$$$
Cumhuriyet Caddesi, Harbiye, 34367 **Tel** *(0212) 315 60 00* **Fax** *(0212) 240 41 65* **Rooms** *498*   **Map** 7 F2

One of Turkey's first luxury hotels, the Hilton provides superb service and comfort. It has lovely rooms, restaurants, bars and tennis courts. Outside there is a peaceful, attractive garden, which has a pool and jogging track. It also has a world-class conference centre. **www.hilton.com**

Istanbul International Airport Hotel
🖥 ⏸ ♨ ⛷ 📺 🖥 $$$$$
Atatürk Airport International Terminal, Yeşilköy, 34831 **Tel** *(0212) 465 40 30* **Rooms** *85*

This is the first hotel within Atatürk Airport and is accessible by foot from the baggage claim area. It has everything you are likely to want, but at a cost. Nevertheless, the bars, food and excellent service exceed anything available elsewhere in the airport. **www.airporthotelistanbul.com**

Swissotel The Bosphorus
🖥 ⏸ ♨ ⛷ 📺 🖥 🅿 $$$$$
Bayıldım Caddesi 2, Maçka, 34104 **Tel** *(0212) 326 11 00* **Fax** *(0212) 326 11 22* **Rooms** *600*   **Map** 8 A4

Run by the Raffles Group, Swissotel is the choice of many globetrotters when in Istanbul. Set within 65 acres (26 ha) of grounds and with Bosphorus vistas, it also has ten restaurants and bars, a spa and wellness centre and tennis courts. The glamorous shopping arcade will entice serious shoppers. **www.swissotel.com**

THE BOSPHORUS

Bebek
⏸ ⛷ 🖥 🅿 $$$$
Cevdetpaşa Caddesi 34, Bebek, European side, 34342 **Tel** *(0212) 358 20 00* **Fax** *(0212) 263 26 36* **Rooms** *21*

This is the ultimate in sea breezes and sumptuous living, as well as dining and clubbing. The bar at Bebek has been legend for several decades and the renovated hotel has roomy, designer rooms. The restaurant is first rate and the setting, overlooking a bay, is particularly fine. **www.bebekhotel.com.tr**

A'jia Hotel
⏸ ⛷ 🖥 🅿 $$$$$
Ahmet Rasim Paşa Yalısı, Çubuklu Caddesi 27, Kanlıca, Asian side **Tel** *(0216) 413 93 00* **Rooms** *16*

This luxury boutique hotel redefines simplicity and minimalist design. Gone are authentic Ottoman interiors or pasha's rooms; it boasts cool, calm, subdued and restful elegance. It is remote from the crowds in a district with no other hotels. Seclusion and anonymity are assured. **www.ajiahotel.com**

Bosphorus Palace
🖥 ⏸ ⛷ 🖥 🅿 $$$$$
Yalıboyu Caddesi 64, Beylerbeyi, Asian side, 34676 **Tel** *(0216) 422 00 03* **Fax** *(0216) 422 00 12* **Rooms** *14*

A meticulously restored summer house on the Bosphorus waterfront, this is one of Istanbul's "ultra" hotels. High ceilings, gilded furniture and fabulous chandeliers set the imperial tone and it is more European than Ottoman in style. A private boat commutes to central Istanbul. **www.bosphoruspalace.com**

Çırağan Palace Kempinski
🖥 ⏸ ♨ ⛷ 📺 🖥 🅿 $$$$$
Çırağan Caddesi 32, Beşiktaş, European side, 34349 **Tel** *(0212) 326 46 46* **Rooms** *315*   **Map** 9 D3

Designed to make guests feel like a sultan, the Çırağan is one of the city's leading hotels. A restored residence of the last Ottoman sultans, it retains its glory and brims with five-star opulence. It has a glorious summer terrace with the Bosphorus lapping below. **www.ciragan-palace.com**

BEYOND ISTANBUL

Anzac
⏸ ⛷ 🅿 $
Saat Kulesi Meydanı 8, Çanakkale **Tel** *(0286) 217 77 77* **Fax** *(0286) 217 20 18* **Rooms** *27*

The Anzac has become almost as legendary as its namesake *(see p170)*. Neat, clean rooms are decorated with Gallipoli themes. There is a popular roof terrace with reasonably priced snacks. It gets very crowded during the period around 25 April, ANZAC Day. **www.anzachotel.com**

Key to Price Guide *see p184* **Key to Symbols** *see back cover flap*

Büyük Ada Princess
İskele Caddesi 28, Büyük Ada **Tel** *(0216) 382 16 28* **Fax** *(0216) 382 19 49* **Rooms** *24*

Established in 1895, the Princess is an elegant Neo-Classical stone building in the town square on the largest of the Princes' Islands. Rooms are comfortable and some have balconies overlooking the sea. There is an outdoor swimming pool and children's playground. The atmosphere is relaxing and appealing. **www.buyukadaprincess.com**

Geçim
Türkeli, Avşa Ada **Tel** *(0266) 896 14 93* **Fax** *(0266) 896 14 93* **Rooms** *15*

This is a popular family hotel and one of the better places to stay in Türkeli. Located in a peaceful neighbourhood and set back from the beach, it offers shared self-catering facilities and some well-equipped apartments. This is an excellent base from which to enjoy the delights of Avşa.

Hotel Maşukiye
Soğuksu Mahallesi, Sarmaşık Sokak 18, Maşukiye, Kartepe, Kocaeli, 41295 **Tel** *(262) 354 21 74* **Rooms** *10*

Maşukiye means "village of lovers" and this snug hotel inspires romance. Nestling amongst forests, lakes and mountains, this rural inn delights in every way. There are plenty of winter and summer outdoor pursuits, unique local history and splendid food and vintage wines. **www.hotelmasukiye.com**

Polka Country Hotel
Cumhuriyet Yolu 36, Polonezköy, 81650 **Tel** *(0216) 432 32 20* **Fax** *(0216) 432 30 42* **Rooms** *15*

This stone and timber lodge is brimming with atmosphere. The town and surrounding area are untouched by development. Settled by Polish migrants in the 19th century, the area gets extremely busy on the weekends but guests can walk, bike, picnic, hike, or just sit and play chess. **www.polkahotel.com**

Rüstempaşa Kervansaray
Kikapalıhan Caddesi 57, Eski Camii Yanı, Edirne, 22100 **Tel** *(0284) 225 21 95* **Fax** *(0284) 214 85 22* **Rooms** *75*

This historic *caravanserai* (travel lodge) dating from the 16th century was a creation of the prolific imperial architect Sinan (*see p155*). It is Edirne's most venerable hostel and has thick stone walls, rows of rooms and creature comforts. In the past commercial traders could overnight here under the sultan's protection. **www.kervansaray.net**

Safran
Ortapazarı Caddesi, Arka Sokak 4, Bursa, 16040 **Tel** *(0224) 224 72 16* **Fax** *(0224) 224 72 19* **Rooms** *10*

Easily recognized by its saffron colour, this charming hotel is over 100 years old and is situated in the centre of Bursa. Its rooms are small but thoughtfully furnished. The restaurant is renowned for producing well-cooked meals and mezes and, on some evenings, there is live music. **www.charminghotelsofturkey.org**

Sığnak (The Retreat)
İbrice Limanı Yolu, Mecidiye, Keşan, 22800 **Tel** *(0284) 783 43 10* **Fax** *(0284) 783 43 86* **Rooms** *8*

Opposite the Gallipoli Peninsula on the Gulf of Saroz is an unspoilt, largely uninhabited region of Turkey. The Retreat is remote and some minutes away from a deserted beach and coastline. Accommodation is homely with a few ethnic decorations. Guests can enjoy fresh air, splendid food and wine here. **www.siginak.com**

İznik Çini Vakfı
Sahil Yolu Vakıf Sokak 13, İznik, 16860 **Tel** *(0224) 757 60 25* **Fax** *(0224) 757 57 37* **Rooms** *9*

This remote guesthouse is run by the foundation that restores the traditional İznik tile-making traditions. Do not expect five-star trappings but it is peacefully artistic, reasonably comfortable and guests can always meet interesting scholarly, cultural types. It is well recommended for independent adventures.

Splendid Palace
Yirmiüç Nisan Caddesi 71, Büyük Ada, 81330 **Tel** *(0216) 382 69 50* **Fax** *(0216) 382 67 75* **Rooms** *70*

The Splendid Palace was opened in 1908. Though influenced somewhat by Art Nouveau, it clearly displays a fusion of East and West architectural designs with a bright inner courtyard encircled with rooms, and pillars around the courtyard. The silver domes and red shutters add a festive touch to the hotel.

Acqua Verde
Kurfallı, Şile, 81740 **Tel** *(0216) 721 71 43* **Fax** *(0216) 721 72 33* **Rooms** *25*

This tranquil, leafy backwater is located on the Ağva River at Şile. Wildlife, trees and a wilderness atmosphere make this spot enormously popular. There are bungalows and picnic areas, and their own restaurant is excellent. At weekends, city dwellers arrive in numbers. Visit mid-week if you prefer solitude. **www.acquaverde.com.tr**

Almira Hotel
Ulubatlı Hasan Bulvarı 5, Bursa, 16200 **Tel** *(0224) 250 20 20* **Fax** *(0224) 250 20 38* **Rooms** *235*

The Almira Hotel has more than a hint of Regency, but with so many restorations to be found, this is a comforting hotel that does not shout about heritage. The rooms are large and well furnished and the lounge areas are spacious and atmospheric. There is an excellent restaurant and bars. **www.almira.com.tr**

Çelik Palas
Çekirge Caddesi 79, Çekirge, Bursa, 16070 **Tel** *(0224) 233 38 00* **Fax** *(0224) 236 19 10* **Rooms** *161*

The most opulent of Turkey's many spa resorts (*see p168*) the Çelik Palas is now run by the Swissotel/Raffles Group. The setting is spectacular with dramatic mountain ranges and views over Bursa. The constant flow of thermal waters reputedly relieves many common ailments. **http://celikpalasbursa.swissotel.com**

RESTAURANTS, CAFÉS AND BARS

Istanbul's restaurants range from the informal *lokanta* and kebab house, which are found on almost every street corner, to the gourmet restaurants *(restoran)* of large hotels. There are also many international restaurants in the city offering a choice of almost every other kind of cuisine, from French to Japanese. Pages 194–7 illustrate the most typical Turkish dishes and the phrase book on pages 279–80 will help you tackle the menu. On page 197

Simit seller

you will find a guide to drinks available. The restaurants listed on pages 198–207 have been chosen from the best that Istanbul has to offer across all price ranges, from bistros to award-winning restaurants. They have been recommended for their quality of food, service and value for money. A detailed description is provided with examples of signature dishes. Light meals and snacks sold by street vendors and served in cafés and bars are described on pages 208–9.

WHERE TO LOOK

Istanbul's smartest and most expensive restaurants are concentrated in the European parts of the city: in and around Taksim; in the chic shopping districts of Nişantaşı, Maçka and Teşvikiye; and in the modern residential suburbs of Levent and Etiler, west of the Bosphorus. The best gourmet restaurants for both Western and Turkish food are usually in five-star hotels.

Beyoğlu district has the trendiest restaurants, cafés and fast-food eateries, particularly around İstiklal Caddesi *(see pp102–3)*, which cater for a young and lively crowd.

Sultanahmet, and the neighbouring districts of Sirkeci, Eminönü and Beyazıt, are full of cheap restaurants serving the local population. In recent years, however, some stylish restaurants with modern decor have opened in these areas.

Further afield, in areas such as Fatih, Fener, Balat and Eyüp, there are plenty of cheap restaurants, cafés and pudding shops.

TYPES OF RESTAURANT

The most common type of restaurant is the traditional *lokanta*. This is an ordinary restaurant offering a variety of dishes, often listed by the entrance. Home-made dishes comprise hot meat and vegetable dishes displayed in steel containers. Other dishes on the menu may be *sulu yemek* (a broth or stew) and *et* (meat – meaning grilled meat and kebabs).

Equally ubiquitous is the Turkish kebab house *(kebapçı* or *ocakbaşı)*. As well as grilled meats, almost every kebab house serves *lahmacun*, a very thin dough base with minced meat, onions and tomato sauce on top *(see*

Pierre Loti café in Eyüp *(see p120)*

p194). Cheaper restaurants and kebab houses also serve *pide*, a flattened bread base, served with various toppings such as eggs, cheese or lamb. There are also a few specialist *pide* restaurants.

If you have had too much to drink you may welcome a tripe soup *(işkembe)*, a Turkish cure for a hangover, before going to bed. *İşkembe* restaurants stay open until the early hours of the morning.

The atmosphere is always informal and lively in Istanbul's innumerable fish restaurants *(balık lokantası)*. The best of these are located on the shores of the Bosphorus *(see pp205–7)* and in Kumkapı on the Sea of Marmara, which is like one large open-air restaurant in summer. A typical fish restaurant will offer a large variety of mezes *(see p196)* before you order your main course from the day's catch. Baby tuna *(palamut)*, fresh sardines *(sardalya)* and sea bass *(levrek)* are the most

Körfez, a luxury restaurant overlooking the Bosphorus *(see p206)*

Diners eating at the Konyalı Restaurant in Topkapı Palace *(see p198)*

popular fish. Also popular are Black Sea *hamsi* (a kind of anchovy), *istarrit* (bluefin) and *mezgit* (whiting). However, as fish are becoming scarcer and more expensive, farmed fish has become more widely accepted, particularly *alabalik* (trout) and a type of bream known as *cipura*. Fish is served fried or grilled and often accompanied by a large plate of salad and a bottle of *rakı* *(see p197)*. The majority of fish restaurants in these busy and popular areas will not accept reservations. However, if you cannot find a table at one restaurant, you will probably find one at another nearby.

International culinary experiences are encouraging local chefs to be adventurous and innovative. Many restaurants are known for superb, original food in a beautiful ambience. Turks frequent the many foreign

restaurants found all over Istanbul, while global icons such as Starbucks and Gloria Jean's are part of everyday life. A *meyhane* is more like a tavern, serving alcohol and a large choice of *mezes*. They are usually more casual than some of the traditional restaurants and often attract a younger crowd. The accent is mostly on drinking and there is almost always *fasil* music and musicians who play atmospheric tunes on a zither or drum.

OPENING HOURS

Turks eat lunch between 12:30 and 2pm and have dinner around 8pm. Ordinary restaurants and kebab houses are open from about 11am to 11pm, while fish restaurants serve all day but stay open later. International restaurants have strict opening hours, usually from noon to 3:30pm and 7:30pm to midnight. *Meyhanes* will be open from 7pm until well after midnight. Most restaurants are open seven days a week, but some are closed on either Sunday or Monday. During Ramazan *(see p47)*, when Muslims fast from sunrise to sunset, many restaurants are closed. Some only shut during daylight hours and then serve special Ramazan meals,

while others, especially in religious areas such as Fatih and Eyüp, will close altogether for the whole month. In sight-seeing areas, however, you will always find somewhere open.

WHAT TO EXPECT

Most restaurants in Istanbul cater for special requirements such as high chairs for children. Also, it is increasingly common for there to be a smoke-free area, but there are no hard-and-fast rules.

When choosing a place to eat, bear in mind that some cheaper restaurants and kebab houses do not serve alcoholic drinks. Many restaurants in the city are equipped for wheelchairs but most are on the ground floor making easy access possible.

Most restaurants also cater for vegetarians and designer vegetarian restaurants seem to be causing much interest.

In local Turkish restaurants outside Istanbul, such as in Edirne and Bursa, women should look for the *aile salonu* sign. This denotes an area

A selection of pastries

set aside for women and children, and single women will be unwelcome in the main restaurant.

Turks are proud of their hospitality and service. Good service is always found in the upmarket restaurants which can afford well-trained staff. You may find that the same standards do not always apply to the cheaper places.

SERVICE AND PAYING

The major credit cards are widely accepted, except in the cheaper restaurants, kebab houses, local *bufés* (snack kiosks) and some *lokantas*. Restaurants usually display the credit card sign or symbol at the entrance if they accept this form of payment. Value-added tax (KDV in Turkish) is always included. Some places add 10 per cent for service while others leave it to the discretion of the customer.

Delicious fried and grilled mackerel sold on Eminönü quayside *(see p208)*

The Flavours of Istanbul

The wide range of climatic zones across Turkey make it one of the few countries that can grow all its own food. Tea is cultivated in the mountains by the Black Sea and bananas in the sultry south. The Anatolian plain in between is criss-crossed by wheat fields and rich grasslands on which cattle graze, providing top quality meat and dairy produce. Fruit and vegetables flourish everywhere and fish abound in the salty seas that lap the nation's shores. Freshness is the hallmark of this varied cuisine, drawn from the many cultures that were subject to nearly five centuries of Ottoman rule.

Pomegranates

A stall in the Spice Bazaar, one of Istanbul's oldest markets

THE ANATOLIAN STEPPE

The steppe stretching from Central Asia to Anatolia is one of the oldest inhabited regions of the world. Dishes from this vast area are as varied as the different ethnic groups that live here, but are mainly traditional and simple. To fit in with a mainly nomadic way of life, food generally needed to be quick and easy to prepare. Turkey's most famous culinary staples, yogurt, flat bread and the kebab, originate in this region. The common use of fruits, such as pomegranates, figs and apricots, in Turkish savoury dishes stems from Persian influences, filtering down with the tribes that came from the north of the steppe. From the Middle East, further south, nomads introduced the occasional fiery blash of chilli. Its use was once an essential aid to preserving meat in the searing desert heat.

OTTOMAN CUISINE

It was in the vast, steamy kitchens of the Topkapı Palace that a repertoire of mouthwatering dishes to rival the celebrated cuisines of France and China grew

Lamb şiş kebab
Stuffed aubergine (eggplant)
Chicken şiş kebab
Prawn (shrimp) kebab
Chilli sauce
Lamb cutlet
Doner keba

A selection of typical Turkish kebabs

LOCAL DISHES AND SPECIALITIES

Because of Istanbul's proximity to the sea, fresh fish is readily available and is a key ingredient on the city's menus. Since ancient times the Bosphorus has been known for its excellent fishing. In the winter months especially, there is a bounty of oil-rich fish, such as bluefish, bream, bonito tuna, sea bass, mullet and mackerel, waiting to be reeled in. From the Black Sea, Istanbul is also provided with a steady supply of juicy mussels and *hamsi*, a type of anchovy.

Turkish Delight

Sweets are also popular and eaten throughout the day, not just after a meal. They are sold in shops, on stalls and by street vendors. Istanbul is renowned for its *baklava*, sweet pastries coated with syrup and often filled with nuts.

Midye dolmasi *Mussels are stuffed with a spiced rice mixture, steamed and served with a squirt of lemon juice.*

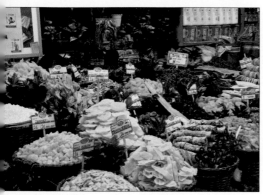

A splendid array of fruit, vegetables and dried goods in the Spice Bazaar

up. At the height of the Ottoman Empire, in the 16th and 17th centuries, legions of kitchen staff slaved away on the Sultan's behalf. Court cooks usually specialized in particular dishes. Some prepared soups, while others just grilled meats or fish, or dreamed up combinations of vegetables, or baked breads, or made puddings and sherberts. As Ottoman rule expanded to North Africa, the Balkans and parts of southern Russia, influences from these far-flung places crept into the Turkish imperial kitchens. Complex dishes of finely seasoned stuffed meats and vegetables, often with such fanciful names as "lady's lips", "Vizier's fingers" and the "fainting Imam", appeared. This imperial tradition lives on in many of Istanbul's

restaurants, where dishes such as *karniyarik* (halved aubergines (eggplant) stuffed with minced lamb, pine nuts and dried fruit) and *hünkar beğendili köfte* (meatballs served with a smooth purée of smoked aubergine and cheese) grace the menu.

Fresh catch from the Bosphorus on a fish stall in Karaköy

BAZAAR CULTURE

A visit to the market that spills out around Istanbul's Spice Bazaar *(see p88)* is an absolute must. A cornucopia of fine ingredients is brought here daily from farms that surround the city. Apricots, watermelons, cherries and figs sit alongside staple vegetables, such as peppers, onions, aubergines and tomatoes. Fine cuts of lamb and beef, cheeses, pickles, herbs, spices and honey-drenched pastries and puddings are also on offer.

KNOW YOUR FISH

The profusion of different species in the waters around Istanbul makes the city a paradise for fish lovers:

Barbunya	Red mullet
Çupra	Sea bream
Dilbaligi	Sole
Hamsi	Anchovy
Kalamar	Squid
Kalka	Turbot
Kefal	Grey mullet
Kiliç	Swordfish
Levrek	Sea bass
Lüfer	Bluefish
Midye	Mussels
Palamut	Bonito tuna
Uskumru	Mackerel

Imam bayildi *Aubergines, stuffed with tomatoes, garlic and onions, are baked in the oven until meltingly soft.*

Levrek pilakisi *This stew is made by simmering sea bass fillets with potatoes, carrots, tomatoes, onions and garlic.*

Kadayif *Rounds of shredded filo pastry are stuffed with nuts and doused with honey to make a sumptuous dessert.*

Mezes

As in many southern European countries, a Turkish meal begins with a selection of appetizing starters known as *mezes*, which are placed in the middle of the table for sharing. In a basic *meyhane* restaurant, you may be offered olives, cheese and slices of melon, but in a grander establishment the choice will be enormous. Mainly consisting of cold vegetables and salads of various kinds, *mezes* can also include a number of hot dishes, such as *börek* (cheese pastries), fried mussels and squid. *Mezes* are eaten with bread and traditionally washed down with *rakı* (a clear, anise-flavoured spirit).

Humus with *pide* bread

Zeytinyağli enginar
(artichokes cooked in olive oil)

Coban salatasi (tomato, red onion and cucumber salad)

Ayse fasulye (green beans with tomato sauce)

Melon with beyaz peynir
(melon with a creamy, feta-like cheese)

Yalaci yaprak dolmasi
(stuffed vine leaves)

Tarama (a dip made with cod's roe, garlic and olive oil)

TURKISH BREADS

Bread is the cornerstone of every meal in Turkey and comes in a wide range of shapes and styles. Besides *ekmek* (crusty white loaves) the other most common types of Turkish bread are *yufka* and *pide*. *Yufka*, the typical bread of nomadic communities, is made from thinly rolled sheets of dough which are cooked on a griddle, and dried to help preserve them. They can then be heated up and served to accompany any main meal as required. *Pide* is the type of flat bread that is usually served with *mezes* and kebabs in restaurants. It consists of a flattened circle or oval of dough, sometimes brushed with beaten egg and sprinkled with sesame seeds or black cumin, that is baked in an oven. It is a staple during many religious festivals. In the month of Ramadan, no meal is considered complete without *pide*. Another popular bread is *simit*, a crisp, ring-shaped savoury loaf that comes covered in sesame seeds.

A delivery of freshly baked *simit* loaves

What to Drink in Istanbul

The most common drink in Istanbul is tea *(çay)*, which is normally served black in small, tulip-shaped glasses. It is offered to you wherever you go: in shops and bazaars, and even in banks and offices. Breakfast is usually accompanied by tea, whereas small cups of strong Turkish coffee *(kahve)* are drunk mid-morning and also at the end of meals. Cold drinks include a variety of fresh fruit juices, such as orange and cherry, and refreshing syrup-based sherbets. Although Turkey does produce its own wine and beer, the most popular alcoholic drink in Istanbul is rakı, which is usually served to accompany mezes.

Fruit juice seller

SOFT DRINKS

Bottled mineral water *(su)* is sold in corner shops and served in restaurants everywhere. If you are feeling adventurous, you may like to try a glass of *ayran*, salty liquid yoghurt. *Boza*, made from bulgur wheat, is another local drink to sample (*see p92*). There is always a variety of refreshing fruit and vegetable juices available. They include cherry juice *(vişne suyu)*, turnip juice *(şalgam suyu)* and şıra, a juice made from fermented grapes.

Vişne suyu   **Ayran**

COFFEE AND TEA

Turkish coffee *(kahve)* is dark and strong and is ordered according to the amount of sugar required: *az* (little), *orta* (medium), or *çok şekerli* (a lot). You may have to ask for it especially, as some restaurants may give you instant coffee. The ubiquitous drink is tea *(çay)*. It is served with sugar but without milk, and in a small, tulip-shaped glass. Apple *(elma)*, is the most popular flavour, but there are also linden *(ıhlamur)*, rosehip *(kuşburnu)* and mint *(nane)* teas.

Traditional samovar for tea

ALCOHOLIC DRINKS

The national alcoholic drink in Turkey is rakı – "lion's milk" – a clear, anise-flavoured spirit, which turns cloudy when water is added. It is drunk with fish and mezes. The Turkish wine industry produces some good reds and whites, served in many restaurants. Doluca and Kavaklıdere are two of the leading brands. Foreign and imported wines are widely available at high prices. Turkey's own Efes Pilsen beer is widely sold. Note that alcohol is not served in some of the cheaper restaurants and kebab houses.

Rakı   **Beer**   **Red wine**   **White wine**

Turkish coffee is a very strong drink and an acquired taste for most people.

Apple tea   **Limeflower tea**

Sahlep is a hot, winter drink made from powdered orchid root.

Choosing a Restaurant

The restaurants in this guide have been selected for their good value, exceptional food, or interesting location. These listings highlight some of the factors that may influence your choice, such as whether you can opt to eat outdoors or if the venue offers live music. Entries are alphabetical within each price category.

PRICE CATEGORIES
Price categories include a three-course meal for one, and all unavoidable extras including service and tax
$ under US$15
$$$ US$15–US$20
$$$ US$20–US$25
$$$$ US$25–US$35
$$$$$ Over US$35

SERAGLIO POINT

Backpackers Restaurant
$

Yeni Akbıyık Caddesi 14/1, Sultanahmet, 34400 **Tel** *(0212) 638 55 86*   **Map** *3 E5 (5 E5)*

Simple, upbeat snacks are served here with the accent more on wines and beer than food. This is very much a cheerful and informal budget gathering place. People congregate to drink, eat hearty snacks, swap travel stories and plan their next journey. Backpackers is a great staging post in the budget area of Sultanahmet.

Doy-Doy
$

Şifa Hamamı Sokak 13, Sultanahmet, 34110 **Tel** *(0212) 517 15 88*   **Map** *3 D5 (5 D5)*

An impressive selection of soups, kebabs, *pide* (flat bread) in abundance, colourful salads, vegetarian dishes and rich desserts is on offer here. Everything is prepared very authentically. Doy-Doiy is a cheerful venue with great prices but alcohol is not served. The rooftop terrace is perfect in summer with inviting views and sea breezes.

Group Restaurant
$

Şehit Mehmet Paşa Yokuşu 4, Sultanahmet, 34110 **Tel** *(0212) 517 47 00*   **Map** *3 D5 (5 D5)*

Part gift shop, part café and restaurant, this is a magnet for tourists and is always bustling. The coffee and sticky pastries are popular but more substantial fare is also served. Grills, salads and stews are on the menu and served in generous portions at reasonable prices. Alcohol is available.

Ahırkapı Lokanta
$$$

Armada Hotel, Ahır Kapı Sokak, Sultanahmet, 34110 **Tel** *(0212) 638 13 70*   **Map** *3 F3 (5 F5)*

This restaurant has the atmosphere of a 1930s Turkish tavern and live *fasıl* music. In keeping with the decor, the cuisine is typically Turkish with a variety of delicious mezes and main dishes, such as *yoğurtlu yaprak dolması* (minced meat in vine leaves with yoghurt). The rooftop terrace boasts views over Sultanahmet.

Konyalı
$$$

Topkapı Palace, Sultanahmet, 34110 **Tel** *(0212) 513 96 96*   **Map** *3 F3*

This gastronomic landmark has been in business for four decades, serving appetizing mezes, meats, salads and fish. There is an award-winning à la carte menu. Located within the Topkapı Palace, it has commanding views of the Bosphorus. Try the elegant "afternoon tea" menu. Konyalı is open for lunch only and closed on Tuesdays.

Sarnıç
$$$$

Soğukçeşme Sokak, Sultanahmet, 34110 **Tel** *(0212) 512 42 91*   **Map** *3 E4 (5 F3)*

Converted from a Byzantine cistern with lofty columns and a domed ceiling, Sarnıç is dimly lit by wrought-iron chandeliers and candles and has an impressive fireplace. Piano music is often played in the evenings. The menu has variety but diners come here more for the atmosphere than the top cuisine.

Seven Hills Restaurant
$$$$

Tevkifhane Sokak 8, Sultanahmet, 34110 **Tel** *(0212) 516 94 97*   **Map** *3 E4 (5 E4)*

The chef here is from Bolu, a region that nurtures Turkey's most creative chefs. The food is outstanding and the choice is sumptuous – try the fresh fish, lobster and seafood, or the star dish, the Sultan's Lamb. Top it off with well-chosen wines and a view over Haghia Sophia. This restaurant is part of the Seven Hills Hotel.

SULTANAHMET

Café Camille
$

Bab-i Ali Caddesi 8, Cağaloğlu, 34110 **Tel** *(0212) 527 81 77*   **Map** *3 D4 (5 D3)*

This small café, with its industrious, bustling kitchen, is the place to grab a cup of coffee or a foaming cappuccino and home-made cakes. Simple lunches with quiche, omelettes and salads are popular. They serve delicious fresh fruit juices and milk shakes. The service is brisk and friendly.

Key to Symbols *see back cover flap*

Cafe Müze

Divanyolu Caddesi 84, Çemberlitaş, 34110 **Tel** *(0212) 512 00 80*   **Map** *2 C4 (4 C4)*

Lacking any pretensions, this is a small café adjacent to the old printing presses at the Press Museum. Omelettes, hot and cold snacks and sandwiches and a few salads are on offer and the coffee is good. They also serve draft beer. It is a relief to come here to escape the bustle of the busy street outside.

Cağaloğlu Paksut

Bab-i Ali Caddesi 16, Cağaloğlu, 34110 **Tel** *(0212) 528 63 94*   **Map** *3 D4 (5 D3)*

Diners will find good, honest cooking here. Stews, salads, rice and vegetable dishes are freshly cooked each day at this popular neighbourhood *lokanta* (traditional restaurant). It is best to go at lunch time. No alcohol is served but there are fruit juices and mineral water.

Cennet

Divanyolu 90, Çemberlitaş, Sultanahmet, 34110 **Tel** *(0212) 513 14 16*   **Map** *3 D4 (5 C3)*

Cennet means heaven and here they specialize in Anatolian dishes such as *mantı* (meat-filled ravioli topped with yoghurt) and *gözleme* (pancakes) cooked over a griddle. Women wear traditional costume and diners sit on the ground on colourful cushions and watch the food being prepared. This is a great place for filling up on snacks.

The Cure

Divanyolu Caddesi, Ticarethane Sokak 35, Sultanahmet, 34110 **Tel** *(0212) 528 19 22*   **Map** *3 D4 (5 D3)*

There is a staggering selection of truly creative international dishes to sample here. Liver with an onion and spinach sauce is popular, the fajitas are delicious and so is the hot corn soup. The service is enthusiastic. Prices for exotic cocktails are high and light jazz is played on occasion.

Sultanahmet Köftecisi

Divanyolu Caddesi 12A, Sultanahmet, 34110 **Tel** *(0212) 513 14 38*   **Map** *3 E4 (5 E4)*

Almost an institution in Sultanahmet, this restaurant has been going since the 1920s and turns out simple, trademark dishes such as *köfte* (meatballs), *piyaz* (beans in sauce) and *pilav* (rice). Locals crowd in here for lunch and queues mean there is no lingering.

The Pudding Shop

Divanyolu Caddesi 6, Sultanahmet, 34110 **Tel** *(0212) 522 29 70*   **Map** *3 E4 (5 E4)*

In the 1950s, nowhere else in Istanbul provided food and tourist information to backpackers. They serve wonderfully cooked Turkish fare. There is an excellent choice of soups, grilled meats, salads, stews and sautéed dishes and, of course, rich puddings. Former customers frequently return.

Valide Sultan Konak

Kutlugün Sokak 1, Sultanahmet, 34110 **Tel** *(0212) 638 06 00*   **Map** *3 E4 (5 E4)*

The semicircular rooftop restaurant of the Valide Sultan Konağı Hotel *(see p186)* commands stunning views of the sea and historic surrounding area. Menus are well balanced with meat, vegetables, meze, kebabs and stews. The stuffed vegetables are particularly creative and taste as good as they look. They also serve seafood and pizzas.

Balıkcı Sabahattin

Seyt Hasankuyu Sokak 1, Sultanahmet, 34110 **Tel** *(0212) 458 23 02*   **Map** *3 E3 (5 F5)*

Everything works well at this delightful fish restaurant. They have a long and delicious menu, having been in business since 1927. The fish and seafood are mouthwatering and other creative dishes include spicy squash with yoghurt. Recommended for smart service and consistently good food. There is a no smoking section.

Kathisma

Yeni Akbıyık Caddesidesi 26, Sultanahmet, 34400 **Tel** *(0212) 518 97 10*   **Map** *3 E5 (5 C3)*

This stylish restaurant takes its name from the Byzantine emperor's lodge which once overlooked the Hipppodrome *(see p80)*. Turkish dishes include *mücver* (fried courgettes), *fırında kuzu* (roast lamb) and some typical and delicious desserts such as *sakızlı sutlaç* (rice pudding with gum mastic).

Rami

Utangaç Sokak 6, Sultanahmet, 34110 **Tel** *(0212) 517 65 93*   **Map** *3 E4 (5 E4)*

Dedicated to a 20th-century painter, Rami Uluer, this romantic restaurant is one of the prettiest in the area. It excels in traditional Ottoman cuisine. *Hünkar beğendi* (meat with a creamy aubergine purée) is a popular dish. Evening diners can see the sound and light display at the Blue Mosque from the terrace.

Rumeli Café

Ticarethane Sokak 8, Sultanahmet, 34110 **Tel** *(0212) 512 00 08*   **Map** *3 E4 (5 D3)*

This is a delightfully atmospheric restaurant just off the busy Divanyolu. Housed in an old printing factory, the Rumeli has a strong Greek flavour to it as well as Mediterranean aromas. Vegetarian dishes are popular and specialties include grilled lamb with various sauces. Tomatoes, herbs and yoghurt feature in many dishes.

Türkistan Aşevi

Tavukhane Sokak 36, Sultanahmet, 34110 **Tel** *(0212) 638 65 25*   **Map** *3 E5 (5 D5)*

A converted Ottoman mansion house, Türkistan Aşevi is furnished with exquisite carpets and textiles. Diners eat in nomadic style using copper trays for tables and wearing the slippers provided. Central Asian-style *mantı* (ravioli) and *gözleme* (pancakes) are favourites and done well. No alcohol is served.

BAZAAR QUARTER

Akdeniz Restaurant   ⑤

Mustafa Kemalpaşa Caddesi 48, Aksaray, 36420 **Tel** *(0212) 458 13 00*   **Map** *2 A4*

This is an unassuming, mid-range *lokanta* (traditional restaurant) serving a large range of appetizers, kebabs, *lahmacun* (thin-crust crepe), *pide* (flat bread) and pizzas. The specialty is tandoor lamb. Ask for a table away from the TV screen if you prefer peace and quiet with meals. Alcohol is available.

Havuzlu   ⑤

Gani Çelebi Sokak 3, Grand Bazaar, Beyazıt, 36420 **Tel** *(0212) 527 33 46*   **Map** *3 C4 (4 B3)*

Havuzlu is where you head when hunger interrupts a shopping spree. It is a small restaurant serving honest local food. Everything is cooked freshly. The soups, *dolma* (stuffed vine leaves) and different kinds of kebabs and grills are great snacks. Havuzlu means "with pool" and is named for the burbling fountain found inside.

İskender Saray   ⑤

Atatürk Bulvarı 116, Aksaray, 36420 **Tel** *(0212) 520 34 04*   **Map** *2 A3*

This classic restaurant serves döner kebabs and signature dishes include *İskender kebab* (döner meat on bread with a rich sauce) and *saç kavurma* (lamb and vegetables flambéed at the table). The white table cloths and cheerful, friendly staff lend a professional touch. They do a handy takeaway service. No alcohol is served.

Karaca   ⑤

Gazi Sinan Paşa Sokak, Vezir Han 1/A, Nuruosmaniye, 36420 **Tel** *(0212) 512 90 94*   **Map** *3 D4 (4 C3)*

This large restaurant is part of an authentic Ottoman caravanserai. Diners eat very well here and dishes such as *pazı dolması* (stuffed chard) and *islim kebabı* (lamb with aubergine) are hearty and filling. Save room for the calorific *kabak tatlısı* (pumpkin pudding). The clientele includes shopkeepers from the Grand Bazaar.

Özbolu Kebap House   ⑤

Hoca Paşa Sokak 33, Sirkeci, 34430 **Tel** *(0212) 522 46 63*   **Map** *2 E3 (5 D2)*

In a street of budget kebaberies, this one stands out with an amazing choice of hot and cold dishes. The grills, stews seasonal fish and puddings are hearty, fresh and delicious. Succulent and juicy kebabs are the dish of the house. The atmosphere here is cheerful. Sour cherry juice and soft drinks are available instead of alcohol.

Subaşı   ⑤

Nuruosmaniye Caddesi, Kılıççılar Sokak 48, Çarşıkapı, 36420 **Tel** *(0212) 522 47 62*   **Map** *3 D4 (4 C3)*

Located near the Nuruosmaniye Gate of the Grand Bazaar, Subaşı is an uncomplicated traditional eatery serving up freshly cooked dishes every day. This is mainly a lunch place and diners will find the food at its freshest and tastiest a this time. You can select various stews, meat and baked dishes before you are seated.

Borsa Lokanta   ⑤⑤

Yalı Köşkü Caddesi, Yalı Köşkü Han 60, Sirkeci, 36420 **Tel** *(0212) 511 80 79*   **Map** *3 D2 (5 D1)*

There are two eateries here, a fast-food, self-service one on the ground floor and a more formal one on the level above. Borsa Lokanta has many branches in Istanbul. One of their trademark recipes is *beğendili kebabı* (meat with a creamy aubergine sauce). The service is extremely competent. Alcohol is served.

Dârüzziyafe   ⑤⑤⑤

Şifahane Caddesi 6, Süleymaniye, 36420 **Tel** *(0212) 511 84 14*   **Map** *4 A1 (2 B2)*

The former kitchens of the Süleymaniye Mosque *(see pp90–91)* house this excellent restaurant, serving unusual and elaborate Ottoman dishes. The nourishing house soup is made with spinach, vegetables and meat. Mezes are available. For dessert, try *keşkül* (milk pudding with pistachios and almonds). It is best to reserve. No alcohol served.

Pandeli   ⑤⑤⑤

Mısır Çarşı 1, Eminönü, 36420 **Tel** *(0212) 527 39 09*   **Map** *3 D2 (4 C1)*

Pandeli is one of Istanbul's most venerable restaurants and they have a crisp and brisk attitude to their business. They are ideally located in the middle of the Spice Bazaar; so it is always crowded and lively. Locals come for the *patlıcan böreği* (aubergine pastry) and sea bass steamed in wax paper (*kağıtta levrek*). Reservations advised.

BEYOĞLU

Nature and Peace   ⑤

Büyükparmakkapı Sokak 21, Beyoğlu, 34430 **Tel** *(0212) 252 86 09*   **Map** *7 E4*

Nature and Peace was one of Istanbul's first vegetarian restaurants and it has stayed in the forefront when it comes to providing wholesome, healthy foods. Vegan dishes are also served. Chicken and fish are on the menu but red meat is not on offer. Desserts, tea-time treats and fresh fruit juices are available all day. Highly recommended.

Key to Price Guide *see p198* **Key to Symbols** *see back cover flap*

Özkonak   ⑤

Akarsu Caddesi 60 Cihangir, Taksim, 34430 **Tel** *(0212) 249 13 07*   **Map** *7 E5*

Istanbul's celebrity journalists, writers and fashion models flock here for the freshly cooked, honest stews, *pilavs* (rice dishes), salads and baked puddings. Some come just for the tastiest *tavuk göğsü* (milk pudding made with shredded chicken breast) in the city. This is mainly a lunch-time spot with speedy service. Alcohol is not served.

Tadım   ⑤

Meşelik Sokak, Taksim, 34430 **Tel** *(212) 249 82 28*   **Map** *7 E4*

Set below street level, this bright and friendly restaurant serves a good selection of Turkish stewed meats, vegetables, heart-warming soups and grills. The obligatory salad and *pilav* (rice) appears with each dish. It is deservedly popular with local office workers who crowd in for lunch. No alcohol is served.

Zencefil   ⑤

Kurabiye Sokak 3, Beyoğlu, 34430 **Tel** *(0212) 243 82 34*   **Map** *7 E4*

This is one of the premier vegetarian restaurants in Istanbul. Daily specials are marked on a blackboard. Everything is fresh and wholesome and the service is skillful. Baked vegetable dishes, home-made breads, soups and herb teas do not disappoint. There are also delicious desserts available. Alcohol is served.

Chez Vous   ⑤⑤

Firuzağa Mahallesi, Cezayir Sokak 21, Galatasaray, Beyoğlu, 34430 **Tel** *(0212) 245 95 32*   **Map** *7 D4*

Part of the rebirth and design revolution sweeping most of Beyoğlu, this small café (part of a restored period mansion) clings to the steep steps of trend-setting French Street. Light snacks and salads are served. The service is rushed and the table wines are expensive, but trendy Chez Vous is great for fun.

Curry House   ⑤⑤

Lamartin Caddesi 33, Taksim, 80090 **Tel** *(0212) 361 48 07*   **Map** *7 E3*

Istanbul's only Pakistani restaurant serves delicious spicy curries. Lamb, vegetarian, beef, shrimp and chicken are prepared to any degree of spiciness you desire. The biryani rice is a masterpiece. Ask for the masala tea afterwards. The family waits on the tables. Top Pakistani singer, Hadika Kiyani, heads here when in Istanbul. Alcohol is served.

Hac ı Baba   ⑤⑤

İstiklâl Caddesi 49, Beyoğlu, 34430 **Tel** *(0212) 244 18 86*   **Map** *7 E4*

This busy and popular restaurant on two floors turns out the most amazing variety of tasty, colourful dishes – over 40 different hot main meals, mezes and 25 different desserts. Try the star dish, *kuzu tandır* (slow-baked lamb) The service is polished and professional, however, the decor is somewhat drab.

Hacı Salih   ⑤⑤

İstiklâl Caddesi 201/1-2, Beyoğlu, 34430 **Tel** *(0212) 243 45 28*   **Map** *7 E4*

The Hacı Salih has been delighting diners for over 60 years with honest, fresh Anatolian dishes. The *İmam bayıldı* (stuffed aubergine) is fantastic. Classic choices with lamb or aubergine will outflavour other dishes. Great stews are baked in earthenware, and there is a wide range of baked and sweet desserts. Alcohol is discreetly available.

Natural Grill House   ⑤⑤

Şehit Muhtar Caddesi 38/A, Taksim, 34430 **Tel** *(0212) 238 33 61*   **Map** *7 E3*

Rustic tables and talented cooking are the appeal here. Fresh salads, grilled meats and baked vegetarian dishes are well cooked and presented. Mexican steak is one of the house specialties. The Grill House is popular with locals and also guests from the nearby hotels. Several different beers are served.

Rum-eli Meyhane   ⑤⑤

Faik Paşa Sokak 37, Çurkurcuma, Taksim, 34430 **Tel** *(0212) 244 38 01*   **Map** *7 E4*

A vibrant symbol of recent Turkish/Greek bonds, this is a hugely popular Greek taverna. Ten choices of meze, main courses and desserts are offered. Their whimsical website gives interactive updates on menus and news about their gourmet shop. All types of alcohol are served. Rum-eli is recommended with gusto.

Taksimoda Café   ⑤⑤

Siraselviler Caddesi 9, Taksim, 34430 **Tel** *(0212) 334 85 00*   **Map** *7 E4*

You will find a wonderful variety of food at Taksimoda, including excellent pastries and afternoon tea cakes. It is part of the Taksim Hill hotel and makes a convenient meeting point and refreshment station. Service is frenetic, more often chaotic, but the well-prepared food compensates. Alcohol is served and there is a small bar.

Asır Rest   ⑤⑤⑤

Kalyoncu Kulluk Caddesi 94, Beyoğlu, 34430 **Tel** *(0212) 297 05 57*   **Map** *7 D4*

Asır is the kind of friendly, convivial place you hope to find on holiday. The staff are friendly and attentive and the food is outstandingly good and economical. Over 50 varieties of mezes are offered amongst many innovative dishes with fish, chicken and chick peas. Typical of *meyhane* (wine bar) culture, there is live *fasıl* music in the evenings.

Leb-i-Derya   ⑤⑤⑤

İstiklâl Caddesi, Kumbaracı Yokuşu, Kumbaracı Han 115/7, Beyoğlu, 34430 **Tel** *(0212) 293 49 89*   **Map** *7 D5*

It is hard to beat this restaurant's marvellous view over Istanbul. Glass, wood and soft lighting are the backdrop for the abundance of appetizers and well-cooked Mediterranean-style healthy main courses, vegetable dishes and salads. There is a lively bar that attracts a dedicated happy hour crowd.

Refik
$$$

Sofyalı Sokak 10-12, Tünel, 34430 **Tel** *(0212) 243 28 34*   **Map** *7 D5*

Refik is an icon of Bohemian Beyoğlu. The restaurant retains its faded plastic tablecloths and bygone era ambience. Intellectuals and media types frequent it every evening. It is an authentic *meyhane* (wine bar) that favours Black Sea dishes. The mezes here are large enough for a main meal. Plenty of alcohol is served.

Restaurant Nuova Rosa
$$$

Cumhuriyet Caddesi 131/, Elmadağ, 34430 **Tel** *(0212) 241 28 27*   **Map** *7F2*

The refreshed and rejuvenated Rosa has traded its 1980s dark interior for gleaming ultra modern decor. The fixed menus are popular and economical. The food has Italian overtones but many of the dishes look and taste more Turkish and Mediterranean. There is an excellent bar where a happy-hour crowd meet. Reservations are advised.

Rio Bravo
$$$

İstiklâl Caddesi 303, Beyoğlu, 34430 **Tel** *(0212) 292 92 69/70*   **Map** *7 D4*

The accent at Rio Bravo is on Tex-Mex, including a huge tap room and bar. The fajitas, western salads and burritos are hearty and delicious, as are the guacamole dishes and lime pie. Tequila and cocktails are a treat for connoisseurs. Sometimes impromptu music is played.

Yakup 2
$$$

Asmalımescit Sokak 35-37, Tünel, 34430 **Tel** *(0212) 249 29 25*   **Map** *7 D5*

Once the most popular restaurant amongst the journalistic and media elite, Yakup now caters more for groups and tourists. It is in the atmospheric and upbeat backstreets of Beyoğlu. The food is of a high quality with excellent salads, grills and impressive mezes. There are drinks of all sorts and many just come to enjoy this.

Zindan
$$$

İstiklâl Caddesi 13, Beyoğlu, 34430 **Tel** *(0212) 252 73 40*   **Map** *7 E4*

Terracotta bricks and vaulted ceilings form the interior at Zindan. It is handy for Taksim and the cooking is classic Ottoman with intriguing variations. Stinging-nettle *börek* (pastry) is rare and tasty and they spruce up the meaty kebabs with fruit. Everything looks and tastes appetizing, and there are good wines.

Çatı
$$$$

Asmalı Mescit Mah, Orhan Adli Apaydın Sokak 20 (7th floor), Beyoğlu, 34430 **Tel** *(0212) 251 00 00*   **Map** *7 D5*

This is a popular rendezvous spot for locals and visitors alike. The walls are covered with photos of celebrity journalists, actors and poets who have eaten here. Çatı has won gourmet awards and the mainly Turkish menu is reliable and beautifully prepared. There is live music in the evenings and belly dancing staged for groups.

China Plaza
$$$$

Recep Paşa Caddesi 5, Taksim, 34430 **Tel** *(0212) 256 36 45*   **Map** *7 E3*

If you need a break from rich Turkish foods, China Plaza is a local landmark that offers Cantonese and Szechuan cooking at its finest. This is a Chinese restaurant with urban flair and exotic fare. The chicken with oyster sauce or the pineapple duck are superb. Alcohol is served – the Chinese beer is first rate and there are many wines on offer.

Feşmeken
$$$$

İnönü Caddesi 53/A, Gümüşsuyu, Taksim, 34430 **Tel** *(0212) 251 02 03/04*   **Map** *7 F4*

A short distance from the hub of Taksim, this lively restaurant and bar specializes in Turkish classic dishes with meat, aubergines and rice, but also does an excellent steak and chips. The service is better when the enormous TV is switched off. The happy hour and late night music attract a young crowd.

Fisher
$$$$

İnönü Caddesi 51/A, Taksim, 34430 **Tel** *(0212) 245 25 76*   **Map** *7 F4*

Fisher was one of the first middle European restaurants in Istanbul. The clientele has stayed loyal after decades and dishes such as borscht, schnitzel, pirogies and strudel seem as popular today as they have always been. It is a little crab, even austere, but the owners seem reluctant to renovate or change too much of a good thing.

Four Seasons
$$$$

İstiklâl Caddesi 509, Beyoğlu, 34430 **Tel** *(0212) 293 39 41*   **Map** *7 D5*

A symbol of cross-cultural Pera, the Four Seasons has reinforced its international image and menu. Its reputation is built on chateaubriand, French onion soup and similar dishes. The fixed lunch menu attracts nearby consular staff, however it is also ideal for a romantic dinner for two.

Gitane
$$$$

Firuzağa Mah, Cezayir Sokak 3 (French Street), Galatasaray, 34430 **Tel** *(0212) 245 92 63*   **Map** *7 D4*

Gitane is owned by one of Turkey's most renowned fashion designers. The extensive menu has choices for breakfast, brunch, lunch and festive dinners and there is excellent local wine on offer. The cheese platter highlights the new interest in Anatolian cheeses.

Great Hong Kong
$$$$

Dünya Sağlik Sokak 12/B, Taksim, 34430 **Tel** *(0212) 252 42 68*   **Map** *7 F4*

A taste of imperial China in the middle of Taksim, the Great Hong Kong is easily recognized by its imposing pagoda-shaped entrance. Dragons, lanterns and rich trappings add to the decoration. The spicy Szechuan dishes, beef with hot pickles and delicious rice are good choices. Chinese beer and rice wines are available.

Key to Price Guide *see p198* **Key to Symbols** *see back cover flap*

Rejans

İstiklâl Caddesi, Emir Nevruz Sokak 17, Beyoğlu, **Tel** *(0212) 244 16 10*

Map 7 D4

One of the most respected eateries in Istanbul, Rejans has been in business since the 1920s when it was established by homesick Russian immigrants. Come here to sample the fine regional dishes such as beef stroganoff, chicken Kiev and *piroshki* (vegetables in pastry). The owners often serve caviar and always vodka.

Şeref

Cumhuriyet Caddesi. Seyhan Apt. No. 12/1 Elmadağ, Taksim, 34430 **Tel** *(0212) 291 99 55*

Map 7 F2

The carefully prepared menu at this very stylish up-to-the-minute café-bar cum restaurant has masterful touches. Appetizers, hamburgers and pizzas are good, and the steak, vegetable dishes, stews, fries and salads come in generous portions. Şeref has domestic wines and a well-stocked bar.

Sofra

Cartoon Hotel Yanı, Tarlabaşı Bulvarı 36 Taksim, 34430 **Tel** *(0212) 297 21 78*

Map 7 E3

The Turkish owner at Sofra has made a great impact on the London restaurant scene and brought his culinary concepts back home. The accent is on colourful Neo-Mediterranean dishes with assertive flavours. Meat and fish courses are flawless and the presentation exciting. There are fine views of the Bosphorus from the terrace in summer.

Sofyalı

Sofyalı Sokak 9, Tünel, Beyoğlu, 34430 **Tel** *(0212) 245 03 62*

Map 7 D5

Tucked away in a leafy alleyway where restaurant competition is fierce, Sofyalı has delicious home-made mezes, pretty tables and a solid reputation for skillful, professional cooking. The menu is not large but quality dominates. Try the stuffed fish. Their stuffed chard creation is also legendary. Domestic wines and other alcoholic drinks are served.

Asmalımescit Balıkçısı

Asmalımescit Mah. Sofyalı Sokak 5/A Tünel, Beyoğlu, 34430 **Tel** *(0212) 251 39 39*

Map 7 D5

The pulse of Beyoğlu beats at this popular fish-only restaurant. Linen, silver service and candles add class to the stone walls and cheerful, chic atmosphere. Every kind of fresh daily catch in Istanbul is served here. Desserts are good and here is a reasonable wine list. There are monthly art exhibitions that adorn the walls.

Flamm

Sofyalı Sokak 16/1, Asmalımescit, 34430 **Tel** *(02120 245 76 04/05*

Map 7 D5

One of the pioneer "nouveau" restaurants, Flamm is small and intimate with a casual, friendly cocktail bar. The owner came to Istanbul from Bodrum, and imported some dishes from sunny Med-side kitchens, including ingenious ways with pasta and rice. You will want to return for the excellent honest cooking and convivial ambience.

41 Paralel

İstiklâl Caddesi, Hüseyin Ağa Mah, Ezine Apt 1/3 Beyoğlu, 34430 **Tel** *(0212) 244 74 22*

Map 7 D4

Extensive and imaginative menus are offered at 41 Paralel. Many dishes have irresistible gourmet sauces. The leek and spinach *köfte* is divine and the Eastern dessert with baked cheese, *künefe*, is a masterpiece, arguably rivaled by the chocolate soufflé. This is a remarkable restaurant in an already trendy area.

Mikla

Marmara Pera Hotel, Meşrutiyet Caddesi 167/185, Tepebaşı, Beyoğlu, 34430 **Tel** *(0212) 293 56 56*

Map 7 D5

Mikla provides a magnificent dining experience – if you can get a reservation. It offers a predominantly seafood menu but unusual culinary influences mingle and the results are exquisite. The decor is subtle and the mood dignified. There are stunning vistas from the bar at the top of the Marmara Pera Hotel.

Panorama

Marmara Hotel, Taksim Square, Taksim, 34430 **Tel** *(0212) 251 46 96*

Map 7 E4

This restaurant with fine views on the top floor of the Marmara Hotel was one of the first in the city to embrace international cuisine. It still deserves its original praise for creative cuisine. Visitors revel in the truly outstanding French and Italian food and authentic decor. Live jazz and dance music is played on weekends.

Ta Nhcia

Asmalı Mescit Mah, Orhan Adli Apaydın Sokak 36-42, Beyoğlu, 34430 **Tel** *(0212) 245 93 66*

Map 7 D5

This successful gourmet Greek restaurant serves dazzling Mediterranean creations that combine the best of Greek and Turkish cookery. The decor, presentation and signature touches make this a real treasure. Fish is recommended and the lamb dishes redefine gourmet tastes. There is an extensive wine list and Greek music after hours.

GREATER ISTANBUL

à la Turka

Hazine Sokak 8, Ortaköy, 34349 **Tel** *(0212) 258 79 24*

Map 9 F3

Tucked away on a side street near Ortaköy mosque, à la Turka is a modest but attractive restaurant. It serves mostly classic Turkish dishes done to perfection. Particularly good are the *dolma* (stuffed vine leaves), and the chef uses herbs very creatively. It is recommended as a reliable favourite.

Beyti   🚶 🍽 $$
Orman Sokak 8, Florya, 34710 **Tel** *(0212) 663 29 92*

Beyti is a 60-year-old Istanbul institution and award-winning legend when it comes to meat and kebabs. There is a vast dining area, with 12 dining rooms and secluded nooks. It is crowded here for lunch and dinner and the good service matches the unerringly excellent food. Beyti kebab is the speciality. There is a good wine selection.

Bolkepçe   🚶 🍽 $$
Muallim Naci Caddesi 41/9, Ortaköy, 34349 **Tel** *(0212) 259 82 61*   **Map** *9 F2*

Eating at Bolkepçe is like eating in your own home. The hand-made curtains and hospitality reflect the home-cooked dishes that have made this place so popular. They routinely serve traditional hearty Turkish dishes, grills and stews, and are known for their *mantı* (ravioli) and tasty *böreks* (stuffed pastry parcels).

Da Mario   ♿ 🚶 🍽 $$
Dilhayat Sokak 7, Etiler, 56730 **Tel** *(0212) 265 15 96*

This was one of Istanbul's first Italian restaurants and is still recognized for its refined and tasty cuisine. The up-market chic decor is in harmony with the contemporary cooking. Veal is especially well prepared. There are some interesting wines. Super desserts and impeccable service round it off. Reservations are advised.

Il Piccolo   ♿ 🚶 🚇 🎵 🍽 $$
Bağdat Caddesi, Ogün Sokak 2, Caddebostan, 95230 **Tel** *(0216) 369 64 43*

An established favourite that has been serving well-cooked dishes for many years and keeping up with trends. Located in an energetic shopping district on the Asian side, meals are served outdoors in summer and a live band plays on weekends. They have simple pizzas and pasta dishes with great sauces plus good wines and Italian cheeses.

Koşebaşı Ocakbaşı   ♿ 🚶 🚇 🍽 $$
Çamlık Sokak 15/3, Levent, **Tel** *(0212) 270 24 33*   **Map** *7 F1*

This internationally-acclaimed prize-winning kebab restaurant has many branches around Turkey and in Istanbul. Bright and airy with absolutely delicious kebabs in the tradition of eastern Turkey. They prepare *künefe* (a rich angel hair dessert baked with cheese) better than anybody in Istanbul.

Zeyrekhane   ♿ 🚶 🚇 🍽 $$
Sinanağa Mahallesi, Ibadethane Arkası Sokak 10, Zeyrek, Fatih, 35600 **Tel** *(0212) 532 27 78*   **Map** *2 B2*

This café for tasty snacks and light meals is combined with a restaurant in a restored Ottoman building. The cool, leafy outdoor courtyard is used in summer. The main restaurant succeeds spectacularly with traditional Ottoman recipes. Alcohol is served. It is best to make a booking for an evening meal.

Develi   🚶 🚇 🍽 $$$
Gümuşyüzük Sokak 7, Samatya, Kocamustafapaşa, 35420 **Tel** *(0212) 632 79 82*   **Map** *off map*

It is no exaggeration to say that you have not really eaten a kebab until you have tucked into a Develi one. Kebabs here are prepared in unusual ways and the quality keeps getting better. The service is slick and all the touches that make dining a great experience are found here. Develi easily tops the kebab charts.

House Café   🚶 🍽 $$$
Salhane Sokak 1, Ortaköy, 34349 **Tel** *(0212) 227-26 99*   **Map** *9 F3*

There are no restaurants that epitomize Istanbul's dynamic revival quite like this one. The colourful salads, snacks and main courses are excellent and the funky decor is amazing, especially the ornately carved bar and octopus chandeliers. It is a magnet for celebrities and always busy.

Hünkar   ♿ 🚶 🍽 $$$
Akdeniz Caddesi 21, Fatih, 35600 **Tel** *(0212) 621 64 33*   **Map** *1 C4*

This family-run restaurant has an admirable record for serving tasty Turkish food, including delightful and little known Ottoman dishes. The walls are decorated with jars of bright pickled fruits and a small fountain sits in the midst of diners. *Böreks* (stuffed pastry parcels) , *köfte* (meatballs), *pilavs* (rice dishes) and salads are well prepared and served.

Sedef   ♿ 🚶 🚇 🍽 $$$
Fevzipaşa Caddesi 19, Fatih, 35600 **Tel** *(212) 532 82 33*

This is a bright and spacious restaurant that prides itself on its meat dishes. Grilled meats are the most popular but do not overlook the delicious vegetable stews. The chef does great things with hamburgers and, of course, kebabs. Children's portions are available. Like most establishments in the Fatih area, alcohol is not served.

Uludağ Et Lokantası   ♿ 🚶 🚇 🍽 $$$
Istanbul Caddesi 12, Florya, 34710 **Tel** *(0212) 579 02 94*

One of several well respected kebaberies in Istanbul, this one also serves up its own local kebab specialty. The restaurant is on the waterfront, not far from the airport, and has space for over 1,000 guests. Come here for a typical Turkish evening and unfailingly good food. The service is smart and the wines reasonable.

Asitane   🚶 🚇 🎵 🍽 $$$$
Kariye Hotel, Kariye Camii Sokak 18, Edirnekapı, 38100 **Tel** *(0212) 534 84 14*   **Map** *1 B1*

This is an outstanding eatery specializing in Ottoman cuisine. They serve some rare and obscure recipes inspired by records found in the Topkapı Palace. Steaks, fish and creative rice dishes are also on offer. Save room for the filling desserts. Asitane is highly recommended.

Key to Price Guide *see p198* **Key to Symbols** *see back cover flap*

Denizkızı $$$$

Çakmaktaşı Sokak 3/5, Kumkapı, 28601 **Tel** *(0212) 518 86 59*   **Map** *2 C5*

The cobbled streets of the old fishing neighbourhood of Kumkapı are dense with fish restaurants and *meyhanes* (traditional taverns). Denizkızı (which means mermaid) is one of these in a lively district. Diners select fish from the tank and the chef will fry, grill or steam it for you with vegetables. There are tables outdoors in summer.

Doğa Balık $$$$

Akarsu Caddesi 46, Cihangir, Taksim, 34433 **Tel** *(0212) 293 91 44*   **Map** *7 E5*

This is a highly regarded fish restaurant in an attractive area. Everything is friendly and comfortable here. Mezes are freshly prepared and colourful, and there is a daily set menu available. The salads are masterful. Domestic wines are available but rakı goes best with the many fish selections.

Galatelia $$$$

Galata Köprüsü, Karaköy Altı (Boğaz Tarafı) 11/12, Eminönü, 34120 **Tel** *(0212) 243 82 54*   **Map** *3 D1*

This is Istanbul's premier fish and seafood restaurant beneath the Galata Bridge. The prices for daily specials and fresh catch are great and there is a generous selection of home-made mezes, salads, wine and rakı. Locals flock here and you may be the only tourist. Gypsy music is played on weekends. It is highly recommended for authenticity.

Hacıbey $$$$

Teşvikiye Caddesi 156/B, Teşvikiye, 80400 **Tel** *(0212) 231 71 34*   **Map** *8 A2*

A bright and modern restaurant on two floors, Hacıbey caters to shoppers and ladies who lunch in Istanbul's shopping district. Try the succulent and substantial Bursa kebab, which has butter, tomato sauce and is topped with yoghurt. All grills are done over traditional charcoal. It is great fun here but can be very loud.

La Maison $$$$

Müvezzi Caddesi 63, Beşiktaş, 82500 **Tel** *(0212) 227 42 63*   **Map** *9 D3*

This is a thoroughly reliable and no-nonsense restaurant with a studious attitude to classical French cooking, enhanced by splendid vistas over the Bosphorus to the Asian side. La Maison is just as popular for power lunches as it is for receptions and intimate dining. It is hugely popular, so a reservation is essential.

Mezzaluna $$$$

Abdi İpekçi Caddesi 38/1, Nişantaşı, 80400 **Tel** *(0212) 231 31 42*   **Map** *8 A3*

Mezzaluna attracts shoppers and strollers at lunch and a serious social set in the evenings. With branches in other Turkish cities also, they cater for the upwardly mobile who crave well-cooked continental dishes. The accent is on Italian cooking and the mussels are first rate. Finish a refined meal with a potent grappa.

Café du Levent $$$$$

Rahmi M. Koç Museum, Hasköy Caddesi 27, Hasköy, 69800 **Tel** *(0212) 235 63 28*

Long before others, Café du Levent initiated the trend for serving gourmet food in a museum setting. The standards have not changed over the years and this is one of the most efficient restaurants in Istanbul. It is not cheap but it is worth paying for this calibre of inspired cooking, with Turkish touches and global influences.

Divan $$$$$

Elmadağ Caddesi 2, Elmadağ, Taksim, 80090 **Tel** *(0212) 231 41 00*   **Map** *7 F3*

Do not be put off by the drab 1950s edifice as its austere appearance belies inner luxury. Local people who want to celebrate a special occasion often make reservations here. The menu is extensive and the cooking is done to perfection. Bookings are essential.

Halat Café $$$$$

Rahmi M. Koç Museum Kumbarhane Caddesi 2, Hasköy, 69800 **Tel** *(0212) 297 66 44*

Halat Café boasts French cooking with whimsical Mediterranean touches and flavours. The steak is a top choice and the separate dessert menu features flamboyant, highly original masterpieces. This restaurant offers memorable dining with the Golden Horn lapping below its terrace.

Şans $$$$$

Hacı Adil Caddesi 6, Aralık, Levent **Tel** *(0212) 280 38 38*

Visitors to Şans love the cozy atmosphere and restful garden. Şans, in fact, leaves nothing to chance and is an award-winning restaurant serving crisp Mediterranean dishes. The menu changes frequently but favourites such as spinach roots endure. The outstanding wine list is selected from around the world.

THE BOSPHORUS

Çınaraltı $$

İskele Meydanı 44, Ortaköy, European Side **Tel** *(0212) 261 46 16*   **Map** *9 F3*

This is one of the cluster of restaurants on the picturesque waterfront in Ortaköy. Freshly prepared, colourful mezes, salads, meat and fish are all smartly served. The tables are close together and they pack in trendy customers, particularly at weekends. Try elsewhere if you are looking for a more romantic or intimate dining experience.

Pafuli　　　　🔲🔲🔲🔲　　ⓈⓈⓈ

Kuruçeşme Caddesi 116, Kuruçeşme, European Side. **Tel** *(0212) 263 66 38*

In business for over two decades, Pafuli has indoor and outdoor tables. Fish and seafood, such as shrimp and squid, are freshly cooked and the superb Black Sea dishes are first rate. *Mıhlama* (corn bread), *hamsi* (anchovy) and cheese dishes are legendary. There is an extensive menu and wine list.

Deniz Restaurant　　　　🔲🔲🔲🔲　　ⓈⓈⓈⓈ

Kefeliköy Caddesi 23, Kefeliköy, European Side **Tel** *(0212) 262 67 77*

Located on the seafront, Deniz Restaurant follows seaside trends in offering excellent fresh fish and seafood specialities. This is an ideal place to enjoy a meal by the Bosphorus (outdoors in summer) with smart, knowledgeable service. It is well patronized by locals and reservations are recommended.

Hidiv Kasrı　　　　🔲🔲　　ⓈⓈⓈⓈ

Hidiv Yolu 32, Çubuklu, Asian side **Tel** *(0216) 425 06 03*

Perched high on a hill with sweeping vistas of the straits, this former palace stands in the midst of a beautiful park. There is a large, formal restaurant that keeps up Turkish culinary traditions, while the terrace is open for buffet brunches on weekends. Come here for the view and sea breezes. No alcohol is served.

Kız Kulesi　　　　🔲🔲🔲🔲　　ⓈⓈⓈⓈ

Leander's Tower, off Üsküdar ferry pier, Asian Side **Tel** *(0216) 342 47 47* 　　　　**Map** *10 A3*

Located just offshore from Üsküdar on its own little islet in the Bosphorus, this old building is a self-service cafeteria during the day, and it rebounds spectacularly at night with a full-service restaurant, gourmet food and live music. Bookings for the restaurant and ferry service are advised.

Konak　　　　🔲🔲🔲🔲　　ⓈⓈⓈⓈ

İstinye Caddesi 23-25, Emirgan, European Side **Tel** *(0212) 32 65 00/01*

This restored wooden mansion house is set on three floors on the water's edge. There is a comprehensive selection of meat, salad and international favourites, but fish is the dish of choice. There is alfresco dining under umbrellas on the breezy terrace in summer. The wines are unremarkable but the sea air and talented cooking compensate.

Kordon　　　　🔲🔲🔲🔲　　ⓈⓈⓈⓈ

Kuleli Caddesi 51, Çengelköy, Asian Side **Tel** *(0216) 321 04 73*

This romantic restaurant is located in a smart and cleverly modernized warehouse. Seafood dishes are artistically presented and there is a fine selection of fresh fish daily. People come for the tempting food as much as for the stunning views of Istanbul's European shores. There is outdoor dining in summer.

Sardunya Fındıklı Restaurant　　　　🔲🔲🔲　　ⓈⓈⓈⓈ

Meclisi Mebusan Caddesi 22, Salıpazarı, Fındıklı, European Side **Tel** *(0212) 249 10 92* 　　　　**Map** *7 F4*

The accent here is on regional Italian cuisine with some unusual international classics. Outdoor dining on the terrace is available in summer. The staff have a thoroughly professional attitude to their wines. A highly successful twin establishment is in Gayrettepe.

A'jia　　　　🔲🔲🔲🔲　　ⓈⓈⓈⓈⓈ

A'jia Hotel, Kanlıca, Asian Side **Tel** *(0216) 413 93 53*

Remote from the urban crush, this beautiful restaurant is part of a hotel of the same name in a refurbished *yalı* on the Asian shore of the Bosphorus. The design is starkly minimalist and clinical but the food superb. Dishes draw on classic Italian recipes and new Mediterranean cooking with subtle flavours and colours. Reservations are advised.

İskele Çengelköy　　　　🔲🔲🔲🔲　　ⓈⓈⓈⓈⓈ

Wharf No. 10, Çengelköyü, Asian Side **Tel** *(0216) 321 55 06*

The indoor restaurant has a nautical theme but it is more fun to eat on the pretty outdoor terrace or garden in summer. The sea air and fishing village atmosphere complement the excellent fresh fish choices and seafood and everything is beautifully cooked, as expected at this popular venue. The service is polished and the wines reasonable

Körfez　　　　🔲🔲🔲　　ⓈⓈⓈⓈⓈ

Körfez Caddesi 78, Kanlıca, Asian side **Tel** *(0216) 413 43 14*

The talented chef here turns out sublime creations. Go for the *levrek* (sea bass) and mouthwatering selection of mezes. The polished service, fine glass- and tableware and candles hint at romance, and the restored villa that houses the restaurant is steeped in history. Körfez offers dining at its best.

Les Ambassadeurs　　　　🔲🔲　　ⓈⓈⓈⓈⓈ

Bebek Hotel, Cevdet Paşa Caddesi 34, Bebek, European side **Tel** *(0212) 358 15 65*

Diners pay for the sea air and waterfront view but Les Ambassadeurs has a well-chosen menu and abundance of typically Turkish and international dishes. There are also a few Russian dishes on the menu and accompanying vodka. Bebek is a small village along the sea shore, so dining here is an intimate, neighbourhood experience.

Poseidon　　　　🔲🔲🔲🔲　　ⓈⓈⓈⓈⓈ

Cevdetpaşa Caddesi 58, Bebek, European Side **Tel** *(0212) 263 38 23*

Poseidon boasts a dream location on a wooden terrace jutting out over the Bosphorus with geraniums and charming tables. There is an extensive Turkish and transnational menu but the staff encourage diners to order fish dishes. The fish chowder is sublime but can come with a large price tag so beware.

Key to Price Guide *see p198* **Key to Symbols** *see back cover flap*

Süreyya 🏃🔲 ⑤⑤⑤⑤

İstinye Caddesi 26, İstinye, European Side **Tel** *(0212) 277 58 86*

Originally established by a Russian immigrant, this restaurant is one of the premier landmarks along the Bosphorus, overlooking the pretty bay at İstinye. Its name comes from the original master chef and some of his recipes still feature on the menu. Caviar blinis, chicken Kiev and beef Stroganoff go down well with lemon vodka.

Urcan ♿🏃🔲 ⑤⑤⑤⑤⑤

Kireçburnu Caddesi 13, Tarabya, European Side **Tel** *(0212) 262 00 24*

Urcan is a neighborly Bosphorus landmark on the European side, best known for its wonderful seafood dishes. The service is polished and the staff are always eager to please. The chef is wonderfully skilled and the creations are stylish, colourful and generous. This is a satisfying dining experience.

BEYOND ISTANBUL

Doyum Pide ve Kebap Restaurant 🏃🔲 ⑤

Cumhuriyet Meydanı 13, Çanakkale, 17100 **Tel** *(0286) 217 48 10*

Pide (flat bread) with various baked toppings and döner kebabs are very serious business here. Simple, delicious and filling foods, on which Turkey practically runs, are cooked to perfection with enormous pride and traditional skill. No alcohol is served. If you cannot actually eat here, ask them to make up a tasty takeaway.

Kebapçı İskender ♿🏃🔲 ⑤

Ünlü Caddesi 7, Bursa, 16020 **Tel** *(0224) 221 46 15*

A local landmark and one of the oldest kebab restaurants in Bursa, everybody comes here and all are welcomed almost like family. The restaurant is known for kebabs and they serve nothing else. Try the *patlıcan kebabı* (aubergine kebab) for the most satisfying main course. No alcohol is served.

Kitap Evi 🏃🔲 ⑤

Burç üstü 21, Tophane, Bursa, 16020 **Tel** *(0224) 225 41 60*

Kitap Evi is the ideal place to eat when in Bursa. They combine a culture centre with a reading room, bookstore and café. There are always papers to read, coffee to sip, friends to meet, and plenty of well-prepared snacks and cakes on hand when hunger strikes. The atmosphere here is great.

Yalova Liman Restaurant ♿🏃🔳 ⑤⑤

Gümrük Sokak 7, Çanakkale, 17100 **Tel** *(0286) 217 10 45*

Overlooking the harbour in Çanakkale, this restaurant brims with character. It is popular with locals who come for the stews and soups for lunch and then fill the place for more formal grills, fish and steaks in the evening. Alcohol is served and they have a separate bar area below ground. Yalova Liman is recommended for great dining.

Yusuf Restaurant ♿🏃🔳🔲 ⑤⑤

Kültür Parkı içinde, Bursa, 16020 **Tel** *(0224) 234 49 67*

As with many of Bursa's restaurants, this one has been around a long time. They serve some of the city's best food and locals flock here for the tandır lamb (lamb cooked in a charcoal pit). The huge choice of mezes, grills and vegetarian food keeps the place packed. Tables spill over into the garden in summer. Alcohol is available.

Çamlık Motel ♿🏃🔳 ⑤⑤⑤

Sahil Yolu, İznik **Tel** *(0224) 757 16 31*

İznik is beautiful with lakes and mountains and wonderful undiscovered gems begging to be explored. Çamlık Motel is one gem that you may want to keep all to yourself. It is a tranquil and simple countrified retreat with a secluded garden. The local speciality, *İnegöl köfte* (meatballs) will tempt you to return.

Canakkale Balık Restaurant ♿🏃🔳🔲 ⑤⑤⑤

Opposite the Piri Reis fountain, Çanakkale, 17100 **Tel** *(0286) 218 04 41/42*

Located near the university campus, this is one of the premier local venues to enjoy excellent fish. The ahtapot şiş (octopus kebab) is one of the dining highlights. Meze choices and salads are vast but try to leave room for traditional desserts, such as quince and pumpkin compote. Alcohol is served. This is a highly recommended eatery.

Balezar ♿🏃🔳🎵🔲 ⑤⑤⑤

Karaağaç Yolu, Edirne **Tel** *(0284) 213 06 00*

This is one of the most pleasant places in Edirne. It is a little way out of town but, after visiting local sights, there is nothing better than to sit here on the banks of the Meriç River and enjoy one of their fine dishes. Try to get a waterside table. Food is not exotic but the meze, kebabs and main courses are well cooked and served.

Leonardo Restaurant 🏃🔳🔲 ⑤⑤⑤⑤

Köyiçi Sokak 32, Polonezköy **Tel** *(0216) 432 30 82*

Leonardo has been going for years and seems to become ever more popular. There is a wonderful garden and also picnic areas and a small swimming pool. The food combines French and Austrian cuisine. They do a generous open buffet brunch on weekends. It gets very crowded because it is so close to the city centre.

Light Meals and Snacks

Eating on the streets is very much a part of life in Istanbul. You cannot go far without coming across a café, street stall or pedlar selling snacks to appease the hunger of busy passers-by. Savoury snacks like kebabs, *lahmacun*, *pide* and *börek* (see pp192–7) are eaten at any time of day, as are sweets and puddings. On every street corner you will find a *büfe* (sandwich kiosk). If you want to sit down, try a traditional *kahve*, or one of the increasing number of European-style cafés in the more affluent and cosmopolitan parts of Istanbul. There are also dozens of American-style restaurants in the city, selling hamburgers, pizzas and other types of fast food.

STREET FOOD

A common sight on the streets of Istanbul is the seller of *simits* – chewy bread rings coated with sesame. The traditional *simit*-seller *(simitçi)* carries his fare on his head on a wooden tray; better-off ones push a glass-fronted cart from which they also sell *poğaça* (flaky pastry filled with cheese or mince), *su böreği* (filled layered pastry), *açma* (a fluffy *simit* shaped like a doughnut) and *çatal* (sweeter, eye-shaped *simits* without sesame seeds). They are all best eaten fresh.

During the summer street vendors sell grilled or boiled corn on the cob *(mısır)*, generously sprinkled with salt. In winter they sell roast chestnuts.

Kağıt helvası, a sweet, is another summer snack. *Kağıt* means "paper", and the thin, crumbly layers of pastry filled with sugar melt in your mouth.

SANDWICH AND PASTRY SHOPS

Delicious sandwiches are on sale from small kiosks or *büfes*, usually near bus stops. They include inexpensive thin, toasted sandwiches *(tost)* and hot dogs *(sosisli sandviç)* with pickles and ketchup.

The snack bars of Ortaköy *(see p122)* specialize in pastries from southern Turkey like *gözleme* and *dürüm*. Both consist of thin layers of bread, grilled on a hot sheet of iron and stuffed with meat, cheese and vegetables. *Dürüm* bread is cooked first, then stuffed and rolled, while *gözleme* is cooked with the ingredients inside, then folded over in a triangle.

FISH

Fish sandwich sellers offer delicious grilled or fried fresh fish inside a large piece of bread. Their small boats line the jetties in Eminönü to meet the passing ferry passengers. *Midye tava* (fried mussels), dressed with ground hazelnuts, garlic and oil, are also served inside bread or on a stick.

Fish and mussel sandwiches are sold at the Galatasaray Fish Market in Beyoğlu *(see p215)*. Here you can also buy *midye dolma*, mussels stuffed with pine nuts, rice and currants *(see p196)*. However, be vigilant when purchasing food that may have had a long street life, particularly in the summer months.

KAHVEHANES

The typical Turkish café, *kahvehane* (or *kahve*), is a male-dominated local coffee shop. The original Ottoman name, *kıraathane*, means "a place to read", but such cafés are more a place where men play backgammon and cards, puff on a nargile (bubble pipe) and drink endless cups of coffee and tea. No alcoholic drinks or food are served.

In tourist areas like Beyazıt and Sultanahmet, however, female foreigners will be welcome in *kahves* and, although they may be stared at, they will not be disturbed. **Çorlulu Ali Paşa Medresesi** *(see p96)* is a *kahve* popular with artists and students. The **Basilica Cistern Café** offers a cooling retreat in an unusual setting although you have to pay to get into the cistern *(see p76)*.

Café Kafka is named after Franz Kafka and is frequented by academics and intellectuals. They serve delicious coffee, cake and snacks in a convivial atmosphere. In Eyüp *(see p120)* the **Pierre Loti Café** is another traditional *kahve*. Decorated with memorabilia and antique wall tiles, it serves good apple tea and claims to have been the haunt of Pierre Loti *(see p42)*. **İsmail Ağa Café**, by the waterside in Kanlıca *(see p141)*, is famous for delicious yoghurt.

Next to the Bebek ferry jetty *(see p138)* is **Bebek Kahvesi**. This café is a favourite with students and middle-class families who read their Sunday newspapers on the terrace while enjoying the breeze of the Bosphorus.

PATISSERIES AND PUDDING SHOPS

The best patisseries are in Beyoğlu, particularly in two hotels: the Divan *(see p188)* and Pera Palas *(see p104)*. **Divan** is known for its chocolates. **Patisserie de Pera** retains its charm with period decor, classical music and tasty biscuits. It has a good selection of English teas. **İnci Patisserie** is famous for its excellent profiteroles and baklava. Despite its run-down appearance, it is always busy.

Next door to the Atatürk Cultural Centre *(see p220)*, **Gezi Istanbul Café** sells handmade confectionery such as truffles and rich torte.

Pudding shops *(muhallebici)* sell traditional sweet milk puddings *(see p195)*. **Sütiş Muhallebicisi** is a long-established chain.

ICE CREAM SHOPS

Itinerant ice cream vendors are a common sight in residential districts in the summer. Turkish ice cream *(dondurma)* is thick and very sweet. It comes in milk chocolate and fruit varieties and is served in cones. One of the best places to eat ice cream is **Mado**, which has several outlets. Also try **Mini Dondurma** in Bebek.

EUROPEAN-STYLE CAFÉS

European-style cafés serving light meals such as salads, croque monsieur, omelettes and crepes are now common in Istanbul. Sweets usually include cheesecake, chocolate brownies, tiramisu and ice cream in summer.

The best are around Taksim and İstiklal Caddesi in Beyoğlu *(see pp102–3)*. The elegant, late 19th-century **Lebon** serves savoury dishes such as vol-au-vent and also sumptuous Viennese cakes. **Gramofon** is a cosy and relaxed café, which overlooks the square in Tünel.

Sultanahmet has a few chic, designer cafés. The **Lale Restaurant**, a hippie spot in the 1970s, now serves inexpensive casseroles and grilled chicken, as well as Turkish milk puddings.

Zanzibar, in the smart shopping district of Nişantaşı, is popular with a stylish young clientele. It serves dishes such as vegetable grill, Waldorf salad and toast provençale. Also in Nişantaşı is the **Next Café**, which offers European-style cakes and pies as well as savoury dishes such as *börek*.

The area around Ortaköy *(see p122)*, with its market, many craft shops and a good nightlife scene, is a haven of street food and light snacks.

Further up along the shores of the Bosphorus, in Rumeli Hisarı *(see p140)*, there is an exclusive English café called **Tea Room**. Decorated in a colonial style, it serves scones and, of course, a variety of English teas.

Among a new generation of internet cafés *(see p235)* springing up in the city, one of the best is **Antique**.

Cafés are now beginning to open on the Asian side, too. One of the most interesting is **Kadife Chalet** near Moda. Housed in a 19th-century wooden building, it offers home-made cakes and dishes made with home-grown ingredients, as well as a range of herbal teas.

BARS

Despite the Islamic edict against alcohol, there are plenty of bars in Istanbul. The majority of the city's fashionable cafés turn into bars in the evening, signalled by a change of music from soft tunes to loud pop. It is possible just to sit with a drink, but for those who wish to have food, many serve pasta, steaks, grills and salads at the bar. Even bars that are not cafés during the day will serve snacks.

Pano Şaraphanesi is one of several historic wine houses found in the back streets of Beyoğlu which serve wine by the glass or bottle in convivial surroundings. A few hotel bars, such as **City Lights** at the Ceylan Inter-Continental Hotel *(see p189)*, offer more elaborate dishes. Other bars, like **Zihni's**, have restaurant sections. Many bars feature live bands playing rock or jazz music. For further details see page 221.

DIRECTORY

KAHVEHANES

Basilica Cistern Café
Yerebatan Sarayı,
Yerebatan Cad 13,
Sultanahmet.
Map 3 E4 (5 E4).
Tel (0212) 512 18 77.

Bebek Kahvesi
Cevdetpaşa Cad 137,
Bebek.
Tel (0212) 257 54 02.

Café Kafka
Yeni Çarşi Cad 26/1,
Galatasaray. **Map** 7 D4.
Tel (0212) 245 19 58.

Çorlulu Ali Paşa Medresesi
Yeniçeriler Cad 36,
Çemberlitaş.
Map 2 C4 (4 B3).
Tel (0212) 528 37 85.

İsmail Ağa Café
Simavi Meydanı,
Kanlıca.

Pierre Loti Café
Gümüşsuyu Karyağdı Sok
5 (inside Eyüp cemetary),
Eyüp.
Tel (0212) 581 26 96.

PATISSERIES AND PUDDING SHOPS

Divan
Cumhuriyet Cad 2,
Elmadağ. **Map** 7 F3.
Tel (0212) 315 55 00.

Gezi Istanbul Café
İnönü Cad 5/1, Taksim.
Map 7 F4.
Tel (0212) 292 53 53

İnci Patisserie
İstiklal Cad 124–2,
Beyoğlu. **Map** 7 E4.
Tel (0212) 243 24 12.

Patisserie de Pera
Pera Palas Hotel,
Meşrutiyet Cad 98–100,
Tepebaşı. **Map** 7 D5.
Tel (0212) 251 45 60.

Sütiş Muhallebicisi
Sıraselviler Cad 9/A,
Taksim. **Map** 7 E4.
Tel (0212) 252 82 68.

ICE CREAM SHOPS

Mado
Osmanzade Sok 26,
Ortaköy. **Map** 9 F3.
Tel (0212) 227 38 76.

Mini Dondurma
Cevdetpaşa Cad 107,
Bebek.
Tel (0212) 257 10 70.

EUROPEAN-STYLE CAFÉS

Antique
Kutlugün Sokak 51,
Sultanahmet. **Map** 3 E4.
Tel (0212) 517 67 89.

Gramofon
Tünel Meydanı 3, Beyoğlu.
Map 7 D5.
Tel (0212) 293 07 86.

Kadife Chalet
Kadife Sok 29, Kadıköy.
Tel (0216) 347 85 96.

Lale Restaurant
Divanyolu Cad 6,
Sultanahmet.
Map 3 E4 (5 E4).
Tel (0212) 522 29 70.

Lebon
Richmond Hotel,
İstiklal Cad 445, Beyoğlu.
Map 7 D5.
Tel (0212) 252 54 60.

Next Café
Ihlamur Yolu 3–1,
Nişantaşı.
Map 7 D5.
Tel (0212) 247 80 43.

Tea Room
Yahya Kemal Cad 36A,
Rumeli Hisarı.
Tel (0212) 257 25 80.

Zanzibar
Teşvikiye Cad 43–57,
Reassürans Çarşısı No.60,
Teşvikiye. **Map** 8 A2.
Tel (0212) 233 80 46.

BARS

City Lights
Ceylan Inter-Continental
Hotel, Asker Ocağı Cad 1,
Taksim. **Map** 7 F3.
Tel (0212) 231 21 21.

Pano Şaraphanesi
Hamalbaşı Cad, Beyoğlu.
Map 7 D4.
Tel (0212) 292 66 64.

Zihni's
Muallim Naci Cad 119,
Ortaköy. **Map** 9 F2.

SHOPPING IN ISTANBUL

Istanbul's shops and markets, crowded and noisy at most times of the day and year, sell a colourful mixture of goods from all over the world. The city's most famous shopping centre is the Grand Bazaar and there are many other bazaars and markets to browse around *(see pp214–15)*. Turkey is a centre of textile production, and Istanbul has a wealth of carpet and fashion shops. If you prefer to do all your

Contemporary glass vase

shopping under one roof, head for one of the city's modern shopping malls which offer a variety of international and Turkish brand goods. Wherever you shop, be wary of imitations of famous brand products – even if they appear to be of a high standard and the salesman maintains that they are authentic. Be prepared to bargain where required: it is an important part of a shopping trip.

Brightly decorated candle lanterns in the Grand Bazaar

OPENING HOURS

Shops are open, in general, from 9am to 8pm Monday to Saturday; open-air markets from 8am onwards. Large shops and department stores open slightly later in the morning. The Grand Bazaar and Spice Bazaar open their gates at 8:30am and close at 7pm. Big shopping malls open from 10am to 10pm seven days a week. Shops do not close for lunch, although a few small shops may close briefly at prayer times, especially for the midday prayers on Fridays. Most shops close for the religious holidays of Şeker Bayramı and Kurban Bayramı, but remain open on national holidays *(see pp44–7)*.

HOW TO PAY

Most shops that cater to tourists will be happy to accept foreign currency. If you can pay in cash, you can usually get a discount. Exchange rates are often displayed in shops and also appear in daily newspapers.

Credit cards are widely accepted (except in markets and smaller shops) and most vendors do not charge a commission. Resist any attempts to make you pay a small compensatory commission. It is not unusual to be asked to draw the money out from a bank on your card. Very few shops now accept travellers' cheques. Cash and haggling are expected in the markets and bazaars. Start by offering half the asking price. In rural markets merchants may accept foreign currency.

VAT EXEMPTION

If you spend at least 118 YTL in one shop, you can claim back VAT (known as KDV in Turkey), which is 18 per cent. More than 2,200 retail outlets display the Tax Free Shopping logo. The retailer will give you a Global Refund Cheque, which you should then present to the customs officials with your invoices and purchases for a cash refund when leaving Turkey.

Fezes for sa a street s

SIZES AND MEASURES

Turkey uses continental European sizes for clothes and shoes. Food and drink are sold in metric measures. This book has a conversion chart on page 227.

BUYING ANTIQUES

Before purchasing antique items, it is important to know what can and cannot be taken out of Turkey. The rule is that objects which are over 100 years old may be exported only when a certificate stating their age and granting permission to remove them from the country has been issued by the relevant

Turkish delight and boiled sweets, sold by weight at market stalls

Antiques shop in Çukurcuma

authority. Museums issue these certificates, as does the Ministry of Culture in Ankara, who will also undertake to authenticate the correct age and value of an object, if necessary. The shopkeeper from whom you bought your goods will often know which museum will be authorizing your purchases for export. In theory, a seller should already have registered with a museum all goods for sale that are over 100 years old. In practice, sellers usually only seek permission after a particular item has been sold. In the past, antiques could be removed from Turkey without a certificate. Although this has changed, the export of antiques is not forbidden, as some believe. If the proper authorities permit your purchase to be exported, you can either take it with you or send it home, whether or not it is over 100 years old. Do take note, however, that taking antiques out of Turkey without proper permission is regarded as smuggling, and is a punishable offence.

Van cats and Kangal dogs have recently been included in this category.

HOW TO BARGAIN

In up-market shops in Istanbul, bargaining is rarely practised. However, you will probably do most of your shopping in the Grand Bazaar and the shops located in or around the old city (Sultanahmet and Beyazıt). In these places haggling is a necessity, otherwise you may be cheated. Elsewhere you can try making an offer but it may be refused.

Bazaar shopkeepers, characterized by their abrasive insistence, expect you to bargain. Always take your time and decide where to buy after visiting a few shops selling similar goods. The procedure is as follows:

• You will be invited inside and offered a cup of tea. Feel free to accept, as this is the customary introduction to any kind of exchange and will not oblige you to buy.

• Do not feel pressurized if the shopkeeper turns the shop upside down to show you his stock – this is normal practice and most salesmen are proud of their goods.

• If you are seriously interested in any item, be brave enough to offer half the price you are asked.

• Take no notice if the shopkeeper looks offended and

Haggling over the price of a rug

refuses, but raise the price slightly, aiming to pay a little more than half the original offer. If that price is really unacceptable to the owner he will stop bargaining over the item and turn your attention to other goods in the shop.

SHOPPING MALLS AND DEPARTMENT STORES

Istanbul's modern shopping malls are popular with Turkish families and foreigners alike, for their entertainment as well as their shopping facilities. They have multi-screen cinemas, "food courts" selling fast food and chic cafés, as well as hundreds of shops.

Akmerkez in Etiler is an ultra-modern skyscraper where, besides branches of almost all the leading Turkish fashion companies, outlets for famous international names can be found. **Galleria**, next to the yacht marina in Ataköy, also offers a wide range of well-known clothes stores. The complex contains a branch of the French department store, Printemps, as well as an ice rink (see p222). **Carousel**, close to Galleria, in Bakırköy, is a smaller mall with branches of foreign shops, including Mothercare and British Home Stores.

International names alongside Turkish shops in Akmerkez

SEASONAL SALES

Clothes shops are the main places for seasonal sales (indirim), although department stores and a number of speciality shops also have them. They begin in June or July and continue to the end of September. The winter sales start as soon as New Year shopping is over in early January and continue until mid-April. There are no sales in bazaars – every day of the year offers bargains depending on your haggling skills.

Where to Shop in Istanbul

Caviar in the Spice Bazaar

Istanbul is home to a vast range of shops and bazaars. Often shops selling particular items are clustered together, competing for custom. The Grand Bazaar *(see pp98–9)* is a centre for carpets and kilims, gold jewellery and leather jackets, as well as every type of handicraft and souvenir. Nişantaşı and İstiklal Caddesi on the European side, and Bağdat Caddesi on the Asian side, have a good range of clothes and shoe shops. The best choices for food are the Spice Bazaar *(see p88)* and the Galatasaray Fish Market *(see p215)*.

CARPETS AND KILIMS

One of the best places to buy carpets and kilims in Istanbul is in the Grand Bazaar *(see pp98–9)*, where **Şişko Osman** has a good range of carpets, and **Galeri Şirvan** specializes in Anatolian tribal kilims. The **Cavalry Bazaar** *(see p71)* has many kilim shops, and **Hazal Halı**, in Ortaköy, is run by a wonderfully professional lady who knows the history of almost all of the carpets.

FABRICS

As well as rugs, colourful fabrics in traditional designs from all over Turkey and Central Asia are widely sold. **Sivaslı Yazmacısı** sells village textiles, crocheted headscarves and embroidered cloths. **Muhlis Günbattı** *(see p98)* has rare Central Asian textiles,

Brightly coloured Central Asian *suzani* wall hangings

Uzbek and Turkmen *suzanis* (large hand-appliqued cloths), silk ikats, and Ottoman kaftans, as well as carpets. The antiques dealer **Aslı Günşiray** sells both original Ottoman and re-production embroidered cloths.

JEWELLERY

Istanbul's substantial gold market centres on Kalpakçılar Başı Caddesi in the Grand Bazaar. Here gold jewellery is sold by weight, with a modest sum added for craftsmanship, which is generally of good quality. The daily price of gold is displayed in the shop windows. Other shops in the Grand Bazaar sell silver jewellery, and pieces inlaid with precious stones.

Urart stocks collections of unique gold and silver jewellery inspired by the designs of ancient civilizations. **Antikart** specializes in restored antique silver jewellery made by Kurds and nomads in eastern Turkey.

LEATHER

Turkish leatherwear, while not always of the best quality hides, is durable, of good craftsmanship and reasonably priced. The Grand Bazaar is full of shops selling leather goods. **B B Store**, for example, offers a good range of ready-to-wear and made-to-order garments.

Meb Deri sells designer handbags and small leather goods, and **Desa** has classic and fashionable designs.

ANTIQUES AND BOOKS

The best area for antiques is Çukurcuma *(see p107)*, in the backstreets of Beyoğlu. Shops worth a visit are **Aslı Günşiray**, **Antikhane** and **Antikarnas** for their Turkish, Islamic and Western stock. A vast array of Ottoman antique brassware, furniture and pottery, including Turkish coffee cups and vases, are sold in the Grand Bazaar.

The antiquarian bookshops, such as **Librairie de Pera** sell old postcards and prints. One of the very best shops for new books is **Galeri Kayseri**, which sells a wide selection of English-language titles.

HANDICRAFTS AND SOUVENIRS

All types of Turkish arts and crafts can be found in the Grand Bazaar. Ideal gifts and souvenirs include embroidered hats, waistcoats and slippers, mother-of-pearl inlaid jewellery boxes, meerschaum pipes in the shape of heads, prayer beads made from semi-precious stones, alabaster ornaments, blue-eye charms to guard

Icons for sale in the Grand Bazaar

against the evil eye, nargiles (bubble pipes) and reproductions of icons. At the **Istanbul Crafts Centre** *(see p76)*, watch the traditional art of calligraphy being practised. **Rölyef** in Beyoğlu, the **Book Bazaar** *(see p94)*, **Artrium** and **Sofa** also sell antique and reproduction calligraphy, as well as *ebru* (marbled paintings) and reproductions of Ottoman miniature paintings.

POTTERY, METAL AND GLASSWARE

Hundreds of shops in the Grand Bazaar are stocked with traditional ceramics, including many pieces decorated with exquisite blue-and-white İznik designs *(see p161)*. Other types of pottery come from Kütahya – distinguished by its free style of decoration – and Çanakkale *(see p170)* – which uses more modern designs, often in yellows and greens. To purchase a modern piece of Kütahya ware, visit **Mudo Pera** which stocks a collection by Sıtkı Usta, a master of Kütahya pottery. Most museum shops also have a good range of pottery for sale, including reproduction pieces.

The Grand Bazaar and the Cavalry Bazaar *(see p215)* are centres of the copper and brass trade and offer a huge selection to the browsing visitor. For glassware, **Paşabahçe**, the largest glass manufacturer

in Turkey, creates delicate *çeşmibülbül* vases (decorated with blue and gold stripes) and Beykoz-style ware (with gilded decoration).

FOOD, DRINK, HERBS AND SPICES

The spice bazaar *(see p88)* is the place to buy nuts (especially pistachios) and dried fruits, herbs and spices, jams and the many types of herbal tea produced in Turkey. These include sage

(adaçayı), linden *(ıhlamur)* and camomile *(papatya)*. However, other foods can be bought here as well, including such luxuries as caviar. Another place with a wide variety of good quality herbs, jams, teas and spices is the Galatasaray Fish Market.

Several shops specialize in particular foods. **Şekerci Hacı Bekir** is renowned for its delectable Turkish delight and baklava. Also popular is **Bebek Badem Ezmesi**, on the Bosphorus, widely acclaimed for its pistachio and almond fondants. Over the course of more than a century in business, **Kurukahveci Mehmet Efendi** *(see p86)* has become the best known producer of Turkish coffee. The quintessential Turkish spirit, raki *(see p197)*, can be bought in any grocery.

Pickled fruits and vegetables, sold in markets and on street stalls

DIRECTORY

Istanbul's Markets

İznik-style plate, Cavalry Bazaar

Whether you want to lose yourself in the aromas of exotic spices, rummage for old prints and miniatures among secondhand books, hunt for souvenirs or just shop for food, you will find a market or bazaar catering to your tastes somewhere in Istanbul. An obvious first stop is the Grand Bazaar, but several others are well worth visiting for their more specialized produce and their atmospheric settings. Every neighbourhood in Istanbul has its own open-air market on a specific day of the week. At these markets, crowded with budget-conscious housewives, you will find a huge variety of merchandise at the cheapest possible prices.

Spice Bazaar
The Spice Bazaar is an exotic trading house for dried herbs, spices and other foodstuffs (see p88).

GOLDEN HORN

THE BAZAAR QUARTER

Wednesday Street Market
One of Istanbul's colourful neighbourhood markets, the Wednesday market, is next to the Fatih Mosque (see p113) and sells everything from fresh produce and household goods to bulbs and seeds.

SULTAN

Book Bazaar
Next to the Grand Bazaar, the Book Bazaar (Sahaflar Çarşısı) offers a wealth of printed matter in various languages, from tourist guides to academic tomes and old magazines (see p94).

Grand Bazaar
The largest market in the world, the Grand Bazaar contains about 4,000 shops. In this roofed labyrinth of passages you can find every commodity associated with Turkey, from costly jewellery to basic foodstuffs. It has operated for hundreds of years (see pp98–9).

Beşiktaş Square Market
A splendid array of fruit, vegetables and fish is found in this interesting market near Dolmabahçe Palace (see pp128–9).

YOĞLU

BOSPHORUS

Ortaköy Flea Market
Every Sunday the main square of Ortaköy is filled with stalls selling souvenirs to suit every budget, from junk to fine jewellery and original Turkish handicrafts (see p122).

Galatasaray Fish Market
The best fish market in Istanbul runs along a historic alleyway. Constantly sprinkled with water to keep them cool, fresh fish from the Sea of Marmara and elsewhere lie waiting to be sold (see p103).

THE ASIAN
SIDE

ḼLIO
NT

Kadıköy Street Market
The main market on the Asian side of the city fills the streets around Mahmut Baba Sokağı. Clothes are sold on Tuesdays, and food on Fridays.

Cavalry Bazaar
Converted Ottoman stables are the setting for this bazaar below the Blue Mosque (see pp78–9). Carpets (see pp218–9) are the main items touted, but handicrafts and jewellery are also on sale (see p71).

0 metres	500
0 yards	500

What to Buy in Istanbul

Turkish slippers

With its endless bazaars, markets, shops and stalls, Istanbul is a souvenir hunter's paradise. If you are seeking a bargain, jewellery and leather can be worth investing in. For something typically Turkish, there is a wide selection of ceramics and copperware based on the designs of traditional Ottoman handicrafts and arts. The city's antique shops *(see p212)* are also worth a visit. Istanbul is possibly most famous for its carpets and kilims *(see pp218–9)*, but check the quality before you buy.

Copperware

Antique copperware can be very expensive. Newer items, however, are also available, at more affordable prices.

Copper goblets

Pipes

Classic nargiles (bubble pipes) are still used by older Turkish men. They make attractive ornaments even if you do not smoke.

Antique copper water ewer

Jewellery

Jewellery includes pendants made from gold, silver, semi-precious stones and other materials. A simple blue glass eye is said to ward off evil.

Blue glass-eye pendants

Ceramics

Ceramics form a major part of Turkey's artistic tradition. The style varies according to the area of origin. Blue and white pottery is in the İznik style (see p161); other areas of production include Kütahya and Çanakkale (see p170).

Colourful Kütahya ware

Green jugs from Çanakkale

Blue and white decorated plate

İznik-style tile

Miniatures

Istanbul has a history of miniature painting, examples of which can be seen in the city's museums, especially Topkapı Palace (see p57). These tiny works of art, often depicting the sultan at court, were once bound in books. Those for sale are copies of originals.

Miniature from the Grand Bazaar

Box inlaid with mother-of-pearl

Box with painted scenes on bone inlay

Handicrafts

Jewellery boxes crafted from wood or bone, alabaster figurines and other hand-made ornaments make unusual souvenirs.

Textiles

Hand-woven cloths, including ikat work (where the cotton is dyed as it is woven), fine embroidery and knits are just some of the range of textiles that can be bought.

Embroidered scarves, known as *oyalı*

Cotton ikat work

Glassware

This elegant jug is an example of the blue and white striped glassware, çeşmibülbül, made in the Paşabahçe works (see p147).

Çeşmibülbül jug

Local Delicacies

Delicious sweets such as halva, Turkish delight and baklava are very popular. A huge range of fragrant spices, dried fruit and nuts are sold loose by weight in the city's bazaars.

Halva

Nuts in honey

Turkish delight

Dried red peppers and aubergines

Mulberries

Sunflower and pumpkin seeds

Chickpeas

Apricots

Almonds

Pistachio nuts

Turkish Carpets and Kilims

The ancient skill of weaving rugs has been handed down from generation to generation in Turkey. Rugs were originally made for warmth and decoration in the home, as dowry items for brides, or as donations to mosques. There are two main kinds of rug: carpets *(halı)*, which are knotted, and kilims, which are flat-woven with vertical (warp) and horizontal (weft) threads. Many foreign rugs are sold in Istanbul but those of Turkish origin come in a particularly wide range of attractive colours. Most of the carpets and kilims offered for sale will be new or almost new; antique rugs are rarer and far more expensive.

A carpet may be machine-made or handmade. Fold the face of the rug back on itself: if you can see the base of the knots and the pile cannot be pulled out, it means that it is handmade.

Wool is the usual material for making a rug, although some carpets are made with silk.

Weaving a Carpet
Wool for rugs is washed, carded, spun and dyed before it is woven. Weaving is a cottage industry in Turkey; the women weave in winter leaving the summer months for farming duties.

RUG-MAKING AREAS OF WESTERN TURKEY

The weaving industry in Turkey is concentrated into several areas of production, listed below. Rug designs are traditional to their tribal origins, resulting in a wide range of designs and en-abling the skilled buyer to identify the area of origin.

ISTANBUL ①
ANKARA
② ③ ⑥
④ ⑦
⑤
⑫
⑪ ⑩ ⑬
⑧ ⑨

CARPETS
① Hereke
② Çanakkale
③ Ayvacık
④ Bergama
⑤ Yuntdağ
⑥ Balıkesir
⑦ Sındırgı
⑧ Milas
⑨ Antalya
⑩ Isparta

KILIMS
⑪ Denizli
⑫ Uşak

CARPETS AND KILIMS
⑬ Konya

CARPET
This reproduction of a 16th-century Uşak carpet is known as a Bellini double entrance prayer rug.

Indigo

Madder

Camomile

Dyes
Before chemical dyes were introduced in 1863, plant extracts were used: madder roots for red; indigo for blue; and camomile and other plants for yellow.

The "prayer design" is inspired by a mihrab, the niche in a mosque that indicates the direction of Mecca *(see pp38–9)*.

The tree of life motif at the centre of the kilim is symbolic of immortality.

BUYING A RUG

Before you buy a rug, look at it by itself on the floor, to see that it lies straight – without waves or lumps. Check that the pattern is balanced, the borders are of the same dimensions, and the ends are roughly the same width. The colours should be clear and not bleeding into one another. Bargaining is essential *(see p211)*, as the first price given is likely to be at least 30% higher than the seller really expects.

Buying a good quality old rug at a reasonable price, however, is a job for an expert. The age of a rug is ascertained from its colour, the quality of the weaving and the design. Check the pile to make sure that the surface has not been painted and look for any repairs – they can easily be seen on the back of the rug. The restoration of an old carpet is acceptable but the repair should not be too visible. Make sure the rug has a small lead seal attached to it, proving that it may be exported, and ask the shop for a receipt.

KILIM

Kilims are usually made using the slit weave technique by which a vertical slit marks a colour change.

Kilim pieces are used to make a variety of smaller craft objects, also for sale in carpet shops.

The width of a rug is limited by the size of the loom. Most rugs are small because a large loom will not fit into a village house.

Burdock motif

Chest motif

Motif from wolf track, crab or scorpion

Modern motif of a human figure

Motifs

The recurring motifs in rugs – some of them seemingly abstract, others more figurative – often have a surprising origin. For instance, many are derived from marks that nomads and villagers used for branding animals.

ENTERTAINMENT IN ISTANBUL

Istanbul offers a great variety of leisure pursuits, ranging from arts festivals, folk music and belly dancing to sports centres and nightclubs. The most important event in the cultural calendar is the series of festivals organized by the Istanbul Foundation for Culture and the Arts *(see pp44–6)*. The festivals take place between March and November, and have been drawing international performers and large audiences since 1973. Throughout the year, traditional Turkish music, opera, ballet, Western classical music and plays are performed

Belly dancer, Galata Tower

at the Atatürk Cultural Centre (AKM), the Cemal Reşit Rey Concert Hall (CRR) and other venues around the city. Beyoğlu is the main centre for entertainment of all kinds. This area has the highest concentration of cinemas in the city as well as several cultural centres, both Turkish and foreign. In the evening the bars and cafés here play live music. Ortaköy, on the European shore of the Bosphorus, is another popular venue where, on summer nights, dining, music and dancing continue into the small hours of the morning.

Copies of *The Guide*

ENTERTAINMENT GUIDES

Istanbul has a bi-monthly entertainment and listings magazine in English called *The Guide*. This publishes the programmes of the AKM and CRR, and information on other cultural events, as well as bars and nightclubs around the city. *The Guide* is sold at the larger, central newsagents and book shops. The English-language newspaper *Turkish Daily News*, available from newsstands, also has information on entertainment in Istanbul.

Lists of events taking place at individual theatres and cultural centres (including those attached to foreign consulates) can be obtained from tourist information offices *(see p229)*.

The Turkish Airlines in-flight magazine, *Skylife*, has details of major events, and the daily Turkish newspaper *Hürriyet* has listings in Turkish.

BOOKING TICKETS

Tickets for performances at the Atatürk Cultural Centre and Cemal Reşit Rey Concert Hall can be purchased one week in advance from their box offices. Perhaps one of the fastest and most convenient ways to book and pay for tickets to any event is through **Biletix**. **Vakkorama** department store and **Galleria, Akmerkez** and **Capitol** shopping centres sell tickets for large pop and jazz concerts, and also for performances at the Atatürk Cultural Centre and Cemal Reşit Rey Concert Hall.

LATE-NIGHT TRANSPORT

The last late-night buses and dolmuşes leave at midnight from Taksim, which is close to many entertainment venues. Taxis run throughout the night. During the music festivals in June and July there is a special bus service which runs between show venues and central parts of Istanbul.

FESTIVALS

Five arts festivals, four annual and one biennial, are organized by the Istanbul Foundation for Culture and the Arts. The Film Festival runs from March to April every year, the Theatre Festival is in May and June, the Music and Dance Festival – the original and biggest festival – is in June

and July and the Jazz Festival is in July. The biennial Fine Arts Festival takes place in the autumn. Tickets for all these festivals can be bought over the phone from the **Istanbul Festival Committee**, which also has programme details, and from the venues.

The Yapı Kredi Arts Festival, Akbank Jazz Festival and Efes Pilsen Blues Festival are also in the autumn *(see p46)*.

WESTERN CLASSICAL MUSIC AND DANCE

Every season the Istanbul State Opera and Ballet companies, State Symphony Orchestra and State Theatre perform a wide repertoire of classical and modern works. The companies share the same venue: the purpose-built, 900-seat **Atatürk Cultural Centre** in Taksim. Early booking is essential for shows here. The **Cemal Reşit Rey Concert Hall** stages concerts of

Classical concert in the church of Haghia Eirene *(see p60)*

Folk dancing at Kervansaray, a long-established venue

Western classical music as well as hosting a wide variety of music and dance groups from all over the world. Concerts, operettas and ballets are also performed at smaller venues throughout the city.

Laser disc screenings of opera, ballet and classical music performances are held most days at 2pm and 6pm at the **Aksanat Cultural Centre**. It also sometimes stages live plays and music recitals.

ROCK MUSIC AND JAZZ

Istanbul has an increasing number of bars and clubs playing good live music. **Hayal Kahvesi** is a bar dedicated to jazz, rock and blues by groups from Turkey and abroad. It also has an outdoor summer branch next to the Bosphorus in Çubuklu. The **Q Jazz Bar**, located in the grounds of the Çırağan Palace Hotel Kempinski (see p190), is an exclusive jazz bar which regularly invites well-known performers. Further up the Bosphorus, in Ortaköy, the **Rock House Café** is an imitation of the famous Hard Rock Café. It has live bands on certain nights of the week.

In the city centre, **Kemancı** features live rock and heavy metal performers. In **Sappho** they play softer, more

Musicians at the Jazz Festival

sophisticated jazz and quality Turkish pop music. Other venues for Turkish pop are **Tribunal** and **Vivaldi**, while at **Beyoğlu Sanat Evi** they play Turkish pop with strong folk music influences.

NIGHTCLUBS

The luxurious, summer-only **Club 29** is probably the most glamorous nightclub in Istanbul. It has a restaurant, swimming pool and torch-lit garden with glorious views of the Bosphorus. Every half-hour a boat ferries guests to and from İstinye on the European side. The bar becomes a disco after midnight. **Laila**, also open in summer only, is the city's biggest nightspot, with a large dancefloor right beside the Bosphorus, as well as several bars and restaurants. **Majesty**, a chic bar and restaurant complex next to the Bosphorus, has a delightful outdoor balcony. Live bands play in the bar and there is dancing to Caribbean music. The restaurant features Turkish music and dance. **Milk** is a popular club open on Thursday, Friday and Saturday nights which plays House, Garage and other electronica.

Avoid the seedier-looking clubs in Beyoğlu, as these have been known to coerce clients into paying extortionate bills.

TRADITIONAL TURKISH MUSIC AND DANCE

Traditional Turkish music is regularly performed at the Cemal Reşit Rey Concert Hall. This includes Ottoman classical music, performed by an ensemble of singers and musicians, mystical Sufi music and folk music from various regions of Turkey. In summer, recitals of Turkish music are occasionally organized in the Basilica Cistern (see p76), which has wonderful acoustics. The Sultanahmet Tourist Office (see p229) has details.

Fasıl is a popular form of traditional music best enjoyed live in *meyhanes* such as **Ece, İstanbulin Dinner Show** and **Asır Rest** (see p201). It is usually performed by gypsies on instruments which include the violin, *kanun* (zither), *tambur* and *ut* (both similar to the lute).

Belly dancing is performed mainly in nightclubs. Though often underrated, the sensuous movements of the female dancers are considered an art. Many clubs and restaurants stage belly dancing together with Turkish folk music and dance. Dinner is often included in the show. One of the best venues is the restaurant in the **Galata Tower** (see p105). Other venues featuring top performers are **Kervansaray, Orient House** and **Manzara**.

A folkloric whirling dervish troupe gives a public performance at the Mevlevi Monastery (see p104) once a month.

The traditional *ut*, a lute-like instrument played in *fasıl* music

CINEMAS

The latest foreign films are on general release in Istanbul at the same time as other European countries. They are screened in their original languages with Turkish subtitles. Only a few cinemas show Turkish-made films.

The majority of the city's cinemas are on İstiklal Caddesi. Of these, **Alkazar**, **Emek** and **Beyoğlu** tend to show art-house films. There are also numerous cinemas in Kadıköy, on the Asian side, while all the main shopping centres have multi-screen cinemas.

The first screening of the day is half-price and many cinemas offer tickets at half-price all day on Wednesdays. Students with a valid card are entitled to a discount for all showings. Films tend to stop about halfway through for an interval.

THEATRE

Plays by both Turkish and international playwrights are staged in Istanbul's theatres, but only in Turkish. One of the most popular companies is the Istanbul State Theatre, which is based at the **AKM**. The theatre season runs from September to June.

HEALTH CLUBS AND SPORTS CENTRES

There are a number of establishments with public sports facilities in and around Istanbul. All the main five-star hotels have good swimming pools and welcome non-residents for a daily fee. Health clubs such as the **Vakkorama Gym** and the **Alkent Hillside Club** can also be used by non-members for a daily fee.

At the edge of the Belgrade Forest, the **Kemer Country Riding and Golf Club** has stables and a 9-hole golf course. It also offers riding and golf lessons. For iceskaters, there is a rink in the **Galleria** shopping centre *(see p211)* which is open to the public after 7pm. Skates are available for hire.

SPECTATOR SPORTS

Football has a very large following in Turkey. The three Istanbul teams, **Beşiktaş**, **Fenerbahçe** and **Galatasaray**, all compete at international level and play in Istanbul most Sundays. Horse racing takes place at the **Veli Efendi** racecourse on Wednesdays and at weekends. The state-of-the-art Istanbul **Formula One** racing circuit is on the Asian side of the city, and is where the Turkish Grand Prix is held in August. In the summer months there are yacht regattas in the Sea of Marmara *(see p45)*. For an unusual spectator sport, head to Edirne at festival time, to see the grease wrestling *(see p154)*.

Galatasaray team logo

BEACHES

The best place to swim, water-ski and windsurf in Istanbul is the Princes' Islands *(see p159)*. Yörükali Plajı, on Büyükada, is a public beach, but it is safe to swim anywhere around the islands.

There are large beaches at Kilyos *(see p158)* and Gümüşdere on the Black Sea, about 30 minutes' drive from central Istanbul, and Şile *(see p158)*. The Black Sea can be rough at times, however, with big waves and dangerous undercurrents, so always exercise caution on these beaches. The Marmara Islands *(see p169)*, are also popular for their beaches.

CHILDREN

Little in istanbul has been designed with children in mind. Nevertheless, there are many things to interest children and increasingly activities and sights that will attract them.

However, children are welcome and will be made a fuss of almost everywhere they go. With a little thought you can find plenty of things for children to do. The State Opera and Ballet puts on children's musicals at the **AKM**, on Saturdays at 11am or 3pm.

The Archaeological Museum *(see pp62–5)* has a special children's section tracing the history of mankind, with a medieval castle and a Trojan horse to climb on.

There are parks at Yıldız *(see pp124–5)* and Emigran *(see p141)*. Another park near Emirgan, the **Park Orman**, is a family complex situated in woods, with picnic areas, a swimming pool and a theatre. **Miniatürk** in Sütlüce boasts an extensive model village, as well as restaurants, shops and a pool. On the Princes' Islands, where there are no cars, children can cycle safely, or take a tour in a horse-drawn carriage or on a donkey. **Tatilya**, 35 km (22 miles)from Istanbul, is a theme park with roller coasters and other rides. The **Toy Museum** in Göztepe is the first of its kind in Turkey. In Darcia, 28 miles (45 km) from Istanbul, the **Bosphorus Zoo** has a variety of exotic animals in their natural habitats.

Roller-coaster ride at Tatilya, a theme park near Istanbul

DIRECTORY

BOOKING TICKETS

Akmerkez
Nispetiye Cad, Etiler.
Tel (0212) 282 01 70.

Biletix
Tel (0216) 556 98 00.
www.biletix.com

Capitol
Tophanelioğlu Cad 1,
Altunizade.
Tel (0216) 391 19 20.

Galleria
Sahil Yolu, Ataköy.
Tel (0212) 559 95 60.

Vakkorama
Osmanlı Sok 13, Taksim.
Map 7 E4.
Tel (0212) 251 15 71.

ISTANBUL FESTIVAL COMMITTEE

Tel (0216) 454 15 55.
www.istfest.org

WESTERN CLASSICAL MUSIC AND DANCE

Aksanat Cultural Centre
İstiklal Cad 16, Taksim.
Map 7 D4.
Tel (0212) 252 35 00.

Atatürk Cultural Centre (AKM)
Taksim Meydanı, Taksim.
Map 7 F3.
Tel (0212) 251 56 00.

Cemal Reşit Rey Concert Hall (CRR)
Darülbedayi Cad,
Harbiye.
Map 7 F1.
Tel (0212) 231 54 97.

ROCK MUSIC AND JAZZ

Beyoğlu Sanat Evi
Abdullah Sok 22/1,
Beyoğlu. **Map** 7 E4.
Tel (0212) 252 61 96.

Hayal Kahvesi (Beyoğlu)
Büyükparmakkapı Sok 19,
Beyoğlu. **Map** 7 E4.
Tel (0212) 244 25 58.

Hayal Kahvesi (Çubuklu)
Burunbahçe Mevkii,
Çubuklu.
◻ *May–Oct.*
Tel (0216) 413 68 80.

Kemancı
Sıraselviler Cad 69/1–2,
Taksim. **Map** 7 E4.
◻ *May–Jun.*
Tel (0212) 251 27 23.

Q Jazz Bar
Çırağan Palace Hotel
Kempinski, A Blok,
Beşiktaş. **Map** 9 D3.
Tel (0212) 236 24 89.

Rock House Café
Princess Hotel, Dereboyu
Cad 36–8, Ortaköy.
Map 9 F2.
Tel (0212) 227 60 10.

Sappho
İstiklal Cad, Bekar Sok 14,
Beyoğlu. **Map** 7 E4.
Tel (0212) 245 06 68.

Tribunal
Muammer Karaça Çıkmazı
3, Beyoğlu. **Map** 7 D5.
Tel (0212) 249 71 79.

Vivaldi
Büyükparmakkapı Sok
29/1, Taksim. **Map** 7 E4.
Tel (0212) 293 25 99.

NIGHTCLUBS

Club 29
A. Adnan Saygun Cad,
Ulus Parki içi, Ulus.
Tel (0212) 358 29 29.
www.club29.com

Laila
Muallim Naci Cad 142,
Kuruçeşme. **Map** 9 F2.
Tel (0212) 227 17 11.

Majesty
Muallim Naci Cad,
Salhane Sok 10/2,
Ortaköy.
Map 9 F3.
Tel (0212) 236 57 57.

Milk
Akarsu Yokuşu 5,
Galatasaray.
Map 7 E5.
Tel (0212) 292 11 19.

TRADITIONAL TURKISH MUSIC AND DANCE

Ece
Tramvay Cad 104,
Kuruçeşme.
Tel (0212) 265 96 00.

Galata Tower
İişhane, İstanbul.
Map 3 D1.
Tel (0212) 293 81 83.

Hasır
Beykoz Korusu, Beykoz.
Tel (0216) 322 29 01.

Istanbulin Dinner Show
Cumhuriyet Caddesi,
Cebel Topu Sokak 2,
Harbiye.
Tel (0212) 291 84 40.
www.istanbulin.org

Kervansaray
Cumhuriyet Cad 30,
Elmadağ. **Map** 7 F2.
Tel (0212) 247 16 30.

Manzara
Conrad Hotel, Yıldız Cad,
Beşiktaş. **Map** 8 C3.
Tel (0212) 227 30 00.

Orient House
Tiyatro Cad 27, next to
President Hotel, Beyazıt.
Map 2 C4 (4 A4). *Tel
(0212) 517 61 63.* www.
orienthouseistanbul.com

CINEMAS

Alkazar
stiklal Cad 179, Beyoğlu.
Map 7 E4.
Tel (0212) 293 24 66.

Beyoğlu
İstiklal Cad 140, Halep
Pasajı, Beyoğlu. **Map** 7 E4.
Tel (0212) 251 32 40.

Emek
İstiklal Cad, Yeşil Çam Sok
5, Beyoğlu. **Map** 7 D4.
Tel (0212) 293 84 39.

HEALTH CLUBS AND SPORTS CENTRES

Alkent Hillside Club
Alkent Residential
Complex, Tepecik Yolu,
Etiler.
Tel (0212) 257 78 22.

Istanbul Sailing Club

Fenerbahçe.
Tel (0212) 336 06 33.

Kemer Country Riding and Golf Club
Göktürk Beldesi,Uzun
Kemer Mevkii, Eyüp.
Tel (0212) 239 79 13.

Vakkorama Gym
Osmanlı Sok 13, Taksim.
Map 7 E4.
Tel (0212) 251 15 71.

SPECTATOR SPORTS

Beşiktaş FC
Spor Cad 92, Beşiktaş.
Map 8 A4.
Tel (0212) 227 87 80.

Fenerbahçe FC
Fenerbahçe Spor Kulübü,
Kızıltoprak, Kadıköy.
Tel (0216) 345 09 40.

Formula One
www.formula1-istanbul.
org

Galatasaray FC
Galatasaray Spor Kulübü,
Hasnun Galip Sok 7,
Galatasaray. **Map** 7 E4.
Tel (0212) 251 57 07.

Veli Efendi Hipodromu
Türkiye Jokey Kulübü,
Osmaniye, Bakırköy.
Tel (0212) 543 70 96.

CHILDREN

Bosphorus Zoo
Daricia.
Tel (0216) 653 83 15.

Miniatürk
İmrahor Cad, Sütlüce.
Tel (0212) 222 28 83.
www.miniaturk.com.tr

Park Orman
Fatih Çocuk Ormanı,
Maslak Cad, Maslak.
Tel (0212) 223 07 36.

Tatilya
E5 Motorway,
Büyükçekmece.
Tel (0212) 852 05 05.
www.tatilya.com

Toy Museum
Dr. Zeki Zeren Sokak 17,
Göztepe.
Tel (0216) 359 45 50.

SURVIVAL GUIDE

PRACTICAL INFORMATION

In recent years Istanbul's infrastructure has greatly improved and it now has the transport, banking and medical facilities of any large modern city. However, it is still worth taking a few precautionary measures, especially if you intend exploring remoter suburbs of the city. A few bus tickets, a phone card, and at least one day's supply of hard currency or Turkish lira are a basic survival kit to carry at all times. Credit cards are still

BüyükSaray Mozaikleri Müzesi

Official sign to a tourist sight

not accepted everywhere, and it can be difficult to get cash outside bank opening hours away from the city centre. Certain aspects of Turkish culture may seem strange to the foreign visitor, especially if you have never travelled in a Muslim country. It is not considered rude to stare and foreigners are often objects of attention. In general, however, Turks are friendly and hospitable, and will appreciate any effort to show respect for their traditions.

VISAS

The situation changes, depending on political circumstances. Most tourist visas are issued for three calendar months, and bar the holder from working. Overstaying incurs a fine, which escalates rapidly. Most tourist visas can be obtained at the airport or overland entry point, but the process is more complicated if you arrive by sea. Citizens of some countries need a visa before arrival. For up-to-date requirements, contact the Turkish consulate in your country.

CUSTOMS

Only airports and main road entry points offer full customs service. At major ports or marinas, customs hours are 8:30am–5:30pm on weekdays. Outside these hours a fee must be paid to activate a customs official. Import limits are generous. You can buy duty-free items at the airport on entering. However, it is often more economical to buy cigarettes and local spirits from retail stores. Visitors over 18 years old can bring in generous amounts of coffee, perfume (5 bottles), spirits (5 litres/180 fl oz) and 500 cigarettes. There is no limit on the amount of foreign currency or Turkish lira you can bring in. The maximum when leaving is US$5,000 (or Turkish lira equivalent). In practice, this is rarely enforced.

Turkey is very strict with regard to drugs. Sniffer dogs are used at Atatürk Airport.

You need to have a permit to export antiquities *(see p210)*. Visitors on a three-month tourist visa can bring in most personal items, including electronics, laptops and their own car. Contact the Turkish consulate or the embassy in your country for details.

SİGARA İÇİLMEZ
NO SMOKING

No smoking sign

LANGUAGE

As a rule, Turks will make every effort to communicate with foreigners. In areas frequented by tourists it is easy to find English speakers.

ETIQUETTE

In cities, Turkish women usually cover their arms and legs in public and, though it is a matter of choice, many cover their heads. Visitors are not expected to cover up in this way, but some Turks may be offended at exposed limbs

in public places. Mosques are less strict about head covering, and often supply disposable plastic covers for shoes.

Traditional rules of etiquette and hospitality are still an important aspect of Turkish society. Even though officials can often seem rude and the persistence of carpet salesmen can be annoying, always try to remain polite while firm. Always show respect for Atatürk *(see p31)*, whose picture you will see often.

Discreet gay and lesbian visitors are unlikely to experience problems, though overt displays of affection are best kept to a minimum. Istanbul, indeed, has a lively gay scene.

Smoking is now prohibited in government offices, on public transport, Turkish Airlines domestic flights and inside airport terminals.

Wearing the veil, a matter of personal choice for Turkish women

◁ **The area between the New Mosque and Galata Bridge in Eminönü, a busy hub of trade and transport**

Newspaper stand where bus tickets and phonecards are also sold

Increasingly, restaurants are providing non-smoking areas and some hotels have non-smoking rooms or floors.

PUBLIC CONVENIENCES

Public toilets are found all over Istanbul. Entrances are marked *Bay* for men and *Bayan* for women. The attendant sitting outside, whom you pay on exit (a sign generally shows the charge), may supply toilet paper, but it is a good idea to carry tissues with you.

If you are particularly squeamish or reluctant about using the old-fashioned squat toilets, you can always go to any restaurant, hotel or café and ask to use their modern flush toilets. Also, motorway service areas have excellent, pristine washroom facilities, and there is no charge for their use.

Sign for a public toilet

TV, RADIO AND NEWSPAPERS

The state-owned TRT (Türk Radyo ve Televizyon) has four television channels and three radio stations. Of these, TRT2 television has news bulletins in English, French and German at 7pm and 10pm. TRT3 radio (FM 88.2) broadcasts news in English, French and German at 9am, midday, 5pm, 7pm and 9pm.

Recent deregulation of the airwaves means that there are now hundreds of private satellite channels from Turkey and abroad.

Foreign channels which can be received include CNN, BBC Prime and MTV. Most hotels receive global satellite television. Check before booking if you particularly want foreign channels.

There is also a wide variety of private radio stations, which play the usual range of Western music, as well as Turkish pop, jazz and classical music. Voice FM (FM 90.6) broadcasts Voice of America programmes in Turkish, and news in English at 3pm. The BBC World Service can be received on short wave.

One English language daily paper published in Turkey is the *Turkish Daily News*, however, foreign newspapers can be obtained throughout the city, as can *The Guide (see p220)*. This has good features on Istanbul and Turkish culture.

CONVERSION CHART

Imperial to Metric
1 inch = 2.54 centimetres
1 foot = 30 centimetres
1 mile = 1.6 kilometres
1 ounce = 28 grams
1 pound = 454 grams
1 pint = 0.6 litres
1 gallon = 4.6 litres

Metric to Imperial
1 centimetre = 0.4 inches
1 metre = 3 feet, 3 inches
1 kilometre = 0.6 miles
1 gram = 0.04 ounces
1 kilogram = 2.2 pounds
1 litre = 1.8 pints

ELECTRICITY

As in Europe, the electric current is 220V AC. Plugs have two round pins, and there are two diameters in use. The smaller one is more common. Adaptors are readily available in Turkey.

TIME

Turkey is two hours ahead of GMT. Between the end of March and the end of October it is three hours ahead.

DIRECTORY

CONSULATES

Australia
Askerocaği Cad 15, Şişli.
Tel (0212) 243 13 33.

Canada
Istiklâl Cad 373/5, Beyoğlu.
Tel (0212) 251 98 38.

United Kingdom
Meşrutiyet Cad 34, Tepebaşı.
Map 7 D4.
Tel (0212) 334 6500.

United States
Kaplıcalar Mevkii 2.
Tel (0212) 335 90 00.

RELIGIOUS SERVICES

Anglican
Christ Church
Serdar-ı Ekrem Sok 82, Tünel.
Map 7 D5.
Tel (0212) 251 56 16.

Greek Orthodox
St George's Cathedral
Sadrazam Ali Paşa Cad 35, Fener.
Tel (0212) 525 21 17.

Jewish
Neve Shalom Synagogue
Büyük Hendek Cad 61, Sişhane.
Map 6 C5.
Tel (0212) 293 75 66.

Presbyterian
All Saints Church
Yusuf Kamil Sok Paşa 10, Moda.
Tel (0216) 449 39 74.

Roman Catholic
St Anthony of Padua
İstiklal Cad 325, Galatasaray.
Map 7 D4.
Tel (0212) 244 09 35.

Tips for Tourists

The major monuments and museums of Istanbul are
state-owned and charge a moderate entrance fee.
Students and senior citizens are entitled to reduced or
free entry to most sights, and should always carry proof
of their status with them. In some museums there is a
separate charge for a special section within the building,
for example the Harem in Topkapı Palace *(see pp58–9)*.
Most sights are closed at least one day a week, usually
Monday or Tuesday. Exhibits in museums are generally
labelled in Turkish only, but some are labelled in English
as well. If you intend to visit mosques *(see pp38–9)*
remember that they close regularly for prayer, although
people may be worshipping in them at any time of day.

Queuing for the Harem guided tour
in Topkapı Palace *(see pp58–9)*

Sign for Sultanahmet tourist office

TOURIST INFORMATION

The sign for a tourist information office is a white "i"
on a light green background
in a white box. The offices
themselves are named in
English and Turkish. They
rarely have much printed information to give out, least of all
public transport timetables,
but the main office in Sultanahmet Square, in particular,
will be able to answer ques-
tions on all aspects of your
stay in Istanbul. The Directorate of Tourism in Beyoğlu
does not give out information
to casual passers-by, but if
you book an appointment
with them they will help with
planning longer trips to places
outside Istanbul and with
mountaineering, walking and
yachting expeditions. It is
open on weekdays only.

Edirne, Bursa, İznik and
Çanakkale all have tourist

**Entrance tickets for some of
Istanbul's public monuments**

offices near the town centre. Most information offices
are open from 9am to 5pm,
Mon–Sat. Some stay open
later in summer, while the
one at the airport is open 24
hours every day of the year.

OPENING HOURS

Museum opening times are
generally 8:30 or 9am to
5:30 or 6pm, with a break for
lunch in smaller establishments.
Private businesses are open
from 9am to 6pm,
and government
offices from 8am
to 5pm. Shops
open from 8:30
or 9am to 7 or
8pm *(see p210)*.
Most banks are
open 8:30am to noon and
1:30 to 5pm, Monday to Friday,
while exchange offices *(döviz)*
are usually open until 8 or
9pm *(see p232)*.

Public offices are closed
on Saturdays and Sundays,
and most shops on Sundays,
although small grocers' are
often open seven days a week.

Sign showing opening hours

GUIDED TOURS

Several tour operators run
special-interest tours of
Istanbul, as well as general
guided tours of the city and
further afield. **Plan Tours** has
a variety of tours, including
trips to Gallipoli, Troy and
Bursa, Jewish heritage tours,
and private yacht cruises along
the Bosphorus *(see pp144–9)*.
GençTur, which does "green"
tours of Istanbul, offers discounts for young people.
Companies running city tours

include **Fest Travel** and
Turkland Travel Agency. For
more companies offering trips
outside Istanbul see page 245.

While sightseeing, you may
be approached by people
offering their services as tour
guides. Some of these will be
official guides licensed by the
Greater Istanbul Municipality.
Others may not be. Before
you go anywhere with a guide,
make it clear
what you want
to see and agree
the fee. If you
have little time,
or do not wish
to travel by
public transport,
it is often worth negotiating a
private tour or visit to a sight
with a taxi driver.

WOMEN TRAVELLERS

Women travelling in
Turkey may receive
unwelcome attention from
men, but are rarely in danger
of physical attack. It is possible
to avoid harassment by dressing respectably and looking
purposeful when walking
around. Avoid being out alone
at night. Traditional cafés *(see
pp208–9)* tend to be male
preserves, but restaurants
often have a section reserved
for women *(see p193)*.

VISITING MOSQUES

Although large mosques
are open all day, closing
after last prayers in the evening, smaller ones open only

five times daily, at prayer times *(namaz)*. At these mosques it may be difficult to gain entrance outside prayer times unless there is a caretaker around to open up for you. Non-Muslims should not enter any mosque during prayers. Instead, wait until most of the worshippers have left.

The times of prayer change throughout the year. They may be chalked up on a board outside the mosque, but they are always signalled by the call to prayer *(ezan)* from a loudspeaker fixed to the minaret of the mosque.

Student with local women

When visiting a mosque women and men should dress appropriately *(see p37)*. Some mosques can provide suitable attire at the door. Take your shoes off before entering and either leave them outside or carry them in with you. Make as little noise as possible inside and show consideration for anyone who is praying there.

Attendant on duty outside the Blue Mosque *(see pp78–9)*

STUDENTS

A Federation of International Youth Travel Organisation (FIYTO) Card will usually ensure free entry to sights, and an International Student Identity Card (ISIC) a 50% reduction. Reduced-price bus tickets are only available to those attending Turkish educational institutions, with a card to prove it. Non-Turkish students can get discounts on

inter-city trains with an ISIC card. Officially, there are no discounts on coaches for non-Turkish students, but if you say you are a student when buying your ticket, you may be given a small reduction. Budget accommodation is easy to find. In July and August you can get a bed in a student dormitory through Sultanahmet tourist information office. There are also a few youth hostels *(see p183)*, and some cheap hotels and guesthouses in the city centre *(see pp184–91)*.

DISABLED VISITORS

Istanbul has few facilities for disabled people and the poor state of the streets can make it difficult to get around. Most mosques will not allow wheelchairs in, and very few museums have disabled access. Toilets with special facilities are also very rare. Conversely, museum staff and the public will go to great lengths to assist with entry to buildings, and there are some low-level public telephones and special-access buses *(see p239)*.

The **Turkish Tourist Office** in London publishes a guide to facilities for the disabled in Turkey. This contains specific details of hotels as well as general information. The **Turkish Association for the Disabled** (Türkiye Sakatlar Derneği) helps disabled people living in Istanbul, and can arrange bus tours around the city for small groups of disabled tourists.

PHOTOGRAPHY

Museums often charge for the use of a video camera, and sometimes even for cameras. Check whether or not a flash is allowed before paying. Flash is often forbidden in mosques, but discreet photography is usually allowed.

Avoid paying extortionate prices for film at tourist sights; you can buy film much cheaper in camera shops.

DIRECTORY

TOURIST INFORMATION

Atatürk Airport
International Arrivals Hall.
Tel (0212) 663 07 98.

Hilton Hotel Arcade
Cumhuriyet Cad, Elmadağ.
Map 7 F2. *Tel (0212) 233 05 92.*

Karaköy
International Maritime Passenger Terminal (Terminal 2). **Map** 3 E1.
Tel (0212) 249 57 76.

Sirkeci Station
Sirkeci İstasyon Cad, Sirkeci.
Map 3 E3 (5 E1).
Tel (0212) 511 58 88.

Sultanahmet Square
Divanyolu Cad 3, Sultanahmet.
Map 3 E4 (5 E4).
Tel (0212) 518 18 02.

United States
821 United Nations Plaza,
New York, NY 10017, US.
Tel (212) 687 2194.

TOUR OPERATORS

Gençtur
Prof Kazım İsmail Gürkan Cad,
Kardeşler Han 14/4, Sultanahmet.
Map 3 D4 (5 D3).
Tel (0212) 520 52 74.

Fest Travel
Barbaros Bulvarı, 44/20,
Beşiktaş. *Tel (0212) 216 10 36.*
www.festtravel.com

Plan Tours
Cumhuriyet Cad 131/1,
Elmadağ. **Map** 7 F3.
Tel (0212) 234 77 77.
www.plantours.com

Turkland Travel Agency
Cankurtaran Mahallesi,
Seyit Hasan Sokak 18,
Sultanahmet. **Map** 3 E4 (5 E4).
Tel (0212) 458 09 80.
www.turklandtravel.com

DISABLED VISITORS

Turkish Association for the Disabled
Tel (0212) 521 49 12.

Turkish Tourist Office
170–73 Piccadilly,
London W1V 9DD, UK.
Tel (020) 7629 7771.

Personal Security and Health

Badge of the Turkish police

Istanbul is as safe as other European cities, and visitors rarely encounter violence or theft. However, lone travellers should avoid certain suburbs of the city, especially those bordering the city walls and, as in any city, particular care should be taken at night. At all times be alert for pickpockets in crowded areas. In the event of any trouble, contact the Tourist Police.

There are public and private health clinics all over the city (some with English-speaking doctors) and a number of excellent private hospitals. For minor complaints, pharmacists will be able to provide advice.

POLICE

There are several police forces in Turkey, distinguishable by their uniforms. The Security Police *(Emniyet Polisi)* is the main force in Istanbul. Its officers wear dark blue uniforms and caps, and pale blue shirts. The Tourist Police *(Turizm Polisi)* is a branch of the *Emniyet Polisi*. Most officers have some knowledge of one or two European languages. The Tourist Police station in Sultanahmet, opposite the Basilica Cistern *(see p76)*, is open 24 hours a day, and has an English-Turkish translator available Monday to Friday, 8:30am to 5pm.

The Dolphin Police *(Yunus Polisi)* is a rapid-reaction branch of the *Emniyet Polisi*. Dolphin officers ride motor-

Dolphin Motorbike Police badge

bikes and wear black biking leathers with a red stripe.

The Traffic Police *(Trafik Polisi)* has the same blue uniform as the *Emniyet Polisi* but with white belt, hat and gloves. You will see these officers patrolling the streets in black and white cars equipped with loud-speakers. The Falcon Police *(Şahin Polisi)* is the motorbike branch of the *Trafik Polisi*. Their black leather uniform is similar to that of the Dolphin Police, but has a yellow stripe on the leathers instead of a red one.

The navy blue uniformed Market Police *(Zabıta)* is a municipal police force which patrols bazaars and other areas of commerce.

The Military Police *(Askeri İnzibat)*, distinguished by an army uniform and white helmet bearing the abbreviation "As İz", is responsible for the large numbers of military conscripts on city streets. The Gendarme *(Jandarma)*, also a branch of the army, mainly polices rural areas and is unlikely to be found in the city.

PERSONAL SECURITY

Turks are honest people and will go to great lengths to return lost property. It is always worth returning to the last place the item was seen, or going to the Tourist Police. Property left on public transport can be reclaimed from **IETT Buses**. The level of petty crime has risen, especially picking pockets and purse snatching, so be aware and take sensible precautions. Avoid leaving valuables lying around in your hotel room, avoid lonely places, and always try to travel in groups when visiting remote areas.

HEALTH PRECAUTIONS

Before leaving, make sure that your basic inoculations (diphtheria, polio, typhoid and tetanus) are all up-to-date. Check with your doctor about hepatitis A and hepatitis B vaccinations.

Bottled spring water

Mosquitoes are more annoying than dangerous in Istanbul. Lorries run by the municipality spray the streets with repellent in the early evening, particularly in residential areas, but it is a good idea to bring some repellent lotion, spray or gel from your home country. ESEM Mat machines, electric vaporizers which release an effective repellent into the atmosphere, are available in Turkey. You can buy the machine and spare tablets in pharmacies, supermarkets and local groceries.

Many travellers to Turkey experience stomach upsets; this is often a result of the amount of oil used in Turkish cooking. Try to eat lightly for

Security policeman

Traffic policeman

Dolphin policeman

Turkish Security Police *(Emniyet Polisi)* patrol car

State ambulance in Istanbul

a few days and keep alcohol intake to a minimum. It is best to avoid drinking tap water altogether (bottled water is readily available everywhere), and some care should be taken when choosing restaurants and meals. Do not eat food that looks as if it could have been standing around for any length of time, especially seafood. If you have a sensitive stomach avoid half-cooked meats (usually grilled), salads, and milk products other than yoghurt and *ayran (see p197)*.

MEDICAL TREATMENT

Should you suffer from stomach troubles, remedies available from pharmacies include Lomotil, Ge-Oral (oral rehydration salts) and Buscopan. Drink lots of fluids – like bottled water, flat cola, weak black tea or soda water – and stick to a bland diet, eating only bread, yoghurt and rice until you recover. More serious bouts will require antibiotics.

The first port of call with a minor complaint should be a pharmacy *(eczane)*. Pharmacists are well-trained

Typical sign for a pharmacy in Istanbul

and many speak some English. If you need advice outside opening hours, look for a note in the window of a pharmacy giving the address of the local *nöbetçi eczane* (duty pharmacist).

There are excellent free public clinics *(poliklinik)* all over Istanbul, offering treatment for minor ailments. Private doctors often specialize in a particular branch of medicine, but there are general practitioners, called *tıbbi doktor*. Their clinics, located above shops in all the main shopping areas, are advertised by prominent signs outside.

Sign for a state hospital in Şişli

HOSPITALS

The Turkish health system has public and private hospitals. Private hospitals are well equipped and have highly professional staff (the doctors are also more likely to speak English and other languages), and are more comfortable than the state hospitals. Private hospitals may also run their own ambulance services. It is strongly recommended that you take out both travel and medical insurance before you leave, or a policy that covers both. It may also be useful to have a policy that covers repatriation costs in an emergency. The state health system has few reciprocal agreements with other countries. You have to pay for treatment and then make a claim with your insurance company.

DIRECTORY

EMERGENCY NUMBERS

Ambulance
Tel 112.

Hospital Call Line
Tel (0212) 444 09 11.

Medline
Tel (0212) 444 12 12.
www.medline.com.tr

Police
Tel 155.

TOURIST POLICE

Yerebatan Cad 6, Sultanahmet.
Map 3 E4. *Tel (0212) 527 45 03* or *528 53 69.*

LOST PROPERTY

IETT Buses
Tünel, Beyoğlu. **Map** 7 D5.
Tel (0212) 245 07 20 ext 3205.

HOSPITALS

American Admiral Bristol Hospital
Güzelbahçe Sok 20, Nişantaşı.
Map 8 A2.
Tel (0212) 311 20 00.

Cerrahpaşa Hospital
Koca Mustafa Paşa Cad,
Cerrahpaşa. **Map** 1 C5.
Tel (0212) 414 30 00.

European (Avrupa) Hospital
Mehmetçik Cad, Cahit Yalçın
Sok 1, Mecidiyeköy. **Map** 8 A1.
Tel (0212) 212 88 11.

German Hospital
Sıraselviler Cad 119, Taksim.
Map 7 E4.
Tel (0212) 293 21 50.

International Hospital
İstanbul Cad 82,
Yeşilköy.
Tel (0212) 663 30 00.

Banking and Currency

There is no limit to the amount of currency (foreign or Turkish) you can bring into Turkey. Although inflation and exchange rates once made headlines, Turkey now has a modest inflation rate of about nine per cent. The New Turkish Lira (YTL) was introduced in January 2005 – a source of pride for all Turks, as the many zeros that humbled the old currency were eliminated. Since January 2006, only the new currency has been accepted as legal tender. Exchange rates have remained steady for several years and there is no longer a need to gain from rising exchange rates. Visitors will have few problems in paying for almost everything by credit card, using ATMs or making their usual banking transactions.

Cash dispenser with instructions in a range of languages

BANKS

Most banks are open from 9am until noon. They close for lunch and reopen at 1pm and close for the day at 5pm. A few banks, such as Garanti Bank, may stay open at lunch and some banks are experimenting with limited Saturday opening. Banks can be found in all main areas, on Divanyolu Caddesi and on İstiklâl Caddesi in Beyoğlu. The İş Bankası at Atatürk airport is open 24 hours. Apart from Turkish banks, many foreign banks like Citibank and HSBC can be found in Turkey with familiar logos and services.

If you want to change money at a bank, you do so by lining up with other customers and waiting your turn for a teller. Queues are usually quite long, so allow extra time for your transactions.

Several Turkish banks have outlets at airports, offering a full range of banking services.

EXCHANGE OFFICES

With lower inflation, you will not need to worry about exchanging foreign currency at the most beneficial time. There are still exchange offices but these are not found in the numbers that they once were. Well established offices include

Para Döviz in the Grand Bazaar, **Bamka Döviz** in Taksim and **Çetin Döviz** on İstiklâl Caddesi. These will offer a somewhat better rate of exchange than banks and are open for longer hours and also on Saturdays. You will not be charged commission on cash exchanges and the rates being offered are prominently posted.

TRAVELLER'S CHEQUES AND CREDIT CARDS

Credit and debit cards and ATM machines have made traveller's cheques almost

Rates of exchange outside a *döviz*

obsolete. It is difficult to find anyone who will cash them, and if they do, they will ask for a high commission. You are advised not to bring them into Turkey. If you need to have large sums of money in hand but do not want to carry it with you, consider using a money order (*havale*) service such as Western Union. They have an association with the Turkish Post Office (PTT) and with some banks, and this is a safe and speedy, although expensive, way to transfer money.

Credit cards, such as VISA, Mastercard, American Express and, to a lesser extent, Diners Club are universally accepted. Many debit cards issued by international banks such as HSBC and Citibank are also

accepted, but check that your card is valid internationally. Even if a smaller restaurant or establishment does not take credit cards, they will often be able to run it through the data line of a neighbour. However, be aware that some smaller establishments may not accept cards in winter even if they do so in summer.

There is no commission on credit cards; even places that used to charge it, such as petrol stations, now display signs saying *kredi kartı komisyonu sıfırdır* (without commission). If you buy an airline ticket from a travel agent, however, they will charge about 3 per cent commission on the fare. Note that many of the new chip and PIN cards require you to enter your PIN number.

CURRENCY

You can take up to US$5,000 out of Turkey in cash. The new currency is known as the New Turkish Lira (YTL) or, more officially, as your credit card statement will show, TRY. The new coins are made of nickel and are not unlike the euro. These are known as *kuruş*. The higher denomination notes contain many advanced and high technology security features that are not visible to the naked eye. The old-style notes ceased to be legal tender on 1 January 2006.

Banknotes

The new Turkish banknotes come in six denominations: 100 YTL, 50 YTL, 20 YTL, 10 YTL, 5 YTL and 1 YTL, and each denomination has its own distinctive colour. All the notes display the head of Atatürk on one side, with some of Turkey's most important touristic highlights on the reverse.

1 lira

5 lira

10 lira

20 lira

50 lira

100 lira

Coins

There are six new coins now in circulation, ranging in value from 1 kuruş, 10 kuruş, 25 kuruş and 50 kuruş to 1 lira (100 kuruş). Those shown here (at their actual size) are for 1 lira and 50 kuruş.

50 kuruş

1 lira

Telephone and Postal Services

Postal service logo

The telephone and postal services in Turkey used to operate as a single unit until 1996, when they were split up to create Türk Telekom (telephone) and the PTT (the postal service). To prepare for privatization, the telephone monopoly made tremendous improvements to its infrastructure and levels of service. Over 80 per cent of Turkey has fibre-optic technology and major cities enjoy easy access to efficient high-speed internet and broadband connections. Many businesses now have numbers beginning with '444' and you can call one contact office in any local area.

Post offices are clearly identified by the letters PTT and although the postal service can often be slow it is reliable. Making phone calls from counter-top metred phones is economical. Many PTT outlets will change foreign currency and also offer the Western Union service for sending and receiving money.

Small, independent kiosk selling phonecards and telephone tokens

USING A CARD PHONE

1 Lift the handset and wait for the dialling tone.

2 Insert your card.

3 Select instructions in the language of your choice and then dial the telephone number you require, using the key pad above the card slot.

4 To make another call press the follow-on button (second from left). If you have finished, replace the handset and the card will be ejected.

USING PUBLIC TELEPHONES

Telephone calls in Istanbul can be made from a variety of locations – public call boxes, post offices or telephone "boutiques". Mobile (cellular) phones have helped to relieve some of the congestion typically experienced at public call boxes. The most economical way to telephone locally or internationally is by using a phonecard. The newest cards have a concealed scratch-off code and this allows you to make calls locally and internationally from any landline in Turkey. Cards come in units of 30, 60, 100, 120 and 180. These can be purchased from all post offices and, for an additional charge, from street sellers and kiosks. After you pick up the receiver, the display screen will prompt you to select the language of your choice, and insert your card. A panel then shows the number of units remaining on your card.

MOBILE PHONES

Turkey has many mobile (cellular) phone operators but the main one is **Türkcell**. This operator has GSM roaming agreements with 180 countries on three different MHz bands, which means that most people can use their existing mobile phone as they would at home. The major exception is North America, where wireless standards and frequencies are less integrated with global ones, even if you have a tri-band mobile phone. An alternative operator to try is **Türk Telekom**.

Requiring only a few formalities, visitors have a flexible option of purchasing prepaid SIM cards from all local mobile operators. These SIM cards can be used with any handset, but you must use the telephone

Akıllı phonecards, featuring portraits of historical figures

REACHING THE RIGHT NUMBER

- Istanbul is divided into two area codes:
  0212 (European side)
  0216 (Asian side).
- To call a number in the same area, do not use the code. For another area, dial the code first.
- To call another city in Turkey, use the appropriate area code. For example, 0224 for Bursa.
- To call Turkey from abroad, dial 00 90 followed by the last three digits of the area code.
- To make an international call from Turkey, dial 00 followed by the code for the country eg: Australia: 61; Canada: 1; New Zealand: 64; Republic of Ireland: 353. UK: 44; US: 1.

number assigned to individual cards. Units can be topped up at many convenient kiosks, bufés and teleboutiques. The cards self-cancel if not used after three months.

OPERATOR SERVICES

Directory Enquiries
Tel 118.
Inter-City Operator
Tel 131.
International Operator
Tel 115.
Wake-Up Call Service
Tel 135.

Note: only international operators are guaranteed to speak English.

INTERNET ACCESS

Istanbul has plenty of internet cafés and most of these are connected at high speeds on a broadband frequency. They charge by the hour but you can usually negotiate a half-hour rate for minimal usage.

Wireless internet connection is now found in many hotels and pensions. In luxury hotels, this will be in your room and included in the price. Even in more modest hotels, you will be able to access the web and check your emails.

BROADBAND AND VOI PROTOCOL

The introduction of broadband and high-speed internet access is refining calling-home and keeping-in-touch options for those abroad. There are now few hotels without internet access of some kind and the upmarket hotels usually offer as standard broadband access in every room. VOI (voice-over-internet) protocol means that you can use your computer for making phone calls anywhere in the world and all for the cost of the internet connection. This is providing you have the right software installed and all the necessary adapters and hardware.

SENDING LETTERS

Stamps are available only from post offices and PTT kiosks. These kiosks, found in tourist areas, also sell tokens and phonecards.

Post offices are found throughout Istanbul. There are large branches, with a full range of postal services, in **Sirkeci**, **Taksim** and **Beyoğlu**. Further locations are marked on the Street Finder (*see pp238–48*). Letters and postcards can be handed over the counter at post offices or

Stamps in 70 and 80 kuruş denominations

posted in letter boxes, which are yellow and labelled PTT. Common signs indicating which box or slot to put your letter in are: *Şehiriçi* (local), *Yurtiçi* (domestic) and *Yurtdışı* (international).

POSTAL SERVICES

It is best to use air mail (*uçak ile*) when posting items abroad as surface post is very slow. If you want to send a parcel by surface mail, use registered (*kayıtlı*) post.

The contents of a package must be inspected at the post office, so take tape to seal your parcel at the counter. Letters between Turkey and Europe average seven to ten days in transit. For other continents, you should allow for around 14 days or more in some cases.

A recorded delivery service (called APS) is available from post offices, with delivery in three days within Turkey. Local courier companies will deliver letters and parcels inland in a day or so at a comparable price.

International mail box

POSTE RESTANTE

Poste restante mail should be sent to the central post office in Sirkeci. Mail should be addressed with the recipient's name, then: poste restante, Büyük Postane, Büyük Postane Caddesi, Sirkeci, Istanbul, Turkey. A nominal fee is payable on collection.

DIRECTORY

MOBILE PHONE OPERATORS

Türkcell
Tel 444 05 32.
www.turkcell.com.tr

Türk Telekom
Tel 444 14 44.
www.telekom.com.tr

POST OFFICES

Beyoğlu
www.ptt.gov.tr
Yeni Çarşı Caddesi
Map 7 D4

Sirkeci
Şehin Şah Pehlevi Caddesi
Map 5 D1

Taksim
Taksim Square
Map 7 E3
www.ptt.gov.tr

TRAVEL INFORMATION

The easiest way to get to Istanbul is to fly directly to the city's international airport, Atatürk Airport, on the European side of the city. Turkish Airlines (THY) has regular, direct flights from 113 destinations throughout the world. Several major European carriers, such as Lufthansa and KLM, also fly direct to Istanbul. Most carriers fly into Atatürk Airport,

Turkish Airlines (THY) aeroplane

but a few charter firms use Sabiha Gökçen, near Pendik on the Asian side. Coaches and trains also offer frequent and well-established services between Istanbul and several European capitals. There are no direct ferry sailings from Europe, although cruises of the Aegean and Mediterranean usually include a one-day stopover for sightseeing in Istanbul.

ARRIVING BY AIR

Turkey's main international airline, **Turkish Airlines** (THY), has direct flights to Istanbul from all major cities in Europe and some in Asia. Major European carriers, such as **Lufthansa**, **KLM**, **Austrian Airlines** and **British Airways** all have at least one flight daily to Istanbul.

Turkish Airlines flies direct to Istanbul from Chicago and New York, and **Delta Airlines**, among others, also has regular direct flights from New York. **American Airlines**, **Qatar Airways** and several other international carriers also serve Istanbul, but not always directly.

ATATÜRK AIRPORT

Istanbul's **Atatürk Airport** (Atatürk Hava Limanı) lies 25 km (16 miles) west of the city centre, in Yeşilköy. Its huge international (*Dış Hatları*) terminal opened in 2000 and is separate from the domestic (*İç Hatları*) terminal.

Atatürk Airport

Services provided in both terminals include duty-free shops open 24 hours where, on arrival as well as departure, you can buy perfume, cigarettes, alcoholic drinks, sweets, personal stereos, watches and cosmetics. There are also gift shops, a café, a restaurant, a post office, 24-hour banking facilities, car hire outlets, a tourist information office and a hotel reservation desk.

Leave plenty of time (at least 2 hours) to check in for departures from Istanbul, particularly during the summer, as there may be queues to get through security checks.

Emblem of Turkish Airlines

TRANSPORT FROM THE AIRPORT

Taxis (*see p238*) are easy to find outside the arrivals hall of the international terminal. They are the most convenient means of reaching the city centre from the airport; the fare to Taksim or Sultanahmet will be about US$35. The airport bus is an efficient, cheaper way of getting to the city centre. Buses depart every half-hour between 6am and midnight. The bus stop is marked '**Havaş**' and is

situated outside the main doors of the arrivals hall. The service into Istanbul stops at Ataköy Marina and at Aksaray, from where you can take a tram or taxi to Sultanahmet and Eminönü. It terminates in Taksim Square (*see p107*). If you wish to get off somewhere else along the route, tell the driver before boarding.

Alternatively, there is a suburban rail service from Yeşilköy to Sirkeci, also handy for Sultanahmet. The fastest and most economical way to the city centre is to use the tramway, which runs directly from the airport all the way to Aksaray.

PACKAGE HOLIDAYS

A number of travel companies organize package deals to Istanbul. These offer substantial savings on a stay in some of the city's top hotels, as well as the reassurance of having a company rep on hand to deal with any problems. Among the specialist firms which do package deals to Istanbul are **Anatolian Sky Holidays, President Holidays** in the UK, and **International Tours and Cruises** in the US.

ARRIVING BY TRAIN

The Orient Express (*see p66*) no longer runs as far as Istanbul. At present, the only

Sirkeci Station in Eminönü, where trains from Europe terminate

direct train route is from Thessaloniki, in Greece. The main overland route is from Munich via Salzburg, Vienna and Budapest, which is a journey lasting two-and-a-half days. Passengers travelling from London can book through Eurail.

Istanbul has two main-line stations: Sirkeci on the European side and Haydarpaşa on the Asian side. Trains from Europe arrive at Sirkeci Station (see p66). Trains from Anatolia and Middle-Eastern cities terminate at Haydarpaşa Station (see p133), from where you can take a ferry to the European side.

Motorway sign showing Turkish and European road numbers

ARRIVING BY COACH

The leading Turkish coach companies **Ulusoy** and **Varan** operate direct services from several European cities to Istanbul. Ulusoy coaches run from Paris, Vienna, Munich, Milan and Athens.

Travelling by coach you will arrive at Esenler coach station (otogar), 10 km (6 miles) northwest of Istanbul city centre. Esenler is also the main terminal for domestic connections (see p244). Your coach company will probably take you into town in a courtesy minibus. If not, take the tramway (see pp240–41) from the station in the centre of the otogar, getting on at the platform marked Aksaray. The 83E and 91 buses also go to the city centre. Kâmil Koç has a daily service between Istanbul and Athens.

ARRIVING BY CAR

Drivers taking cars into Turkey are asked to show registration documents and a valid driving licence at the port of entry. You will be given a certificate by the Turkish customs authorities and this should be carried at all times, together with your driving licence and passport. You must have a Green Card (available from your insurance company) if arriving from Europe, and appropriate insurance if you wish to drive in the Asian part of Turkey. The car should be equipped with a fire extinguisher, a first-aid kit and two hazard warning triangles. Foreign drivers may find driving in Istanbul difficult as local traffic travels at dangerously fast speeds. There are public car parks (otopark or katlıotoparkı), although it can be difficult to get a space.

DIRECTORY

AIRLINES

American Airlines
www.americanairlines.com

Austrian Airlines
www.aua.com

British Airways
Tel (0212) 310 66 00.
www.britishairways.com

Delta Airlines
Tel (0212) 310 20 00.
www.delta.com

KLM
Tel (0212) 310 19 00.
www.klm.com.tr

Qatar Airways
Tel (0212) 296 58 88.
www.qatarairways.com

Turkish Airlines (THY)
Tel (0212) 444 08 49.
www.turkishairlines.com

AIRPORTS

Atatürk Airport
Tel (0212) 444 08 49.

Havaş
Tel (0212) 465 47 00.

Sabiha Gökçen Airport
Tel (0216) 585 50 00.

PACKAGE TOURS

Anatolian Sky Holidays
IMEX House, 52 Blucher Street, Birmingham, B1 1QU, UK.
Tel (0121) 633 4018.

International Tours and Cruises
184 Fifth Avenue, 4th floor New York, NY 10010, US.
Tel (800) BUY-TRAVEL.

President Holidays
92 Park Lane, Croydon, CR0 1JF, UK. Tel (020) 8688 7555.

TRAIN TRAVEL

Haydarpaşa Station
Tel (0216) 336 04 75.

Sirkeci Station
Tel (0212) 527 00 50.

INTERNATIONAL COACH SERVICES

Kâmil Koç
Tel (0212) 444 05 62.

Ulusoy
Tel (0212) 658 30 00.

Varan
Tel (0212) 444 05 62.

Coaches parked in front of their company offices at Esenler

GETTING AROUND ISTANBUL

It is possible to walk between most major sights in Istanbul, and central areas are well served by an expanding system of metro and tram lines. Buses and dolmuşes provide city-wide transport, but take care to avoid travelling by road at rush hour times, when the main roads in and out of the city are congested with traffic.

Street sign at a junction in central Sultanahmet

As the public transport network grows, it becomes ever more confusing to work out the best means of transport for any one journey, but the various forms of transport all link up so you can always get where you want to go somehow. See the map inside the back cover for more information. Each type of transport has an individual ticket system, but there is also a travel pass, AKBİL *(see p241)*, which can be useful whatever the length of your stay. Bus passes can be bought more economically by the week. If time is short, take taxis, which are relatively cheap.

ISTANBUL ON FOOT

The development of semi-pedestrianized areas, such as İstiklal Caddesi and central Sultanahmet, has made it possible to walk with ease around some parts of Istanbul. This can be particularly pleasant in spring and autumn, when the weather is mild. It is also possible to walk around the city's quieter backwaters – like the area around the antiques shops of Çukurcuma, near Galatasaray, or Eyüp *(see pp120–21)* – without encountering much traffic. For specialist tour companies offering walking tours around the city see page 229.

Sign for a pedestrian underpass

Wherever you walk, bear in mind that traffic only stops at pedestrian crossings controlled by lights, and always make use of pedestrian overpasses and underpasses on main roads.

Istanbul, like any city, has parts that should be avoided. If you are planning to walk in areas off the usual tourist track seek local advice, take extra care and try not to be walking in unfamiliar streets after dark.

TAXIS

Taxi cabs are ubiquitous in Istanbul, and fares are cheap in relation to other major European cities. Taxis operate day and night, and can be hailed in the street or found at taxi ranks *(see pp246–56)*. Hotel and restaurant staff can always phone for a taxi.

Cabs are bright yellow, with the word "taksi" on a sign on the roof. They take up to four passengers. In all licensed taxis the fare is charged according to a meter. The daytime *(gündüz)* fare is applied between 6am and midnight; the night-time *(gece)* rate is 50% higher. If you cross the Bosphorus Bridge the bridge toll will be added to the fare at the end of your journey. The driver will not expect a sizeable tip unless he has helped you load luggage. The normal procedure for tipping is just to round up the fare to the nearest convenient figure.

Most taxi drivers do not speak much English, if any. Some drivers may not be familiar with routes to lesser-known sights, so it is a good idea to carry a map. It may also help to have the name of your destination written down.

DOLMUŞES

Dolmuşes are a useful means of transport outside the city centre. These shared taxis with fixed routes are cheaper than regular taxis and more frequent than buses. In Turkish the word *dolmuş* means "full", and drivers usually wait until every seat is taken before setting off. In the past, dolmuş passengers would travel in huge 1950s Chrysler or Chevrolet cars. Today minibuses or SUVs have largely replaced these enormous, fuel-hungry dinosaurs. Dolmuşes run throughout the day until mid-evening, and later on busy routes, such as those starting from Taksim.

Old-style dolmuş, a rare sight these days

Points of origin and final destinations are displayed in the front windows of all dolmuşes, and passengers can get in and out anywhere en route. The fare depends on the length of your journey. State your destination, then hand your

Licensed Istanbul taxi cab with its registration number on the side

USEFUL DOLMUŞ ROUTES

Taksim – Ataköy
(from Taksim Caddesi)
Taksim – Beşiktaş
(from Gümüşsuyu Caddesi)
Taksim – Kadıköy
(from behind the Atatürk Culture Centre – AKM)
Taksim – Teşvikiye
(from Gümüşsuyu Caddesi)
Beşiktaş – Taksim
(from Beşiktaş Caddesi)
Eminönü – Topkapı
(from Sobacılar Caddesi)
Kadıköy – Üsküdar
(from Haydarpaşa Rıhtım Caddesi)
Kadıköy – Bostancı
(from Kumluk Meydanı)
Üsküdar – Beykoz
(from Paşa Limanı Caddesi)
Beşiktaş – Sarıyer
(from Barbaros Bulvarı)
Yedikule – Edirnekapı
(the underpass beneath the city walls at Kale İçi)

money to the driver or another passenger to pass forward. To stop the vehicle, simply say to the driver "*inecek* (pronounced eenejek) *var*" ("somebody wants to get out").

Dolmuş ranks are marked by a blue sign with a black "D" on a white background. A main centre for dolmuşes is Taksim. Dolmuşes from here cross the Bosphorus Bridge and the bridge tariff is reflected in your fare.

GETTING AROUND BY BUS

Inner-city buses are operated by two companies, both under municipal jurisdiction. I.E.T.T. (Istanbul Omnibus company) buses are red and the environmentally friendly ones (*yeşil motor*) are green and run on natural gas. Özel Halk (public) buses are orange and cream. Both ply similar routes and depart from the same depots and charge equal fares. There is little difference from a commuter's point of view.

I.E.T.T. buses accept paper tickets which you must purchase before boarding, as

well as the electronic AKBİL *(see p241)*. Bus tickets can be purchased from main bus departure centres, newsagents, kiosks and private vendors, who are usually found around bus shelters. If you plan to travel extensively by bus to see the city, you can save money by purchasing a weekly pass, available at major bus depots, such as Taksim, Beşiktaş, Kadıköy or Eminönü.

If you cross either of the Bosphorus bridges, expect to pay double fare, or two tickets. You queue and enter at the front of the bus and exit by the middle or rear doors. Push the button above the door or, on the later models, attached to the railings or support poles, to alert the driver that you wish to alight at the next stop. A list of stops is displayed on a board on the side of buses or on a video

An Özel Halk city bus, on which you pay a conductor on boarding

Full-fare and student bus tickets

screen on newer buses. Bus shelters have more details of routes and stops. Most buses run from 6am until 10 or 11pm.

Plan Tours operates a Hop-On-Hop-Off double-decker tourist bus service around all the main sights. Outlying parts of Istanbul can easily be seen by bus, for example, the No. 40 bus from Taksim Square runs beside the Bosphorus as far as Sarıyer.

I.E.T.T. bus advertising a brand of tomato purée

DIRECTORY

TAXI COMPLAINTS

Tel (0212) 283 65 46.

BUS COMPANIES

I.E.T.T. (Istanbul Omnibus Company)
Erkan-ı Harp Sok No: 4, Beyoğlu.
Map 7 D5.
Tel (0800) 211 60 68,
(0800) 211 61 20.
www.iett.gov.tr

BUS TOURS

Plan Tours
Cumhuriyet Cad 131/1,
Elmadağ.
Map 7 F3.
Tel (0212) 230 22 72.
www.plantours.com

Sultanahmet Office (across from Haghia Sophia):
Map 3 E4 (5 E4).
Tel (0212) 458 18 00.

Getting Around by Metro, Tram and Train

Metro sign

Although Istanbul can seem hectic at times, the public transport system runs remarkably efficiently and punctually, and is open until around 11pm. The underground Metro and the extensive overground tramway system and its branch lines are comfortable and affordable. Atatürk Airport and the bus station are accessible by tram. A third Bosphorus Bridge is in the planning stage and excavation has started on the Marmaray Project, which is a subterranean, intercontinental commuter tunnel under the Bosphorus.

the bus station at Esenler and to the World Trade Centre and Atatürk Airport. For the bus station, be sure to alight at the Otogar stop, not Esenler. Inevitably, trams get packed during the rush hour. The line is being extended on the Asian side from Kadıköy to Kartal. The tramway and its branch lines are officially known as the *Raylı Sistemi* (Rail system).

To access the tramway you purchase a token which operates the turnstile (these also accept the AKBİL pass).

Trams travel on the right hand side of the street, so be sure to stand on the correct platform. To board a tram, buy a flat-fare token from the booth *(gişe)* near the platform, and put it into the receptacle at the top of the platform steps. Trams are frequent, running every 5 minutes between 5am and midnight.

Modern tram at a stop in Sultanahmet

THE TRAMWAY

Istanbul's tramway system is clean and modern, and is the fastest way to get around the city. The main line runs from Kabataş, across the Galata Bridge *(see inside back cover)*, up through the main tourist area of Sultanahmet to Aksaray. Feeder lines, sometimes called the Hafif Tramway (light tramway), go above and below ground to

THE METRO

The Metro system has only six stops, but it is a source of pride to the city that it has an

TRAM AND METRO ROUTE MAP

The Metro goes from Taksim to IV Levent and an extension will open in 2007 between Taksim and Yenikapı. The Metro is an underground system. The Tramway is mainly an above-ground, electrified rail system.

KEY

— Metro

- - Metro planned or under construction

— Tünel funicular

— Tramway

- - Tramway planned or under construction

— Nostalgic Tram

— Underground funicular

İkitelli

Otogar

Esenler

IV Levent

Gayrettepe

Sisli

Mecidiyeköy

Osmanbey

Taksim　Kabataş

Tünel

Karaköy

Golden Horn

Aksaray　Eminönü

Yusufpaşa

Yenikapı

Zeytinburnu

Airport

Sea of Marmara

Harem

Kartal

Bosphorus

underground transport system. The Taksim to IV Levent line opened in 2000 and helps to relieve some of the pressure on traffic moving north of Taksim Square. The Metro is clean, well run and the cars are air conditioned. Journey tokens, purchased on entry, operate the turnstiles. The line runs deep underground and is accessed by many walkways and escalators. Platforms tend to be much longer than the two or three cars used on the route, so wait near the middle of the platform where the trains stop. An extension to the line is under construction from Taksim to Yenikapı and is due to come into service at the end of 2007.

Turkish Railways sign on the side of a train

TÜNEL

Inaugurated in 1875, this French-built underground railway climbs steeply uphill for a distance of 500 m (550 yards) from Karaköy to Tünel Square in Beyoğlu, from where you can get the old tram up İstiklâl Caddesi. The Karaköy station is set back from the main road just off the Galata Bridge *(see p101)*. The best way to get to it is through the underpass at the end of the bridge. Look out for the exit marked "Tünel". To board it at either station you need to buy a token *(jeton)* from the booth to operate the turnstile. The Tünel closes at 9pm.

THE NOSTALGIC TRAM

The nostalgic tram *(Nostaljik Tramvay)* covers a distance of just over 1 km (just under 1 mile) along İstiklâl Caddesi from Tünel to Taksim Square. The trams are the original early 20th-century vehicles, taken out of service in 1966 but revived in 1989 for their historical value. The ticket collectors wear period costume. Tickets can be purchased from kiosks at either end of the line.

SUBURBAN TRAINS

Suburban trains *(banliyö)* run beside the Sea of Marmara between Sirkeci and Halkalı (on the European side), and Haydarpaşa and Gebze (on the Asian side). The service is slow, and stations are generally not close enough to tourist sights to be of much use to visitors. Exceptions are Yedikule (for Yedikule Museum, *see p115*), Ataköy (near Galleria shopping mall, *see p211*) and Yeşilköy (the airport station, *see p236*). On the Asian side, Bostancı is one of the ferry piers for the Princes' Islands.

A train ticket costs the same flat rate as a bus ticket, and should be retained for the whole journey. Suburban trains start daily at 6am and stop at 11:30pm. For further information on the rail network, see the map inside the back cover.

THE AKBİL TRAVEL PASS

The Akbil is a type of travel pass which can be used on almost all forms of public transport in Istanbul. Short for *akıllı bilet*, or "intelligent ticket", this metal token can be purchased from main bus stations and other public transport ticket offices. It can be used on the Tramway, ferries and sea buses, and city buses.

When purchasing an AKBİL, you pay for a number of units in advance and also a deposit, which is refundable, for the token itself. More units can be added to the token at any time. The distinctive orange-coloured AKBİL machines are located at the entrances to stations and on buses. To use the AKBİL place the metal token in the socket on the front of the machine, near the display panel. The fare will then be deducted in units.

AKBİL passes

Nostalgic tram travelling along İstiklâl Caddesi in Beyoğlu

Getting Around by Boat

Token (*jeton*) for iDO ferry

Perhaps the most pleasant and relaxing means of getting around Istanbul is by the innumerable water-borne craft which ply the Bosphorus between the European and Asian sides. These range from small, privately operated motor boats to a fleet of high-speed catamarans. Travelling by boat, you will avoid the traffic jams and tariffs of the Bosphorus road bridges. As well as being a relatively fast way to get around, a ride on a boat will also provide some great views of the city.

Old ferries at Karaköy

FERRIES

A constant traffic of ferries crosses the Bosphorus and the Golden Horn. Called *vapur*, they are run by the **Istanbul Sea Bus Company (iDO)**. The principal ferry terminus on the European side is at Eminönü *(see p87)*. Each of the six piers here has a boarding hall, with the destination written in large black letters on the outside. The three main piers are numbered. Pier 1 serves Üsküdar; pier 2 serves Kadıköy; and pier 3, labelled "Boğaz Hattı", is for all ferries travelling up the Bosphorus, including the special cruise. The other three piers are a short distance from Eminönü proper. On the west side of the Galata Bridge is the pier

Passengers boarding a ferry

for ferries up the Golden Horn (Haliç Hattı). To the east of pier 1, at Sirkeci, across the road from the station, is the departure point for car ferries to Harem. Further along from this, at Sarayburnu, is the final pier, labelled "Adalar", from which long-distance ferries depart. This is the pier for ferries to the Princes' Islands.

Another main terminus is Karaköy, opposite Eminönü, from which ferries run to Haydarpaşa and Kadıköy.

FERRY AND SEA BUS ROUTE MAP

There are numerous ferry and sea bus services departing daily from Eminönü and the other ports. In addition, a number of smaller, privately operated motor boats serve the same destinations as the state-run ferries.

EMİNÖNÜ PIERS

① Üsküdar
② Kadıköy
③ Bosphorus, Beşiktaş
④ Harem
⑤ Princes' Islands, Marmara, Yalova
⑥ Balat-Üsküdar

Galata Bridge

Sea Bus

KEY

— Ferry
— Sea bus
— Car ferry
— Motor boat

Balat · Golden · Horn · Fener · Kasımpaşa

Kabataş

BEYOĞLU

Bosphorus

Beşiktaş · Anadolu Kavağı

Üsküdar

Karaköy

Eminönü Piers

BAZAAR QUARTER

SERAGLIO POINT

Harem

Yenikapı

SULTANAHMET

Marmara · Princes' Islands · Princes' Islands Yalova Marmara Islands · Kadıköy

The international dock, where cruise liners berth, is also here.

There are ferries from Eminönü to Kadıköy between 7:30am and 9pm, and from Eminönü to Üsküdar between 6am and 11:30pm, every 15 minutes (20 minutes at weekends). Other services are less frequent. If you want to explore independently using ferries, especially to hop between the villages along the Bosphorus, you will need to arm yourself with a timetable.

MOTOR BOATS

A number of privately run craft cross the Bosphorus and Golden Horn at various points, and run up the Bosphorus. These routes are also served by İDO ferries, but private motor boats are more frequent, though slightly more expensive. A conductor will come and collect your fare after the boat leaves the pier.

SEA BUSES

The modern, Swedish-built catamarans which are known as sea buses *(deniz otobüsleri)* are also run by İDO, a private company. Their interiors resemble aircraft cabins, with long rows of comfortable, reclining seats, piped music and air-conditioning. Sea buses are considerably faster and more comfortable than ferries, but cost two or three times as much.

The most useful routes are Eminönü to Kadıköy (half-hourly from 7:40am to 7pm Monday to Friday, and 8:15 am to 6:10pm at weekends); and Bakırköy to Bostancı (hourly between 8:15am and 10pm). In the summer, sea buses run

Ferry for Kadıköy, docked at Eminönü's pier 2

from Kabataş and Bostancı to Büyükada on the Princes' Islands. For destinations outside Istanbul see pages 244–5.

THE BOSPHORUS TRIP

İDO runs daily excursions up the Bosphorus *(see pp136–49)*. These are normal ferries on which light refreshments are served (although at considerably inflated prices) but no meals. They get crowded in the summer months, especially at weekends, so it is a good idea to arrive early to ensure that you get a deck seat with a view. You should retain your ticket during the journey, as you must show it when boarding for the return trip. You can disembark at any pier along the way, boarding the next ferry that comes along with the same ticket; but if you make a second stop you will need to buy a new ticket. İDO also offers a trip from Kadıköy in summer at weekends only.

There are several alternatives to the official Bosphorus trip. The small private boats, which leave Eminönü just after the İDO ferry sails in the summer months, only go halfway up the straits and do not stop on the way. If you decide to book a private cruise through a tour company, be sure to choose a reputable company, such as **Hatsail Tourism**.

İDO logo

BUYING BOAT TICKETS

For ferries and sea buses, you need to buy a flat-fare *jeton* from the booth *(gişe)* at the pier or alternatively from one of the unofficial street vendors who sit nearby and sell them at slightly higher prices. These *jetons* can be used for all local journeys. For ferries to the Princes' Islands or for the Bosphorus trip, you still need to buy a jeton which will cover the outward and return journeys, but it is more expensive than the normal İDO fare.

To enter the pier put the *jeton* into the slot beside the turnstile, and then wait in the boarding hall for a boat.

A schedule of sailing times is on view at each pier and a copy of the timetable *(tarife)* can usually be bought at the ticket booth.

A sea bus catamaran, Istanbul's fastest form of water transport

Travelling Beyond Istanbul

The best way of getting from Istanbul to other towns and cities is by long-distance coach. A bewildering number of companies offer services to every conceivable destination in Turkey, with several companies serving any one intercity route. It is worth paying a bit extra to travel with a reputable company, to ensure a safe and comfortable journey.

Courtesy minibus to and from the city centre

The rail network is much more limited than the coach network. Trains go to only a limited number of cities in Turkey and the service is less efficient. Even express trains take longer than the same journey by coach. For destinations across the Sea of Marmara, ferries and sea buses are a relaxing means of transport.

INTERCITY COACHES

The main coach station / for both domestic and international destinations is at Esenler, 14 km (9 miles) northwest of the city centre. The Otogar is poorly maintained; public conveniences and restaurants are dirty and it is generally unkempt. Unless you are staying in this part of Istanbul, you will probably not need to use it at all. All coach companies have city centre branches where you can buy tickets, and they run a shuttle service to one of their collection points near the motorway. On the Asian side, too, they will stop at one of their own terminals.

You must make a booking for all coach journeys. Most companies accept credit cards. **Varan** and **Ulusoy** *(see p237)*, the two most reputable bus companies, can make bookings and issue tickets for any of their destinations around Turkey from any of their city centre offices. They operate services between main centres such as Ankara, Antalya and İzmir, as well as to destinations along the Black Sea coast. **Kamil Koç** has a service to Bursa. The journey goes via Gebze, boarding the ferry to Yalova

and takes about four hours. **Çanakkale Truva Seyahat** is the best company to use for getting to Gelibolu (Gallipoli), which takes about five hours, or Çanakkale, which takes about six hours. **Metro Turizm** is a large and reliable coach company that runs regular schedules to many destinations outside Istanbul.

One of the many inter-city coaches from Esenler

Smoking is not permitted on any coaches. Single passengers will usually be seated next to someone of the same sex. Couples can sit together. Mineral water, and sometimes other refreshments, are available on board free of charge. There will be frequent rest and meal stops. On most coaches, the attendant will offer a refreshing bottle of cologne to passengers.

LONG-DISTANCE FERRIES

Ferries and sea buses are a convenient means of travelling long distances from a city surrounded by water. **İDO** ferries *(see p242)* are very good value, and cars are carried on some routes. Few concessions are made to comfort, however; seating is often basic and the buffets offer only snacks.

The trip to Bursa can be made by a combination of sea bus or ferry, and coach. The fastest route is to take one of four daily sea buses from Kabataş to Yalova, just an hour away. Ferries also sail from Sarayburnu, in Eminönü, to Yalova. The port of Mudanya is even closer to Bursa but boats are much less frequent. Sea buses go there from Yenikapı, ferries from Sarayburnu. Frequent buses meet incoming boats at Yalova and Mudanya.

In the summer, sea buses go from Yenikapı to Marmara. IDO also has ferries to the Marmara Islands, departing from Sarayburnu. A car ferry runs from Kabataş to Avşa.

TRAINS TO EDİRNE

There is a daily train to Edirne from Sirkeci Station *(see p66)*. However, the

Sea bus coming in to dock at Eminönü pier

journey takes six hours, twice the length of time taken by the coach. Advance reservations can be made at the railway stations in either city, or in certain travel agencies displaying the **TCDD** (Turkish State Railways) sign. Unfortunately, Bursa is not on the rail network.

CAR HIRE AND ROAD TRAVEL

Car rental office in the arcade of the Hilton Hotel, Taksim

Turkey's comprehensive intercity coach network means that a car is not necessary for travelling to other cities. However, if you do wish to drive, car hire companies such as **Avis**, **Budget** and **Sixt** have offices in the airport, as well as in the city centre. You do not need an international driving licence; a normal licence from your own country is all that is required.

All roads in Turkey, both in and outside cities, are made hazardous by reckless driving, and caution is recommended at all times. Traffic drives on and gives way to the right, even on roundabouts.

The Turkish Touring and Automobile Club (Türkiye Turing ve Otomobil Kurumu, or **TTOK**), based in Istanbul, is happy to give visiting motorists advice on driving in Turkey, as well as offering assistance with breakdowns, accidents and insurance. It has reciprocal agreements with the British AA and RAC.

DAY TRIP TOURS

A number of companies offer day trips from Istanbul to the Princes' Islands, the Dardanelles, Bursa and villages on the Black Sea. These are often good value and offer an efficient and hassle-free method of simplifying your travel arrangements.

Reputable tour operators with English-speaking guides include **Plan Tours**, **VIP Turizm** and **Türk Expres**. All offer classical, biblical and heritage tours in Istanbul as well as to regions throughout Turkey. Some companies offer personalized tours all over Turkey. Plan Tours also operates a double-decker bus service around Istanbul. **CARED** (Çanakkale Tour Guide Association) can provide tour guides who speak many languages.

LOCAL TRANSPORT OUTSIDE ISTANBUL

The main means of public transport in both Bursa and Edirne is the dolmuş. These are either minibuses or saloon cars, with the destination displayed on signs on the roof. If you stay in the centre of either city and are moderately fit, you will find that all of the major sights are within easy walking distance.

In Bursa city centre, Heykel, at the eastern end of Atatürk Caddesi, is the main dolmuş terminus. From there you can get dolmuşes to most other parts of the city. There is also an efficient bus service.

Edirne is much smaller than Bursa, and the public transport system is not as comprehensive. To get from the coach station to the town centre, a distance of 2 km (1 mile), take a Merkez–Garaj minibus dolmuş, or a taxi.

There are no motor vehicles on the Princes' Islands. On Büyükada and Heybeliada there are phaeton carriages; otherwise you have to get around on foot or by bicycle.

Horse-drawn carriage (phaeton) on Büyükada

DIRECTORY

STREET FINDER

The map references that are given throughout this guide refer to the maps on the following pages. Some small streets with references may not be named on the map. References are also given for hotels *(see pp180–91)*, restaurants *(see pp192–209)*, shops *(see pp210–19)* and entertainment venues *(see pp220–23)*. The map

Visitor to Istanbul consulting a map

below shows the area covered by the ten maps and the key lists the symbols used. The first figure of the reference tells you which map page to turn to; the letter and number indicate the grid reference. For an overview of Greater Istanbul see pages 108–9. The map on the inside back cover shows public transport routes.

KEY TO STREET FINDER

■ Major sight	**D** Dolmuş terminus	═ Motorway
■ Place of interest	🚖 Taxi rank	··· Pedestrian tunnel
■ Other building	**i** Tourist information	— City walls
⛴ Ferry boarding point	**H** Hospital	
▭ Sea bus boarding point	🚓 Police station	**SCALE OF MAPS**
🚆 Railway station	🛁 Turkish baths	**1–3 & 6–10**
Ⓜ Metro station	**C** Mosque	0 metres 250
🚠 Underground funicular stop	✡ Synagogue	0 yards 250
🚋 Tram stop	**†** Church	
🚋 Nostalgic tram stop	⊠ Post office	**SCALE OF MAPS 4 & 5**
🚠 Cable car station	═ Railway line	0 metres 200
🚌 Main bus stop	— Tram line	0 yards 200

Street Finder Index

In Turkish, Ç, Ğ, İ, Ö, Ş and Ü are listed as separate letters in the alphabet, coming after C, G, I, O, S and U respectively. In this book, however, Ç is treated as C for the purposes of alphabetization and so on with the other letters. Hence Çiçek follows Cibinlik as if both names began with C. Following standard Turkish practice we have abbreviated Sokağı to Sok and Caddesi to Cad. References in brackets refer to the enlarged section of the Street Finder (maps 4 and 5).

General Index

Acknowledgments

Dorling Kindersley would like to thank the following people whose assistance contributed to the preparation of this book:

Main Contributors

Rosie Ayliffe lived in Turkey for three years, during which time she worked as a freelance writer in Istanbul for the English-language weekly *Dateline Turkey* and as a tour guide travelling all over western Turkey. She is one of the authors of the *Rough Guide to Turkey*, and has also contributed to the *Rough Guide to France* and to Time Out's London guides.

Rose Baring is a travel writer who has spent many months exploring Istanbul. She is the co-author of *Essential Istanbul* (AA) and has also contributed to guides to Tunisia, and Moscow and St Petersburg.

Barnaby Rogerson has travelled, written and lectured extensively in the countries of the eastern Mediterranean. He is, with Rose Baring, co-author of *Essential Istanbul* (AA), and has contributed to several other AA and Cadogan guides. He is the author of *A Traveller's History of North Africa*.

Canan Silay worked for many years as the editor-in-chief of the English-language magazine *Istanbul, The Guide*. Previously, she had worked as a journalist with the Turkish daily newspaper *Hürriyet*. She has contributed to several books on Turkey, including Insight guides to Istanbul, Turkey and the Turkish coast.

MANAGING EDITOR Georgina Matthews
MANAGING ART EDITOR Annette Jacobs
SENIOR MANAGING EDITOR Vivien Crump
DEPUTY ART DIRECTOR Gillian Allan

Additional Contributors

Ghillie Başan, Krysia Bereday Burnham, Professor Anthony A M Bryer, Jim Crow, José Luczyc-Wyhowska, Colin Nicholson, Venetia Porter, Dott. A Ricci, Professor J M Rogers, Sargasso Media Ltd, London, Suzanne Swan, Tina Walsh.

Additional Cartography

Robert Funnell, Emily Green, David Pugh, Lee Rowe (ESR Cartography Ltd).

Design and Editorial Assistance

Didem Mersin Alıcı, Gillian Andrews, Gary Cross, Mehmet Erdemgil, Sally Hibbard, Hasan Kelepir, Francesca Machiavelli, Sam Merrell, Ella Milroy, Mary Ormandy, Marianne Petrou, Mani Ramaswamy, Lee Redmond, Nicola Rodway, Anna Streiffert, Rosalyn Thiro, Dutjapun Williams, Veronica Wood.

Proofreader

Stewart Wild.

Indexer

Hilary Bird.

Additional Photography

DK Studio/Steve Gorton, John Heseltine, Dave King, Ian O'Leary, Clive Streeter.

Artwork Reference

Kadir Kir, Remy Sow.

Special Assistance

The Publisher would like to thank staff at museums, mosques, churches, local government departments, shops, hotels, restaurants and other organizations in Istanbul for their invaluable help. Particular thanks are also due to: Feride Alpe; Halil Özek, Archaeological Museum, Istanbul; Hamdi Arabacıoğlu, Association of Mevlevis, Istanbul; Veli Yenisoğancı (Director), Aya Sofya Museum, Istanbul; Nicholas Barnard; Ahmet Kazokoğlu, Bel Bim A.Ş., Istanbul; Poppy Body; Banu Akkaya, British Consulate, Istanbul; Vatan Ercan and Mine Kaner, Bursa Tourist Office; Hanife Yenilmez, Central Bank of the Republic of Turkey, London; Reverend Father Ian Sherwood, Christ Church, Istanbul; Father Lorenzo, Church of SS Peter and Paul, Istanbul; Münevver Ek and Muazzez Pervan, Economic and Social History Foundation of Turkey, Istanbul; Edirne Müze Müdürlüğü; Emin Yıldız, Edirne Tourist Office; Tokay Gözütok, Eminönü Belediyesi, Istanbul; Mohammet Taşbent, Eminönü Zabıta Müdürlüğü, Istanbul; Orhan Gencer, Protocol Department, First Army HQ, Istanbul; Robert Graham; Cengiz Güngör, şevki Sırma and Mustafa Taşkan, Greater Istanbul Municipality; Hikmet Öztürk, İETT Genel Müdürlüğü, Istanbul; Bashir Ibrahim-Khan, Islamic Cultural Centre, London; İsmet Yalçın, İstanbul Balık Müstahsilleri Derneği; Nedim Akıner, İstanbul Koruma Kurulu; Sühela Ertürk Akdoğan and all staff of the Istanbul Tourist Offices; Abdurrahman Gündoğdu and Ömer Yıldız, İstanbul Ulaşım A.Ş.; İznik Tourist Office; Mark Jackson; Sibel Koyluoğlu; Semra Karakaşlı, Milli Saraylar Daire Başkanlığı, Istanbul; Akın Bavur and Recep Öztop, Cultural Department, Ministry of Foreign Affairs, Ankara; staff at the Edirne Müftülüğü and Eyüp Müftülüğü; Mehmet Sağlam and staff at the İstanbul Müftülüğü; Professor Kemal İskender, Museum of Painting and Sculpture, Istanbul; Öcal Özerek, Museum of Turkish and Islamic Arts, Bursa; Dilek Elçin and Dr Celia Kerslake, Oriental Institute, Oxford University; Kadri Özen; Dr İffet Özgönül; Cevdat Bayındır, Public Relations Department, Pera Palas Hotel; Chris Harbard, RSPB; Rosamund Saunders; John Scott; Huseyin Özer, Sofra; Ahmet Mertez and Gülgün Tunç, Topkapı Palace, Istanbul; Doctor Tüncer, Marmara Island; Mr U Kenan İpek (First Secretary), Turkish Culture and Tourism Office in London and Istanbul, Turkish Embassy, London; Orhan Türker (Director of International Relations), Turkish Touring and Automobile Club, Istanbul; Peter Espley (Public Relations Counsellor) and all staff at the Turkish Tourist Office, London; Mustafa Coşkan, Türkiye Sakatlar Derneği, Istanbul; Dr Beyhan Erçağ, Vakıflar Bölge Müdürlüğü, Istanbul; Yalova Tourist Office; Zeynep Demir and Sabahattin Türkoğlu, Yıldız Palace, Istanbul.

Photography Permissions

Dorling Kindersley would like to thank the following for their kind permission to photograph at their establishments: the General Directorate of Monuments and Museums, the Ministry of Culture, the Ministry for Religious Affairs, İstanbul Valiliği İl Kültür Müdürlüğü, İstanbul Valiliği İl Müftülüğü, the Milli Saraylar Daire Başkanlığı and Edirne Valiliği İl Müftülüğü; also the many churches, restaurants, hotels, shops, transport services, and other sights and establishments too numerous to thank individually.

Picture Credits

t = top; tl = top left; tlc = top left centre; tc = top centre; trc = top right centre; tr = top right; cla = centre left above; ca = centre above; cra = centre right above; cl = centre left; c = centre; cr = centre right; clb = centre right below; cb = centre below; crb = centre right below; bl = bottom left; b = bottom; bc = bottom centre; bcl = bottom centre left; br = bottom right; d = detail

The publisher would like to thank the following individuals, companies, and picture libraries for their kind permission to reproduce their photographs:

A Turızm Yayınları: 158b; Archaeological Museum 42b, 62b, 63tr, 64tr, 65t/c; *Aya Sofia from Fossart Album* 74tr; Topkapı Palace 56b; ABC Basin Ajansı A.ş.: 44t, 47c/b, 215cr; The Advertising Archives: 102t; Aisa Archivo Icongrafico, S.A., Barcelona: 19, 20c, 24c, 32tr, 33br, 119t, 171t; Louvre Museum 21c; Topkapı Palace 55bl, 57c, AKG, London: 31tl; Erich Lessing 30t, Erich Lessing/Kunsthistoriches Museum, Vienna 32c; Alamy Images: David Crossland 196br, Jeff Greenberg 107br; Ali Kabas 195c; John Stark 194cl, 195tl; Ancient Art and Architecture Collection Ltd: 20tr, 23tr;

Aquila Photographics: Hanneand Jens Eriksen 169b; Archive Photos: 179 inset; Tahsın Aydoğmuş: 4t, 17b, 21b, 22tl, 43b, 71ca, 72t, 75b, 78t, 86tl, 86tr, 119ca, 144b, 170b; Jon Arnold Images: Walter Bibikow 11tr.

Bel Bım İstanbul Beledıyelerı Bılgı İşlem San Ve Tıc A.Ş: 241c; Benaki Museum, Athens: 25t; Bridgeman Art Library, London: British Library *A Portrait of Süleyman the Magnificent* (1494–1566), Persian 32br; National Maritime Museum, London *Battle of Lepanto, 7th October, 1571*, Anonymous 27t; Private Collection *Constantine the Great (c.274–337 AD, Roman Emperor 306–337AD), gold aureus* 20tl; Stapleton Collection *Ibrahim from a Series of Portraits of the Emperors of Turkey, 1808*, John Young (1755–1825) 33tl; Victoria and Albert Museum, London *Sultan Mahmud II: Procession*, Anonymous 33tc, 161cbl/cbr; © The Trustees of the British Museum: 161cla; Directorate of Museums, Bursa: 162tl.

Çalikoğlu Reklam Tunzm Ve Tıcaret Ltd.: 220b; Jean Loup Charmet: 29t, 33cr; Manuel Çıtak: 46b, 103c, 141t, 162b; Bruce Coleman Collection: 141b; Corbis: Lynsey Addario 175br; Paul Hardy 172cl; Michael Nicholson 10br; Adam Woolfitt 10cla; Alison Wright 177tr; Zefa/Herbert Spichtinger 176cla.

C.M Dixon Photo Resources: 62tr.

ET Archive, London: 18; Bibliotheque de L'Arsenal, Paris 24t; National Gallery 32bl; Mary Evans Picture Library: 142b, 171b, 225 inset; ES Collection/Vatican Library 23tl.

First Army HQ, Istanbul: 133b.

Getty Images: 9 inset, 30c, 32tl, 49 inset; Photographie Giraudon, Paris: 26c; Bibliotheque Nationale, Paris 33bl; Lauros 29bl; Topkapı Palace 26b, 27c, 28c, 28–9, 32tc; Ara Güler: 23bl, 26tl, 35br, 87b, 128c, 219tr, 224–5; Mosaics Museum 77c; Topkapı Palace 1, 57t/b, 81t, 95bl, 161bl; Şemsı Güner: 43t, 129ca, 140t, 158t.

Sonia Halliday Photographs: 29br, 127b; engraved by Thomas Allom, painted by Laura Lushington 23c, 28br, 59tr; Bibliotheque Nationale, Madrid 21t; drawn by Miss Pardoe, painted by Laura Lushington 104c; Topkapı Palace 33tr, 76b; Robert Harding Picture Library: Robert Francis 35cla; David Holden 150; Michael Jenner 3 inset, 55br; Odyssey, Chicago/Robert Frerck 40br, 168b; JHC Wilson 129cb; Adam Woolfitt 39cl, 91tr, 210b; Hutchison Library: Maurice Harvey 240cl.

İDO-Istanbul Sea Bus Company: 243c; Istanbul Foundation for Culture and the Arts: 221b; Istanbul Hilton: 182t; Istanbul History Foundation: 30br; Istanbul Library: 66b, 95tl.

Gürol Kara: 2–3, 98c, 115b, 146ca, 153t, 169t; İzzet Kerıbar: 5b, 16tr, 47t, 48–9, 50, 52ca, 118tl, 128tr, 134–5, 138b, 139t, 146cb, 172tc, 173br, 173ca, 174tr, 174cl, 174bc, 175tc, 177bc, 214br, 234tl, 240tl.

José Luczyc-Wyhowska: 218tr, 219cl/cr/bl/blc/brc/br.

Magnum Photos Ltd.: Topkapı Palace/Ara Güler 8–9, 28bl, 33cl, 41b, 55t, 56t; Military Museum, Istanbul: 127t.

Nour Foundation, London: The Nassar D. Khalili Collection of Islamic Art Ferman (MSS801) 95tr, Mahmud II (CAL 334) 95cr, Leaf (CAL 165) 95cl; Burnisher (SC1210) 95bra, Knife (SC1297) 95brb.

Dick Osseman: 175clb; Güngör Özsoy: 60t, 70b, 157t/cr, 170c.

Paşabahçe Glassworks: 146t; Pera Museum: 103bc; Pictures Colour Library: 44b, 214tr, 218cl; Private Collection: 135 inset.

Science Photo Library: CNES, 1993 Distribution SPOT image 12t; Neil Setchfield: 84; Antony Souter: 53b; Remy Sow: 180c; Spectrum Colour Library: 153b; The Stockmarket: 130t.

Tatılya: 222b; TAV Investment Holding Co.: 236bl; Travel Ink: Abbie Enock 35bc; Trip Photographic Library: 154b; Marc Dubin 45t; Turkish Airlines: 236t; Turkish Information Office: Ozan Sadık 45b. Peter Wilson: 56c, 75t/c, 79tl, 118c. Erdal Yazici: 34, 44c, 167r, 169c.

Front endpaper: all special photography except Robert Harding Picture Library: David Holden tc; İzzet Keribar: c; Neil Setchfield: cl.

JACKET
Front Cover: DK Images: Tony Souter clb; Getty Images: Photonica/Jake Rajs.
Back Cover: DK Images: Tony Souter cla, clb, bl; Francesca Yorke tl.
Spine: DK Images: Tony Souter b; Getty Images: Photonica/Jake Rajs t.

All other images © Dorling Kindersley.
For further information see: www.dkimages.com

Phrase Book

Pronunciation

Turkish uses a Roman alphabet. It has 29 letters: 8 vowels and 21 consonants. Letters that differ from the English alphabet are: **c**, pronounced "j" as in "jolly"; **ç**, pronounced "ch" as in "church"; **ğ**, which lengthens the preceding vowel and is not pronounced; **ı**, pronounced "uh"; **ö**, pronounced "ur" (like the sound in "further"); **ş**, pronounced "sh" as in "ship"; **ü**, pronounced "ew" as in "few".

In an Emergency

Help!	İmdat!	*eem-dat*
Stop!	Dur!	*door*
Call a doctor!	Bir doktor çağrın!	*beer dok-tor chah-ruhn*
Call an ambulance!	Bir ambulans çağrın!	*beer am-boo-lans chah-ruhn*
Call the police!	Polis çağrın!	*po-lees chah-ruhn*
Fire!	Yangın!	*yan-guhn*
Where is the nearest telephone?	En yakın telefon nerede?	*en ya-kuhn teh-leh-fon neh-reh-deh*
Where is the nearest hospital?	En yakın hastane nerede?	*en ya-kuhn has-ta-neh neh-reh-deh*

Communication Essentials

Yes	Evet	*eh-vet*
No	Hayır	*h-'eye'-uhr*
Thank you	Teşekkür ederim	*teh-shek-kewr eh-deh-reem*
Please	Lütfen	*lewt-fen*
Excuse me	Affedersiniz	*af-feh-der-see-neez*
Hello	Merhaba	*mer-ha-ba*
Goodbye	Hoşça kalın	*hosh-cha ka-luhn*
Good morning	Günaydın	*gewn-'eye'-duhn*
Good evening	İyi akşamlar	*ee-yee ak-sham-lar*
Morning	Sabah	*sa-bah*
Afternoon	Öğleden sonra	*ur-leh-den son-ra*
Evening	Akşam	*ak-sham*
Yesterday	Dün	*dewn*
Today	Bugün	*boo-gewn*
Tomorrow	Yarın	*ya-ruhn*
Here	Burada	*boo-ra-da*
There	Şurada	*shoo-ra-da*
Over there	Orada	*o-ra-da*
What?	Ne?	*neh*
When?	Ne zaman?	*neh za-man*
Why?	Neden	*neh-den*
Where?	Nerede	*neh-reh-deh*

Useful Phrases

How are you?	Nasılsınız?	*na-suhl-suh-nuhz*
I'm fine	İyiyim	*ee-yee-yeem*
Pleased to meet you	Memnun oldum	*mem-noon ol-doom*
See you soon	Görüşmek üzere	*gur-rewsh-mek ew-zeh-reh*
That's fine	Tamam	*ta-mam*
Where is/are ...?	... nerede?	*... neh-reh-deh*
How far is it to...?	... ne kadar uzakta?	*... neh ka-dar oo-zak-ta*
I want to go to ...	... a/e gitmek istiyorum	*... a/eh geet-mek ees-tee-yo-room*
Do you speak English?	İngilizce biliyor musunuz?	*een-gee-leez-jeh bee-lee-yor moo-soo-nooz?*
I don't understand	Anlamıyorum	*an-la-muh-yo-room*
Can you help me?	Bana yardım edebilir misiniz?	*ba-na yar-duhm eh-deh-bee-leer mee -see-neez?*

Useful Words

big	büyük	*bew-yewk*
small	küçük	*kew-chewk*
hot	sıcak	*suh-jak*
cold	soğuk	*soh-ook*
good/well	iyi	*ee-yee*
bad	kötü	*kur-tew*
enough	yeter	*yeh-ter*
open	açık	*a-chuhk*
closed	kapalı	*ka-pa-luh*
left	sol	*sol*
right	sağ	*saa*
straight on	doğru	*doh-roo*

near	yakın	*ya-kuhn*
far	uzak	*oo-zak*
up	yukarı	*yoo-ka-rub*
down	aşağı	*a-shah-uh*
early	erken	*er-ken*
late	geç	*gech*
entrance	giriş	*gee-reesh*
exit	çıkış	*chuh-kuhsh*
toilets	tuvaletler	*too-va-let-ler*
push	itiniz	*ee-tee-neez*
pull	çekiniz	*cheh-kee-neez*
more	daha fazla	*da-ha faz-la*
less	daha az	*da-ha az*
very	çok	*chok*

Shopping

How much is this?	Bu kaç lira?	*boo kach lee-ra*
I would like ...	... istiyorum	*... ees-tee-yo-room*
Do you have ...?	... var mı?	*... var muh?*
Do you take credit cards?	Kredi kartı kabul ediyor musunuz?	*kreh-dee kar-tuh ka-bool eh-dee-yor moo-soo-nooz?*
What time do you open/ close?	Saat kaçta açılıyor/ kapanıyor?	*Sa-at kach-ta a-chuh-luh-yor/ ka-pa-nuh-yor*
this one	bunu	*boo-noo*
that one	şunu	*shoo-noo*
expensive	pahalı	*pa-ha-luh*
cheap	ucuz	*oo-jooz*
size (clothes)	beden	*beh-den*
size (shoes)	numara	*noo-ma-ra*
white	beyaz	*bay-yaz*
black	siyah	*see-yah*
red	kırmızı	*kubr-muh-zub*
yellow	sarı	*sa-rub*
green	yeşil	*yeh-sheel*
blue	mavi	*ma-vee*
brown	kahverengi	*kah-veh-ren-gee*
shop	dükkan	*dewk-kan*
till	kasa	*ka-sa*
bargaining	pazarlık	*pa-zar luhk*
That's my last offer	Daha fazla veremem	*da-ha faz-la veh-reh-mem*

Types of Shop

antiques shop	antikacı	*an-tee-ka-jub*
bakery	fırın	*fuh-ruhn*
bank	banka	*ban-ka*
book shop	kitapçı	*kee-tap-chub*
butcher's	kasap	*ka-sap*
cake shop	pastane	*pas-ta-neh*
chemist's/ pharmacy	eczane	*ej-za-neh*
fishmonger's	balıkçı	*ba-luhk-chub*
greengrocer's	manav	*ma-nav*
grocery	bakkal	*bak-kal*
hairdresser's (ladies)	kuaför	*kwaf-fur*
(mens)	berber	*ber-ber*
leather shop	derici	*deh-ree-jee*
market/bazaar	çarşı/pazar	*char-shuh/pa-zar*
newsstand	gazeteci	*ga-zeh-teh-jee*
post office	postane	*pos-ta-neh*
shoe shop	ayakkabıcı	*'eye'-yak-ka-bub-jub*
stationer's	kırtasiyeci	*kubr-ta-see-yeh-jee*
supermarket	süpermarket	*sew-per-mar-ket*
tailor	terzi	*ter-zee*
travel agency	seyahat acentesi	*say-ya-hat a-jen-teh-see*

Sightseeing

castle	hisar	*hee-sar*
church	kilise	*kee-lee-seh*
island	ada	*a-da*
mosque	cami	*ja-mee*
museum	müze	*mew-zeh*
palace	saray	*sar-'eye'*
park	park	*park*
square	meydan	*may-dan*
theological college	medrese	*med-reh-seh*
tomb	türbe	*tewr-beh*
tourist information office	danışma bürosu	*da-nuhsh-mah bew-ro-soo*
tower	kule	*koo-leh*
town hall	belediye sarayı	*beh-leh-dee-yeh sar-'eye'-ub*
Turkish bath	hamam	*ha-mam*

Transport

airport	havalimanı	*ha-va-lee-ma-nuh*
bus/coach	otobüs	*o-to-bewss*
bus stop	otobüs durağı	*o-to-bewss doo-ra-uh*
coach station	otogar	*o-to-gar*
dolmuş	dolmuş	*dol-moosh*
fare	ücret	*ewj-ret*
ferry	vapur	*va-poor*
sea bus	deniz otobüsü	*deh-neez o-to-bew-sew*
station	istasyon	*ees-tas-yon*
taxi	taksi	*tak-see*
ticket	bilet	*bee-let*
ticket office	bilet gişesi	*bee-let gee-sheh-see*
timetable	tarife	*ta-ree-feh*

Staying in a Hotel

Do you have a vacant room?	Boş odanız var mı?	*bosh o-da-nuhz var muh?*
double room	iki kişilik bir oda	*ee-kee kee-shee-leek beer o-da*
room with a double bed	çift kişilik yataklı bir oda	*cheeft kee-shee-leek ya-tak-luh beer o-da*
twin room	çift yataklı bir oda	*cheeft ya-tak-luh beer o-da*
for one person	tek kişilik	*tek kee-shee-leek*
room with a bath	banyolu bir oda	*ban-yo-loo beer o-da*
shower	duş	*doosh*
porter	komi	*ko-mee*
key	anahtar	*a-nah-tar*
room service	oda servisi	*o-da ser-vee-see*
I have a reservation	Rezervasyonum var	*reh-zer-vas-yo-noom var*
Does the price include breakfast?	Fiyata kahvaltı dahil mi?	*fee-ya-ta kah-val-tuh da-heel mee?*

Eating Out

A table for … please	… kişilik bir masa lütfen	*… kee-shee-leek beer ma-sa lewt-fen*
I want to reserve a table	Bir masa ayırtmak istiyorum	*beer ma-sa 'eye'-uhrt-mak ees-tee-yo-room*
The bill please	Hesap lütfen	*heh-sap lewt-fen*
I am a vegetarian	Et yemiyorum	*et yeh-mee-yo-room*
restaurant	lokanta	*lo-kan-ta*
waiter	garson	*gar-son*
menu	yemek listesi	*ye-mek lees-teh-see*
fixed-price menu	fiks menü	*feeks meh-new*
wine list	şarap listesi	*sha-rap lees-teh-see*
breakfast	kahvaltı	*kah-val-tuh*
lunch	öğle yemeği	*ur-leh yeh-meh-ee*
dinner	akşam yemeği	*ak-sham yeh-meh-ee*
starter	meze	*meh-zeh*
main course	ana yemek	*a-na yeh-mek*
dish of the day	günün yemeği	*gewn-ewn yeh-meh-ee*
dessert	tatlı	*tat-luh*
rare	az pişmiş	*az peesh-meesh*
well done	iyi pişmiş	*ee-yee peesh-meesh*
glass	bardak	*bar-dak*
bottle	şişe	*shee-sheh*
knife	bıçak	*buh-chak*
fork	çatal	*cha-tal*
spoon	kaşık	*ka-shuhk*

Menu Decoder

badem	*ba-dem*	almond
bal	*bal*	honey
balık	*ba-luhk*	fish
bira	*bee-ra*	beer
bonfile	*bon-fee-leh*	fillet steak
buz	*booz*	ice
çay	*ch-'eye'*	tea
çilek	*chee-lek*	strawberry
çorba	*chor-ba*	soup
dana eti	*da-na eh-tee*	veal
dondurma	*don-door-ma*	ice cream
ekmek	*ek-mek*	bread
elma	*el-ma*	apple
et	*et*	meat
fasulye	*fa-sool-yeh*	beans
fırında	*fuh-ruhn-da*	roast
fıstık	*fuhs-tuhk*	pistachio nuts
gazoz	*ga-zoz*	fizzy drink
hurma	*hoor-ma*	dates
içki	*eech-kee*	alcohol
incir	*een-jeer*	figs
ızgara	*uhz-ga-ra*	charcoal grilled

kahve	*kah-veh*	coffee
kara biber	*ka-ra bee-ber*	black pepper
karışık	*ka-ruh-shuhk*	mixed
karpuz	*kar-pooz*	water melon
kavun	*ka-voon*	melon
kayısı	*k-'eye'-uh-suh*	apricots
kaymak	*k-'eye'-mak*	cream
kıyma	*kuhy-ma*	minced meat
kızartma	*kuh-zart-ma*	fried
köfte	*kurf-teh*	meatballs
kuru	*koo-roo*	dried
kuzu eti	*koo-zoo eh-tee*	lamb
lokum	*lo-koom*	Turkish delight
maden suyu	*ma-den soo-yoo*	mineral water (fizzy)
meyve suyu	*may-veh soo-yoo*	fruit juice
midye	*meed-yeh*	mussels
muz	*mooz*	banana
patlıcan	*pat-luh-jan*	aubergine
peynir	*pay-neer*	cheese
pilav	*pee-lav*	rice
piliç	*pee-leech*	roast chicken
şarap	*sha-rap*	wine
sebze	*seb-zeh*	vegetables
şeftali	*shef-ta-lee*	peach
şeker	*sheh-ker*	sugar
su	*soo*	water
süt	*sewt*	milk
sütlü	*sewt-lew*	with milk
tavuk	*ta-vook*	chicken
tereyağı	*teh-reh-yah-uh*	butter
tuz	*tooz*	salt
üzüm	*eu-zewm*	grapes
vişne	*veesh-neh*	sour cherry
yoğurt	*yob-urt*	yoghurt
yumurta	*yoo-moor-ta*	egg
zeytin	*zay-teen*	olives
zeytinyağı	*zay-teen-yah-uh*	olive oil

Numbers

0	sıfır	*suh-fuhr*
1	bir	*beer*
2	iki	*ee-kee*
3	üç	*ewch*
4	dört	*durt*
5	beş	*besh*
6	altı	*al-tuh*
7	yedi	*yeh-dee*
8	sekiz	*seh-keez*
9	dokuz	*doh-kooz*
10	on	*on*
11	on bir	*on beer*
12	on iki	*on ee-kee*
13	on üç	*on ewch*
14	on dört	*on durt*
15	on beş	*on besh*
16	on altı	*on al-tuh*
17	on yedi	*on yeh-dee*
18	on sekiz	*on seh-keez*
19	on dokuz	*on doh-kooz*
20	yirmi	*yeer-mee*
21	yirmi bir	*yeer-mee beer*
30	otuz	*o-tooz*
40	kırk	*kuhrk*
50	elli	*eh-lee*
60	altmış	*alt-muhsh*
70	yetmiş	*yet-meesh*
80	seksen	*sek-sen*
90	doksan	*dok-san*
100	yüz	*yewz*
110	yüz on	*yewz on*
200	iki yüz	*ee-kee yewz*
1,000	bin	*been*
100,000	yüz bin	*yewz been*
1,000,000	bir milyon	*beer meel-yon*

Time

one minute	bir dakika	*beer da-kee-ka*
one hour	bir saat	*beer sa-at*
half an hour	yarım saat	*ya-ruhm sa-at*
day	gün	*gewn*
week	hafta	*haf-ta*
month	ay	*'eye'*
year	yıl	*yuhl*
Sunday	pazar	*pa-zar*
Monday	pazartesi	*pa-zar-teh-see*
Tuesday	salı	*sa-luh*
Wednesday	çarşamba	*char-sham-ba*
Thursday	perşembe	*per-shem-beh*
Friday	cuma	*joo-ma*
Saturday	cumartesi	*joo-mar-teh-see*